PROPERTY, POWER AND POLITICS

Why We Need to Rethink the World Power System

Jean-Philippe Robé

BRISTOL
UNIVERSITY
PRESS

First published in Great Britain in 2020 by

Bristol University Press
University of Bristol
1-9 Old Park Hill
Bristol
BS2 8BB
UK
t: +44 (0)117 954 5940
e: bup-info@bristol.ac.uk

Details of international sales and distribution partners are available at bristoluniversitypress.co.uk

© Bristol University Press 2020

British Library Cataloguing in Publication Data
A catalogue record for this book is available from the British Library

ISBN 978-1-5292-1316-4 hardcover
ISBN 978-1-5292-1317-1 paperback
ISBN 978-1-5292-1318-8 ePub
ISBN 978-1-5292-1319-5 ePdf

Cover design: Liam Roberts
Front cover image: Alamy W7XBXR

Contents

Detailed Contents   v

List of Figures and Tables   ix

Acknowledgements   x

General Introduction   1

PART I   Property

Introduction to Part I   39

1   The Meaning of Property   53

2   The Modern Constitutional Mode of Government   87

3   Sovereignty and Property   107

4   From Political Enterprise to the Modern State   137

5   The Mixing of Democracy and Despotism   163

PART II   Firms in the World Power System

Introduction to Part II   185

6   Firms   195

7   The Features of Business Corporations   227

8   The Spreading of the Corporate System and its Consequences   241

9   Coping with Firms   293

10   Towards a Sustainable World Power System   327

Epilogue   353

Bibliography   355

Index   387

Detailed Contents

General Introduction		**1**
	The State System	3
	Property and Government	5
	Property, Things and Rights	8
	Autonomy and Efficiency	11
	Property in the Power System and the Perturbing Development of Corporate Law	14
	Negative Externalities	20
	The Concentration of Property and the Evolution of the Power System	24
	Content	27
PART I	**Property**	
Introduction to Part I		**39**
	Law Matters	42
	A Deeply Embedded Legal Institution	44
	Property Today	46
	The Notion of 'Economic Property Rights' is a Distraction	47
	Property and Legal Personality	49
1	**The Meaning of Property**	**53**
	1.1 Property as a Constitutional Prerogative	56
	1.2 The Secondary Importance of Possession	62
	1.3 Property as a Value-enhancing Institution	64
	1.4 Property and the State	65
	1.5 Possession and Agency	67
	1.6 A Right to Exclude and its Contractual Consequences	69
	1.7 Prices versus Orders	72
	1.8 Owners as Lawmakers	75
	1.9 A Right as a Matter of Principle, not a 'Bundle of Rights'	78

1.10 A Rejoinder: Oliver Hart's Theory of Ownership 83
1.11 A Similar Concept in Civil Law and Common 84
Law Systems
1.12 Property as a Building Block of the Power System 85

2   The Modern Constitutional Mode of Government   87
2.1 The State and the 'Organs of the State' 90
2.2 Private Prerogatives 94
2.3 Property and the Autonomy from the 'Organs 100
of the State'
2.4 The Small-scale Despotisms 102
2.5 Power in Times of Peace, Power in Times of War 104

3   Sovereignty and Property   107
3.1 North, Wallis and Weingast's Thesis 110
3.2 The Role of Organized Violence 113
3.3 Property Rights and Sovereignty 118
3.4 International Sovereignty 121
3.5 Internal Sovereignty 126
3.6 Political Organs of the State, Administrative 133
Organs of the State and Law

4   From Political Enterprise to the Modern State   137
4.1 Coalitions 138
4.2 The Provision of Services by the State and 142
the Need for Market Exchange
4.3 Modern Taxes and Modern State 148
4.4 Practical Issues in Taxation 151
4.5 From Compulsion to Modern Taxation 154

5   The Mixing of Democracy and Despotism   163
5.1 Property and Legal Pluralism 166
5.2 From Official to Unofficial Legal Pluralism 168
5.3 Relays in the Power System 171
5.4 Acceptability 174
5.5 Correcting Unbalances 175
5.6 The Constitutional Revolutions of the 176
Twentieth Century

PART II Firms in the World Power System

Introduction to Part II   185

    A World of Corporations   187
    The Corporate Danger   188
    From Liberalism to Capitalism   189

6   **Firms**   **195**
    6.1   The Need to Differentiate Firms from   195
           Corporations
    6.2   The World Wide Web of Contracts   201
    6.3   Contracts and Stable Exchange   205
    6.4   Firms   207
    6.5   The Unincorporated Business   208
    6.6   The Firm in the World Wide Web of Contracts   211
    6.7   The Firm's Limits   214
    6.8   The Importance of Firms   216
    6.9   The Incorporation Process   217
    6.10 The Consequences of Incorporation   218
    6.11 Corporations   220
    6.12 Corporate Personality versus Notions it Should   221
           Not be Confused with
    6.13 The Importance of Being a Legal Person   223
    6.14 Incorporation and the Multiplication of   224
           Property Rights

7   **The Features of Business Corporations**   **227**
    7.1   Legal Personality   229
    7.2   Shares as Autonomous Objects of Property   231
    7.3   Assets and Liability Partitioning   234
    7.4   Locking in Capital   235
    7.5   The Elimination of the Haggling over Residual 236
           Control Rights
    7.6   The Concentration of Property and the Nature   238
           of Corporate Prerogatives

8   **The Spreading of the Corporate System and**   **241**
    its Consequences
    8.1   State Affairs   243
    8.2   Modern Capitalism   246
    8.3   The Interaction Between Firms and States   249
    8.4   The Financial Structure of Firms   259
    8.5   Firms versus Corporations   268

8.6	Corporate Governance in a Globalized World	282
8.7	The Recent Dynamic of the Power System	285

9   Coping with Firms   293

9.1	Competing Firms and Competing States	297
9.2	From Despotisms to Constitutional Government	301
9.3	The Rise of 'Private' Government in the US and Berle and Means' Real Message	305
9.4	Legal Institutionalism in Europe	310
9.5	Agency Theory and an Improper Mandate to Maximize Short-term Shareholder Value	313
9.6	Rules of Accounting	320

10   Towards a Sustainable World Power System   327

10.1	The Challenge to Address the Global Issues	330
10.2	Re-engineering Multinational Enterprises	332
10.3	Starting with What We Have	334
10.4	True Cost Accounting	336
10.5	Curing the Deficiencies of Accounting	338
10.6	Concluding Remarks	349

Epilogue   353

List of Figures and Tables

Figures

8.1	The initial structure of the enterprise	250
8.2	The legal structure of the firm at Step 5	253
8.3	The legal structure of the firm at Step 6	254
8.4	The legal structure of the firm at Step 7	256
8.5	The financial structure of the firm at the starting position	260
8.6	The acquisition structure	262

Tables

8.1	The simplified presentation of profits and losses at the starting position	251
8.2	The impact of labour costs increases at Step 2	251
8.3	The impact of the production delocalization in Country B at Step 3	252
8.4	The impact of the new environmental law at Step 4	252
8.5	The impact of the increased production delocalization in Country B at Step 5	254
8.6	The impact of the offshoring of the IP in Country C at Step 6	255
8.7	The impact of the offshoring of management services in Country D at Step 7	256

Acknowledgements

The research having led to the drafting of this book has spanned so many years that it is impossible for me to acknowledge all the individuals and institutions I am indebted to. I do apologize for anyone I have missed but I want to acknowledge my gratitude to the European University Institute in Florence (Italy), the University of Michigan Law School in Ann Arbor, the Collège des Bernardins in Paris and Alexia Autenne, Larry Cata Baker, Jean-Baptiste Barfety, Alexandra Bidet, Jean-Cassien Billier, Yuri Biondi, Sandrine Blanc, Aurore Chaigneau, Valérie Charolles, Christian Chavagneux, David Ciepley, Terence Daintith, Simon Deakin, Bertrand Delaunay, Anne Donnot, José Engràcia Antunes, Aude-Solveig Epstein, Olivier Favereau, Isabelle Ferreras, Benoît Fleury, Robert Freeland, Patrick Fridenson, Benoît Frydman, Antoine Garapon, Marcel Gauchet, Paul du Gay, Corine Gendron, Pierre-Yves Gomez, Filip Gregor, Christopher Halburd, Charley Hannoun, Geoffrey Hodgson, Daniel Hurstel, Paddy Ireland, Katsuhito Iwai, Christophe Jamin, Larissa Katz, Patricia Kelso, Jean-Marc Le Gall, Antoine Lyon-Caen, Jens Lowitzsch, Jean De Munck, Birgitta Nedelman, André Orléan, Ronen Palan, Elsa Peskine, Hannah Petersen, Richard Phillips, Gaetano Piepoli, Nicolas Postel, Antoine Rebérioux, Sandra Rigot, Kristal Robé, Baudoin Roger, John Gerard Ruggie, Tatiana Sachs, Jean-Michel Saussois, Philip Scranton, Richard Sobel, Susan Strange, Lynn Stout, Alain Supiot, Gunther Teubner, Bertjan Verbeek, Bertrand Valiorgue, Stéphane Vernac, Lynne Wurzburg and Mikhail Xifaras. I would also like to extend my thanks to the students in my class 'Globalization and Legal Pluralism' at the Sciences Po Law School in Paris.

A very special thanks goes to John Gerard Ruggie and Philip Scranton for their encouraging and detailed comments on the last version of the manuscript.

Finally, two anonymous reviewers provided relevant and useful detailed comments.

General Introduction

Humanity is facing unprecedented challenges. Climate change is threatening the survival of our species, alongside many other forms of life. Democratic States are increasingly run by populist politicians elected by angered majorities rejecting traditional political parties. Existing international institutions are under pressure with a rise of unilateralism and protectionism. And inequality has never been as high at both domestic and international levels. War used to be the worst form of violence humanity imposed upon itself. Today, we are peacefully destroying our natural environment, our democratic institutions and the inclusiveness of our societies.

Over the last decades, political parties from right and left have had the opportunity to implement their programmes in most democratic States. It has not made much of a difference to the most important issues of ecological survival, societal inclusiveness and the preservation of effective democratic institutions.

Our institutions do not work. With regards to climate change, scientists have alerted us for decades. It is obvious that whatever has been achieved via international negotiations is far too insufficient.[1] The end of history could be quite different from the one contemplated by Francis Fukuyama some 30 years ago.[2] The collapse of the Soviet Union was supposed to herald a bright future for liberal democratic institutions. But although communism has certainly demonstrated its ineptness as a political and economic system, Western-style institutions are now next in line if we do not seriously adapt them to the issues of our time.

The deep reason for all this is that our institutions have been by-passed by the historical development of a World Power System creating overwhelming constraints, and the politicians in charge of our local political institutions do not have the levers to effectively act on its course.

---

[1] Christiana Figueres, Hans Joachim Schellnhuber, Gail Whiteman, Johan Rockström, Anthony Hobley and Stefan Rahmstorf, 'Three Years to Safeguard our Climate', 546 *Nature*, 29 June, pp. 593–597 (2017).

[2] Francis Fukuyama, 'The End of History?', 16 *The National Interest*, pp. 3–18 (1989).

The daunting challenges we are facing are the result of the process of globalization of markets and firms without a parallel development of proper countervailing rules and institutions. The so-called 'Washington consensus' in its blind reliance on markets to resolve problems of resource generation and allocation bears a heavy burden of responsibility for the resistance or unwillingness to address significant areas of market failures.[3] Global firms, global markets and investment funds play States against each over, which reduces their means of action. And the ability to *govern*, at the local, State or international level has been seriously eroded. But if neoliberal ideas bear their share of responsibility for today's predicament, the alternative thought movements do not have much to offer. The various social sciences, which should explain the operation of the institutions of our societies and provide a description of available levers of action, seem incapable of living up to the task. We are going through times when even a bare understanding of what is happening to us is lacking.

Most of the intellectual production in the social sciences is the outcome of an implicit assumption that we are still living in a State System when in fact the globalization of the economy is reducing the States' ability to adopt proper rules to address societal issues (1). To understand this state of affairs, it is important to understand the role played by property in the operation of the liberal Power System (2). Property is a right of autonomy constitutionally protected (3). Its justification can be found either in the defence of the individual's autonomy or via efficiency considerations (4). The fact is, however, that a sizable proportion of productive property today is concentrated in large, corporate organizations (5). The exploitation of the possibilities offered by an international open economy to these organizations has led to the production of potentially deadly negative externalities such as climate change, unbearable inequalities and the impoverishment of public institutions (6). The development of these large organizations has induced changes in the operation of the Power System. They must be understood to identify the existing potential means of action, in particular via proper rules of accounting for the impact of their activities (7). This is the ambition of this book.

---

[3] David Held, 'Reframing Global Governance: Apocalypse Soon or Reform!', in David Held and Anthony McGrew, *Globalization Theory – Approaches and Controversies*, Cambridge: Polity Press (2007), pp. 240–260, at pp. 243–244.

The State System

The existing world political system is structured around what is called the 'State System'. Or, maybe more appropriately, the 'State System' has been serving as a substitute to a non-existing world political system. The State System, born in Europe in the seventeenth century, is the only global system of authority that has ever existed.[4] The planet's surface and population were, and still are in many respects, divided among sovereign States. States, as the combination of a territory, a population and an effective government over the first two components, are usually further divided internally between a 'public' (governmental) sphere of action and a 'private' one.[5] The dominant paradigm in modern social science separates political and economic actors into distinct, well-defined spheres.[6] Power is being understood as being exercised in the 'public sphere' via political institutions exercising executive, legislative and judicial authority. In the 'private sphere', a combination of property rights and liberties (freedom of contract, of movement, of thought, in particular) operate to entitle private persons to enjoy their autonomy.

In fact, the seeming independence of the private (and economic) and political systems is only apparent. These systems are deeply intertwined.[7] In democracies, when the private sphere is dysfunctional and the electorate demands changes, this normally leads to remediation via the political institutions. Laws are changed via democratic government and are enforced by the power forces existing in the 'public' sphere. As a matter of example, the mere operation of 'freedom of contract' can lead to low wages or poor working conditions. If the electorate and its representatives consider that these are issues to be addressed, minimum wages and protective laws can be adopted. Or 'freedom of enterprise' can lead to abuses of the natural environment; here again, in our classical

---

[4] Robert Jackson, *Sovereignty*, Cambridge: Polity Press (2007), p. x.

[5] In the United Kingdom and in the United States of America, the word 'government' is preferred to the word 'State', a reason being that in the US the word 'State' refers to the governmental units united by the federal constitution which also created the 'federal government', which is not called a 'State' although it is clearly a 'State' in international public law.

[6] Douglass C. North, John Joseph Wallis and Barry R. Weingast, *Violence and Social Orders – A Conceptual Framework for Interpreting Recorded Human History*, Cambridge: Cambridge University Press (2009), pp. 268–269. *See also* Saskia Sassen, *Territory, Authority, Rights – From Medieval to Global Assemblage*, Princeton: Princeton University Press (2006), p. 184.

[7] *E.g.* North, Wallis and Weingast, *op cit*, note 6, p. 269. *See also* Marcel Gauchet, *L'avènement de la démocratie – I – La révolution moderne*, Paris: Gallimard (2007), p. 182.

understanding of the operation of our institutions, laws can be adopted to redress the situation. This is the reason why we have consumer protection laws, antidiscrimination laws, antitrust laws, labour laws, zoning laws, environmental laws, or why we regulate insurance and banking, and so on.

Even neo-classical economists, usually 'pro-market', are in line with this view of how society should operate. As Roland Bénabou and 2014 economics Nobel prizewinner Jean Tirole phrase it:

> Economists' view of how society should be organized has traditionally rested on two pillars. The invisible hand of the market, described in Adam Smith, harnesses consumers' and corporations' pursuit of self-interest to the pursuit of efficiency. The State corrects market failures whenever externalities stand in the way of efficiency, and redistributes income and wealth, as the income and wealth distribution generated by markets has no reason to fit society's moral standard. In industrialized democracies, much of the political spectrum has converged on this division of labor, albeit with some sharp divergences of opinion as to the relative roles of the market and the State.[8]

In this 'view of how society should be organized', the market should do most of the coordination work; but there is still need for a 'State' to correct negative externalities and redistribute wealth and income. This thread of analysis was started by Arthur Cecil Pigou in 1920[9] and is now mainstream. Most of the coordination work in society should be done by the market, which works by itself; except when it doesn't, which is when governmental intervention is required. The market operates as a matter of principle; the government intervenes as a matter of exception. A few paragraphs later in their article, Roland Bénabou and Jean Tirole acknowledge, however, that there are also 'Government failures'

---

[8] Roland Bénabou and Jean Tirole, 'Individual and Corporate Social Responsibility', 77(305) *Economica*, pp. 1–19 (2010), p. 1. On the internalizing role of the State, *see also* the position of Kenneth Arrow for whom the State's responsibility in this area is obvious, although difficult in practice; Kenneth J. Arrow, *The Limits of Organization*, New York: WW Norton & Co. (1974), p. 24. And on justice issues, the same Arrow writes: '... there are profound difficulties with the price system, even, so to speak, within its own logic, and these strengthen the view that, valuable though it is in certain realms, it cannot be made the complete arbiter of social life. One point, and a difficult one indeed, (...) is that the price system does not in any way prescribe a just redistribution of income.' *Ibid*, p. 22.

[9] Arthur Cecil Pigou, *The Economics of Welfare*, London: Palgrave Macmillan (1920, reprint 2013).

preventing the State from properly fulfilling its roles. They mention the role of lobbies, inefficiency and the territoriality of jurisdiction, i.e. the fact that State norms apply on the States' territories only. Implicitly, they acknowledge that in a global economy, there is a major issue with the generally agreed division of labour between 'markets' and 'government'. There is no world State to fulfil the governmental function of internalizing negative externalities and correcting inequalities that are not and cannot be addressed locally. But they do not elaborate further. This is quite unfortunate because this is where the difficulties of our time start ...

This major issue is what the developments in this book address. Unfortunately, the World Power System does not operate in a Pigovian fashion. We are living in a global economy, in a World Power System, in a globalized world in which we cannot oppose 'the market' to 'the State'. There is no world State and the State System is insufficient to operate as a surrogate of a 'world State'. In the real-world economy, the second pillar described by Bénabou and Tirole is non-existent. The simple conclusion is that so-called 'market economies' cannot properly operate at the world level with the present institutional arrangement.[10]

To understand how we got where we are and what can be done about it, we need to start from the building block of all the political/economic systems based on liberal institutions, i.e. property.

Property and Government

Property is intrinsically linked to government. This idea is certainly not new. In John Locke's *Two Treatises of Government*, published in 1690, government is created to protect property. Property comes first, as the outcome of man's work over nature. Government comes second – the purpose of government being to protect property, alongside life and liberty.

Locke, like most property philosophers, argued from the point of view of an imagined 'state of nature'. He viewed property as a right already in existence in a world without government. Man owned what he created. Government was only needed because property was at risk from the violence of other men, and therefore in need of protection.

In this book, I will not explain property and its role in the structuring of what I call the World Power System starting from an imagined 'state

---

[10] *See also* R. Edward Freeman, Jeffrey S. Harrison, Andrew C. Wicks, Bidhan L. Parmar and Simone De Colle, *Stakeholder Theory – The State of the Art*, Cambridge: Cambridge University Press (2010), p. 4.

of nature'. None has ever existed and, given the state of our knowledge about the historical processes of institutional development, I have doubts about the wisdom of any modern analysis starting from an imagined 'state of nature'.[11] We are better off starting from the institutional world as it effectively developed. It is, of course, beyond dispute that 'state of nature' theories played a key role in the design of *real* institutions, particularly those created by the Constitutions first adopted in the late eighteenth century in the United States and in France. And in virtually all effective constitutional systems of governments, a Bill of Rights purports to protect property rights (and some other rights) and to put them out of the reach of capricious governments. The Fifth Amendment of the US Constitution promulgated in 1791, for example, provides that 'No person shall be … deprived of property, without due process of law'. Article 2 of the French Declaration of the Rights of Man and Citizen of 26 August 1789 is even clearer: 'The aim of every political association is the preservation of the natural and imprescriptible rights of Man. These rights are Liberty, Property, Safety and Resistance to Oppression.' These provisions purporting to protect 'natural rights', rights deemed to have been already in existence in a 'state of nature', are still today part of the constitutional laws of the US and France. Parliaments, when they adopt new statutes, must respect these rights. Whatever their historical merit or lack thereof, state of nature theories clearly played a key role in long-lasting institutions and in their operations.

These great constitutional texts and the principles they embody were adopted in the context of an agricultural economy with artisans, shopkeepers but no large-scale industrial production and distribution – no large business firms. With the subsequent industrialization of the economy and the social issues linked to it, competing views developed about the extent to which property deserves protection. In polities having liberal institutions, rules reducing the owners' autonomy to make room for social, environmental or consumption laws and the like were seen as an attack on property. And there was, of course, a major historical divide in the twentieth century between polities having nationalized the 'means of production' and liberal ones, protecting private property, including the property over businesses. Interestingly, socialism was also advocated based on the natural law doctrine – private property being declared as *against* nature.[12] It shows how this method of reasoning can be used to declare

---

[11] *See also*, concurring, Norberto Bobbio, *The Age of Rights*, Cambridge: Polity Press (1996), p. 53.

[12] Hans Kelsen, *General Theory of Law and State*, Clark, New Jersey: The LawBook Exchange (1945, 2007), p. 11.

and maintain the most opposite postulates. But this opposition about two competing world views regarding property also underlies the importance of the concept of property as a primary rule of social organization.

The fact is that in today's world, most political systems accept private property, including China, which is managing to combine an officially communist political system with private property. Property was and still *is* the keystone right in the Power System.[13]

The notion of 'Power System' I use in this book refers to the fact that 'power' does not exist in isolation, in either the 'public' or the 'private' spheres of life. Today, for example, one often opposes political power to 'civil society'.[14] Power, in this simple construction, is 'State power', the power of the government, of the 'constituted bodies', of the various 'public' authorities vested with powers by the constitutional system of government. Power in this sense is, in democracies, the articulation of the executive, legislative and judicial branches of government, the method of selecting those who will be their members, the procedures for the preparation and enforcement of mandatory rules and the use of State resources in compliance with these rules. In this construction, 'civil society' is the area of the private, of individual autonomy, of the free exercise by each individual person of his or her prerogatives, rights and freedoms in an autonomous, supposedly non-political, 'private' sphere.

The notion of 'Power System' goes beyond this dichotomy. The 'Power System' is much denser, has a much broader base and goes much further than the public authority understood in this fashion. It is a combination of large- and small-scale powers, of macro- and micro-authorities, the ones existing thanks to the others.[15] They evolve together – changes in the operation and rules created within small-scale powers leading to adaptation in the operations and rules created by large-scale powers. And *vice versa*.[16] Today, the macro-powers are, primarily, the States. The

---

[13] Carol M. Rose, 'Property as the Keystone Right?', 71 *Notre Dame Law Review*, pp. 329–369 (1996), pp. 337–338.

[14] On the origin of this dichotomy, *see generally* Rafe Blaufarb, *The Great Demarcation – The French Revolution and the Invention of Modern Property*, Oxford: Oxford University Press (2016). On the rejection of this dichotomy, *see* Michel Foucault, *Dits et écrits – 1954–1988*, tome IV (1976–1979), Paris: Éditions Gallimard, Bibliothèque des sciences humaines (1994), p. 89.

[15] A distinction has been made between 'power' and 'authority'. To take the analogy of a car, power is what resides under the bonnet; authority is who is in the driver's seat. This distinction is interesting for certain purposes. In my usage in this book, the word 'power' covers the combination of both concepts – or functions.

[16] Serge Audier, *Le colloque Lippmann – Aux origines du néo-libéralisme*, Editions Le Bord de l'Eau (2008), p. 95.

micro-powers are those of everyday life, mediocre in their importance relative to macro-powers, of course, but essential for those who are subject to them daily and for the orderly functioning of society. The micro-powers are, in different forms at different times in history, to be found in families, schools, universities, monasteries, armies, business firms and many other kinds of power organizations. They are essential for the existence of the Power System to which they belong in a different mode than macro-powers, with whom they exist in a form of symbiosis. The 'Power System' is the system of relationships linking macro- and micro-powers in an evolutionary dynamic. In a Power System, participants in the system enjoy more or less *autonomy*. But they are not *independent*; they *depend* on each other. States, for example, protect property and thus increase its value; they provide services which justify at least in part the amount of taxes paid by the beneficiaries of the services. The property of owners depends on the effective existence of the protection service and owners will be more or less content to pay for the protection service depending on its efficiency. And States will get more in tax resources if the protection service provided is such that property values are effectively protected and therefore enhanced, that contractual exchanges are enforced and develop. And so on. States' access to resources is facilitated by the effective operation of the services they offer. This is important because no freedom is possible without a State having the resources required to guarantee freedom's existence. This coexistence and coevolution of micro- and macro-powers is constitutive of the Power System. As Michel Foucault once wrote, 'the State, with its great judicial, military and other systems, represents only the guarantee, the armature of a whole network of powers that passes through other channels, different from these main ways'.[17]

Property, Things and Rights

The central importance of property in systems of government protecting its existence is clear.

[17] Michel Foucault, *Dits et écrits – 1954–1988*, tome II (1970–1975), Paris: Éditions Gallimard, Bibliothèque des Sciences Humaines (1994), p. 812. *See also* Braudel, *Civilisation matérielle, économie et capitalisme, XVe–XVIIIe siècles*, tome 2 'Les jeux de l'échange', Paris: A. Colin (1979), p. 494.

But what *is* property? Constitutions do not define it.[18] Property is one of these notions which seem so obvious that we do not tend to think about them. Property, however, becomes highly problematic when one tries to understand what it is. It is certainly not self-defining.[19]

For most political thinkers, economists or lawyers, property is a direct relationship between a person and a thing. I own the objects I can call mine: this is my pen, this is my car, this is my house. Property is the relationship I have to these objects. What else could there be to it? Such a conception was clearly the one of John Locke. As we will see in more detail in this book, it is also the way most economists treat property today, considering it is the same thing as 'possession', the actual physical control over things. A notable exception is Hernando De Soto who, in his search for the *Mystery of Capital*, clearly states that 'the crucial point to understand is that property is not a physical thing'.[20]

The widespread notion of property as a direct relationship between a person and an object of property (be it a car, a patent, a share of stock, a painting or any other object of property) is mistaken.[21] My contention is that this mistake is at the root of fundamental misunderstandings in political science, economics and law. It is so significant that it prevents understanding globalization and how the present World Power System operates.

---

[18] Of the four human rights proclaimed by Article 2 of the French Declaration of the Rights of Man and Citizen of 26 August 1789 – liberty, property, security, and resistance to oppression – only liberty is defined. In relation to other individuals, Article 3 states that liberty is 'the power to do anything that does not harm others' while, in relation to State power, Article 5 provides that 'everything which is not prohibited by the law cannot be impeded and no one can be forced to do that which the law does not order'. And Article 4 limits the role of the State by providing that 'the law has only the right to prohibit those actions which are harmful to society'. But nothing is said about what property is. *See also* Katharina Pistor, *The Code of Capital – How the Law Creates Wealth and Inequality*, Princeton and Oxford: Princeton University Press (2019).

[19] *E.g.* Ronald A. Cass, 'Property Rights Systems and the Rule of Law', in *The Elgar Companion to the Economics of Property Rights*, Cheltenham, UK: Edward Elgar (2004), Enrico Colombatto (ed.), pp. 222–248, at p. 222. For Jean Carbonnier, it is a mistake to study property in general. There are only categories of properties, as diverse as the categories of things. His error is the classical one of considering property as a right over things; Jean Carbonnier, *Flexible droit*, Paris: Librairie Générale de Droit et de Jurisprudence (4ème éd. 1979) (9ème éd. 1998), p. 325.

[20] *E.g.* Hernando de Soto, *The Mystery of Capital – Why Capitalism Triumphs in the West and Fails Everywhere Else*, New York: Basic Books (2000), p. 157.

[21] *See also* Richard Theodore Ely, *Property and Contract in Their Relations to the Distribution of Wealth*, Vol. 1, New York: The Macmillan Company (1914), p. 96.

Property is first of all a *legal* concept, a *right* persons have in connection with the object of property, things in particular (although of course one can also own immaterial objects of property which are not 'things', such as a patent). There is general agreement on the fact that, as a minimum, property is protected by law and, as we have seen, for thinkers like John Locke, the whole *purpose* of creating governments was to protect property. That makes of property a *legal* concept, an enforceable *right*, i.e. a right which can potentially be enforced, whose respect can be forced using the coercion and physical force available to the State. And the point is that rights potentially enforced by the State are not direct, straightforward relationships. As far as *property* rights are concerned, they are not a right of a person over a thing: they are a mode of relationship of a person – the owner – towards the world as a whole in connection with the object of the property right. As we will see, property is this ability of the owner to be the decision-maker as a matter of principle in connection with the object of property. I do what I want with my pen, I do what I want with my car, I do what I want with my house – as a matter of principle – because I own them. There are only limited rules reducing my ability and they operate as a matter of exception. The principle is that I do what I want with what I own; the exception is the set of rules I need to obey when exercising my property right. And this right of mine is enforceable against the world at large because in case my right is disregarded, I can trigger the operation of several parts of the State's institutions to protect my right: go to court, get an injunction and have police forces impose upon others the respect of my right. Or I can do nothing and let others enjoy my property; because this – also – is my (property) right.[22]

This right of autonomy – of decision-making as a matter of principle towards the object of the property right – translates into an ability for the owner to define the conditions under which others can make use of his or her property. For productive assets, such as a farm or a factory, property entitles the owner to organize the productive activities of those who are making use of his or her property. The owner will set, as a matter of principle, the production process and indirectly its consequences over the workforce, society at large and its natural environment.

In today's world, with regards to the largest productive assets, this ability is now concentrated into very large organizations, into very large enterprises. This concentration of property rights into large private global enterprises has fundamentally changed the operation of the Power System. But our understanding of the operation of the Power System has not

---

[22] Although this form of adverse possession may lead to the loss of property for lack of use by the original owner and the acquisition of property by the (long-time) user.

evolved accordingly. We remain stuck with an understanding of the Power System which is outdated, considering it is centred on the State System.

Autonomy and Efficiency

There are two classical ways of dealing with and defending property.

For some, the objective of having property as an institution is to preserve individuals' *autonomy* with no efficiency considerations. Based on ideas of personhood and liberty, property is first of all a right of autonomy, a right to do what one wants with what one owns. A variation of this theme is that property entitles the individual to develop one's specific abilities – one's own self. It creates a sphere within which an individual may exercise his or her will with full sovereignty and discretion, without needing to account for either government authorities or to other individuals for his or her wishes, tastes, preferences and choices.

For others, private property – as a fundamental institution of a market economy – leads to an *efficient use and allocation of resources*. Owners have an interest in preserving and developing their property, and by doing so, they incidentally serve as the guardians, keepers and developers of the assets existing in society which are put under their watch. By decentralizing the right of decision-making to the lowest level possible – at the level of the individual – we collectively benefit from the productive and innovative energies which can express themselves. Owners can do what they want with what they have, and this enables them to create new activities, new products, new services. Potential users of the new products or services will buy them, or they won't. Their collective choice – the 'market' – will decide whether the new product or service, at the price and level of quality proposed, meets enough demand (a 'market') to justify their production or not. In this utilitarian view, property creates incentives to use resources efficiently.[23]

There is probably a little bit of both in the institution of property. Libraries have been written about these two aspects of property but none of these two conceptions has priority in my starting point. Private property may be an instrument needed to preserve individuals' autonomy; it may be a key institution of a market economy. The fact is that in today's World Power System, private property over the most important productive

---

[23] *See generally* Meir Dan-Cohen, *Rights, Persons and Organizations: A Legal Theory for Bureaucratic Society*, Berkeley: University of California Press (1986), pp. 85–86.

assets has been reallocated via what can be called the 'corporate system',[24] and this reallocation has dramatically changed the way property operates in large business organizations – and in society at large.

With regards to autonomy, productive property in large business organizations is not an instrument of the autonomy of *the individual*. On the contrary, property allows organizations to create mandatory rules individuals have to follow when they are working for them. These individuals' autonomy is reduced and is subjected to the heteronomy of the rules created within large organizations thanks to their control over property.[25] Kenneth Arrow (1972 economics Nobel prizewinner) made interesting remarks about the *coercive* power of firms:

> the government is … only one of a large number of collective institutions. It is distinguished from the others primarily by its monopoly on coercive power, although even that monopoly is not absolute. A firm, especially a large corporation, provides another major area within which price relations are held in partial abeyance. The internal organization is … hierarchical and bureaucratic. … internally, and especially at lower levels, the relations among the employees of a firm are very different from the arm's length bargaining of our textbooks. As Herbert Simon has observed, an employment contract is different in many ways from an ordinary commodity contract; an employee is selling willingness to obey authority.[26]

'Obeying authority' means obeying the *owner* or his *agent*, who is managing the property on behalf of the owner.[27] And the concentration

---

[24] This expression has been used by several authors dealing with the same phenomenon as the one we are addressing. Adolf Berle described the dominance of collective capitalism as the 'corporate system'; *see* Adolf A. Berle, Jr., 'Property, Production and Revolution', 65 *Columbia Law Review*, pp. 1–20 (1965).

[25] Alain Laurent, *Histoire de l'individualisme*, Paris: Presses Universitaires de France (1993), p. 121.

[26] Arrow *op cit*, note 8, p. 25. Herbert Simon won the Nobel Prize in Economics in 1978.

[27] '… property is a form of social organization, whereby the labour of those who have it not is directed by and for the enjoyment of those that have. … the control of the owner is essentially a control of labour.' Leonard T. Hobhouse, 'The Historical Evolution of Property in Fact and in Idea', in *Property, its Duties and Rights*, pp. 1–31, The Bishop of Oxford (ed.), London: Oxford University Press (1913), p. 10.

of productive property has in effect reduced individual autonomy.[28] It may have increased it for the few but has reduced it for the many.[29] This is quite contrary to the constitutional principles of our society in the sense that the first ground for the protection of property – the protection of individuals' autonomy – is not available for *corporations* or *firms* which, of course, are not *individuals*. And while productive property is now owned in great proportion by corporations (companies, in English), the organizations within which the decisions are made about their use cannot make the same autonomy claims as individuals. The paradigm of autonomy is directly concerned with *individuals only*, and it provides moral grounds for legal claims made by *individuals only*.[30] For the main part, however, the legal system has treated corporations as if they were 'individuals', granting them the protections, immunities and liberties of individuals.[31] These rights designed to protect real-life individuals, made of flesh and blood, in fact turned out to be constitutional grounds for the creation of large and repressive systems of governance: firms, in which the activities of individuals are organized, subject to rules made by others than themselves.[32] Via property, *auto*nomy has been turned into widespread *hetero*nomy: the rules one makes for oneself have left the stage for rules made by others.

Let's now turn to the other claim in defence of property: efficiency in the use of resources. Irrespective of the *market's* efficiency as an allocator of resources, the fact is that most large productive resources today are allocated *by firms, within firms*. And it is clear to most of those studying firms as organizations that resources allocated *within* firms are not allocated as a result of market mechanisms. Contrary to an idea which is widespread

---

[28] For Adams, 'the tyranny of corporations, which grew naturally from conditions of "industrial freedom", was as grievous as any tyranny ever established by government agency.' Henry Carter Adams, *Relation of the State to Industrial Action and Economics and Jurisprudence. Two Essays*, New York: Columbia University Press (1954), p. 66.

[29] 'The institution of property has, in its modern form, reached its zenith as a means of giving to the few power over the life of the many, and its nadir as a means of securing for the many the basis of ... freedom and self-support.' Hobhouse, *op cit*, note 27, p. 23.

[30] Dan-Cohen, *op cit*, note 23, p. 62.

[31] In a 1978 interview of Hayek by Judge Robert Bork, Hayek declared that "we have very blindly applied the rules of law which have been developed to apply to individuals to legal persons".

[32] The governing power is repressive when it does not care about the interests of the governed, that is to say when it is disposed to neglect these interests or to deny their legitimacy. The result is that the subject's position is precarious and vulnerable. *E.g.* Philippe Nonet and Philip Selznick, *Law and Society in Transition – Toward Responsive Law*, New York: Octagon Books (1978), p. 29.

among many economists,[33] firms do not operate as 'markets', as we will see in more detail. Consequently, a vast proportion of the allocation of resources does *not* take place via market mechanisms in our society; it takes place via organized action, via the exercise of power within organizations.[34] And the fact is that today the operation of property rights by large organizations leads to the production of negative externalities in colossal amounts.[35] The most significant and potentially deadly one is climate change. The claim that the operation of property rights in organizations is efficient when all of us can witness that extraordinary amounts of negative externalities are being produced by these organizations is hard to make.

Property in the Power System and the Perturbing Development of Corporate Law

Via the operation of property and the evolution of the rules applicable to economic exchange, markets and modern States are part of the same institutional arrangement. Historically, they have developed together. Initially, the liberal State only played the role of a nightwatchman, protecting property rights and enforcing contracts. Then, with the development of industrialization, increased negative externalities and increased inequalities, the State gradually became a regulatory and welfare State.

With the American and French revolutions, the general architecture of the constitutional mode of government which ensued was articulated around these structuring principles: individuals have fundamental rights – and rights of autonomy, in particular – as a matter of principle; the

---

[33] Geoffrey M. Hodgson, 'Taxonomic Definitions in Social Sciences, with Firms, Markets and Institutions as Case Studies', *Journal of Institutional Economics*, pp. 1–18 (2018), p. 11.

[34] The word 'power' in this book will be used to designate the ability of A to obtain from B the performance of actions B would otherwise not have been performing. It is the ability for some to structure the field of what is possible for others; *see* Foucault, *op cit*, note 14, pp. 236–238. *See also generally* Paddy Ireland, 'Property, Private Government and the Myth of Deregulation', in Sarah Worthington (ed.), *Commercial Law and Commercial Practice*, Oxford: Hart (2003), pp. 85–123.

[35] In general, the term 'externality' is used to refer to a cost (negative externality) or a benefit (positive externality) involving 'secondary' effects felt by third parties to which producers would not attend except under regulatory incentives or controls – effects such as pollution, noise, job experience, or safer neighborhoods. *See, e.g.*, R.R. Nelson and S.G. Winter, *An Evolutionary Theory of Economic Change*, Cambridge: The Belknap Press of Harvard University Press (1982), p. 367.

government is a *residual* organization designed to address by laws and regulations the general interest when it is not properly taken care of by the autonomous actions of individuals.[36] But regulation is not something *external* to property. *It is part of the notion*, although it can be minimal or very extensive.[37] Increased regulation of property in any form *reduces* the degree of autonomy of the owner; it does not affect property as a right to decide about the use, disposition of or regulation of the object of property *as a matter of principle* – unless the regulation becomes so extensive that it amounts to a deprivation of property, to a 'taking'.[38] Similarly, 'deregulation' does not eliminate 'regulation': it just takes it away from the 'public' regulator to put it back into the hands of the 'private' owner.[39] The amount of 'law' in society is not determined by official rules only, but rather by all the rules in existence, whether public or private.[40]

The whole system, however, was predicated on one thing: that private property and rights of autonomy would be the prerogatives of *individuals*. When the US Constitution was adopted, there were only seven business corporations in existence and nowhere does the word 'corporation' appear in it. Corporations were not considered to represent a political issue at the time, although this changed rapidly. Originally, most American lawyers considered that a variety of institutions – business corporations, municipal corporations, guilds, churches etc. – were partly private and partly public in character. This changed progressively. Business corporations were stripped of some of their more public powers and

---

[36] *See also* Bobbio, *op cit*, note 11, p. 16; Jacques Chevallier, *L'État de droit*, Revue de Droit Public, pp. 313–380 (1988), p. 371 and Pistor, *op cit*, note 18, pp. 218–219.

[37] As noticed by Anthony Honoré, 'it is striking that the French Civil Code, enacted in an atmosphere of liberal individualism, defines ownership as "the right of enjoying and disposing of things in the most absolute manner, provided that one abstains from any use forbidden by statutes or subordinate legislation", while the Soviet Civil Code, framed in a socialist context, provides, in very similar language, that "within the limits laid down by law, the owner has the right to possess, to use, and to dispose of his property". Obviously much here depends on what limits are laid down by law in each system.' *See* in Geoffrey M. Hodgson, 'Editorial introduction to "Ownership" by A.M. Honoré' (1961), followed by 'Ownership' by A.M. Honoré, 9(2) *Journal of Institutional Economics*, pp. 223–255 (2013), p. 229.

[38] *See* in Section 1.1, the notion of Property as a Constitutional Prerogative.

[39] *See* Ireland, *op cit*, note 34, pp. 85–123. As a consequence, 20 years of privatization, deregulation and liberalization have simply increased the economic power of private firms; *see* Groupe de Lisbonne, *Limites à la concurrence – pour un nouveau contrat mondial*, Lisbonne: Fondation Gulbenkian, La Découverte (1995), p. 120.

[40] *E.g.* Lawrence M. Friedman, *Total Justice*, New York: Russell Sage Foundation (1985), p. 149.

general incorporation statutes made the corporate form available to all persons.[41] In the process, corporations became 'privatized' and were provided constitutional protections against governmental regulations comparable to the protections enjoyed by individual persons.

In France, business corporations were originally not even conceived as legal instruments belonging to private law. The legal commentators of French commercial law prior to the French Revolution only mention corporations (*sociétés de capitaux*) in passing, and often ignore them. Pothier makes no mention of them; Jousse no more; Savary and Bornier do not devote any doctrinal development to them. The attitude of these commercialists appears surprising to us. But they had difficulties integrating this new type of legal instrument into their understanding of private commercial companies. This is due to their semi-public nature. From the middle of the seventeenth century, corporations were constituted in France under the impulse of the royal power at the imitation of what already existed abroad, in Holland and England. A company could not have legal personality if there was no incorporation.[42] In France, it required a royal charter. But the King only consented to it if there was a *public interest* in doing so: the exploitation of the colonies or the development of maritime trade. Later, the King gave it protection, was personally interested in it, often as a shareholder, granted nobility to those who collaborated.[43] In 1664, Colbert created the *Compagnie des Indes Occidentales* and the *Compagnie des Indes Orientales*. In 1686, he created the Compagnie Générale for Insurance and Big Adventures. What was setting these companies apart was, from the point of view of their formation, the preponderant part played by the royal power. Not only was their constitutive charter an act of a legislative nature (edict or letter patent) signed by the King, duly countersigned and registered by the Parliament; but it also was, in essence, a real concession often pushed very far since, in some of these charters, the King divested himself in favour of the company of some of his rights of sovereignty, such as the right to wage war or render justice.[44] Characteristically, these great companies were

---

[41] William W. Fisher III, Morton J. Horwitz and Thomas A. Reed (eds.), *American Legal Realism*, New York: Oxford University Press (1993), p. 98.

[42] And not only in France. *See* Raymond Saleilles, *De la personnalité juridique*, Paris: Librairie Nouvelle de Droit et de Jurisprudence A. Rousseau (1910) (Editions La Mémoire du Droit, 2003), p. 209.

[43] Georges Ripert, *Les aspects juridiques du capitalisme moderne*, Paris: Librairie Générale de Droit et de Jurisprudence (1951), p. 56.

[44] Henri Lévy-Bruhl, *Histoire juridique des sociétés de commerce en France aux XVIIe et XVIIIe siècles*, Paris: Domat Montchrestien (1938), pp. 42–44.

legally considered as vassals of the King, owing him faith and homage (East India Company, Article 29, West India Company, Article 21).

With the French 1789 Revolution, the French declaration of human rights was concomitant with the destruction of all the intermediary, mandatory, corporate bodies of the *Ancien Régime*. Hence, the birth of legal monism – this idea that individuals are all equals under State law and that all intermediary groupings between individuals and States should be dissolved.[45] With regards to corporate legal vehicles, the antagonism was eased when the Directory allowed the formation of joint-stock companies in 1795. And under the regime of the 1807 Code of Commerce, limited liability corporations could be created; but their creation required the approval of the *Conseil d'État* and the demonstration that the corporation was used for a project of *public interest*. Initially, these legal entities were perceived as marginal and of limited importance.[46] The contemplated post-revolutionary society was a construction in which *individuals* enjoy their freedoms and their properties. They contract among themselves as equal parties. And *individuals* – although it took time to make this side of the institutional system effective via a succession of setbacks and political revolutions – participate in the process of collective rule-making via democratic institutions. The liberal constitutional system of government was conceived as a coherent Power System, with the *individual* rights proclaimed in the Bill of Rights or Preamble to the Constitution being intrinsically connected with the combined operations of the Organs of the State in the main body of the Constitution.[47]

In the liberal Power System, it was generally envisaged that in situations where the autonomous contracting activity of *individuals* would lead to undesired outcomes, *individuals* could, as voters, collectively act to correct the situation. In this fashion, economic liberalism was intrinsically linked to liberal democracy, which progressively developed and led to the introduction of regulatory laws.

---

[45] Léon Ingber, 'Le pluralisme juridique dans l'œuvre des philosophes du droit', in *Le pluralisme juridique*, Bruxelles: Editions de l'Université de Bruxelles, J. Gilissen (éd.) (1972), p. 58. *See also* Blaufarb, *op cit*, note 14, *especially* p. 128.

[46] Claude Fohlen, 'Société anonyme et développement capitaliste sous la monarchie censitaire', *Histoire des entreprises*, pp. 65–77 (1960), p. 67.

[47] In the US, the addition of a Bill of Rights was the price paid by the supporters of the remainder of the document to secure its ratification by the States. *See also* Rose, *op cit*, note 13, pp. 337–338. In Luhmann's expression, 'The constitution constitutes [*konstituiert*] and at the same time makes invisible the structural coupling of law and politics'; in Niklas Luhmann, 'La constitution comme acquis évolutionnaire', 22 *Droits*, pp. 103–125 (1995), p. 118.

Progressively also, however, corporate law was introduced into the laws of liberal Power Systems. It is one of the outcomes of a divided World Political System: States have always competed among themselves to provide businesses with laws attractive to them. We are very much aware of this issue in the world of the twenty-first century. States compete across the board to attract economic activity on their territory to provide jobs to their population and collect at least some taxes.[48] The agents of this transformation are primarily multinational firms. They are today the most effective wielding economic power organizations in the world. Their power is not a power to invade: their investments are always seen as a local victory. Their power is a power *not to* invade or to *withdraw*, to exercise an *exit* option. And this option they have is what forces States, for example, to dismantle their systems of social protection or to adjust their tax systems, in particular by reducing corporate taxes and those taxes affecting the mobile global elite.[49] Global enterprises have spread their organizations over most of the planet and, in so doing, they have changed the mode of operation of the World Power System.

But the issue is not new and a major instance of competition among the States to serve the needs of businesses was the development of corporate laws. This is a known story in the US. The concept of a regulatory 'race' emerged during the late nineteenth and early twentieth century, when there was competition among States to attract corporations to incorporate in their jurisdiction. Some described the race as being a 'race to efficiency' while others, such as Justice Louis Brandeis, considered it was a 'race to the bottom'. The 'race to the bottom' metaphor was updated in 1974 by William Cary,[50] then former Chairman of the US Securities and Exchange Commission. But others have responded to defend the State competitive process as efficient.[51]

Although it is a lesser-known story, a similar process took place in Europe. Legislative changes took place in Britain in 1844 and 1856 and within 20 years, the number of British business companies went from

---

[48] For a relatively early account, *see* John M. Stopford, Susan Strange and John S. Henley, *Rival States, Rival Firms – Competition for World Market Shares*, Cambridge: Cambridge University Press (1991).

[49] Ulrich Beck and Johannes Willms, *Conversations with Ulrich Beck*, Cambridge: Polity Press (2004), pp. 46–47.

[50] William L. Cary, 'Federalism and Corporate Law: Reflections upon Delaware', 83 *Yale Law Journal*, pp. 663–705 (1974).

[51] Daniel R. Fischel, 'Race to the Bottom Revisited: Reflections on Recent Developments in Delaware's Corporation Law', 76 *Northwestern University Law Review*, pp. 913–945 (1981).

700 to 10,000.[52] In France, more flexibility was introduced in 1867 in the wake of Britain's relaxation of its laws and the adoption of free trade treaties.[53] One reason for granting freedom of incorporation was that England dictated French economic policy, and that the English companies, formerly subject to the approval of the Parliament and the Crown, had just obtained in 1856 their freedom of incorporation by simple recording. Moreover, they could operate in France. A French Statute of 30 May 1857, initially voted in favour of Belgian companies, made it possible to grant by Imperial Decree the same favour to the companies incorporated in other countries. The treaty of 30 April 1862 granted it to England only months after the two countries had concluded the 1860 Cobden–Chevalier free trade agreement[54] which infuriated French industrialists.[55] For them, it was now necessary to move forward on the corporate law front. A compromise was found in the creation of a new type of company, imitated from the English Private Limited Company and which was named (because of this imitation) the 'limited liability company' by the Statute of 23 May 1863. But the *société à responsabilité limitée* suffered from numerous limitations, including a capital capped at 20 million francs. Four years later, the French Empire had to give full freedom. In 1867, the Government introduced a bill removing the need for authorization. 'Government should not interfere with private transactions', stated Duverger's Explanatory Memorandum. It had taken 60 years to conquer the freedom to incorporate. There was clear understanding that:

---

[52] North, Wallis and Weingast, *op cit*, note 6, p. 219.

[53] Anne Lefebvre-Teillard, 'Liberté d'entreprendre, structures juridiques et rôle de l'État', in Alain Plessis, *Naissance des libertés économiques – Le décret d'Allarde et la loi Le Chapelier*, Paris: Histoire Industrielle, pp. 283–288 (1993), pp. 285–286.

[54] This treaty became the model for numerous subsequent commercial treaties and produced an 'international Bill of Rights'; *see* Ronen Palan, *The Offshore World – Sovereign Markets, Virtual Places and Nomad Millionaires*, Ithaca: Cornell University Press (2003, 2006), pp. 99–100.

[55] To give an idea of the protectionist climate in the *Corps Législatifs*, here are some of the remarks made by the *députés*: 'They delivered to England the future and the industrial fortune of France' (Pouyer-Querties); 'It is a sad day for a number of our industries; I doubt that there has been a more fatal for France since the revocation of the Edict of Nantes; it is that of January 23, 1860 ... that of the Franco-English treaty covering with ruins a whole part of our country' (Lesperut). In the same vein, the *Comité des Forges*, a very powerful lobby group of steel makers, would be created in 1864 to defend the French iron and steel metallurgy against competition brought by free trade; *see generally* M. Tacel, *Restaurations, Révolutions, Nationalités, 1815–1870*, Paris: Masson (3ème ed. 1981), p. 210. For a description of this '*coup d'Etat commercial*', *see* George Duby, *Histoire de la France*, Paris: Flammarion (1970), pp. 454–455.

the commercial prosperity of a country and the advantageous means it will have to compete on the international market depend, first of all, from the value of the instruments of production and commercialization the laws grant it. And of all the instruments of this kind, the commercial corporation ... is one of the most powerful. It is important in this regard not to lose ground.[56]

With the increased competition induced by free trade treaties, industrialists requested a relaxation of local corporate laws. Soon, the whole of Europe was left with no choice but to introduce the freely created limited liability corporation into the various national legal systems.[57]

But with 'free incorporation', what disappeared was the need to demonstrate that the use of this instrument to concentrate financial capital was – at least in part – in furtherance of the *general interest*. The concentration of property rights over productive assets in large corporate enterprises led to a concentration of the right of decision-making as a matter of principle into large organizations having no other concern than the pursuit of purely *private* interests. With globalization, property rights have now been spread all over the world to take advantage of the rich menu of State norms designed to attract businesses. This has led to a privatization of the world and to the rise of global issues which cannot be addressed in classical ways in the existing Power System.

Negative Externalities

Developing a renewed understanding of property is required today because our planet is facing potentially devastating challenges. In 2009, a group of Earth system and environmental scientists[58] identified 'Planetary Life Support Systems' which are essential for human survival. There are nine 'Earth System Processes' which could affect these 'Planetary Life Support Systems'. They are (1) climate change, (2) the biodiversity loss extinction rate, (3) anthropogenic nitrogen removal from the atmosphere and anthropogenic phosphorus going into the oceans,

---

[56] Saleilles, *op cit*, note 42, p. 40.

[57] For a general description of this process is Europe, *see* W.O. Henderson, *The Genesis of the Common Market*, London: Frank Cass & Co. Ltd. (1962).

[58] Including Johan Rockström from the Stockholm Resilience Centre and Will Steffen from the Australian National University, Nobel laureate Paul Crutzen, James Hansen and the German Chancellor's chief climate adviser Hans Joachim Schellnhuber.

(4) ocean acidification, (5) land use (land surface converted to cropland), (6) freshwater consumption, (7) ozone depletion, (8) atmospheric aerosols and (9) chemical pollution (concentration of toxic substances, plastics, endocrine disruptors, heavy metals and radioactive contamination into the environment).

The researchers attempted to quantify how far seven of these Planetary Life Support Systems have been pushed already. Their research was updated in 2015.[59] Their conclusion is that anthropogenic perturbation of four of the Life Support Systems exceeds the Planetary Boundaries they identified. This is the case for climate change, biosphere integrity, biochemical flows and land-system change.

With regards to climate change, an almost worldwide agreement was reached in 2015. The so-called Paris Agreement was concluded in December 2015 within the United Nations Framework Convention on Climate Change (UNFCCC). It has been negotiated by representatives of 196 States, and 184 of them have become party to it.

The Paris Agreement's long-term goal is to keep the increase in global average temperature to 'well below' 2°C above pre-industrial levels.[60] Under the Paris Agreement, each country must determine, plan and regularly report on the contribution that it undertakes to make to mitigate climate change. The contributions each individual country is to make to achieve the 2°C worldwide goal are set individually and are called Nationally Determined Contributions (NDCs). They are supposed to be 'ambitious', represent a 'progression over time' and be set 'with the view to achieving the purpose of this Agreement'. No mechanism, however, forces any country to set any specific target by any specific date.

While the individually set NDCs are not legally binding, the parties are legally bound to have their progress tracked by technical expert review to assess achievement towards the NDCs, and to determine ways to strengthen their ambition. Thus, each country must report every two years on its mitigation efforts, and all parties will be subject to both technical and peer review.

But even the negotiators of the Paris Agreement stated that the NDCs and the 2°C reduction target were insufficient. To start with, they noted

---

[59] Will Steffen et al., 'Planetary Boundaries: Guiding Human Development on a Changing Planet', 347 (6223) *Science*, p. 736 (2015).

[60] 'Trajectories of the Earth System in the Anthropocene', Will Steffen, Johan Rockström, Katherine Richardson, Timothy M. Lenton, Carl Folke, Diana Liverman, Colin P. Summerhayes, Anthony D. Barnosky, Sarah E. Cornell, Michel Crucifix, Jonathan F. Donges, Ingo Fetzer, Steven J. Lade, Marten Scheffer, Ricarda Winkelmann, Hans Joachim Schellnhuber, *Proceedings of the National Academy of Sciences*, August 2018.

'with concern' that the estimated aggregate greenhouse gas emission levels in 2025 and 2030 resulting from the intended NDCs do not fall within the 2°C scenario. Studies in the highly respected review *Nature* have shown subsequently that, as of 2017, *none* of the major industrialized nations were implementing the policies they had envisioned and they have not met their pledged emission reduction targets.[61] Further, as everybody knows, Donald Trump announced in June 2017 his intention to withdraw the US from the Agreement. The Emissions Gap Report 2017 published by the United Nations Environment Programme (UNEP) makes it clear that:

> current State pledges cover no more than a third of the emission reductions needed [and] even if the current NDCs are fully implemented, the carbon budget for limiting global warming to below 2°C will be about 80 percent depleted by 2030.[62]

To make things worse, a 2018 study points at the risk of crossing a *'threshold'* at which temperatures could rise to 4 or 5 degrees compared with the pre-industrial levels, through self-reinforcing feedbacks in the climate system.[63] The *'threshold'*, or climatological tipping point, is the value at which a very small increment for the control variable (like CO_2) produces a large, possibly catastrophic, change in the response variable (climate change). The study suggests that this threshold could be *below* the 2°C temperature target, agreed upon by the Paris climate deal. Study author Katherine Richardson stresses:

> we note that the Earth has never in its history had a quasi-stable state that is around 2° C warmer than the preindustrial and suggest that there is substantial risk that the system itself

---

[61] David G. Victor et al., 'Prove Paris was more than paper promises', *Nature Magazine* (1 August 2017); Joeri Rogelj et al., 'Paris Agreement climate proposals need a boost to keep warming well below 2° C', 539 *Nature*, pp. 631–639 (2016); Mooney, Chris, 'The world has the right climate goals – but the wrong ambition levels to achieve them', *Washington Post* (29 June 2016).

[62] *The Emissions Gap Report 2017*, United Nations Environment Programme (UNEP), Executive summary.

[63] 'Trajectories of the Earth System in the Anthropocene', Will Steffen, Johan Rockström, Katherine Richardson, Timothy M. Lenton, Carl Folke, Diana Liverman, Colin P. Summerhayes, Anthony D. Barnosky, Sarah E. Cornell, Michel Crucifix, Jonathan F. Donges, Ingo Fetzer, Steven J. Lade, Marten Scheffer, Ricarda Winkelmann, Hans Joachim Schellnhuber, *Proceedings of the National Academy of Sciences*, August 2018.

will continue warming because of all of these other processes even if we stop emissions. This implies not only reducing emissions but much more.

Co-author Johan Rockström called into question the wisdom of the Paris Agreement: even if greenhouse gas emissions are substantially reduced to limit warming to 2°C, that might still be above the 'threshold' at which self-reinforcing climate feedbacks add additional warming until the climate system stabilizes in a hothouse climate state. This would make parts of the world uninhabitable, raise sea levels by up to 60 m (200 ft) and raise temperatures by 4–5°C (7.2–9.0°F).[64]

With climate change, we are clearly confronted with the largest negative externality to the economic system ever experienced.[65] And we do not seem to be appropriately institutionally equipped to face it. While the Power System has dramatically changed with the advent of the corporate system, we have not properly adapted our understanding of the operations of our institutions to their mode of operation. And consequently, as written by three major economists, including two recipients of the Nobel Prize:

> The most severe distortions in market prices derive from the incapacity to evaluate the rarity of environmental resources. … The world is depleting rapidly the available 'carbon space' but those using it are not paying the price. As a result, the price of all the goods and services making use of this carbon space (in effect all the goods and services) are distorted.[66]

The point, at this stage of the presentation of my analysis, is that an exchange system destroying our life-supporting environment can hardly be said to be 'efficient'. It is the case only if one incorrectly neglects negative externalities – as we do today – including the largest of all time: climate change.

It would thus appear that the present mode of operation of the productive assets, be it via market mechanisms or within firms, cannot

---

[64] *See also* Nicholas Stern, 'The Structure of Economic Modeling of the Potential Impacts of Climate Change: Grafting Gross Underestimation of Risk onto Already Narrow Science Models', 51(3) *Journal of Economic Literature*, pp. 838–859 (2013).

[65] Craig Deegan, 'The accountant will have a central role in saving the planet … really? A reflection on "green accounting and green eyeshades twenty years later"', 24 *Critical Perspectives on Accounting*, pp. 448–458 (2013), p. 452.

[66] Joseph Stiglitz, Amartya Sen and Jean-Paul Fitoussi, *Richesse des nations et bien-être des individus*, Paris: Odile Jacob (2009), pp. 134–135.

be defended either on autonomy grounds or on efficiency ones. A major challenge of our time is to preserve the autonomy granted to *individuals* via the use of their property rights and freedom while at the same time dealing with the potentially deadly negative externalities we are experiencing due to the autonomous use of property rights by productive organizations.

The Concentration of Property and the Evolution of the Power System

The development of corporate law has completely changed the structure of the economy and of the political and legal systems. By concentrating property rights, corporate organizations have concentrated unrestrained, subjective, autonomous, private powers – property rights – into very large organizations to the point that the reality of the operation of the World Power System is significantly disconnected from the rules officially applicable to it. Institutions originally developed for an agrarian society have been strained by the development of an industrial and financial corporate world economy. In the US context, Felix Frankfurter noted, just before becoming one of the Justices of the US Supreme Court in 1939, that:

> The history of American constitutional law in no small measure is the history of the impact of the modern corporation on the American scene.[67]

But this is true as well for other systems of government. The history of this impact (which spans less than two centuries) has produced two convergent movements – towards the great economic organization, the large enterprise; and towards the extended government. Although different answers were sometimes given to similar issues in different jurisdictions, this history has operated in many parts of the world: the concentration of private property *has* affected the operation of public government; which, of course, has affected the operation of property.

For many, this evolution is linked to the *industrial* revolution and the surge of large industrial production with dramatic changes in the organization of work and on the impact of human activity over the environment, social and natural. But this evolution is also due, and I think more importantly for our purposes, to a *legal* revolution under the form

---

[67] Arthur S. Miller, 'Toward the "Techno-Corporate" State? – An Essay in American Constitutionalism', 14 *Villanova Law Review*, pp. 1–73 (1968), p. 3.

of the introduction and spreading of the *corporate* system. Limited liability corporations are legal tools with extraordinary capabilities. Progressively, but widely introduced into liberal legal systems during the nineteenth century, they allowed the concentration of capital (property rights) into private organizations to an unprecedented level. And because of their legal characteristics, they made it possible to concentrate prerogatives initially designed for *individuals* into *organizations*. They concentrated property – the 'rights of decision making as a matter of principle towards the objects of property' – into organizations which benefited from the same rights of autonomy as *individuals* although they are *not* individuals.[68] The use of autonomy rights by organizations over large concentrations of property rights, such as industrial plants, led to an explosion of negative externalities and inequality and to the need for a change in the role of the State.

With globalization and the spreading of the corporate system, the 'impact of the modern corporation' is now being felt at the global level. But there is no global State in a position to react and adjust its mode of operation. And even worse: the States are now part of a global competitive process which leads to an erosion of their ability to fulfil their required missions. They are pushed into an enhanced competition for the localization of business activity by global business firms on their territory.

So-called 'market economies' in fact comprise both 'markets' and 'organizations': business firms. At the world level, most of *international* economic exchange is in fact *intra-firm* exchange: 80 per cent of world trade takes place *within* organizations, within multinational enterprises. The exchange decisions made within these organizations are not based on *market* prices. They are made *within* organizations seeking to optimize the localization of the various firm activities. Prices are *administered*. Prices internal to firms are not *market* prices: they are *administrative decisions*. And the issues created by the tweaking of prices have increased in seriousness because of a deficient principal/agent economic theory which pushes firms into exploiting as much as possible the loopholes generated by a divided State System to extract more profits. Today, firms are managed by their executives with a mandate to maximize 'shareholder value'. With such a mandate, combined with an improper *accounting* of the firms' effective value creation or destruction, enterprises today often

---

[68] This is one of the two fallacies about corporations: treating them as *individuals* (the other one being to treat them as mere nexuses of contracts); *see generally* Philip Pettit, 'Two Fallacies about Corporations', in *Performance and Progress: Essays on Capitalism, Business, and Society*, pp. 379–394, Subramanian Rangan (ed.), Oxford: Oxford University Press (2015).

operate as destroyers of the natural environment and of the States' access to financial resources. As we will see, this translates into an accounting acknowledgement of 'shareholder value creation' when the reality is that (in particular) our natural capital is being eroded, workforces are impoverished and taxes are being avoided. In the present global economy, 'shareholder value' can be created at the expense of the destruction of natural capital, at the expense of expendable workers and at the expense of the financing of required States' functions.

I will concentrate the presentation of the impact of my analyses mostly on the issue of global climate change. At this stage of our shared history, we are left with a limited amount of CO_2 to emit to reach any given global warming level. This is a form of capital we share. To preserve it, the accounting of economic operations needs to be enriched by the inclusion into the accounting of all the productive organizations of the replacement value of the CO_2 they use in their operations. The challenge is to identify the means via which it is possible to get firms to account for their real economic impact. In this book, I advocate a move away from agency theory as presently understood, i.e. from this notion that firm managers are under a duty to maximize the short-term welfare of the holders of *financial* capital only. In fact, other forms of capital *also* need to be protected in the firm's management of the property rights under its control. The negative externalities firms generate have no *price*; but they can be allocated an accounting *value* – their *replacement cost*. What does it cost to absorb the same quantity of CO_2 as that which has been produced over a period of time by the business firm? The measurement and accounting of this cost is required to give firms an incentive to reduce their CO_2 footprint and achieve what is ultimately required: carbon neutrality. Just like the profits of a firm destroying part of its financial capital are not real profits, the profits of a firm which is not carbon neutral evidence in fact an unpaid for destruction of our CO_2 capital.

All organizations, public or private, are accounting organizations. What does not enter their accounts via prices or laws can enter them via market pressure to include the replacement cost of the other forms of capital being used. Otherwise, market participants cannot discriminate among firms which are environmentally sustainable and those which are not. For investment funds, the case can be made that not requiring this information from the firms they are investing in is a breach of the fiduciary duty they have towards their own investors who need to know whether their savings are invested into sustainable companies or not.

We know that if no serious change occurs in the management of our common capital in CO_2 absorption, a large proportion of the equity existing today will disappear the hard way, via the numerous and chaotic disruptions our planet will experience. *Financial equity* will get destroyed if our CO_2 *capital* is destroyed. Confronted with this reality, equity investors *today* need to have access to the appropriate information to direct their investments. They need to know, for each company, the replacement cost of the CO_2 it is using *now* so as to avoid the destructive ones. And directors will increasingly be under pressure to provide this information. This would give companies a serious incentive to reduce their CO_2 production footprint.

In short, it is possible in the present World Power System to address climate change. But it requires understanding that business firms affect all sorts of values in the management decisions they make and that it is now necessary to properly account for their value creation or destruction via proper accounting rules. What cannot be properly priced by the market for *productive* assets (e.g. because no one owns the CO_2 absorption capacity which therefore cannot be *sold* for a *price*), or via laws which can't be adopted by competing States, can be priced by *financial* markets. Today's equity valuation by financial markets lacks the required information to differentiate firms which are *sustainable* after taking into account the replacement cost of their CO_2 consumption from firms *which are not sustainable*. By providing market participants the information required to make investment decisions in sustainable businesses, a strong incentive would be given to firms to adjust their internal processes. Firms unable to change their ways and to reduce their environmental footprint would lead the way to firms which can, and the best arbitrator should be a properly informed equity market – a properly informed market for the valuation of shares of capital.

Understanding that it is via this type of adaptation that our global society's operations can be adjusted to our natural environment's limits in an open society requires a proper understanding of the operation of today's World Power System, its shortcomings and their origin. This is the objective of this book. It requires a deep understanding of property, of the corporate reconfiguration of property rights into global firms and of their role in the structuring of our Power System. This book provides such knowledge.

Content

This book is structured in two parts. The first deals with the concept of property in today's world. The second deals with the position of global firms in the World Power System and the institutional adjustments needed as a consequence of their existence.

The first part addresses the operation of property today. It disregards debates about the purported appearance of property in a state of nature and the development of government to protect it. It also shows that the notion of 'economic property rights' which some economists have entertained as of late is a costly distraction. Property is a prerogative of legal persons and must be addressed as a legal concept.

The first part (**Property**) is divided into five chapters. They address in turn the meaning of property today (1), the role of property in a modern constitutional mode of government (2), the relationship between sovereignty and property (3), the historical movement of the State from political enterprise to the modern State (4) and, finally, how modern constitutional systems mix political democracy and what can be economic despotisms (5).

To start with, it is important to realize that contrary to the 'common sense' understanding of property, property is not a right over things. Property is a right of property owners against the world at large in connection with the object of property. It is first of all a right of decision- and rule-making in connection with objects of property which is part of the foundations of our Power System. This is how property operates in our modern society. It is part of the constitutional rules required for the operation of a 'State of law'.

In **Chapter 1** (**The Meaning of Property**), property is presented in a constitutional perspective. Property in the modern, present sense, certainly never existed in any 'state of nature', whatever this expression means. Modern property can only exist in an orderly and relatively sophisticated society and is part of what I call the Power System. It is a prerogative which is protected both *by* the State (protecting the owner against theft, trespass and other abuses of property) and it is protected *against* the State (the State being effectively prohibited from unlawfully appropriating private property). I will show that contrary to what most economists think, possession plays a secondary role in the notion of property. From an economic standpoint, property, as a prerogative protected by the State, is a value-enhancing institution. Possession is only of secondary importance and raises issues in the case of *agency* relationship, i.e. when the *possessor* of the property is not its *owner*. Beyond this issue, we will see that property includes a right to exclude which entails considerable contractual and power consequences. It translates, in particular, into a right to hire and to fire. Because of the institution of property, the economic system operates via two sets of separate tools: prices, when resources are sold and purchased; and orders, when individuals work for owners. In this perspective, owners are akin to *lawmakers* in connection with their property. They exercise sovereignty, their prerogatives being rights 'as a matter of principle' and not merely 'bundles of rights'. Laws affecting the use of property are only limited *derogations* to a prerogative – property – which exists *as a matter of principle*. Just like the right to personal liberty is not the sum of the right to sleep, to take a walk, to go to the beach and so on in an endless list, the right to property is not the sum of limited prerogatives. This view is congruent with the theory of ownership developed by Oliver Hart (2016 economics Nobel prizewinner) and applies in both Civil and Common Law legal systems. Understanding property in this fashion is a key to the understanding of the operation of the existing Power System.

In **Chapter 2 (The Modern Constitutional Mode of Government)**, the notions of State and of the 'Organs of the State' are explained in some detail to distinguish their prerogatives from private prerogatives. Private property, in this respect, grants autonomy from the 'Organs of the State'. It is part of the constitutional prerogatives protecting private persons against excessive public governmental encroachments. It is part of a constitutional order which combines both democracy and distrust for democracy, by limiting the prerogatives of the Organs of the State. The approach developed proposes a unitary view of the Constitution as providing for both public and private prerogatives, the first ones being exercised by Organs of the State and the second ones by legal persons which are *not* Organs of the State. Public and private prerogatives operate via fundamentally different rules, private property rights entitling their holders to exercise their prerogatives in a despotic manner, i.e. they can do what they want with what they have without the need to take anybody's advice or authorization – which is the definition of despotism.

Chapter 3 (Sovereignty and Property) deals with the relationship between these two concepts. It first addresses the thesis developed by North,[69] Wallis and Weingast on the role of organized violence in the development of a modern, open access society. Their intuition is that the 'limited access order' of the 'natural state' in which personal relationships form the basis of social organization had to leave the way to an 'open access order' in which impersonal categories of individuals interact. This is generally correct. But they neglected the role of *law* in the process and, in particular, the role of the development of *constitutional* modes of government. Via modern international law, starting in Europe in the middle of the seventeenth century, sovereignty was allocated among States. Via modern liberal constitutions, internal sovereignty was decentralized as a matter of principle to owners, who are decision-makers as a matter of principle towards the objects of property. The operations of political

---

[69] Douglass North received the economics Nobel prize in 1993.

Organs of the State, of administrative Organs of the State and of law can usefully be viewed in this perspective.

Chapter 4 (From Political Enterprise to the Modern State) explains how the State evolved from being merely a type of political enterprise to the institution it is today. In its origins, the State is nothing more than a coalition of powerful people, mostly men, controlling a territory via the use of violence if necessary. Property rights in the modern sense hardly exist at this stage of institutional development. Accessorily, violent coalitions of political entrepreneurs provide a service to the population: order. The political enterprise will extend this service, enlarging its jurisdiction and effective control over competing forces and will facilitate and benefit from the progressive development of market exchange. The modern State is intrinsically linked to modern taxes, payable *in money* and not *in kind*. Via a very long process, the resources needed by States to provide their services will be extracted via taxation and not mere compulsion in the context of the development of a monetary economy developed in part thanks to State action. States developed an inherent interest in protecting property and facilitating monetary exchange as a means to access to more resources via the taxation of a monetary economy.

In **Chapter 5 (The Mixing of Democracy and Despotism)**, I show that constitutional systems of government promoting the protection of property actually lead to a mix of democracy and despotism. This is due to the fact that property, with its absolute prerogatives and the decentralization of sovereignty it represents, was designed to protect individuals' autonomy. With the advent of a corporate economy, however, these prerogatives were concentrated within corporations used to legally structure business firms. A new form of legal pluralism developed, in an unofficial manner. Firms are organizations coordinating the operation of large sectors of the economy. But they do it in an unofficial manner. After each of the major crises of the twentieth century – the two World Wars and the Great Depression of the 1930s, in particular – radical evolutions occurred in the legal systems to equilibrate the imbalanced operation of the private side of the Power System. Protective laws were adopted; social rights were granted. Via the Constitutional Revolutions of the twentieth century, the liberal, nightwatchman State moved to become the welfare and regulatory State. These Constitutional Revolutions are now being challenged by globalization.

The second part of this book (**Firms in the World Power System**) explains the position of global firms in the World Power System and how a renewed understanding of the effective structure of the present Power System could lead to an adjustment of their role.

This part stresses the importance of corporate property. The only type of corporation which is discussed to some extent in the first part of this book is the State. But we now live in a world of corporations and the fact that for most significant economic activities, individual persons act via separate legal, corporate persons, has completely changed the economic and political landscape. When liberal constitutions were put in place, it was not envisioned that the rights of autonomy granted to individuals would be extended to corporate vehicles. Corporations were feared and perceived as incompatible with liberal democracy. But the introduction of the business corporation into the legal system proved irresistible and led to a move from liberalism to capitalism.

The second part is divided into five chapters. They address in turn the concept of *firm* (an economic organization), which is explained and differentiated from the concept of *corporation* (a specific form of legal person used to legally structure most large firms) (6), the features of business corporations which explain their considerable success (7), the spreading of the corporate system and its consequences (8), the need to deal with firms in a renewed manner in an international economy (9) and ways through which it is possible to enrich financial accounting to make our World Power System sustainable (10).

The concept of firm is explained in **Chapter 6 (Firms)**. The chapter starts by making a sharp distinction between the concept of 'firm' and the concept of 'corporation'. The two words are often used as synonyms, in many different languages, but they correspond to radically different notions. The firm is an organization performing an economic activity. The corporation is a type of legal person – most firms of some significance being organized using business corporations. The chapter goes on to explain the notion of the World Wide Web of Contracts, which today connects almost everyone to almost everyone. But the nature of the contracts in this Web vary significantly – pure market sale and purchase contracts being at one end of the contractual spectrum. At the other end, one finds relatively stable *clusters* of long-term contracts. Some are the contractual substratum of households. Some are the contractual substratum of business firms. The chapter goes on to explain the legal structure of the unincorporated business firm, its position in the World Wide Web of Contracts and the notion of the firm's limits. It then explains the incorporation process and what changes when a corporation is used to legally structure a firm. The importance for the corporation to be a legal person is stressed and the fact that the incorporation leads to two separate forms of property rights linked to the same assets – the property right over the productive *assets* owned by the corporation and the property right over the *shares* of stock issued by the corporation and owned by the shareholders – is explained.

In **Chapter 7 (The Features of Business Corporations)**, we will look at some fundamental features of business corporations. One of the key features is that business corporations have what is called 'legal personality': they are treated by the legal system as 'persons' in a position to own assets, to contract and be liable for the torts attributed to them by the legal system. Corporations can issue shares of stock which entitles them to raise equity capital to develop businesses. The shares are autonomous objects of property and with the development of capital markets, two separate forms of property have gained in importance: the ones owned by corporations over *productive assets*; and the ones owned by shareholders over *shares*. Both categories of owners are the decision-makers as a matter of principle over what they own: the *productive assets* for the *corporation*, and the *shares* for the *shareholders*. And contrary to a widespread misconception, shareholders do not own firms, nor corporations, nor their assets. The asset and liability partitioning deriving from the existence of the corporation as a *separate legal person* is a fundamental feature of modern capitalism. Combined with the locking-in of productive assets in the ownership of corporations, this legal structuring of businesses has concentrated residual control rights – property rights – over productive assets into the ownership of potentially eternal corporations. This concentration of power into the hands of firm managers raises the issue of the proper rules of governance applicable to global firms as significant participants in the World Power System.

In **Chapter 8 (The Spreading of the Corporate System and its Consequences)**, we will analyse how business corporations developed in the industrializing world in a legal environment which was initially hostile to them. Competing firms have led competing States to amend initially restrictive corporate laws to transform incorporation from a *privilege* into a *right*. Freedom of incorporation is now widely accepted. The development of corporate law has led to the advent of Financial Capitalism, i.e. a form of capitalism in which two forms of capital exist in connection with any given bundle of assets and contracts concentrated into any given firm structured using a corporation having issued shares of capital. There is first the capital and contracts required by the productive activity; and there is then the financial capital represented by the financial instruments issued by the corporation used to legally structure the firm. To understand the role played by financial markets, I will present the evolving relation between firms and States in a globalized economy. To do this, I will use the simple model of a firm adapting its corporate structure to the opportunities offered by the evolving legal rules in an international economy. This will lead us to a reassessment of the necessity to differentiate firms from corporations and to insist on the importance of the rules of corporate governance in a globalized world. The opportunities offered to multinational firms by the international economy combined with an improper mandate to maximize short-term shareholder value, and the biased accounting rules accompanying it, lead to the accounting acknowledgement of 'shareholder value creation' even when *no* real 'value' is being created.

In **Chapter 9** (**Coping with Firms**), I will address the necessity to cope with firms as participants to the World Power System. The issue raised by the rise of private government has been spotted early on in both the US and Europe. But the development of several schools of thought was stopped by the spread of the simplistic 'agency theory' which has led to biased firm governance worldwide. The bias extends to accounting rules which do not provide a full picture of the impact of a firm's operations and actually prevents firms from adapting their ways to the requirements of today's predicament. Addressing world issues such as climate change requires the making of decisions to change our ways of producing, travelling and consuming. These decisions are made by individuals as individuals or as agents of the institutions of the World Power System. At the roots of this System lie property rights which are protected by the States and which form part of the constitutional systems of government. The concentration of productive assets within corporations which are used to legally structure large business firms has changed the global constitution. Economic decisions within the World Power System are not made based on *prices* only. Within organizations they are made on the basis of an *accounting* of the operations of the organization. To change these decisions, we need to amend the ways organizations account for their operations, considering the various forms of capital being used (financial and environmental – for our purposes). We will look at the issues raised by the fact that in an open economy, the competition among large business firms derivatively leads to a competition among States to offer firms accommodating legal environments. This limits the States' ability to internalize negative externalities and to redistribute income. Given the inherent defects of our divided State System, it is at the firm level that governmental rules must be developed so that firms consider the consequences of their activities to a larger extent than they do today.

Finally, in **Chapter 10 (Towards a Sustainable World Power System)**, we will look at some of the tools available to address the issue of climate change in the present World Power System. We will first present the issue and the daunting task of addressing it in our divided world within a relatively short time frame. We must take seriously the real structure of the Power System and find the way to re-engineer multinational enterprises in a way that they address climate change issues in their day-to-day operations. A flawed agency theory has led to improper firm governance, the maximization of shareholder short-term interests leading to a massive production of negative externalities and to accounting rules which reinforce the pressure of this inadequate mandate. We need to move to true cost (or full-cost) accounting by integrating into the accounts of reporting entities the replacement cost of the CO_2 used in their value chains, via a life-cycle approach encompassing the impacts of products and services from their design to the sourcing of the materials used, the production, transportation, sale and then recycling and waste management. Using the notion of *replacement cost* prevents any attempt at *pricing* environmental services. Pricing would be subjective and/ or artificial. The move allows us to go beyond the financial sustainability of firms, which is a requirement but is insufficient. Firms also need to show that they are compatible with the preservation of natural resources. It is the only way to make firms and our kind of society, with strong rights of autonomy, including property rights, sustainable.

★★★

In conclusion, property rights are legal rights. They are fundamental rights for the individuals enjoying their prerogatives and building blocks for the institutional operation of the polities defining and enforcing them. Owners have the right of decision-making as a matter of principle towards the objects of property. The acknowledged role of political institutions, in connection with the autonomous operation of property, is to correct the negative externalities and inequalities which may ensue. Once this is understood, it becomes clear that market institutions are inseparable from political institutions in a position to correct the undesired outcomes of the autonomous operation of property rights and other liberties. Having democratic political institutions operative over the operations of 'the market' is a requirement for making the price system work.

With globalization, this allocation of prerogatives is fundamentally challenged. The rights of decision-making as a matter of principle over productive assets have been concentrated into large corporate organizations operating at the world level. The internalizing and redistributive functions remain decentralized at the local, State level. Combined with a mandate given to firms to maximize short-term shareholder value and an accounting of the firm's activities concentrating on financial returns and ignoring the costs imposed outside the organization, a perfect storm has been and still is in the making.

Economic theory has not been able to catch up with the developments of the last several decades because of its lack of understanding of property rights and how they operate. They are inseparable from the State System creating them, defending them, enforcing them and making sure that the so-called 'market failures' are corrected. At the global level, this division of functions does not work: there is no world State to make the 'market' work. 'Market failures' combine with 'governmental failures'.

Existing theories of the firm are inadequate to assist us in addressing this issue. Firms do not operate like markets and, having concentrated property rights, they have a governmental function. The agency theory, which is at the root of the present rules of corporate governance and has led to an improper accounting of the firm's operations, is part of the problem.

To cure this issue, more information should be made available about each firm's environmental footprint. What is required, in connection with the climate change issue we are dealing with, is to integrate within the instruments used to make economic decisions *costs* which have no *prices*. This can be done via the accounting system, which can supplement defective markets and a defective State System. Sooner or later, unsustainable businesses will be out of business and equity investors in these firms will lose the value of their investment, employees will lose their jobs, surrounding communities will be left with industrial remnants and so on. Equity investors need to know *today* whether the enterprises in which they are invested are sustainable or whether they are on a path towards unsustainability. They have a *right* to get this information about the business models of the firms they are invested in *now* because this can have a dramatic impact on the long-term value of their investment. And corporate directors and officers have a duty to give market participants a true and fair view of the outcome of the operations. By forcing companies to give this information, concerned investors can make it a market obligation to become sustainable or else, for lack of investment, including equity investment by shareholders, they will have to leave room for firms which can be.

PART I

Property

Introduction to Part I

The first part of this book is divided into five chapters. They address in turn the meaning of property today (1), the role of property in a modern constitutional mode of government (2), the relationship between sovereignty and property (3), the historical movement of the State from political enterprise to the modern State (4) and, finally, how modern constitutional systems mix political democracy and what can be economic despotisms (5).

To start with, it is important to realize that contrary to the common-sense understanding of property, property is not a right over things. It is a right of property owners against the world at large in connection with the objects of property. It is first of all a right of decision- and rule-making as a matter of principle in connection with objects of property. This makes of property part of the foundations of our Power System. Property is part of the constitutional rules required for the operation of a 'State of law'.

$$\star\star\star$$

Contrary to 'common-sense' perceptions of what property is, and to most of the explicit or implicit assumptions in the mainstream economic literature on property rights, property is not a right over things. Property is a right of legal persons (of 'owners') against all other persons in connection with the object of property.[70]

In day-to-day life, one can avoid the pedantry of correcting this widespread misconception and treat property as a right over things.[71]

---

[70] Richard Ely has a close position when he writes that 'strictly speaking, property refers to rights only. Property is an exclusive right. Speaking accurately, then, property is not a thing but the rights which extend over a thing.' Ely, *op cit*, note 21, p. 108. The slight difference is that I do not think property is the rights which extend over a thing; it is a right against others (a right of decision-making as a matter of principle) in connection with a thing.

[71] I use the word 'thing' for convenience only. There are many objects of property which are not physical, such as a patent, a trademark, a copyright, a share of stock, a bond, and so on.

Making the mistake of thinking that rights exist over things and not against legal persons in connection with things, however, prevents the development of a proper understanding of property rights and of their role in today's society.[72]

Most economists treat property as a spontaneous institution.[73] They start their analyses with some notion of hunters and gatherers acquiring property by hunting rabbits or gathering berries. Then the hunters and gatherers meet and barter. They agree that on this particular day, so many berries are worth one rabbit. Then money is introduced in the system to facilitate exchange.[74] The market economy is born. With this starting point, what property means is never really addressed. It appears as being mere possession over things: rabbits or berries, obtained via labour.

With rare exceptions, economists generally consign a secondary or epiphenomenal role to law in their analyses.[75] When confronted with evidence that their conception of property may be incomplete, they often retreat by saying that the notion of 'economic' property right is different

---

[72] In *Legal Foundations of Capitalism*, John R. Commons attributed the prominence of physical objects over legal relationship in economics to the concomitance of the development of economics as a science and the industrial revolution. *See* Commons, John R., *Legal Foundations of Capitalism*, Madison: The University of Wisconsin Press (1968, 1st edition 1924), p. 47: 'Modern economic theory started with the Industrial Revolution of the eighteenth and nineteenth centuries. The steam engine was invented by John Watt in the same year that his friend, Adam Smith, published *The Wealth of Nations*. This coincidence of wealth and machinery explains, in part, the prominence of physical things in the form of commodities, rather than legal relations in the form of transactions, which dominated economic theory for a hundred years.'

[73] For example, Steve Pejovich, one of the gurus of the property rights analysis of economics, starts his 'Foreword' to *The Elgar Companion to The Economics of Property Rights*, Cheltenham: Edward Elgar (2004) (ed. Enrico Colombatto) with the sentence 'From the beginning of recorded history, people have understood the importance of property for their survival'. Armen Alchian, Harold Demsetz, Henry Manne, Douglass North, Richard Posner and Oliver Williamson are then listed among the founding fathers of the discipline.

[74] The fact, however, is that in anthropology, no example of a barter economy has ever been described, let alone the emergence of money from it; *e.g.* David Graeber, *Debt – The First 5,000 Years*, Brooklyn and London: Melville House (2011, 2012, 2014), pp. 21–41.

[75] Geoffrey M. Hodgson, 'Much of the "economics of property rights" devalues property and legal rights', 11(4) *Journal of Institutional Economics*, pp. 683–709 (2015), p. 685. For a review of property rights economics, *see* Kirsten Foss and Nicolai Foss, 'Coasian and Modern Property Rights Economics', 11(2) *Journal of Institutional Economics*, pp. 391–411 (2014).

from the legal notion.[76] They thus absolve themselves from any need to explain the function of legal institutions. This can lead to serious misunderstandings. Daniel Cole, for example, rightly asserts that:

> the notion of extra-legal, non-institutionalized 'economic property rights' creates unnecessary confusion that obstructs efforts by legal scholars and economists to advance our understanding of how institutions structure exchange.[77]

With 'extra-legal' notions of property, the same words tend to take a wealth of meanings and it makes it hard to understand each other.[78]

The reality is that for any real-life participant to economic exchange, the meaning of 'property rights' first lies *in the law*. Giving 'property rights' constructed meanings to develop above-ground theories obscures the issues.[79] As will be shown in this book, it is *impossible* to understand economic liberalism and capitalism without understanding the legal system and the role played, inter alia, by property rights in these systems

---

[76] Thomas W. Merrill and Henry E. Smith, 'The Property/Contract Interface', 101(4) *Columbia Law Review*, pp. 773–852 (2001), pp. 775–776.

[77] Daniel H. Cole, '"Economic Property Rights" as "nonsense upon stilts": a comment on Hodgson', 11(4) *Journal of Institutional Economics*, pp. 725–730 (2015), p. 729.

[78] *See also* Sabine Hoffmann, 'Property, possession and natural resource management: towards a conceptual clarification', 9(1) *Journal of Institutional Economics*, pp. 39–60 (2013). The issue goes beyond semantics and the mere confrontation of different paradigms. Confusing possession and property leads to serious errors, in particular with regards to the important issue of firm governance.

[79] Douglas Allen holds the exact opposite view, which shows how far we are, today, from a consensual understanding of property rights. Allen writes that 'contrary to Hodgson's claim that "it is impossible to understand capitalism … without an adequate conception of [legal] property", it is quite the opposite'; Douglas W. Allen, 'Comment on Hodgson on Property Rights', 11(4) *Journal of Institutional Economics*, pp. 711–717 (2015), p. 712. This is a strange position: how could an 'adequate conception of legal property' prevent an understanding of capitalism? Having such an 'adequate conception' may not be sufficient; but how could having an adequate conception of something prevent one from properly understanding something else? Maybe Allen really meant to write that it is possible to understand capitalism without having an adequate concept of legal property. That assumes Allen understands capitalism, or at least that Allen thinks he understands capitalism. But maybe if he would understand 'legal property', he would know better. Suffice to notice here that, on second thoughts apparently, in the conclusion of his article, Allen agrees that 'perhaps Hodgson is correct that not enough attention is directed at the law itself'; see *Ibid*, p. 716. This is quite right.

of government. It is quite extraordinary that on this issue, neo-classical economists adopt the same stance as pure Marxists: they treat legal rules as a mere superstructure of secondary importance, their content being supposedly dependent on the production regime – the 'infrastructure' in Marxist terms.[80]

Law Matters

In the reality of the institutional environment in which real-life entrepreneurs, consumers and firms operate, it is the *legal system* which shapes the type of relationships they will have in connection with what they exchange. If and when the time of third-party enforcement comes, only the legal has teeth. Neglecting the importance of the law as is the case in the standard economics of property rights is deeply mistaken. If one wants to develop a real-life economic analysis of property rights, one must think and develop concepts taking into account the institutional and conceptual systems within which *real-life* participants to economic exchange *must* operate. It may be easier to develop theories without going through the rigours of legal analysis. But the relevance of these theories to real-life issues in a world with positive transaction costs is quite limited. Ronald Coase (1991 economics Nobel prizewinner) wrote very clearly that if we move from a regime of zero transaction costs to one of positive transaction costs (i.e. from an unrealistic model to a more real-life situation), what becomes immediately clear is the crucial importance of the legal system. What are traded on 'markets' are not, as is often supposed by economists, physical entities, but the *rights* existing in connection with these objects of property. And these rights and the legal persons owning them are created by the legal system.[81] With regards to property rights, Daniel Cole and Peter Grossman explained that 'it is careless (to say the least) for economists writing about property rights simply to presume that

---

[80] Simon Deakin, David Gindis, Geoffrey M. Hodgson, Kainan Huang and Katharina Pistor, 'Legal institutionalism: Capitalism and the Constitutive Role of Law', 45 *Journal of Comparative Economics*, pp. 188–200 (2017), pp. 191 & 193; *see also* Pistor, *op cit*, note 18, pp. 116. *See also* Geoffrey M. Hodgson, *Conceptualizing Capitalism – Institutions, Evolution, Future*, Chicago and London: The University of Chicago Press (2015), p. 110.

[81] Ronald H. Coase, 'The Institutional Structure of Production', 82(4) *The American Economic Review*, pp. 713–719 (1992), p. 717.

such "rights" arise from mere use'.[82] Not using the concept of property rights in its legal sense leads to an absence of consensus about them among economists, which is necessarily an issue with regards to one of our central institutions.

As Walter Lippmann wrote 80 years ago:

> The whole regime of private property and contract, the whole system of enterprise by individuals, partners, and corporations, exists in a legal context, and is inconceivable apart from that context.
>
> Just how the latter-day liberals came to overlook something so obvious as that is rather obscure. ...
>
> Without the implied willingness of the State to intervene with all its power, the rugged individualists who preached laissez-faire would have been utterly helpless. He could not have obtained or given title to any property. He could not have made a contract, however free. He could never have organized a corporation with limited liability and perpetual succession.[83]

In her recent book on *The Code of Capital*, Katarina Pistor provided an overview of the various means through which the law 'codes' assets, in particular to make them tradeable. Her analysis purports to trace the 'making of capital' via this 'coding' process, and she insists on the key importance of law in this regard. I share many of her conclusions. But my analysis is different. It does not make use of any notion of 'coding' which I think can end up being confusing for non-lawyers. The notion covers under one term very different legal processes and institutions. My own analysis starts from a particular legal institution – the notion of property. It explains in details why it is the key legal notion for a joint analysis of economics and politics, which is made possible if one integrates in the analysis the *legal* structuring of society. It then explains the roles of the notion of property in the present institutional structuring of our societies, in particular in what I call the World Power System, which is now in operation at the global level.

---

[82] *See* Daniel H. Cole and Peter Z. Grossman, 'The Meaning of Property Rights: Law versus Economics?', 78 *Land Economics*, pp. 317–330 (2002). *See also* Claude Menard and Mary M. Shirley, 'The Contribution of Douglass North to New Institutional Economics', in Rafe Blaufarb, *The Great Demarcation – The French Revolution and the Invention of Modern Property*, pp. 11–29, Oxford: Oxford University Press (2016), p. 15.

[83] Walter Lippmann, *An Inquiry into the Principles of The Good Society*, Boston: Little, Brown and Company (1938), pp. 189–190.

In this book, I review the work of several key economists having concentrated their attention on institutions. But I do it from a legal perspective. Many of their contributions can be enriched by supplementing their intuitions with a rigorous legal analysis. Adding the legal dimension is important because any business person has to structure business activities in compliance with the law. In my view, the analysis has to start with a proper understanding of what a property right is. It is the foundational right for any sophisticated market economy to exist. Other key concepts like commercial contracts, corporations and firms can then be better explained.

A Deeply Embedded Legal Institution

No economist so far has come close to a proper understanding of property.[84] And there is certainly no consensus on the definition of what property is.[85] One may wonder how this is possible given the centrality of the notion in the economic system and in social life generally. But this is actually not surprising. Understanding property requires a deep understanding of the *legal system* (and not only of that subpart one can call 'the law of property', i.e. the different rules applying to real estate or personal property, conveyancing rules etc).[86] Due to the need to specialize, it is hard to have such a comprehensive view of the legal system, even for lawyers. As we will see, however, modern property is a *legal* notion

---

[84] *See*, for example, Thomas W. Merrill and Henry E. Smith, 'What Happened to Property in Law and Economics?', 111 *Yale Law Journal*, pp. 357–398 (2001). *See also* Geoffrey M. Hodgson, 'What Humpty Dumpty might have said about property rights – and the need to put them back together again: a response to critics', 11(4) *Journal of Institutional Economics*, pp. 731–747 (2015), p. 735; and Gunnar Heinsohn and Otto Steiger, *Ownership Economics – On the foundations of interest, money, markets, business cycles and economic development*, London & New York: Routledge (2014), p. 3, for whom 'an economic theory worthy of that name has been lacking because economists … never made a distinction between possession … and ownership. … they have mainly been concerned with possession and have incorrectly identified it as the main attribute of property rights' (*Ibid*, p. 16).
[85] Antoine Pietri, *'Property' or 'possession': just a matter of semantics … or Paradigm?*, MPRA Paper No. 67096, posted 8 October 22:38 UTC (2015), p. 2.
[86] The law of property in a narrow sense, being that subpart of the legal system determining how property can be acquired, leased, etc.

which is *embedded in the overall system of governance of society*.[87] It is part of the overall *constitutional* mode of allocation of prerogatives. Understanding property rights requires understanding the legal and governance system *as a whole* due to its importance in the institutional structuring of our Power System.

The next problem, however, is that few lawyers understand the economic consequences of their work.[88] According to Walter Eucken, one of the key thinkers of ordoliberalism in Germany, insofar as economic phenomena occur in an institutional and normative context, economic knowledge cannot be dissociated from legal knowledge. The legal system provides the rules for the economic game, and one cannot understand economic processes without incorporating knowledge of these rules. But that's what happened in Western economic and legal thought. Economists have considered legal knowledge as irrelevant to their business, while legal thinkers have failed to recognize the interplay between legal and economic systems. The result is that neither jurists nor economists fully understand the economic-legal phenomena they claim to interpret.[89]

Spontaneously, one would think that the definition and operation of property rights belongs to *private* law and not to the rules of governance of society. An owner does what he wants with what he owns, as long as he is not breaching the law. What could be more private than that? In fact, the operation of property is part of the foundations of our Power System. It is part of a *decision- and rule-making* system, but this is not officially acknowledged, and property is treated as fully belonging to the private side of the Power System. Consequently, for perfectly understandable reasons, most economists have been working with the 'common-sense' approximation that property is the connection between the owner and the thing owned. This error has prevented mainstream economists from developing an adequate theory of property rights and of institutional economics generally. Worse, some economists have embarked on the construction of theories of property rights detached from *any* connection

---

[87] Understanding it goes even beyond what De Soto thought: the process within the formal property system that breaks down assets (objects of property) into capital (their legal representation) is not only hidden in thousands of pieces of legislation, statutes, regulations and institutions that govern the system. *See* de Soto, *op cit*, note 20, p. 48.

[88] De Soto, *op cit*, note 20, p. 199.

[89] *E.g.* David J. Gerber, 'Constitutionalizing the Economy: German Neo-liberalism, Competition Law and the "New" Europe', 42 *American Journal of Comparative Law*, pp. 25–84 (1994), p. 41.

with the concept of property as it operates in the legal system.[90] This is a recipe for failure to address real-life issues in a society structured like ours. Jeremy Bentham's key message in his *Theory of Legislation* is to be remembered: 'property and law were born together and would die together. Before the laws, property did not exist; take away the laws, and property will be no more'.[91]

Property Today

In this book, I am only interested in dealing with property as it operates in the early twenty-first century in societies constitutionally guaranteeing the right to property. Very interesting developments could be and have been made about property at other points in time or in other social contexts.[92] In this book, they would distract from my main argument. How we got where we are is interesting and relevant. And at times I will refer to the historical origin of certain notions when it is helpful to understand them. But an elaborate description of the historical process having led to our present notion of property, taking into account the importance of the evolution of the legal and political systems, has to be for later. We first need to understand where we are now. And this is particularly the case given the dire consequences of where we are going if we do not find the way to change the course of the evolution of our Power System.

Property in its modern sense is an integral part of the legal and governance system of a *specific type* of society. Dealing with property at other points in time and in other social contexts is actually a problem in much of the writings about property rights containing substantial developments about property in a number of circumstances unrelated to the modern operation of property.[93] Going through such a detour, these studies then hardly address the important issues of our time, like the

---

[90] Yoram Barzel shows little regret for this. He writes that 'perhaps economists should have coined a term distinct from the one used for legal purposes, but by now the cost of doing so is too high.' See *Economic Analysis of Property Rights*, Cambridge: Cambridge University Press (1989), p. xi. The fundamental mistake is to think that there is a meaning of property rights 'for legal purposes' as opposed to 'economic purposes'. Property rights cannot be understood in their complexity and subtle entanglement in the political and economic system if one does not face their complex legal meaning.

[91] Etienne Dumont (ed.), Oxford: Oxford University Press (1914), pp. 145–147.

[92] *See generally* North, Wallis and Weingast, *op cit*, note 6.

[93] *See also* Hodgson, *op cit*, note 84, p. 742 and Robert Gilpin, *Global Political Economy – Understanding the International Economic Order*, Princeton: Princeton University Press (2001), p. 64.

relationship of the concept of *property* to the concept of *legal person* and to the concept of the business *firm*. As we will see, this is one of the areas in which a proper understanding of property rights is urgently required for the development of a proper understanding of the firm and of its governance in our World Power System.

The Notion of 'Economic Property Rights' is a Distraction

There is an existing debate about the purported existence of *'economic property rights'* (which would more or less resemble 'possession') as opposed to *'legal property rights'* ('property rights proper').[94] This debate is not particularly fruitful because it starts with the mistaken notion that property is a right over things. Anthony Honoré once wrote that 'to have worked out the notion of "having a right to" as distinct from merely "having" was a major intellectual achievement'.[95] It is not so much that, as he went on, 'without it society would have been impossible'. Numerous societies existed and many still exist today without this distinction. What could *not* have existed is our type of liberal and now capitalist society.[96] Property rights are *rights*; they are *incorporeal*.[97] They are not things nor the possession over things.[98] Notwithstanding this key evolution, the four major schools of economic thought (classical economics, neoclassical economics, Keynesianism and new institutional economics) confuse property with possession.[99] Possession, however, is a direct relationship to things. It

---

[94] *See*, in particular, Yoram Barzel, *Economic Analysis of Property Rights*, Cambridge: Cambridge University Press (1989) and *A Theory of the State: Economic Rights, Legal Rights, and the Scope of the State*, Cambridge: Cambridge University Press (2002). Douglas Allen, who fiercely defends the importance of an economic approach to property rights, also considers that 'possession is essentially another term for economic property right'; *see* Allen, *op cit*, note 79, p. 713.

[95] Hodgson, *op cit*, note 37, p. 225.

[96] Which, I think, are two different things; but this is not essential for my argument here. For further details, *see* Robé in the introduction to *Le temps du monde de l'entreprise – Globalisation et mutation du système juridique*, Paris: Dalloz (2015).

[97] Frédéric Zenati, 'L'immatériel et les choses', 43 *Archives de philosophie du droit*, pp. 79–95 (1999).

[98] On the long dissociation between property and possession, *see* Frédéric Zenati, 'Pour une rénovation de la théorie de la propriété', *Revue Trimestrielle de Droit Civil* (2) avril–juin, pp. 305–323 (1993), starting at p. 310.

[99] Hoffmann, *op cit*, note 78, p. 40. *See also* Heinson and Steiger, *op cit*, note 84, p. 1 & p. 25.

is unsophisticated, simplistic and, if taken in isolation from property, it actually limits the potential uses of the object of possession. Generally, only one person can possess an object of property at a time. 'Having a right to', on the other hand, is a sophisticated notion allowing the structuring of property in many ways offering innumerous opportunities.

Property in this sense facilitates the development of credit (by creating, for example, the possibility to grant a security interest – a mortgage, for example – without losing possession).[100] It offers the possibility of splitting the rights in connection with the objects of property. It entitles to create derivative rights. It enables the securitization of property by the creation of different types of property rights in securities issued by legal vehicles owning the securitized assets. And so on in almost endless combinations.

Confusing possession and property is at the origin of major misunderstandings about the process of economic development. As De Soto remarked in *The Mystery of Capital*, after having collected a wealth of data in Asia, Africa, the Middle East and Latin America:

> most of the poor already possess the assets they need to make a success of capitalism. ... But they hold these resources in defective forms: houses built on land whose ownership rights are not adequately recorded, etc. ... Because the rights to these *possessions* are not adequately documented, these assets cannot readily be turned into *capital*, [they] cannot be used as collateral for a loan. In the West, ... assets can lead an invisible, parallel life alongside their material existence. They can be used as collateral for credit. ... *This is the mystery of capital.*[101] [emphasis added]

It is simply impossible to understand this 'mystery' if one confuses *possession* with *property*, as mainstream economists are doing. Numerous markets and complex organizations can exist *only* thanks to the existence of property rights in the modern sense. I will show this in some detail later on. Both very simple *and* very complex legal relationships towards objects of property can be developed if one understands that 'having' in the modern sense means 'having a right to' against the world at large. This is a key point, and this book will also show why. It is via modern law that a modern society made of impersonal relationships among legal persons via contracts or through the rules of modern property took shape. If one

---

[100] Allowing a lender to have a right over the object of property in case the borrower does not fulfil his promise.

[101] De Soto, *op cit*, note 20, pp. 5–7.

does not understand that the history of the evolution of law as it relates to property is a history of the techniques and means by which the abstract shaping of our societies took place, one misses almost all of the uniqueness of this story, all of the specificity of our legal system and its importance for the development and operation of our specific social system.[102]

Property and Legal Personality

Property is a prerogative of *legal persons*.[103] Property must be thought about in conjunction with the way legal persons operate in the legal system. It is so central to the operation of the legal system that, in his opening discourse presenting the draft of the *Code civil* to the French *Conseil d'État*, his main drafter, Portalis, stated in 1804 that 'all laws either relate to persons or to property, and to property for the utility of persons'.[104]

As we will see also, there are actually two types of property rights: the ones of *public persons*, such as the State, and the ones of *private persons*, such as individual persons or private corporations. They grant very different types of prerogatives and what is generally called 'property' in the literature on property rights is 'private property'. But as we shall see, 'private property' can exist because of the simultaneous existence of 'public property' and of the specific ways public property is being used.[105]

Via an integrated understanding of property rights, both public and private,[106] one can go beyond the type of approach Douglass North, John Joseph Wallis and Barry Weingast have been developing. In their book on *Violence and Social Orders*, they designed a concept of 'open access order' which is very fruitful. In their analysis, our society is an 'open access society' which means that entry into politics and economics is 'open'.[107] North, Wallis and Weingast insist that open access orders are not just improved versions of the societies that preceded them. They state that changes took place in certain societies during the nineteenth century that transformed those societies and produced a new social order with a fundamentally different logic. North, Wallis and Weingast point to the

---

[102] Yan Thomas, 'La valeur des choses. Le droit Romain hors la religion', 6 *Annales, Histoire, Sciences sociales*, pp. 1431–1462 (2002), p. 1433.

[103] The word 'prerogative' meaning here in a general sense an exclusive or special right, power, or privilege.

[104] In François Ewald (ed.), *Naissance du Code civil*, Paris: Flammarion (1989), p. 48.

[105] *See also* Thomas W. Merrill, 'The Property Strategy', 160 *University of Pennsylvania Law Review*, pp. 2061–2095 (2011–2012), p. 2091.

[106] *See also* Ely, *op cit*, note 21, p. 107.

[107] North, Wallis and Weingast, *op cit*, note 6, p. 144.

fact that open access orders 'support' the rule of law, including a judicial system relatively free of corruption.[108] An important consequence they identify is that rule-of-law courts allow the legislative branch to write legislation detailing impersonal rules of policy.[109]

But the importance of law goes well beyond what North, Wallis and Weingast think and describe. In 'open access orders', as opposed to a 'natural state' – as they call it – a significant part of the population is treated equally, which involves treating everyone impersonally without regard to their identity as individual persons.[110] Equality requires that individual persons be treated as *legal persons* having the *same rights and duties* irrespective of their characteristics as *specific* human beings, i.e. irrespective of their age, social origin, family ties, complexion, skin colour and so on. When moving from the pre-legal to the legal world,[111] a society develops rules for curing the defects of a social order based on unofficial norms.[112] As summarized by Lon Fuller, law is 'the enterprise of subjecting the human conduct to the governance of rules'.[113] We will see that the equal protection of property rights with equal meaning no matter the object to which the notion applies and no matter the identity of the person owning the property right is *also* one of the achievements of an 'open access order'. In such an order, individual persons are treated equally and they are being granted uniformly defined and enforced property rights. And, in such an open access order, the enforcement of contracts via a fair, open and consistent 'blind justice' system also plays a key role.

The benign neglect for law in today's mainstream economic analysis I have already mentioned leads to the fact that there are very few developments in the property rights and contracting literature which suggest that formal institutions are necessary for the security of property rights and contract enforcement. The informal alternatives which existed through history via merchants' courts, for example, were however always a poor substitute.[114] The rights existing under the law allow those holding them to enlist the services of the cadaster, judges, bailiffs, policemen, jailers

---

[108] *Ibid*, p. 267.

[109] *Ibid*.

[110] H.L.A. Hart, *The Concept of Law*, Oxford: Oxford University Press (1961), p. 91.

[111] *E.g.* Stephan Haggard, Andrew MacIntyre and Lydia Tiede, 'The Rule of Law and Economic Development', 11 *Annual Review of Political Science*, pp. 205–234 (2008), p. 219.

[112] Philip Selznick, *Law, Society and Industrial Justice*, New York: Russell Sage (1969, 1980, 1983), p. 5.

[113] Lon L. Fuller, *The Morality of Law*, New Haven: Yale University Press (2nd edition 1969), p. 106.

[114] *E.g.* Haggard, MacIntyre and Tiede, *op cit*, note 111, p. 219.

and so on. Without these services provided by the State, entitlements are less precise, less reliable; contracts are much less enforceable, and the value of traded goods and services is made much less certain.

North, Wallis and Weingast are right that changes took place in certain societies in the late eighteenth and early nineteenth centuries which gave birth to a new type of social order. But their approach is limited by their lack of understanding of the deep role played by *law* in this process. They insist on 'institutions' and 'organizations', on 'rules of the game' and 'group behaviour'. But they miss the importance of the evolution of the 'rules of the game' into a constitutional 'State of law'. They refer to it, in passing, but it is *central* to the historical process they were trying to grasp.

We will see why by going deeper into our analysis of property rights and of the legal persons owning them.

1

The Meaning of Property

In this chapter, property is presented in a constitutional perspective. Property in the modern, present sense, certainly never existed in any 'state of nature', whatever this expression means. Modern property can only exist in an orderly and relatively sophisticated society and is part of what I call the Power System. It is a prerogative which is protected both by the State (shielding the owner from theft, trespass and other abuses of property) and against the State (the State being effectively prohibited from unlawfully appropriating private property). I will show that, contrary to what most economists think, possession plays a secondary role in the notion of property. From an economic standpoint, property, as a prerogative protected by the State apparatus, is a value-enhancing institution. Possession is only of secondary importance and raises issues in the case of agency relationships, i.e. when the possessor of the property is not its owner. Beyond this issue, we will see that property includes a right to exclude. Having a right of decision-making as a matter of principle towards the object of property, the owner is entitled to decide who can make use of his or her property and who can't. And how. This has considerable contractual and power consequences. It translates into a right to hire those who are going to make use of the property, to organize their activities and to fire them. Because of the institution of property, the economic system operates via two sets of separate institutions: *prices*, when resources are sold and purchased; and *orders*, when individuals work for owners. In this perspective, owners are akin to lawmakers in connection with their property. They exercise sovereignty, their prerogatives being rights 'as a matter of principle' and not merely 'bundles of rights'. Laws affecting the use of property are only limited derogations to a prerogative – property – which exists as a matter of principle. Just like the right to personal liberty is not the sum of the right to sleep, to take a walk, to go to the beach and so on in an endless list, the right to property is not the sum of limited prerogatives. This view is in phase with Oliver Hart's theory of ownership and applies in both Civil and Common Law legal systems. Understanding property in this fashion is a key to the understanding of the operation of the existing Power System.

★★★

When John Locke wrote his *Second Treatise of Government* (1690), he started with a conception of property in an idealized 'state of nature' in which property is first of all property over *land* and is the result of *labour*:

> Though the Earth, and all inferior Creatures be common to all Men, yet every Man has a Property in his own Person. This no Body has a Right to but himself. The *Labour* of his Body, and the *Work* of his Hands, we may say, are properly his. Whatsoever then he removes out of the State that Nature has provided, and left it in, he hath mixed his *Labour* with, and joined to it something that is his own, and thereby makes it his *Property*.[115]

In this constructed 'state of nature', man has a '*Property* in his own *Person*'. Because of this, in Locke's view, the result of the labour of this body over nature – the Earth and all inferior Creatures [which are] common to all men – also becomes his property.[116]

Property, in this 'state of nature', is first of all property over land:

> *As much Land* as a Man Tills, Plants, Improves, Cultivates, and can use the Products of, so much is his *Property*. He by his *Labour* does, as it were, inclose it from the Common.[117]

In this 'state of nature', man is presented as the 'absolute Lord of his own Person and Possessions, equal to the greatest, and subject to no Body'.[118] The question then is why, if man in the 'state of nature' is such an 'absolute lord':

---

[115] John Locke, *Two Treatises of Government*, Cambridge: Cambridge University Press (1960, 1963, 1988), pp. 287–288.

[116] For Macpherson, the difficulties of modern liberal-democratic theory lie in the seventeenth-century possessive individualism in which the individual is the proprietor of his own person or capacities and owes nothing to society for them. *See* C.B. Macpherson, *The Political Theory of Possessive Individualism – Hobbes to Locke*, Oxford: Oxford University Press (1962, 2011), p. 3.

[117] Locke, *op cit*, note 115, pp. 290–291.

[118] *Ibid*, p. 350.

> Why will he give up this Empire, and subject himself to the
> Dominion and Controul of any other Power? To which 'tis
> obvious to Answer, that though in the state of Nature he hath
> such a right, yet the Enjoyment of it is very uncertain, and
> constantly exposed to the Invasion of others. For all being
> Kings as he, every Man his Equal, and the greater part no
> strict Observers of Equity and Justice, the enjoyment of the
> property he has in this state is very unsafe, very unsecure. This
> makes him willing to quit this Condition, which however
> free, is full of fears and continual dangers: And 'tis not without
> reason, that he seeks out, and is willing to joyn in Society with
> others who are already united, or have in mind to unite for
> the mutual *Preservation* of their Lives, Liberties and Estates,
> which I call by the general Name, *Property*.[119]

So, if one follows Locke's proposition closely, although man is the 'absolute Lord of his own Person and Possessions …', in fact, he is subject to his 'Equals', 'the greater part no strict Observers of Equity and Justice'. An owner he may be, in the 'state of nature', but with only a feeble possession over his 'property' because of the existence of thieves, trespassers and other abusers of property (the 'no strict Observers of Equity and Justice'). As a result, 'the enjoyment of the property he has in this state is very unsafe, very unsecure'. In Locke's construction, man is both the 'absolute Lord of his … Possessions …' whereas the enjoyment of his property 'is very unsafe, very unsecure'. This is quite paradoxical. An 'unsafe and unsecure absolute lord' is an oxymoron. To escape this paradox in his construction, Locke explains that men unite 'for the mutual *Preservation* of their Lives, Liberties and Estates, which I call by the general Name, *Property*'.

The fact is that prior to this 'uniting', men have *no enforceable personal rights*. This is a key point.

It is important to notice that Locke ends up using the word 'property' in a new sense. The notion from then on encompasses 'the mutual *Preservation* of … Lives, Liberties and Estates'. And although the detailed legal situation in present-day constitutional societies is slightly different, as we shall see in the next chapter, in a constitutional system of government, the protection of property is often found in provisions also providing for the protection of other individual personal prerogatives.

This is a clear sign that property in a constitutional system of government goes well beyond the mere protection of the possession over *things*. It is part of the constitutional prerogatives of the individual person.

---

[119] *Ibid.*

1.1 Property as a Constitutional Prerogative

In fact, property as a notion is useful only if there are conflicting claims over the object of property. It is useless otherwise.[120] Whether Robinson Crusoe owns the desert island on which he landed or not is irrelevant as long as no one comes to dispute his use of the island; as long as it is a deserted island. He possesses the island but whether or not he has a property right over it is irrelevant as long as no one comes to challenge his title *and* until he can have recourse to institutions to get his right vindicated. And the same applies to the tools, hut and any other object he will create via labour to help him survive on the island. They are no more his 'property' than the rest of the island, irrespective of the fact of whether he owns himself or not, an irrelevant concept on a desert island. The concept of 'property' makes sense only when the island becomes populated. It is necessarily a social concept.[121] Because it is meaningless on a desert island, 'property' cannot be a direct relationship between and owner and a thing. It can only be a concept created to serve the needs of life in society, in a particular type of society having developed this concept.

And even when potential conflicting claims arise over the island, the objects on it and Robinson's artefacts, property can *still* be an irrelevant concept. In Daniel Defoe's novel, when Friday appears, he does not dispute Robinson's dominion over the island; presumably because he is grateful Robinson saved his life. But even with a less obedient Friday, property would *still* be irrelevant in case of a dispute over the use of the island and the resources on it because it is most likely that *force* would determine who has what, i.e. who decides what to do with what. Even if one imagines Robinson Crusoe and Friday originally negotiating about who owns which part of the island, in case of a dispute, the strongest would prevail, not their original agreement. No one would be present to enforce their original agreement and their allocation of 'property rights' in an informed and balanced way. Robinson, Friday and Locke's man in a state of nature do not have *property*; and they can't conclude enforceable contracts.[122] They only have *possession*, as long as they can

---

[120] Jean-Pascal Chazal, 'La propriété: dogme ou instrument politique? Ou comment la doctrine s'interdit de penser le réel', *Revue Trimestrielle de Droit Civil*, n° 4 (2014).

[121] In his widely cited article, 'Toward a Theory of Property Rights', 57(2) *American Economic Review*, pp. 347–359 (1967), Harold Demsetz made the same point, insisting on the fact that 'In the world of Robinson Crusoe property rights play no role. Property rights are an instrument of society'. *See* p. 347. Demsetz, however, did not conduct his own analysis of property rights using the legal notion of property considering, for example, that the managers of a company are the *de facto* owners. *See* p. 357.

[122] Jacques Ghestin, 'La notion de contrat', *Dalloz*, Chronique, pp. 147–156 (1990).

defend it. No legal and enforcement apparatus – in a position to impose impassionate *force* – is in a position to protect 'rights' against the risk of involuntary dispossession. Before you can get your 'natural rights' asserted in an independent court, free from corruption, with properly trained judges, with proper appeal procedures to ensure that the final decision in any given matter is free from judicial, procedural and reasoning errors, with fair enforcement forces effectively enforcing the judicial decision in a timely and even fashion, the whole on the basis of legal rules created in compliance with the wishes of the individuals affected via an effective democratic process, you need many, many, many (*ad libitum*) Fridays and a very lengthy historical process ...

Mancur Olson made a very similar point when he wrote:

> What do the individuals in an economy need if they are to have the maximum confidence that any property they accumulate will be respected and that any contracts they sign will be impartially enforced? They need a secure government that respects individual rights. But individual rights are normally an artifact of a special set of governmental institutions. There is no private property without government! In a world of roving bandits, some individuals may have possession, but no one has a claim to private property that is enforced by the society. There is typically no reliable contract enforcement unless there is an impartial court system that can call upon the coercive power of the state to require individuals to honor the contracts they have made.[123]

In summary, the notion of 'natural rights' – such as 'property' in a 'state of nature' – is a creation of a specific *society*. I do not mean to weaken their status: they are constitutionally put out of the reach of electoral majorities and Organs of the State for solid reasons. But there is nothing 'natural' about them. On the contrary, it is one of the most sophisticated inventions made within Western legal systems. Writing without qualification – or sources – that 'the first important point to note is that property law in all societies preceded the State', as Norman Barry did in 2004 in his 'Property rights in common and civil law',[124] implies an almost complete ignorance of what property rights are.

---

[123] Mancur Olson, 'Dictatorship, Democracy and Development', 87(3) *American Political Science Review*, pp. 567–576 (1993), p. 571.

[124] In Enrico Colombatto (ed.), *The Elgar Companion to the Economics of Property Rights*, Cheltenham, UK: Edward Elgar (2004), pp. 177–196.

Property can only exist when it is a legal, enforceable right. As phrased by Lippmann:

> No man can hold or enjoy property openly and securely except by virtue of the readiness of the State to enforce his lawful right. Without a lawful title, he has no property; he is merely a possessor without recourse against those who are strong enough to help themselves to his goods.[125]

It also means that, for a market economy and the price system to exist and operate, 'individuals need their property and their contract rights protected from violation not only by other individuals in the private sector but also by the entity that has the greatest power in the society, namely, the government itself'.[126] Otherwise, the 'owner' has no title to transfer and the party seeking his good has an alternative to purchasing it: stealing it.

Property and the economic and political institutions built on it, i.e. the market and the government, can only arise in an *orderly and relatively sophisticated society*. Property is part of a particular *Power System*, a system in which individual physical *force* does not determine who has what.[127] It is part of a system in which the legitimate use of physical violence has been domesticated, concentrated into an institution called the 'State' which, inter alia, defines and enforces property rights as rights of individuals and other legal persons. It is part of a system in which the legitimate use of force has been subjected to the rule of law, so that the owner's prerogatives are protected both *by* the State and *against* the State. It is protected *by the State* in the sense that in case of theft or trespass or any other form of violation of property, the intervention of the judiciary and/or police forces can be triggered to protect property. And it is protected *against the State* in the sense that although the State holds the monopoly of legitimate violence, there are *effective* procedures internal to the State preventing it or those acting in its name from illegally appropriating property.[128]

For example, Article 2 of the French Declaration of the Rights of Man and Citizen of 26 August 1789 – which is strictly speaking *the fundamental*

---

[125] *E.g.* Lippmann, *op cit*, note 83, p. 274. *See also* John Umbeck, 'Might Makes Right: A Theory of the Formation and Initial Distribution of Property Rights', 19(1) *Economic Inquiry*, pp. 38–59 (1981).

[126] Olson, *op cit*, note 123, p. 571.

[127] North, Wallis and Weingast, *op cit*, note 6; *also* Pistor, *op cit*, note 18, p. 209.

[128] Francis Fukuyama, *The Origins of Political Order – From Prehuman Times to the French Revolution*, New York: Farrar, Strass and Giroux (2011), p. 248. *See also* Hodgson, *op cit*, note 80, p. 10.

Article[129] and was adopted by the French National Constituent Assembly a few weeks after the beginning of the French Revolution – provides: 'The aim of every political association is the preservation of the natural and imprescriptible rights of Man. These rights are Liberty, Property, Safety and Resistance to Oppression.' This Article, like the rest of the Declaration, is still part of the French Constitution. The inspiration and content of this Declaration emerged from the philosophers of the Enlightenment and from the ideals of the American Revolution. Key drafts were prepared by Lafayette, working at times with his friend Thomas Jefferson, who himself drew heavily upon the Virginia Declaration of Rights, drafted in May 1776. It was itself based in part on the English Bill of Rights of 1689, as well as Jefferson's own drafts for the American Declaration of Independence.[130] The French and American constitutional documents drafted at the time were born from different political circumstances; but they all purported to embody 'rules of nature' in which individuals have fundamental rights, the political institutions, as a result of a free choice by individuals, being under a duty to respect them.[131] Around the end of the eighteenth century, a set of new ideas were at the root of the creation of new Power Systems in which the protection of property was clearly put forward as one of the purposes of the existence of the State (the *'political association'* in the Declaration's parlance). Article 17 of the Declaration further provides: 'Since the right to Property is inviolable and sacred, no one may be deprived thereof, unless public necessity, legally ascertained, obviously requires it, and just and prior indemnity has been paid.' The State must therefore protect property in all circumstances. The only exception is in case of 'public necessity'. But even then, the existence of an instance of public necessity must be 'legally ascertained'. The deprivation of property must be 'obviously required'. And a just indemnity must be paid prior to the taking of property. These are quite strict conditions.[132]

---

[129] Bobbio, *op cit*, note 11, p. 107.

[130] On Rousseau's influence, *see* Henry Sumner Maine, *L'ancien droit – considéré dans ses rapports avec l'histoire de la société primitive et avec les idées modernes*, translation of *Ancient Law* (1861), NuVision Publication LLC (2008), p. 90.

[131] Jürgen Habermas, *La paix perpétuelle*, Paris: Cerf, coll. 'Humanités' (1996), p. 84. On this continuity, *see also* Michel Foucault, *Naissance de la Biopolitique, Cours au Collège de France, 1978–1979*, Paris: Gallimard-Seuil, collection 'Hautes Etudes' (2004), p. 41.

[132] Conseil constitutionnel, Décision n° 81–132 DC of 16 January 1982: 'the very principles enunciated in the Declaration of Human Rights have full constitutional value both as regards the fundamental character of the right of property whose conservation constitutes one of the aims of political society and which is placed in the same rank as freedom, security and resistance to oppression, as regards the guarantees

It is thanks to this ability to seize private property for the public good that *specific objects of property*, necessary for the development of a modern economy, have been created. Roads, canals, highways, railroads, airports and so on could not have been created as specific objects of property with unique characteristics without State power. Of course, in some cases, their management can be delegated to private parties and the State does not have to deal with day-to-day issues in connection with the *management* of these assets. But the *creation* of these objects of property, without which economic development would be hindered, required and still requires State action, the ability to seize private property.[133]

Similarly, in the US, property ownership was viewed historically as establishing the economic basis for freedom from government coercion and the enjoyment of liberty.[134] The Constitution's Fifth Amendment's Takings Clause states that '*private property* [shall not] *be taken for public use, without just compensation*'. This Amendment – ratified as part of the Bill of Rights in 1791 – also states: '*No person shall ... be deprived of life, liberty, or property, without due process of law*.' Significantly, the language of the Fifth Amendment unites safeguards for both liberty and property.[135] Exactly as Article 2 of the French Declaration does. The protection of

---

given to the holders of this right and the prerogatives of the public authorities; that the freedom which, under Article 4 of the Declaration, consists in being able to do everything that does not harm others, cannot itself be preserved if arbitrary or abusive restrictions are imposed on the freedom of enterprise.' Which is a translation from: '... les principes mêmes énoncés par la Déclaration des droits de l'homme ont pleine valeur constitutionnelle tant en ce qui concerne le caractère fondamental du droit de propriété dont la conservation constitue l'un des buts de la société politique et qui est mis au même rang que la liberté, la sûreté et la résistance à l'oppression, qu'en ce qui concerne les garanties données aux titulaires de ce droit et les prérogatives de la puissance publique; que la liberté qui, aux termes de l'article 4 de la Déclaration, consiste à pouvoir faire tout ce qui ne nuit pas à autrui, ne saurait elle-même être préservée si des restrictions arbitraires ou abusives étaient apportées à la liberté d'entreprendre.' Or under UK law, *see Burmah Oil Co Ltd v Lord Advocate* [1965] AC 75, deciding that the executive cannot deprive people of their property without the payment of compensation.

[133] *See generally* Blaufarb, *op cit*, note 14, especially p. 218. In France, Louis-Philippe passed the first statute on the construction of railways and their management. The State undertook to pay for the land, the embankment and the structures such as tunnels and bridges. Private companies were responsible for the financing of the rails, stations and equipment with, in return, a 99-year concession. *See* Jean-Robert Pitte, *Histoire du Paysage Français*, tome 2, 'Le profane: du XVIe siècle à nos jours', Paris: Tallandier (1989), p. 84.

[134] John Hart Ely, *Democracy and Distrust: A Theory of Judicial Review*, Cambridge: Harvard University Press (1980), p. 3.

[135] *Ibid*, p. 9.

property ownership was an integral part of the American effort to fashion constitutional limits on public governmental authority.[136]

The introduction of these protections against the government bears heavily the mark of Locke's political philosophy. In Locke's grand theory, as we have seen, private property existed *prior* to the creation of political authority. Of course, this is contradictory to the modern notion of property, which is a right against others, which only makes sense in a social setting. But the perception at the time was that property was a *direct* relationship to the object of property, created in a 'state of nature' and that the purpose of government was to protect these *natural* property rights which were fused with liberty.[137] The Fifth Amendment, in addition to its provisions relating to property and liberty, also contains specific procedural safeguards governing criminal trials. Providing *in the same Amendment* for provisions against double jeopardy and self-incrimination is clear evidence of the close association of property rights with personal liberty. Arbitrary punishment and deprivation of property were closely associated as two major risks created by the existence of a federal government.[138] Thus, public *governmental powers* had to be limited by the government's duty to protect *property*.[139]

The Framers of the US Constitution expected that the separation of powers among the branches of the federal government would create checks and balances via which property interests would be safe. Believing that unrestrained democracy posed a threat to liberty and property, the Framers expected a strong executive and an independent judiciary to curb legislative interference with property rights.[140] They certainly did not think that in this manner they were creating an *overall Power System* in which the primary decision-makers would be property owners. In their mind, property was just a direct relationship to physical goods – mostly land at the time. But this is how the Power System effectively evolved through time, as we shall see.

Like the other guarantees of the Bill of Rights, the Fifth Amendment applies against the federal government only. It did not apply against the States. Throughout the nineteenth century, however, State governments were the primary source of economic regulation.[141] For many, these regulations were an encroachment to the autonomy of the individual

---

136 *Ibid*, p. 26.

137 *Ibid*, p. 17.

138 *Ibid*, p. 54.

139 *Ibid*, p. 17; and Pistor, *op cit*, note 18, p. 209.

140 Ely, *op cit*, note 134, p. 47.

141 *Ibid*, pp. 59–60.

person, be it as an owner or as a contracting party. After the Civil War, there was an active movement to make sure that the States could not infringe on the fundamental rights of citizens and, in particular, Afro-Americans. This led to the ratification of the Fourteenth Amendment which provides inter alia that no State shall: 'deprive any person of life, liberty, or property, without due process of law'. But this process, initially designed to protect Afro-Americans after the end of slavery against the risk of discrimination, soon became one of the key constitutional rules protecting the rights of business corporations. Corporations were soon to be construed as 'persons' with all the rights of human beings in any one State.[142] They could claim for themselves the benefit of these rights – which they did with great appetite.

Like the French Declaration of Human Rights, these Amendments are still in force today. Their interpretation has changed over time, allowing the production of the regulatory laws made necessary due to industrialization and the development of large business firms. But these basic rules are still part of the constitutional foundations of our societies.

1.2 The Secondary Importance of Possession

In this book, I will discuss *possession* only to a limited extent. I am mostly interested in property/ownership, which is *the* key notion at the roots of the operation of the World Power System. As I have already mentioned,

---

[142] As is well known, corporations are the greatest users of the Fourteenth Amendment. Alfred F. Conard, 'Federal Protection of the Free Movement of Corporations', in 2 *Courts and Free Markets – Perspectives from the United States and Europe*, T. Sandalow and E. Stein (eds.), Oxford: Clarendon Press (1982), p. 363: '… corporations created under the law of one state have no right, either under the federal constitution or federal laws, to conduct local business in other states. Although the federal constitution gives a right of free movement between states to all "citizens", corporations have been excluded by judicial theory from the benefit of this clause. In spite of the lack of a guaranteed right of migration, corporations are in practice permitted to operate freely in other states by the terms of state laws on admission of out-of-state corporations. Moreover, they are protected against many forms of discriminatory treatment by the operation of the "equal protection" clause of the Fourteenth Amendment, which is framed not in terms of "citizens" but of "persons". The equal protection clause has become the principal instrument for protecting corporations' freedom of movement. A secondary line of protection for free movement comes from the implications of "interstate commerce powers". This is, in form, a power granted to the federal Congress to legislate on interstate commerce; but it has been interpreted to prohibit by implication legislation of the states which unreasonably burden interstate commerce.'

the four major schools of economic thought confuse property with possession.[143] They all ultimately rest on a notion of the spontaneity of the relationship of the subject to the object.[144] Locke also confused property with possession when he considered that property existed prior to the existence of the government when what he describes in the 'state of nature' is merely possession – and a weak possession at that. Possession, however, is of distinctly *secondary* importance. Possession is mostly a factual situation which may be legitimate or not.[145]

For example, a thief possesses the stolen good but does not own it. He has no *property right* over it.[146] The purse he has just stolen is not his property; if another thief steals it from him, the first thief cannot persuade a court to return it to him.[147] Or a tenant paying his rent *legitimately* possesses the apartment he is renting; but he does not own it. The landlord does. *Legitimate* possession is a legal relationship of the possessor towards the rest of the world,[148] *derived from the property right* of the owner and usually resulting from a contract.

Note that in both of these examples of *legitimate* and *illegitimate* possession, the *owner* does not have possession. This shows how little possession has to do with property, contrary to the view shared by most property rights theorists.

---

[143] Hoffmann, *op cit*, note 78, p. 40.

[144] Jean-Pierre Dupuy, 'Epistémologie de l'économie et analyse de système', in *La notion de système dans les sciences contemporaines*, tome 2, Aix-en-Provence: Librairie de l'Université (Jacques Lesourne (ed.), 1981), p. 127.

[145] In French law, there are two different words for possession as a mere 'fact' and possession as 'legitimate possession'. The fact to possess is called '*détention*'. It can be legitimate or not. An owner, a tenant, a thief, all have *détention* of the owned, leased or stolen property. But only the owner or tenant has possession, i.e. legitimate '*détention*'.

[146] This is contrary to what Barzel thinks, for example. In his constructivist *A Theory of the State*, he decided to distinguish 'economic rights' which 'reflect individuals' ability to consume or exchange commodities' from 'legal rights' which are 'rights delineated by the State'. *See* Barzel, *op cit*, note 94, p. 6. This leads Barzel to draw inferences such as 'you own today even the apples you intend to steal from your neighbour's tree tomorrow': *ibid*, p. 15. Only in a theoretical construction can a thief be an owner. But even in Barzel's construction, today the owner of the apple is still the neighbour. He will lose *possession* tomorrow, at the time of the theft. But if he picks up the apple later today and sells it to another neighbour, is he stealing the property of the neighbour who intended to steal from him in the future? Of course not. The approach in this book is totally different. It is not constructivist and, on the contrary, is anchored in the legal system as it effectively operates. Readers will decide which approach is the most useful to address real-life problems.

[147] *E.g.* Lippmann, *op cit*, note 83, p. 245.

[148] Including the owner who can't intrude into the apartment rented by the tenant.

With legitimate possession, the possessor has some of the rights of the owner transferred to him by the owner, usually via a contract and for a consideration. For example, a tenant is free to use the rented house (within the limits set by the lease) and to set the 'rules of the house' (within the same limits). He does not need *ownership* for that. But he needs the owner to grant him the right to use the house. And granting possession for a consideration is one way for the owner to use his property. It is normally temporary whereas ownership is potentially eternal.[149]

The prerogatives granted by legitimate possession are just a sub-part of those granted by ownership. So, I will concentrate on ownership which comprises all the rights of legitimate possession although the two can be separated.

1.3 Property as a Value-enhancing Institution

Illegitimate possession is only marginally interesting for our purposes. But the notion is useful to show how the idea that there can be 'economic property rights' opposed to 'legal property rights' misses a significant contribution of the *legal* notion of property to economic value.

For all we know, the exchange value of a good known to be a stolen good is much less than that of the same good legitimately owned. This would tend to show that legally owning goods *adds* value to the good owned while possessing *illegally* subtracts value to the good illegally possessed. Treating a fief as an owner, as Yoram Barzel does for example,[150] on the basis that 'economic property' is somewhat equivalent to 'possession', is fundamentally flawed.

The reason for this is that for legally owned goods, the whole enforcement system offered by the State (courts and police forces) is freely available to the owner to defend his property. As we have seen, the protection of property is one of the aims of the modern State, of the 'political association'. The protection services available to defend a legally owned object of property will follow the property *in whoever's hands it will legally pass*. Legally owned goods see their value enhanced by the existence of these services which will be freely provided whomever the legitimate owner is.

---

[149] Of course, for individuals, it ceases with death and the heirs become the new owners. But for corporate property, i.e. property owned by corporations, property really can be eternal. What gets transferred through inheritance are the shares issued by the corporation owning the corporate property.

[150] Barzel, *op cit*, note 94.

For goods *possessed* illegally (they are not 'owned'), this is the *reverse*: the State enforcement system can be mobilized *against* the possessor/fief and whomever will purchase the object of property in an illegitimate way. The object has much less value.[151] The possessor does not benefit from the protection services. On the contrary, he must spend resources to protect his feeble possession and whomever will knowingly purchase the stolen good from him will have to do the same. Hence, its reduced value.

Legally owning a good is therefore better than possessing the same good illegally. Even if it were for this simple reason only, 'legal property' is inherently better than merely 'economic property', whatever that means. Treating the two as the same is fundamentally mistaken.

Understanding this is *very* important for an understanding of the economic role of the State and the connection between the economic and the political systems in the Power System. A State properly operating in its basic functions of providing order and protecting property rights *enhances* the value of the assets located within its jurisdiction.[152] It significantly improves the conditions of an exchange economy: the objects exchanged are not merely possessed. They are the objects of rights with a full enforcement system to back their title and the legal agreements (leases, sale contracts) relating to them. All things being equal (taxation in particular), a State improperly operating with regards to the provision of these same services *reduces* the value of the assets under its jurisdiction. And vice versa.

1.4 Property and the State

A properly operating State therefore contributes to the creation and preservation of wealth. As we will see in more detail in Section 5.5, the democratic institutions of the State may affect negatively the value of properties by the adoption of laws reducing their potential uses. For

---

[151] This is the reverse for illegal goods such as illegal drugs (their definition being an evolving one). Illegal goods are more expensive than when they become legal because it is less costly to produce, transport and sell them. Numerous conclusions can be drawn from this fact. For our purposes, the important element is that the legal status of a good affects its value.

[152] And yet, as raised by Bates, institutional economists still have to extract the full implication of the fact that power, if properly deployed, can create value; *see* Robert Bates, 'The New Institutionalism', in Sebastian Galiani and Itai Sened (eds), *Institutions, Property Rights and Economic Growth: The Legacy of Douglass North*, Cambridge: Cambridge University Press (2014), pp. 50–65, at p. 50. *See also* Foss and Foss, *op cit*, note 75, p. 398.

example, a new zoning law can limit the type of constructions which can be erected on certain pieces of land. It may seriously reduce the economic value of the land; or it may increase it. But this reduction of the potential uses of the object of property derives from State functions *additional* to the ones of being a protector of property rights. This is the case for many laws affecting the production of goods and services. The independent operation of firms based on unrestrained property rights has led to issues, such as inhuman working conditions, contamination of the natural environment, the production of unsafe products and so on, which have led to the development of whole sets of laws pursuing the protection of interests affected negatively. States had to intervene, and adopt laws which, in some cases, have reduced the value of property by limiting its potential uses. They had to reduce the autonomy of owners who were making decisions which had serious adverse effects. In circumstances when this happens as the result of the proper operations of the democratic political system, however, this is just one of the normal outcomes of political institutions answering to the demands of the electorate to redress the negative outcomes of autonomous exchange. I will come back to this issue. The autonomous operation of property rights as a system of autonomous decision-making by owners *as a matter of principle* is intrinsically linked to the operation of the State adopting laws *as a matter of exception* to correct issues raised in the economic sphere, improperly addressed by economic firms and needing to be corrected by the democratic process of government.[153] This 'social side' of property is required because, as von Ihering wrote, an 'absolute' right of property would result in the dissolution of society.[154] There is today more or less general agreement on the need to redress adverse issues generated by the autonomous operation of the property system, as indicated above in the Introduction.[155] The problem created by a globalized world is that there is no global 'State' and one has to think about an effective division of functions and the combined operations of institutions in a renewed fashion. As written early on by Eirik Furubotn and Svetozar Pejovich:

> the right of ownership is an exclusive right in the sense that
> it is limited only by those restrictions that are explicitly stated

---

[153] Portalis, in his introductory discourse presenting the draft *Code civil* to the French *Conseil d'État*, phrased a similar idea in a somewhat different language: 'There is no private question in which no issue of public administration is involved; as there is no public issue that does not somehow affect the principles of the distributive justice that regulate private interests'; in Ewald, *op cit*, note 104, p. 49.

[154] *See* Ely, *op cit*, note 21, p. 137.

[155] *See* Bénabou and Tirole, *op cit*, note 8, p. 1

in the law. ... It follows, of course, that a theory of property rights cannot be truly complete without a theory of the State. And, unfortunately, no such theory exists at present.[156]

The situation is, of course, made even more complex when one looks at identifying the proper rules of operation of a World Power System in which the States are only one category of participants to a much wider and complex Power System without a Global State.

1.5 Possession and Agency

Possession will be discussed in this book mostly when it raises *agency* issues: in certain circumstances, an *agent* has possession over an asset or a bundle of assets owned by someone else (a *principal*) and must manage the asset(s) in the principal's interest. This is always the case with corporate law where corporate officers manage assets they do not own. They manage the assets *owned by the corporation*. It gives them 'power without property',[157] and this raises very important and difficult issues. But it is impossible to properly address them (as is the case today) without a proper understanding of what property really is – a right of decision-making as a matter of principle – and of the complex structure of the property rights involved in corporate ownership.

These issues are addressed improperly today because the property relationships involved in business *firms* legally structured using *corporations* are misunderstood or misrepresented. For example, most of the literature on corporate governance and agency theory simply ignores the legal reality of the property relationships within a corporate business firm. The shareholders are deemed to be the *owners of the firm* and the corporate directors and officers are deemed to be their *agents*. It is widely considered that, consequently, their duty is to maximize shareholders' short-term profits. This is totally inaccurate and results from disregarding the reality of the legal relationships within a firm.[158] The shareholders in fact and at

[156] Eirik G. Furubotn and Svetozar Pejovich, 'Property Rights and Economic Theory', 10(4) *Journal of Economic Literature*, pp. 1137–1162 (1986), p. 1140. On this specific issue, *see also* Douglass C. North, *Structure and Change in Economic History*, New York: WW Norton (1981), pp. 17–21.
[157] Adolf A. Berle, Jr., *Power Without Property: A New Development in American Political Economy*, New York: Harcourt, Brace and Company (1959).
[158] Lynn A. Stout et al., *The Modern Corporation Statement on Company Law* (2016), available at https://papers.ssrn.com/sol3/papers.cfm?abstract_id=2848833. Jean-Philippe Robé, 'Being Done with Milton Friedman', 2(2) *Accounting, Economics, and*

law own the *shares* issued by the *corporation* having issued them to collect the equity capital required to build the *firm*. This leads to a complex set of legal relationships among, inter alia:

(a) the shareholders (owning the shares) who have a right to vote in shareholders' assembly meetings and to collect dividends when they are distributed by the *corporation*;
(b) the *corporation* having issued the shares (owning the assets used to produce goods and/or services via the *firm's* operations);
(c) the officers and directors managing and supervising the operations of the *corporation* and, therefore, the use of the assets owned by the *corporation* in the operation of the *firm's* activity;
(d) the internal participants to the operation of the *firm* (officers, managers, employees, certain suppliers, certain distributors) having contracts with one of the *corporations* used to legally structure the *firm*;
(e) the outside interests affected; and
(f) the natural environment.

This complex set of legal relationships (which are not merely 'contracts', as most economists assume) cannot be addressed if one works with the approximation that 'shareholders own firms', and that managers are the 'shareholder's agents'. All this is simply false. As Berle phrased it more than 50 years ago: 'The directors of the corporation are not the "owners"; they are not agents of the stockholders and are not obliged to follow their instructions.'[159] And all the deductions made from these erroneous starting points are necessarily false as well. Even earlier, in 1897, Ernst Freund stated very clearly that:

> ... a shareholder of a railroad company has no direct right of property in the rolling stock, the roadbed, the station houses, etc. of the road; he cannot use the cars at his pleasure, he can give no orders to the employees, and if he performs acts of ownerships, he is a trespasser.[160]

Law (2012), Article 3 and 'The Legal Structure of the Firm', 1(1) *Accounting, Economics, and Law* (2011), Article 5, available at: https://www.degruyter.com/view/journals/ael/1/1/article-ael.2011.1.1.1001.xml.xml?language=en.

[159] Berle, *op cit*, note 24, p. 2.

[160] Ernst Freund, *The Legal Nature of Corporations*, Chicago: The University of Chicago Press (1897), p. 34.

Disregarding the reality of the ownership relationships within a firm as is being done with the prevailing 'agency theory' has led to serious errors in the literature on corporate governance, as we will see later in this book.

1.6 A Right to Exclude and its Contractual Consequences

Property, as a legally enforceable right, includes a right to exclude. So much so that, for many, property is first of all a right to exclude.[161] In his dissenting opinion in the 1918 *International News* case, Justice Holmes wrote that 'Property, a creation of law, does not arise from value ... a matter of fact. ... Property depends upon exclusion by law from interference'.[162] For Justice Brandeis, also dissenting in the same case, 'An essential element of individual property is the legal right to exclude others from enjoying it'.[163] The right to exclude is often seen as the marker of property.

As a matter of illustration, absent any violation of the law leading to the issuance of a warrant, the owner of a house has the absolute freedom to refuse access to his house – to anybody, including police forces and other State officials.[164] The most powerful person on the planet – say, the US President – cannot enter somebody's house if the rightful occupier of the house refuses him.

This dimension of property as a right to exclude translates into a series of rights which is very important for our purposes: the right to hire, to organize the use of the object of property and to fire the users. The owner of a house hires, as a matter of principle, whomever he or she wants to clean the house. He or she is the one entitled to determine who enters her house and therefore who will be able to clean it under a contract. Laws can reduce the ability to discriminate among candidates for the job based on inappropriate criteria (skin colour, gender, seniority). Laws can impose restrictions to the working hours; laws can impose minimal working conditions, and so on and so forth. Irrespective of these limitations, it is the owner who decides whom to hire – or not to hire – as a matter of principle.

---

[161] Thomas W. Merrill, 'Property and the Right to Exclude', 77 *Nebraska Law Review*, pp. 730–755 (1998).

[162] *International News*, 248 U.S. p. 246.

[163] *International News*, 248 U.S. p. 250.

[164] While warrantless arrests in public are constitutional, warrantless arrests in the home are not. *E.g.* Margaret J. Radin, 'Property and Personhood', 34 *Stanford Law Review*, pp. 957–1015 (1982), p. 997.

Similarly, the owner of a factory determines who has access to the factory in the same manner the owner of a house determines who enters his house.[165] The factory owner, because he is an owner, is entitled to hire, organize and fire. The owner is the one determining, as a matter of principle, who has access to the factory and to the tools used by the employees under what conditions. Of course, a contract can be concluded to determine the rights and duties of the hired person and of the employer, the conditions of the employment relationship and so on. Depending on the locally applicable laws, termination of the contract by the owner without proper cause can lead to the payment of damages. But the one deciding who has access to the factory and to the tools required to produce goods and services, how these assets will be used and under whose supervision is the *owner*, or someone acting on behalf of the *owner*. Property grants managerial authority over the object of property and those making use of it.[166]

Consequently, property creates a fundamental difference in the legal position between the two parties to the employment contract. Since the abolition of slavery, nobody is legally forced to work. But those who accept to work either because they want to or like it or because hunger gives them no choice will have to obey the rules set by the owner, as long as they are in compliance with the employment contract and laws. Property is not *only* inequality in terms of *wealth*; it is also inequality in terms of *legal power*.[167] Property determines in part who in society can give orders and who must obey. It is part of the Power System. Robert Hale has pushed this point to the extreme: 'it is the law of property which coerces people into working for factory owners'.[168] It is

---

[165] On the importance of this notion of 'access', *see* Raghuram Rajan and Luigi Zingales, 'Power in a Theory of the Firm', *Quarterly Journal of Economics*, pp. 387–432 (1998).

[166] Merrill, *op cit*, note 105, p. 2068.

[167] Arthur S. Miller, *The Modern Corporate State: Private Governments and the American Constitution*, Greenwood Press (1976), p. 41. It is in this respect that the vision of the revolutionaries of the late eighteenth century that property could be separated from power was utopian. Property conveys power over other people; *see* Blaufarb, *op cit*, note 14, p. 222. And concentrated property creates serious competitors for official political institutions.

[168] Robert L. Hale, 'Coercion and Distribution in a Supposedly Non-Coercive State', 38(3) *Political Science Review*, pp. 470–494 (1923), p. 472. *See, contra*, Larissa Katz, who considers 'that a system of private property introduces a network of public goods that allow those unwilling to submit to private power to sidestep entirely the sphere within which owners are sovereign', in 'Property's Sovereignty', 18 *Theoretical Inquiries in Law*, pp. 299–328 (2017), p. 325. It amounts to saying that everyone has the choice

not contract law. It is not the joint exercise of their 'freedom of contract' by both employer and employee. The process via which property came to carry these prerogatives occurred in historical conjunction with the monopolization of the legitimate use of violence in the hands of the State. *Violence* was 'extruded' from private relationships, concentrated into the hands of State authorities who decentralized *power* via property and freedom of contract.[169] In our system of legal equality among legal subjects, the employment contract presents this astonishing peculiarity of bearing on the body of one of the contractors and of subordinating it to the other, of submitting it, better than would an exhausting system of coercion and, in the very name of his liberty, to a whole system of discipline organized by the comptrollers of property rights.[170] The identity of who obeys and who commands in the employment contract does not derive primarily from the content of the contract. It derives from who owns the assets used in the performance of the producing activity in connection with the fulfilment of the employment contract.[171] The non-owner obeys. The owner orders. The key provisions of the contract which determine for which consideration the employee will be a subordinate, for which activities and for how long derive from this fundamental legal difference.[172] And for anything not specifically provided for in the contract or in the applicable labour laws, the owner decides due to his *residual* control right over the assets involved.

The understanding of this fact sheds a different light on Ronald Coase's analysis in his 1937 article on 'The Nature of the Firm'. Coase questioned why firms do exist at all. Why are there organizations within which

---

to be a beggar living on the streets. Any non-owner making a different choice and not working for a public institution has 'to submit to private power'.

[169] *See also* Anthony Giddens, *The Consequences of Modernity*, Cambridge: Polity Press (1991), p. 62.

[170] Alain Jeammaud and Antoine Lyon-Caen, 'Droit et direction du personnel', *Droit Social*, pp. 56–69 (1982), p. 68.

[171] Oliver D. Hart, *Firms, Contracts and Financial Structure*, Oxford: Oxford University Press (1995), p. 58.

[172] *See* Léon Duguit, *Les transformations du droit public*, Paris: Hachette Livre (1913 edition), p. 7, for whom the King's 'right to command is a right analogous to a property right'. *See also* Alain Supiot, for whom the fundamental difficulty for Occidental law to deal with the employment relationship is the founding distinction between 'things' and 'persons'; in Alain Supiot, *Critique du droit du travail*, Paris: Presses Universitaires de France, Collection 'Les voies du droit' (1994), p. 8. The way out of this enigma is to cut the Gordian knot and to understand property as a mode of relationship among people. *See* in Section 1.1 our developments regarding Robinson Crusoe's evolving position towards things as society develops around him.

production takes place via the issuance of orders? Why is there not only 'market contracts', contracts through which products and services are *bought and sold* among autonomous market participants? His answer was that there must be some cost of operating the market – 'transaction costs'. And to reduce some of these costs, it is better to create an organization, a firm. This led to a whole branch of 'new institutional economics', attempting to identify what these transaction costs are, and which institutional arrangements are best placed to reduce them.

This is interesting in and of itself. But another answer to the question Coase was asking could simply have been: firms exist because of the law of property. Certain employees may not have the means to own or let the premises, the tools, the work in progress needed to be a market participant integrated to the production process via purely market – buy and sell – contractual relationships. They may not be able to bear the risk of failure of their venture. They may have no attractive alternatives to working for others, under their command. And those who will command in the employment relationship are those having the legal control over the objects of property rights the employees need to access to participate in the production process and be compensated in exchange. There may very well be 'transaction costs' explaining recourse to the firm as an alternative to market exchange. But the allocation of property rights certainly plays a role as well and this must be integrated into the analysis.

1.7 Prices versus Orders

In 1972, Armen Alchian and Harold Demsetz denied the importance of the authority of the owner. They took the view that 'the presumed power to manage and assign workers to various tasks' is 'exactly the same as one little consumer's power to manage and assign his grocer to various tasks'.[173] And to try to save the notion that firms are just sub-parts of 'the market', they denied the importance of long-term contracts: 'Long-term contracts between employer and employee are not the essence of the organization we call a firm.'[174] Their view was that 'to speak of managing, directing and assigning workers to various tasks is a deceptive way of noting that the employer <u>continually is involved in renegotiation of contracts on</u>

---

[173] Armen A. Alchian and Harold Demsetz, 'Production, Information Costs and Economic Organization', 62(5) *American Economic Review*, pp. 777–795 (1972), p. 777.
[174] *Ibid.* To be fair, Alchian has since rejected this position in 1984, followed in 1995 by Demsetz.

terms that must be acceptable to both parties'.[175] In the reality of firms'
operations, it is quite the opposite. If in large firms coordinating the
work of hundreds or thousands or even hundreds of thousands employees
there would be constant renegotiations of the terms of each employment
contract, the organization would be unmanageable. The employment
contract submits the employee to the commands of the owner (or his
agent and those receiving a delegation of authority) and this relationship
avoids having to renegotiate all the time. It *avoids* having to negotiate at
length to agree on the details of how discrete tasks will be performed, for
how long, for how much and so on. The employer cannot go beyond the
'zone of acceptance' of the employee, as evidenced by Herbert Simon.[176]
But within that zone, he is the one issuing the orders, and the employee
is the one obeying them. Property plays an important economizing role
in this regard: it allows doing without palaver. Property rights entitle,
as a matter of principle, to easy, simple decision-making processes in
connection with production. They are economical in that they reduce
the need for collective decision-making. As Niklas Luhmann explained:

> the only great delegalizer with a minimum of rules and a
> maximum of effects that has been invented in legal history is
> the institution of property because of its clear and simple way
> of pre-deciding conflicts.[177]

With individual liberalism, property lost its collective nature and became
a component of the rise of the autonomy of the individual person and
of a liberal society.[178] Both legal subjects (individuals) and legal objects
(property) were simplified to the extreme.[179] 'Medieval law did not know
this form of assignation of a thing to a person, except in the case of
movable property. Several persons were capable of having simultaneously

---

[175] *Ibid*, emphasis added.

[176] *See generally* Herbert A. Simon, *Administrative Behavior: A Study of Decision-Making in Administrative Organizations*, New York: Free Press, Fourth Edition (1997).

[177] Niklas Luhmann, 'The Self-Reproduction of Law and its Limits' in *Dilemmas of Law in the Welfare State*, p. 113, Gunther Teubner (ed.), Berlin: De Gruyter (1986), p. 121. For Maurice Hauriou, more generally, 'The rules of law are transactional limits imposed on the claims of the individual powers and on the powers of the institutions; they are anticipated settlements of conflicts.' In Maurice Hauriou, 'La théorie de l'institution et de la fondation (essai de vitalisme social)', *Cahiers de la nouvelle journée* 4, pp. 89–128, Paris: Bloud & Gay (1925), p. 94.

[178] Gwendoline Lardeux, 'Qu'est-ce que la propriété? Réponse de la jurisprudence récente éclairée par l'histoire', *Revue Trimestrielle de Droit Civil*, p. 741 (2013).

[179] Paolo Grossi, *L'Europe du droit*, Paris: Faire l'Europe, Seuil (2011), p. 145.

rights in rem of equal rank in the same piece of land.'[180] With regards to real estate, various rights could be vested on a particular land, mixing what we call today 'public' and 'private' duties and service charges. In France, these various interests reflected vested rights and privileges protected by the law of the *Ancien Régime*. With the French Revolution and the adoption of the Civil Code, the law of property tended to suppress as much as possible any outside interests resting on the property. Before 1789, the essentially rural law of France was characterized by the multiplicity of rights bearing on the same thing. Everywhere, the rights of use were superimposed and intertwined. With the property right 'pure and simple' as it results from Article 544 of the Civil Code, the contrast is absolute.[181] Article 544 of the French Civil Code provides: 'Ownership is the right to enjoy and dispose of things in the most absolute manner, provided they are not used in a way prohibited by statutes or regulations.' In the new legal regime, all powers were concentrated as much as possible into the hands of a sole owner, into the hands of the individual.[182] With the French Revolution, Napoléon and the widely exported Civil Code, a decisive shift in property rights came to Europe. Property rights were now freely acquired, freely traded and divorced from any attachment to birth and status. In England, it is also in the early 1800s that the new concept of absolute property rights was born.[183]

Shared ownership still exists today, but it is a disfavoured form of property.[184] The sharing of ownership rights adds a degree of complexity in the governance of assets because the owners in common must devise a governance system among themselves to determine how the object owned in common will be used, who will benefit from what and who will bear what liability.[185] In some cases, there are default rules provided for by the legal system for the exercise of shared ownership. For example, there are rules about how to manage the shared parts of an apartment building (the corridors, the staircase, the elevator and so on). Or part

---

[180] Karl Renner, *The Institutions of Private Law and their Social Functions*, New Brunswick & London: Transaction Publishers (1949, 2010).

[181] Jehan de Malafosse, *Le droit à la nature*, Paris: Editions Montchrestien, (1973), p. 2. *See generally* Blaufarb, *op cit*, note 14, who rightly speaks about a 'Great Demarcation'.

[182] Simon Deakin and Alain Supiot, *Capacitas – Contract and the Institutional Preconditions of a Market Economy*, Oxford: Hart Publishing (2009), pp. 52–53.

[183] Rose, *op cit*, note 13, pp. 337–338, and Pistor, *op cit*, note 18, pp. 32–33. On the invention of 'Modern Property', *see generally* Blaufarb, *op cit*, note 14.

[184] Saleilles, *op cit*, note 42, p. 7. *See also* Blaufarb, *op cit*, note 14, especially pp. 5, 10–11 and 15.

[185] *See generally* Elinor Ostrom, *Governing the Commons – The Evolution of Institutions for Collective Action*, Cambridge: Cambridge University Press (1990, 2008).

of family law deals with how the family property must be managed by the family members (mostly the parents). But with shared ownership come potential disputes, or even blocked situations among the co-owners which do not exist with individual ownership since, by definition, the owner does what he wants with what he has as a matter of principle. In contradistinction, shared ownership may lead to the need to ask in court the authorization to pursue a particular course of action. It is a much less efficient decentralization of the decision-making power in connection with assets and is rarely encouraged by the modern legal system.[186]

With regards to the 'coercive power' deriving from property, it is important to be aware that the prerogatives granted to the owner via property are *inherent to property as such* and are not affected by the modification in the *identity* of the owner. Taking this control

> from the owner of the plant and to vest it in public officials, in a guild or in a union organization elected by the workers would add nor subtract from the constraints which is exercised with the aid of the government. It would merely transfer the constraining power to a different set of persons.[187]

This is a key consideration to keep in mind. Property is a decentralization of the authority to make the rules in connection with the use of the object of property. The identity of the owner can be modified; property remains the same. Or, as Lippmann put it, communism, when it abolishes private property in productive capital, establishes a new kind of property in the public offices which manage the collective capital. The commissars replace the capitalists, but they exercise the same powers or greater ones. And the struggle for wealth is just transmuted into a struggle for power.[188]

1.8 Owners as Lawmakers

As already mentioned, property entails the right to set 'the rules of the house'. This is a fundamental feature of property which can only be limitedly reduced by laws or judges.

---

[186] Larissa Katz, 'The Regulative Function of Property Rights', 8(3) *Econ Journal Watch*, pp. 236–246 (2011), p. 241.

[187] Hale, *op cit*, note 168, p. 478. Or, as Georges Ripert puts it, 'Nationalization is a lazy solution. It consists of taking the capitalist enterprise as it is and turning it into a State enterprise. Private capitalism disappears, but it is replaced by State capitalism'; Ripert, *op cit*, note 43, p. 328.

[188] *E.g.* Lippmann, *op cit*, note 83, p. 83.

Take, for example, Jeff inviting Bob to his home. Bob sits down and puts his feet on the table. Jeff asks Bob not to put his feet on the table. If Bob goes to court to argue that this is an excessive restriction on his freedom, no judge will change the rule of the house set by Jeff. Bob must obey Jeff or leave the house and no judge will help him obtaining a different result. Jeff on the contrary can get the help of a judge in case Bob refuses to obey and leave the house. When the government is actively protecting a property right, 'it is forcing the non-owner to desist from handling it unless the owner consents'.[189] Except in the limited field of the constraints set by laws, Jeff is the final enactor and judge of the rules applicable in his house.

The same applies in factories, offices or shops.[190] In these various locations, the rules applicable to the use of the premises and other assets used for the firm's operations can take several forms: works rules, inner regulations etc. They can be extremely repressive.[191] Several theories have been developed to give them a *contractual* basis. They are unfounded.[192] The origin of these rules is not to be found in *contracts*; it is to be found in *property*. Laws can provide for procedures to establish these rules, involving employee representatives, for example, or they can limit the content of the rules (prohibiting or limiting the fines the employer can impose on employees, protecting certain fundamental rights of the employees, and so on). But these are *derogations* to the *principle* that, absent rules set by contracts, laws, customs etc. it is the *owner* who sets the rules in connection with the use of his property. It is because of property rights that the management of a firm can make decisions that apply to all the workers or to categories of workers. And these decisions are enforced by sanctions, including firing.[193] It is because of property rights that controllers of property can force others to abide by their rules, to abide by the heteronomy they impose, at the expense of their autonomy. The fact is that nineteenth-century employees were subject to severe private regulations, repression by fines, wage reductions or dismissal; unhealthy

---

[189] Hale, *op cit*, note 168, p. 470.

[190] Hélène Landemore and Isabelle Ferreras, 'In Defense of Workplace Democracy: Towards a Justification of the Firm–State Analogy', *Political Theory*, pp. 1–29 (2015).

[191] Foucault, *op cit*, note 17, pp. 609–615 & 618.

[192] For more details, *see* Jean-Philippe Robé, 'L'ordre juridique de l'entreprise', 25 *Droits*, pp. 163–177 (1997) and 'Enterprises and the Constitution of the World Economy', in 2 *International Corporate Law*, pp. 45–64, Fiona Macmillan (ed.), London: Hart Publishing (2003).

[193] Robert A. Dahl, *A Preface to Economic Democracy*, Berkeley and Los Angeles: University of California Press (1985), pp. 113–115.

and unsafe workplaces, harsh work and long workdays.[194] They did not agree to all this in the joyful exercise of their 'freedom of contract'.

For classical writers about the legal system, this is a very problematic fact. Understanding property as a right over things and the owner's power as deriving from a contract among equals preserves the idea that we live in a society of equals. This is the classical legal construction. But this construction hides the reality of the Power System structuring the operation of our society. It is merely an effort at window dressing the power of owners in the Power System behind the appearance of contracts. Of course, this is a highly problematic conclusion. It is hard to imagine that *any* Supreme Court could acknowledge this difference in *rights*, which is an interesting situation for a legal concept. But the inner foundations of any social order are necessarily arbitrary and what is being evidenced by the identification of property as a right of decision-making as a matter of principle inherently generating legal inequality among legal persons is just an evidence of the unfounded foundations of our specific social order.[195] At the root level of our legal system as it relates to the relationships among individual persons towards objects of property, equality is *not* the rule and the rule-makers are *not* contracting individual persons. There is *inequality in power* and the *rule-makers are owners*.[196] As a consequence, as written by Hale: 'We don't have equal rights. Each of us has his unique set of property and contract rights, and they aren't equal in any significant sense.'[197]

The world surrounding us is a system of prerogatives towards others in connection with objects of property allocated among owners, public and private. Unless we would decide to change the fundamental legal rules structuring our society – in effect get rid of private property altogether – it can't be otherwise, as a matter of principle. In polities having implemented nationalization programmes, the only thing which

---

[194] Sassen, *op cit*, note 6, p. 111. 'In the nineteenth century … rights were shed at the gates of most institutions in society'; Friedman, *op cit*, note 40, p. 85.

[195] The entire law is subordinate to the lawful/unlawful code [*Recht/Unrecht*] with the sole exception of the Constitution; *e.g.* Luhmann, *op cit*, note 47, p. 110. The Constitution cannot be subject to this code; the artificiality of the whole construction would appear which would affect the Constitution's stabilizing effect. This is a direct consequence of the artificiality of any founding principle.

[196] Pierre Bourdieu, 'Les juristes, gardiens de l'hypocrisie collective', in F. Chazel and J. Commaille (sous la direction de), *Normes juridiques et régulation sociale*, Paris: Librairie Générale de Droit et de Jurisprudence (1991), p. 95.

[197] In the *Hale Papers*, as cited by Barbara H. Fried, *The Progressive Assault on Laissez Faire – Robert Hale and the First Law and Economics Movement*, Cambridge: Harvard University Press (1998), p. 96.

changed was the identity of the rule-maker, the identity of the holder of the *'constraining power'*, as explained by Hale. The *'constraining power'* itself remained. Concentrating much of the prerogatives over assets in one single organization, as was the case in most countries of the former communist bloc, may have been inefficient. Organizations can be efficient only up to a size which may vary from organization to organization. But a limit ends up being met. When too many property rights are being concentrated, there are limits to the ability of any organization to gather the precise local knowledge required to make proper decisions about the use of these rights.[198] The right of decision-making must be re-decentralized, i.e. property must be dispersed anew. The point here is different: changing the identity of the owner does not change the constraining power entailed by property, by the control over assets and by the derived control over who has access to them under what terms.

1.9 A Right as a Matter of Principle, not a 'Bundle of Rights'

In twenty-first-century Western societies, this 'right-against-others-in-connection-with-things' we call property extends to the relationship between property owners and the State. It is a feature of 'open access orders', not of 'natural States', to use the terminology developed by North, Wallis and Weingast. In our society, State law can limit the content of the 'rules of the house' or the 'factory rules'. The fact remains that the owner is the rule-maker towards others in connection with his property *as a matter of principle*. Laws are only limited *derogations* to the rule-making right of the owner *as a matter of exception*. Laws are basically a limitation to freedom and to the use of property.[199]

In this respect it is a mistake to view property as a 'bundle of rights', something finite, an addition of identifiable prerogatives. The 'bundle of rights' theory is clearly the currently prevailing understanding of property in mainstream Anglo-American legal philosophy.[200] It is a

---

[198] According to Coase, 'in a competitive system there is an optimum amount of planning, and ... an optimum quantity of market operations'; Ronald H. Coase, 'Accounting and the Theory of the Firm', 12 *Journal of Accounting and Economics*, pp. 3–13 (1990), pp. 12–13.

[199] Carl Schmitt, *Théorie de la Constitution*, Paris: Presses Universitaires de France (1989), p. 286.

[200] J.E. Penner, 'The 'Bundle of Rights' Picture of Property', 43(3) *UCLA Law Review*, pp. 711–820 (1995–96), p. 712.

legacy of the Legal Realism movement in late nineteenth-century and early twentieth-century America, found, in particular, in the works of Wesley Hohfeld.[201] It is also a consequence of the definition given by Ronald Coase. Sometimes, for opposite reasons, this conception has been attractive for Critical Legal authors, Law and Economics scholars and New Institutional economists.[202] In the analysis developed in this book, however, this view of property is misleading and does not appropriately convey the notion of property. The bundle of rights picture obscures more than it illuminates.[203]

To understand property, one must understand the notions of *rights in rem* as opposed to *rights in personam*.

What characterizes a right *in rem* is that it is normally available against the world at large. For example, if I own a house, everybody has a duty to respect my property. My right is not against any specific person; *every* person has a duty not to interfere with my property. It is called a 'real right' and opposite to this right, there is a duty upon *every person* not to interfere with this right. This right creates prerogatives against the world at large and creates obligations for the world at large. It exists against an open and indefinite class of persons.

A right *in personam*, on the contrary, is available only against a particular person or a set of particular persons. For example, I lease the house I own to a tenant. I have a right to receive rent from my tenant only. This right to receive rent is a right *in personam*. The rest of the world is not concerned with this right of mine and my tenant's obligation. Such a right is also called a 'personal right'. Opposite to my right, there is a duty imposed upon *a determinate person*; in the example I used, the tenant.

With the 'bundle of rights' understanding of property, at least ownership is not perceived as a relationship between the owner and the thing owned. As written by Penner:

> my ownership of a car should not be regarded as a legal relation between me and a thing, the car, but as a *series of rights* I hold against all others, each of whom has a correlative duty not to

---

[201] Wesley Newcomb Hohfeld, 'Some Fundamental Legal Conceptions as Applied in Judicial Reasoning', 23(1) *Yale Law Journal*, pp. 16–59 (1913).

[202] *See* Henry E. Smith, 'Property is not just a Bundle of Rights', 8(3) *Econ Journal Watch*, pp. 279–291 (2011). *See also* Daniel B. Klein and John Robinson, 'Property: A Bundle of Rights? Prologue to the Property Symposium', 8(3) *Econ Journal Watch*, pp. 193–204 (2011).

[203] Penner, *op cit*, note 200, p. 724.

interfere with my ownership of the car, by damaging it, or stealing it, and so on.[204]

But with the generally agreed notion of property rights as 'bundle of rights', as a *'series of rights'*, rights *in rem* ('real rights') end up being treated as a myriad of rights *in personam* ('personal rights') among individual persons. This is an inaccurate description of the right to property. The 'bundle of rights' theory strips away from the concept of property one of its *fundamental* attributes, i.e. that it is a right an owner holds against the whole world, not just against specified individual persons.[205] Karl Renner puts it in a slightly different way:

> Ownership is not an aggregate of individual rights, it implies unlimited possibilities of disposal. ... Any restriction of this power of disposal, whether imposed from outside by legislation or self-imposed by contract, only affects the exercise, not the right itself; it affects the owner, not his ownership.[206]

This view is confirmed by looking at the 'twin brother' of the right to property – the right of personal liberty[207] found, like property, for example in Article 2 of the French Declaration of Human Rights or the Fifth Amendment of the US Constitution.[208] Each individual person can, in relation to all others, do as he pleases 'and it would be as meaningless to dissolve the right of personal liberty into the freedom to sleep, to take a walk, to make the sign of the cross, as it would be to dissect ownership into individualized powers'.[209] Treating differently the two rights constitutionally provided for in the same Articles is incomprehensible. Personal liberty is not a bundle of rights. It is a right as a matter of principle. And property operates in the same fashion.

---

[204] *Ibid*, p. 712 (emphasis added). *See also* Hohfeld, *op cit*, note 201, who understood that the entitlements granted by property are relational.

[205] *Ibid*, p. 717. *See also* Kelsen, *op cit*, note 12, p. 86.

[206] Renner, *op cit*, note 180, p. 81.

[207] On the connection between the two, *see* Frédéric Zenati, 'Pour une rénovation de la théorie de la propriété', *Revue Trimestrielle de Droit Civil* (2) avril-juin, pp. 305–323 (1993), p. 316.

[208] In addition to Liberty and Property, the French Declaration also declares 'Safety and Resistance to Oppression' to be among the aims of every political association. But these rights come more as defences of both property and liberty; *see* Carbonnier, *op cit*, note 19, p. 309.

[209] Renner, *op cit*, note 180, p. 82.

Elaborating on the 'bundle of rights' theory, Anthony Honoré has listed 11 incidents of ownership.[210] The list is impressive and covers most of what can be done with a property. But I am not going to discuss it because it does not affect my argument. Rather, the deconstruction of property into a series of incidents gives an inaccurate image of what property is and leads to somewhat irrelevant discussions about the list of items and their detailed content. As already claimed by Penner, 'if property is an aggregative complex, it is a matter of judgment to decide which particular aggregates of more basic elements constitute property ..., then the concept of "property" is a flexible one'.[211] And it reduces the significance of property[212] and obfuscates its importance in the structuring of the Power System.

Today's 'bundle of rights' paradigm has not always been the prevailing mantra. Its present – but contested – dominance is the outcome of two streams of thought.

First, it came out of the Realists' effort *against* property. They sought to undermine the notion of property to smooth the way for activist State intervention in regulating and redistributing property.[213] To correct the unfairness and inefficiencies of 'market' exchange left to itself, they wanted to desacralize property. But attempts to tame the 'sole and despotic dominion' of property are *even more justified* with a more accurate description of property. This may have been a position too aggressive for the Realists at the time of their writings.

The second stream of thought having led to the 'bundle of rights' theory is Ronald Coase's formulation in his 1960 article on 'The Problem of Social Cost' that 'what the land-owner in fact possesses is the right to carry out a circumscribed list of actions'.[214] In the zero transaction cost setting underlying Coase's article, all possible uses of the asset are *known* and *can be contracted about*.[215] But this does not apply in a real, positive transaction cost, world. Coase's influential article, however, paved the way for a (mis)understanding of property as a *collection of rights* to

---

[210] 1. The right to possess, 2. The right to use, 3. The right to manage, 4. The right to the income, 5. The right to the capital, 6. The right to security, 7. The incident of transmissibility, 8. The incident of absence of term, 9. The prohibition of harmful use, 10. Liability to execution, and 11. The residuary character; *see* Hodgson, *op cit*, note 37, pp. 231–242.

[211] Penner, *op cit*, note 200, pp. 722–723.

[212] Zenati, *op cit*, note 207, pp. 315–316.

[213] *See* Merrill and Smith, *op cit*, note 84, p. 365.

[214] Ronald H. Coase, 'The Problem of Social Costs', 3 *Journal of Law and Economics*, pp. 1–44 (1960), p. 44. *See* Merrill and Smith, *op cit*, note 84, p. 398.

[215] Foss and Foss, *op cit*, note 75, pp. 391–411.

carry out certain actions *with respect to resources*. While Coase himself was purportedly exploring the 'influence of the law on the working of the economic system',[216] Coase unfortunately led his followers on the wrong path by misunderstanding what property really is. He treated property as a 'right to perform certain actions'. As a result, property rights economists ended up disregarding the legal notion of property, concentrating on the so-called 'circumscribed list of actions'.

The 'bundle of rights' theory fundamentally misrepresents how property operates in our imperfect world with positive transaction costs. It leads to infinite errors. With property, what is finite at any point in time is *not* the set of prerogatives, the bundles of rights. What is finite is the set of *limitations* to the right to property, to the autonomy it entails. The autonomy of the property owner is *the rule*; the limitations of this autonomy via contracts or laws or other norms created via the political system limiting the uses of property are *the exceptions*. Property is a *right as a matter of principle* with 'bundles of _limits_' evolving when the law evolves, depending on the demands made on the political system, and on its eventual reaction, to adopt norms limiting the potential uses of property.[217] Property is a default rule and is a key to the decision-making rules in a society full of uncertainty.

This is important because with the globalization of firms and of the Power System, the use of property is now subject to fewer rules. The ability to make decisions as a matter of principle which is guaranteed to owners suffers fewer restrictions. There is more autonomy on the part of those controlling property and a reduced ability for officially political institutions to internalize negative externalities and to redistribute income and wealth. Of course, States remain *officially* sovereign with the ability to put limits to the autonomy of property owners. But the competition among States has changed the equilibrium among micro- and macro-powers. The whole operation of the Power System based on property as a prerogative as a matter of principle, and of laws as mere limitations as a matter of derogation, is affected. The ability – real or threatened – to relocate business activities completely upsets the global constitutional scheme of allocation of authority.

---

[216] *See* Merrill and Smith, *op cit*, note 84, p. 367.

[217] *See also* Merrill, *op cit*, note 105, p. 2069.

1.10 A Rejoinder: Oliver Hart's Theory of Ownership

Oliver Hart, who was awarded the 2016 economics Nobel Prize, reached a similar conclusion, explaining that property is important in a less than perfect world with positive transaction costs. His analysis is built on the notion of 'incompleteness of contracts' developed by Oliver E. Williamson (2009 economics Nobel prizewinner) and others. He started with the fact that we live in a world where:

> transaction costs are pervasive and large. As a consequence, ... the parties to a relationship will *not* write a contract that anticipates all the events that may occur and the various actions that are appropriate in these events. Rather, they will write a contract that is *incomplete*, in the sense that it contains gaps or missing provisions. ... A result of this incompleteness is that events will occur which make it desirable for the parties to act differently from the way specified in the contract. As a consequence, the parties will want to *revise* the contract. In addition, the parties may sometimes disagree about what the contract really means; disputes may occur, and third parties may be brought in to resolve them.[218]

For Oliver Hart, the incompleteness of contracts leads to a theory of ownership. If there can be *only* incomplete contracts, *ownership* of the assets involved in the relationship will be an important source of power enhancing the *owner's* bargaining position during renegotiations. The owner is in a strong bargaining position because of the *residual rights of control* characterizing ownership. The owner of an asset may bind himself and the asset via a contract; but for anything which is not specified in the contract, the owner has the residual control rights and therefore has a strong ex-post bargaining position.[219] This is because, as I contend above,

---

[218] Oliver D. Hart, 'Incomplete Contracts and the Theory of the Firm', in Oliver E. Williamson and Sidney G. Winter (eds.), *The Nature of the Firm – Origins, Evolution, and Development*, New York & Oxford: Oxford University Press (1993), pp. 138–158, at p. 141 (emphasis in original).

[219] The ownership of assets is actually at the root of another strand of analysis understood as the 'theory of property rights'. Sanford Grossman and Oliver D. Hart, 'The Costs and Benefits of Ownership: A Theory of Vertical and Lateral Integration', 94(2) *Journal of Political Economy*, pp. 691–719 (1986), Oliver D. Hart and John Moore, 'Property rights and the theory of the firm', 98 *Journal of Political Economy*, pp. 1119–1158 (1990) and Oliver D. Hart, 'Corporate Governance: Some

ownership is a right 'as a matter of principle' and both laws and contracts can only be limitations 'as a matter of exception'.[220]

Hart's analysis in effect goes against the 'bundle of rights' theory and is useful for my purposes in this book because it is in line with what I claim to be the *legal* notion of property.[221] The owner has the residual rights of control. He is the decision-maker as a matter of principle. And this is so because property is not a 'bundle of rights' which can be specified and fully contracted about.

1.11 A Similar Concept in Civil Law and Common Law Systems

Interestingly, this legal definition of property is not dependent on whether we are dealing with a 'civil law' or 'common law' legal system.

To start with, the distinction between the two types of systems is not as severe as is usually thought,[222] with *efficient* 'judge-made law' on the one side and *rigid* 'Code law' on the other. This is a caricature, put forward most recently by the 'legal origins' enthusiasts (according to whom the historical origin of a country's laws is highly correlated with its level of economic development).[223]

---

theory and implications', 105 *Economic Journal*, pp. 678–689 (1995) have developed an analysis pursuant to which the employee obeys the employer because the employer can deprive him of the means of production. In their analysis, the authority of the employer derives from the power conferred by property. Of course, this assumes that the employee needs to have access to the property rights controlled by the employer and that the employee is not necessary to the employer for the efficient use of the assets he controls.

[220] This view has been criticized by Harold Demsetz on several grounds. *See* Harold Demsetz, 'Book review of *Firms, Contracts and Financial Structure*, by Oliver Hart', 106(2) *Journal of Political Economy*, pp. 446–452 (1998), pp. 448–450.

[221] This idea that the incompleteness of contracts explains the importance of property forms the basis of the theory of integration later developed by Grossman and Hart, *op cit*, note 219.

[222] Geoffrey M. Hodgson, 'On the Institutional Foundations of Law: The Insufficiency of Custom and Private Ordering', 43(1) *Journal of Economic Issues*, pp. 143–166 (2009), p. 153.

[223] *See*, in particular, Rafael La Porta, Florencio Lopez-de-Silanes and Andrei Shleifer, 'The Economic Consequences of Legal Origins', 46(2) *Journal of Economic Literature*, pp. 285–332, (2008). For a mild criticism, *see* Haggard, MacIntyre and Tiede, *op cit*, note 111, pp. 205–34.

The notion of rights *in rem*, first developed in civil law systems, used to be prevalent in common law as well.[224] For the famous William Blackstone, who was the first to give lectures on the English Common Law at any university, property is 'that sole and despotic dominion which one man claims and exercises over the external things of the world, in total exclusion of the right of any other individual in the universe'.[225] This notion of 'sole and despotic dominion' has been subsequently heavily criticized to justify encroachments to property. And innumerous laws have reduced the effectiveness of the 'sole and despotic dominion'. They have not changed the fact that property is, *as a matter of principle*, a 'sole and despotic dominion'; with exceptions. It may not be 'sole' anymore; but it is still 'despotic' as a matter of principle.

In a Civil Law system, the provisions of the French Civil Code are quite clear on this 'as-a-matter-of-principle/as-a-matter-of-exception' dichotomy. Article 544 of the French Civil Code (unchanged since the enactment of the Code in 1804) defines ownership (*la propriété*) in the following manner: 'Ownership is the right to enjoy and dispose of things in the most absolute manner, provided they are not used in a way prohibited by statutes or regulations.' A quick reading of the Article could lead to the conclusion that ownership is a right over things. This is not the proper way of understanding the principle set by this Article: owning something means that one has a right *as a matter of principle* against the world at large to '*enjoy and dispose*' of the object of property.[226] But 'statutes and regulations', i.e. the political system through which generally applicable norms are adopted, can limit this right, *as a matter of exception*.

1.12 Property as a Building Block of the Power System

It is this specific character of property as an entitlement to make decisions as a matter of principle with regards to the object of property *which allows developing a unified analysis of politics and economics*.[227] The restrictions

---

[224] *See* Merrill and Smith, *op cit*, note 76, p. 780, and Merrill and Smith, *op cit*, note 84, pp. 358–359.

[225] *Ibid*, pp. 360–361.

[226] On this issue, *see generally* Blaufarb, *op cit*, note 14, especially pp. 208–210. *See also* Marquis de Vareilles-Sommières, 'La définition et la notion juridique de propriété', *Revue Trimestrielle de Droit Civil*, pp. 443–495 (1905).

[227] On this universally recognized but never satisfactorily resolved problem, *see* Susan Strange, *The Retreat of the State: The Diffusion of Power in the World Economy*, Cambridge: Cambridge University Press (1996), p. 37. Susan Strange explains that the issue is to

applicable to the uses of property vary from jurisdiction to jurisdiction. Throughout history, different electorates, via the different political systems of governments, had and still have different views about the proper limitations to the right to property. But the *fundamental* characteristic of property as a right of decision-making as a matter of principle in connection with things is the same *everywhere* there is a constitutional form of government protecting property rights. The restrictions may vary in their significance and nature. The extent of the property right may vary. But the existence of the right as being a right of decision-making as a matter of principle remains.

---

relate the 'political system' of 'States' to the 'economic system' of 'markets'. She cites Gilpin, for whom 'the parallel existence and mutual interaction of "State" and "market" in the modern world create "political economy"'. They both made the mistakes of (1) using 'State' and 'market' in the singular; (2) considering that States and markets are independent, when the ones are in part a creation of the others; and (3) taking it for granted that we are living in 'market economies' whilst large firms in fact are 'counter-markets', i.e. are organizing economic exchanges on the basis of principles other than market competition. But although she was unclear in her terminology, Susan Strange was on the right track when she considered that 'extending the definition of politics beyond States to all sources of authority, to all with power to allocate values, however, allows the two worlds of markets and States, of government and business, to be treated as one, rather than two as in Gilpin's equation.' *Ibid*, p. 38.

2

The Modern Constitutional Mode of Government

In Chapter 1, I have presented the concept of property in a constitutional perspective. Modern property is in no way a 'state of nature' notion. It is part of a highly sophisticated social system. It is a constitutional prerogative towards objects of property protected *by* the State and *against* the State. It has very little to do with possession. Property includes a right to exclude, owners having rights of decision-making as a matter of principle towards what they own. Laws affecting the use of property are only limited derogations to a prerogative which exists as a matter of principle. Understanding property in this fashion is a key to the understanding of the operation of the existing World Power System.

In the coming chapter, the notions of the State and of the 'Organs of the State' are explained in some detail to distinguish their prerogatives from private prerogatives. Private property, as a private prerogative, grants autonomy from the 'Organs of the State'. It is part of the constitutional prerogatives protecting private persons against excessive public governmental encroachments. It is part of a constitutional order which combines both democracy and distrust for democracy, by limiting the prerogatives of the Organs of the State. The approach developed proposes a unitary view of the Constitution as providing for both *public* and *private* prerogatives, the first ones being exercised by Organs of the State and the second ones by legal persons which are *not* Organs of the State. Public and private prerogatives operate via fundamentally different rules, private property rights enabling their holders to exercise their prerogatives in a despotic manner, i.e. they can do what they want with what they have without the need to take anybody's advice or authorization.

★★★

In a modern constitutional system of government protecting property rights, there are two sets of interacting rules. One of the purposes of the Constitution is to define the operation of the branches of public government, usually via democratic institutions. This is the most traditional way of understanding what a 'Constitution' is. But the Constitution also aims at protecting individual persons and minorities against governmental abuses.

There is, therefore, a set of constitutional rules defining fundamental rights, rights of autonomy designed for individual persons. These rights – freedom of thought, of movement, of religion, of association and so on – are to some extent *out of the reach* of the institutions created via the operation of the second set of constitutional rules: those which define the mode of operation of the *political* institutions of a constitutional system of government. One of the Constitution's purposes is to provide protection against unrestrained majorities obtaining control of the legislative and/or executive branches of government which otherwise would have minorities or individual persons at their mercy. Constitutions are conservative in this respect. They are written in such a way that even democratically elected *majorities* do not have total freedom to adopt any kind of legal or regulatory rules. In the rules they adopt, majorities must preserve the fundamental rights placed out of their reach. Courts, and Supreme Courts in particular, are here to ensure that such is the case. All democratic liberal constitutional States combine at the same time democracy *and* distrust for democracy.[228] In Luhmann's terms, any law, with the problematic exception of the Constitution, can potentially be contrary to the law. The whole of the law is therefore put in a contingency situation. And this is the case not only to the extent that the legislator can make law and, if necessary, revise it, but because it is possible for the law to be unlawful [*Unrecht*]. The entire law is subordinate to the lawful/unlawful code [*Recht/Unrecht*] with the sole exception of the Constitution.[229]

In this way, *fundamental rights* are somehow placed out of the reach of the public political institutions. Individual persons benefit from a combination of freedoms and rights of autonomy allowing them to pursue their individual purposes and, in the sphere of economic exchanges, to use their assets with a significantly reduced risk of being illegally deprived

---

[228] Ely, *op cit*, note 134. On this issue, *see also generally* Gregory S. Alexander, *The Global Debate Over Constitutional Property – Lessons from American Takings Jurisprudence*, Chicago and London: The University of Chicago Press (2006). *See also* Léon Duguit, for whom individuals' rights limit the State's sovereignty; in Duguit, *op cit*, note 172, p. 27. *See also* Chevallier, *op cit*, note 36, p. 365.

[229] Luhmann, *op cit*, note 47, p. 110.

of their property. This may lead to issues the electorate wants to see addressed via the adoption of new laws; and part of the democratic process of government is designed to provide procedures to address these issues. This is particularly the case since the State has evolved, especially after the Great Depression of the early 1930s, from a 'nightwatchman' State to a 'regulatory' and 'welfare' State, internalizing negative externalities and redistributing income, in compliance with the Pigovian view of the proper operation of a market democratic society. But there are limits – which are changing via evolutions in the interpretation of constitutional norms – to what the democratic process can do. Unrestrained democracy could lead to absolute public governmental power. The purpose of the fundamental rights protected by the Constitution is to create limits to absolutism. Their existence necessarily limits democracy.[230]

This unitary view of the Constitution, looking at the operation of the rights of autonomy, of the institutions of democracy and of constitutionalism as a whole, is contrary to the traditional one, as expressed for example by Alf Ross. It is classical to consider that the Constitution 'deals with matters such as Parliament, the King, the ministers and the court but not, e.g. ... economic organizations, or private individuals ... because only the former are regarded as "Organs of the State"'.[231] In my own analysis, this is a restrictive view of the Constitution and of a constitutional system of government.[232] If fundamental rights listed in the Constitution or in amendments to the Constitution or in other texts having constitutional ranking are *effectively enforced*, i.e. are effective restraints on the autonomy of the legislative, executive and judicial branches of the State, these rights *are part* of the constitutional system of government. They are part of a complex *Power System* comprising State institutions (Organs of the State) and non-State ones (private persons) which do exist as such *because of* constitutional provisions. Since the French Revolution of 1789 and the first written modern European Constitution – the French Constitution of 1791 – Constitutions typically contain a declaration of fundamental rights, on the one hand, and a description of the separation of State powers, on the other. There is first a definition of certain fundamental rights and principles guaranteed against the State

---

[230] Antonio Negri, *Le pouvoir constituant – Essai sur les alternatives de la modernité*, Paris: Presses Universitaires de France (1992), pp. 2–7.

[231] Alf Ross, 'On the Concepts "State" and "State Organs" in Constitutional Law', 5 *Scandinavian Studies in Law*, pp. 111–129 (1961), p. 115.

[232] *See also* David Kennedy, 'The Mystery of Global Governance', 34 *Ohio Northern University Law Review*, pp. 827–860 (2008), p. 854.

and, second, the description of the political system which can be that of a monarchy, an aristocracy or a democracy or anything else in between.[233]

2.1 The State and the 'Organs of the State'

The constitutional system of government provides for the existence of a series of prerogatives which can, in first approximation, be understood as 'public', for some of them, and as 'private', for the others. Only 'Organs of the State' are entitled to make use of the public prerogatives, with rare exceptions. These prerogatives are being used by individual legal persons who are not acting in their own name but as *agents* of the State. Their actions are imputed to a separate legal person, which is 'the State'.[234] The State, who is the subject of State acts, is a point of legal imputation.[235] It is the outcome of the imputation *by the legal system* of certain human actions not to the human being acting by him- or herself, but to a separate legal person acting, so to speak, *through him or her*: the State.[236] As a legal person, the State needs organs to represent it and express its 'will'. As holder of powers, the State can exercise them only through organs composed of individuals.[237] And equally, the State is this legal person to which certain human actions are imputed.

But the existence of provisions on 'public', and 'private' prerogatives in one *single set* of constitutional rules creates the complex unity of a pluralistic Power System which cannot be reduced to 'the State'. The Power System is operating via an autonomous, private sphere, on the one hand, and a public sphere, on the other. There is not, on the one hand, the realm of freedom in which the exchange economy operates and, on the other, a realm of the law where the State has jurisdiction. Capitalism has developed in the context of an evolving legal system and not in the free realm of Nowhere.[238] Certain private prerogatives are constitutionally protected. But the institutions of the 'public sphere' (a) have some ability

---

[233] Schmitt, *op cit*, note 199, pp. 171–172 & 183.

[234] On this theory of the State, *see generally* the works of Gierke, Jellinek, Michoud and Hauriou. And for a critique, *see* Duguit.

[235] Hans Kelsen, 'L'essence de l'État' (traduction H. Thévenaz), 17 *Cahiers de philosophie politique et juridique*, p. 17, Presses Universitaires de Caen (1990, 1ère édition 1926), pp. 24–26. Saleilles, *op cit*, note 42, pp. 356–357.

[236] Kelsen, *op cit*, note 235, pp. 24–25. Nguyen Quoc Dinh, Patrick Dailler and Alain Pellet, *Droit international public*, Paris: Librairie Générale de Droit et de Jurisprudence (4e édition 1992), p. 402.

[237] Kelsen, *op cit*, note 235, pp. 24–26.

[238] *See* Lippmann, *op cit*, note 83, pp. 190 & 272.

to amend the 'rules of the game' applying to legal persons operating in the 'private' sphere of the Power System when they are politically perceived as requiring changes; and at the same time (b) they can't encroach in an excessive manner on private prerogatives. The positioning of the line between valid legal intervention and unconstitutional infringement of private rights is, of course, a major issue perceived differently in different cultures and at different times in history. The fact remains that in many States, the legal structuring of the 'private' side of the power system has much more stability than the structuring of the public side.[239] In France, for example, since the French Declaration of the Rights of Man and Citizen of 26 August 1789 and the Civil Code of 1804, governments have been emperors, kings and republics (five in total). The unamended 1789 Declaration of the Rights of Man and Citizen is still part of French constitutional law and although the Civil Code has been amended, sometimes substantially in matters of family law, for example, the main principles of the organization of civil, private life have fundamentally remained the same. Or, as Carl Schmitt remarked in the overall European context, wars can lead to a change in the authority holding sovereignty over a given territory and population; private legal arrangements remain fundamentally unaffected by the political changes.[240]

The political 'Organs of the State' can vary significantly from State to State: the executive can be a king, a president directly or indirectly elected by the electorate, a prime minister; the legislative can be composed of one or two chambers; the judiciary can be elected or not, and so on. There is a wealth of possibilities which are *not* of primary concern for my purposes as long as the State operates via generally applicable rules in a democratic manner. The key to a unified understanding of economics and politics – which we need to develop to understand the World Power System – is to understand that underneath the varieties of public governments, there is something more fundamental. At the root of the operation of the State in a constitutional mode of government is a State operating through

---

[239] On the continuity of the constitutional protection of property rights in France irrespective of the many political changes which have occurred since the 1789 Declaration, *see* Jean-Louis Mestre, 'Le Conseil constitutionnel, la liberté d'entreprendre et la propriété', *Dalloz*, Chroniques, pp. 1–8 (1984), pp. 4–8. *See also* Blaufarb, *op cit*, note 14, p. 57, for whom this issue is 'the constitutional history of the French Revolution'. *See also*, *ibid*, p. 119.

[240] Carl Schmitt, *Le nomos de la terre*, Paris: Presses Universitaires de France (1988, 2001), starting at p. 200. On Röpke's views on this, *see also* Quinn Slobodian, *The Globalists – The End of Empire and the Birth of Neoliberalism*, Cambridge: Harvard University Press (2018), pp. 116–117.

Organs of the State abiding by a series of principles applicable to Organs of the State only.

In this context, it is important to precisely understand the concept of 'organ of the State' because it is a necessity to differentiate 'public' prerogatives and 'private' ones.[241] When an act is imputed to the State as a legal person, it is a 'State act' and the individual who is the author of this act is an 'Organ of the State'. The legal person of the State has the same character as other legal persons, public or private: it is a point of legal imputation.[242]

In a constitutional system of government, there are certain prerogatives which are legally attributed to a legal person (the 'State') different from the physical person or persons making use of the prerogatives (the 'organ of the State'). This phenomenon of attributing certain acts of certain *individual persons* holding specific offices to a *legal person* which clearly has no physical existence creates a 'public authority' called 'the State'.[243] These 'public' prerogatives have specific characteristics:

(a) They are powers which are not for everyone but only attach to certain *qualified persons* (a king, a president, a prime minister, a member of parliament, a judge and so on).

(b) These prerogatives entail a capacity to create rules (statutes, regulations, judgments, orders) that *bind others*.

(c) The persons having these prerogatives are not entitled to use them freely at their convenience. They have a legal *duty* to exercise their prerogatives.

(d) These prerogatives can only be used in the *public interest*, as opposed to the individual interest of the person exercising the prerogative. The holders of these prerogatives have an *objective duty*.

(e) These prerogatives are not part of a *right* and are therefore *never transferable*. At most, they can be delegated to other persons, which leaves untouched the holder's own power.[244]

To summarize, public prerogatives are *qualified*, *heteronomous*, *mandatory*, in the *public interest* and *non-transferable*. They are performed by 'Organs

---

[241] For this whole chapter, *see generally* Ross, *op cit*, note 231, pp. 115–119.

[242] Hans Kelsen, *Théorie pure du droit* (traduction H. Thévenaz), Paris: Editions de la Baconnière, collection 'Être et penser, cahiers de philosophie', n° 37 (1953, 1988), p. 171.

[243] Ross, *op cit*, note 231, pp. 115 & 118.

[244] As a matter of illustration, the President of the United States of America cannot transfer the right to be President of the United States of America. He cannot sell his office. He can only delegate the performance of some of his prerogatives.

of the State' in the sense that they are attributed to a *legal person* different from the individual person or collective body performing the act, making use of the prerogative. Each of these authorities – and the beneficiaries of delegations of authority from these authorities – is part of a systematic unity of authorities we call 'the State'. The organs having the privilege to use force are regarded as organs of the same legal subject – the same 'State' – as those, for example, possessing the authority to prescribe norms. This is so because force may ultimately need to be used to enforce the norms created by the competent Organs of the same 'State'. They are interconnected organizations belonging to the same systematic unity of public rule-making, implementing decisions and actions over a given territory and population.[245] Legal personality gives the State political unity and institutional continuity. Various organizations providing services to the population are combined into one political organization[246] which keeps its continuity no matter the changes which may occur in the identity of the political personnel. The institution takes on a timeless character and the exercise of its prerogatives is made impersonal while only mortals can in fact act in its name.[247]

The existence of a 'State' operating in this fashion is a fundamental feature of a 'State of law'. It reduces considerably the possibilities for individual persons holding public offices to use the prerogatives they have for their own individual benefit or for the benefits of clients. It plays a fundamental role in ensuring that the 'rules of the game' are the rules of a 'State of law', of a State operating via law in an *impersonal* manner and itself subject to the law. A 'State of law' operating under the 'rule of law' is a State operating via a government of laws, and not of men and women.[248] In a sense, the modern constitutional State has been invented

---

[245] Ross, *op cit*, note 231, p. 121.

[246] 'The State is a group of individuals possessing a force they have to use to create and manage public services.' *E.g.* Duguit, *op cit*, note 172, p. xix.

[247] Fukuyama insists on the fact that although China during the Ming Dynasty had most of the institutions regarded as critical for economic development, the absence of a rule of law left property rights vulnerable to the government's capriciousness and hindered development. *See* Fukuyama, *op cit*, note 128, p. 315.

[248] *See* Art. XXX of the Declaration of the Rights of the Inhabitants of the Commonwealth of Massachusetts, which is part of the Preamble to the 1780 Constitution of Massachusetts, which states that: 'In the government of this commonwealth, the legislative department shall never exercise the executive and judicial powers, or either of them; the executive shall never exercise the legislative and judicial powers, or either of them; the judicial shall never exercise the legislative and executive powers, or either of them; to the end it may be *a government of laws, and not of men*' (emphasis added). The text was authored by John Adams, one of the Founding Fathers of the United States Constitution.

to prevent individuals from being subjected to other individuals.[249] To be freed from any relationship of personal dependence, individuals must be subjected to the same general laws.[250] For this to be achieved, rules must be applied in an *impersonal* fashion – in a fashion in which neither the person *applying* the norm nor the person to whom the norm in being *applied* – matter. Certainty as to the application of the norm must derive from an understanding of the norm as written and not from the knowledge of the person interpreting or applying the norm. Of course, there are always interpretation issues, exceptions and political scandals. Public prerogatives are sometimes used in furtherance of private interests, be it the personal interest of the holder of the prerogative or of some clients obtaining favours. But the point is precisely that such *abuses* of public offices are perceived as *scandals*, not as something *normal* in a properly operating constitutional system of government.

2.2 Private Prerogatives

With regards to 'private' prerogatives in a constitutional system of government, they create what can be called 'private autonomy'. As we have seen, private property is part of the rights of autonomy. It shares many of its features with other rights of autonomy. It is different in one way, however. It can be at the origin of a form of *heteronomy* which, however, is *not* treated as being 'public', attributable to 'the State'.

As prerogatives, rights of autonomy have characteristics which can be opposed one by one to those enjoyed by 'Organs of the State'.

(a) Whereas public prerogatives are for certain qualified persons only, rights of autonomy create prerogatives which are available for every individual person.[251] As opposed to public prerogatives, they are *not restricted to qualified persons*.

---

[249] In Jean-Jacques Rousseau's words, 'A free people has leaders but no masters; it obeys Laws, but it obeys only Laws, and it is by the force of Laws that he does not obey men.... A people is free ... when in the one who governs them, it does not see the man, but the organ of the Law.' *See* Alain Supiot, *La gouvernance par les nombres – Cours au Collège de France (2012–2014)*, Paris: Fayard (2015), pp. 51–52, and *also* Georges Burdeau, *L'État*, Paris: Editions du Seuil (1970), p. 15, for whom men invented States in order not to obey other men.

[250] Supiot, *op cit*, note 249, p. 51.

[251] With some protective restrictions linked to age, mental sanity and, in the past, gender.

(b) Whereas public prerogatives entail a capacity to create heteronomous rules applicable to others, private prerogatives are, as a matter of principle, rights of *autonomy*. The beneficiary of the rights of autonomy creates his own rules. These rights comprise freedom of movement, of thought, of speech and so on. Private property is one of the rights of autonomy.

(c) Whereas a public official has an obligation to perform the duties of his office, there is no legal *duty* to exercise one's autonomy or to exercise it only in certain ways. In this regard, it is mistaken to consider that ownership is an 'office' and that the owner is an officeholder who happens to be the present occupier of the office.[252] It is misleading because an official in charge of an office *must* fulfil his duties in the interests of the institution to which the office belongs. The owner has no such duty. 'Do whatever you want' is not a mandate and 'choose whomever you want to be your successor' is not a procedure.[253]

(d) Whereas a public prerogative has to be used in the general interest, there is no duty to exercise private prerogatives in any interest other than the one of the person having the prerogative as defined by such person. The holder of the prerogative does not have to take into account the externalities generated by the use of the prerogative.[254] It is a *subjective right*.[255]

(e) Finally, whereas public prerogatives are *not* transferable, private prerogatives – and this is particularly the case with property rights – *are transferable*.

To summarize, while public prerogatives are *qualified, heteronomous, mandatory,* in the *public interest* and *non-transferable*, private prerogatives are generally *unqualified, autonomous, optional,* in the *private interest* and *transferable*.

Private prerogatives are *not* performed by 'Organs of the State'. They enable the individual to shape his legal relationships in accordance with his own choices. As a consequence, the individual person to whom the

---

[252] *See generally* Larissa Katz, 'Governing Through Owners: How and Why Formal Private Property Rights Enhance State Power', 160 *University of Pennsylvania Law Review*, pp. 2029–2059 (2012).

[253] Arthur Ripstein, 'Property and Sovereignty: How to Tell the Difference', 19 *Theoretical Inquiries in Law*, pp. 243–268 (2017), p. 254.

[254] *See also* Merrill, *op cit*, note 105, p. 2089.

[255] One should take notice, however, of the content of article 14 of the 'German Basic Law', which provides that (1) Property and the right of inheritance shall be guaranteed. Their content and limits shall be defined by the laws; and also that (2) Property entails obligations. Its use shall also serve the public good.

exercise of the private prerogatives is imputed *assumes the consequences and potential liabilities* for his actions. For State prerogatives, it is the State which is the point of imputation.

★★★

Ownership is a specific category of private prerogatives. It allows the creation of 'private' heteronomy.

(a) With regards to the *unqualified* nature of rights of autonomy, in connection with property, any owner has the prerogatives of the owner in connection with the object of ownership, no matter who the owner is and whatever the object of property is.

(b) Private property is also a *right of autonomy*. But in connection with certain assets, its content actually leads to a specific form of *heteronomy*. It is inaccurate to consider that 'property is the keystone right because property makes <u>individuals</u> independent and thus capable of self-government'.[256] In fact, property is the keystone right because property makes <u>owners</u> independent and thus capable of self-government. For individuals who are not owners, the situation is radically different. Property does not lead them to autonomy, but to its exact opposite: it leads them to be bound by the heteronomy of owners, by the discipline they impose. The subjective rights protected by the State can be a source for the flourishing of private legal orders based on coercion.[257] As Michel Foucault once wrote:

---

[256] Rose, *op cit*, note 13, p. 345, emphasis added. On this right of autonomy under German constitutional law, *see* Gregory S. Alexander, 'Property as a Fundamental Constitutional Right? The German Example', 88 *Cornell Law Review*, pp. 733–778 (2003).

[257] I use the expression 'legal order' with the same meaning as the one given by Santi Romano: any organized grouping is a legal order. *See* Santi Romano, *The Legal Order*, London: Routledge (1946, 2017) which was first published in Italian in 1917 and translated into English one full century later. For Professor Paulsson, president of the London Court of International Arbitration and of the World Bank Administrative Tribunal, 'It is a scandal of intellectual history that this seminal monograph has never been translated into English.' *See generally* Filippo Fontanelli, 'Romano and l'ordinamento giuridico: The Relevance of a Forgotten Masterpiece for Contemporary International, Transnational and Global Legal Relations', 2(1) *Transnational Legal Theory*, pp. 67–117 (2011). Our world would be a different one if the work of Santi Romano had been better diffused and, also, better translated.

In the workshop, in the school, in the army, there is a whole micro-penal system relating to time (delays, absences, interruptions in tasks), activity (inattention, negligence, lack of zeal), in the way to behave (rudeness, disobedience), to speak (gossip, insolence).[258]

The shop discipline, while remaining a way of enforcing regulations and authorities, preventing theft or dissipation, tends to increase skills, speeds, yields and therefore profits; it always moralizes the behaviors but more and more it finalizes the behaviors, and brings the bodies into a machinery, the forces into an economy.[259]

It is often said that the model of a society whose constituent elements are individuals comes from the abstract legal forms of contract and exchange. Market society is deemed to be a contractual association of isolated legal subjects. ... But we must not forget that there existed at the same time a technique for constituting individuals as correlative elements of a power and knowledge system. The individual is ... also a reality made of this specific technology of power that is called 'discipline'.[260]

... behind the establishment of an explicit legal framework, codified, formally egalitarian, and through the organization of a parliamentary and representative type of regime [there is] the development and generalization of disciplinary types of devices ... The general legal system which guaranteed a system of rights in principle egalitarian was underpinned by minute, daily and physical mechanisms, by all the essentially unequal and dissymmetrical systems of micro-powers that constitute the disciplines. And if, in a formal way, the representative system allows that the will of all forms, directly or indirectly, with or without relay, the fundamental instance of sovereignty, the disciplines give, at the base, a guarantee of the submission of forces and bodies. Real and corporal disciplines have been the subsoil of formal and legal freedoms. The contract could well be imagined as the ideal foundation of law and political power; panoptism was the universally widespread technical process of coercion. ...

---

[258] Michel Foucault, *Surveiller et punir*, Paris: Gallimard (1974), p. 180.

[259] *Ibid*, p. 211.

[260] *Ibid*, p. 195.

> The 'enlightenment' that discovered freedoms also invented the disciplines.[261]

But for all his perspicacity, Foucault sees in the disciplines only an 'infra-law' (*infra-droit*) or even a 'law against the law' (*contre-droit*).[262] He completely missed the constitutional basis of what he was calling the 'disciplines', via the right to property.[263]

The notion that property gives power over people is often associated to Marxism or 'postmodernism'. The fact is that it was a recurrent theme of Republicanism as well, found for example in the writings of Thomas Jefferson. One strain of Republicanism considers that the Republic has to be run by virtuous citizens only by eliminating from the franchise all those lacking property; the other – egalitarian – strain seeks widespread distribution of property so that every citizen gains self-sufficiency and does not need to fall into subservience.[264] There was a clear notion that if property is distributed in a highly unequal fashion, a conflict will tend to arise between democracy and property rights.[265] This was Jefferson's view and, in the Constitution he drafted for Virginia, he included a clause providing that 'every person of full age neither owning nor having owned [50] acres of land, shall be entitled to an appropriation of [50] acres or to so much as shall make up what he owns or has owned [50] acres in full and absolute dominion'.[266]

The fact of the matter is that property entails a right to legislate. *Not* towards the whole public: towards those who are making use of the privately owned property. Below the level of collective consciousness, the right of ownership comprises the power to issue commands and to enforce them.[267]

---

[261] *Ibid*, p. 223.

[262] *Ibid*, (1974), p. 224.

[263] Jean-Yves Grenier and André Orléan rightfully underline Foucault's general disregard for the legal system and the cost for his analysis of his total exclusion of any consideration of property rights; *see* Jean-Yves Grenier and André Orléan, 'Michel Foucault, l'économie politique et le libéralisme', 5 *Annales, Histoire, Sciences Sociales*, pp. 1155–1182 (2007). Attempting to analyse the reality of power relationships beyond legal formalism, Foucault missed the constitutional structuring of the power system at the fringe of the political and formal legal systems, in particular via property rights.

[264] Joan Williams, 'The Rhetoric of Property', 83 *Iowa Law Review*, pp. 277–361 (1997), p. 317.

[265] Dahl, *op cit*, note 193, p. 101.

[266] Williams, *op cit*, note 264, p. 318.

[267] Renner, *op cit*, note 180, p. 107.

This authority is partly hidden behind this right of autonomy called 'freedom of contract'.[268] The 'private' legislative power of the owner often takes the form of a contract with those who will be subject to the authority of the owner. I have already mentioned this phenomenon.[269] A contract is understood as one way to exercise one's autonomy. But it is often actually one way to subject oneself to someone else's *heteronomy*, which exists because of the existence of property.

This is particularly the case for the employment contract which is in direct contradiction with the principle of 'private autonomy'. It is, by definition, a contract of *subordination* pursuant to which the employee becomes the subordinate of the employer. Via the contract, parts of the rights of autonomy of the employee (his freedom of movement, of speech etc.) are being reduced to the benefit of the employer.[270] The identity of who the *employer* is in the relationship is determined by the identification of who is the *owner* of the assets the employee will use in the performance of the employment contract.

This has led Adolf Berle, for example, to distinguish property used in production and property used for consumption.[271] He thought that we were

> well underway toward recognition that property used in production will be made to conform to the conception of civilization worked out through American constitutional democratic process [and that] the right to choose consumption – to spend if and as you please – will be guarded as a defense of the individual's right to order his own life.

The future of this sensible view, however, was buried with the advent of the faulty agency theory, as we will see later.[272]

---

[268] This issue is made even more complex under US constitutional law because some property rights have been qualified as 'contracts', to benefit from the Contracts Clause, and some contracts are treated as property, to benefit from the Taking Clause; *see* Merrill and Smith, *op cit*, note 76, p. 774.

[269] *See* Section 1.8.

[270] Elizabeth Anderson, *Private Government – How Employers Rule Our Lives (and Why We Don't Talk about It)*, Princeton: Princeton University Press (2017).

[271] *See generally* Berle, *op cit*, note 24, pp. 1–20.

[272] *See* Section 9.5.

(c) Like for the other rights of autonomy, the owner, as a matter of principle, has *no duty* to do anything with his property.

(d) The owner is entitled to use his property in his sole *private personal interest*.

(e) The rights of autonomy towards an object of property are obviously *transferable* to another person.[273]

Owners have clearly more of the enabling power provided by the rights of individual autonomy than non-owners do. But owners are *not* part of the systematic unity of authorities we call 'the State'. The State Constitution recognizes their powers but does *not* integrate them in the State apparatus; it does not treat them as 'Organs of the State'.

2.3 Property and the Autonomy from the 'Organs of the State'

The fact that the protection granted to private property comes from the Constitution does not mean that 'economic organizations or private individuals' become 'Organs of the State'. It is quite the opposite. Fundamental rights *limit the ability of governments* to make of individual persons and of any beneficiary of the fundamental rights of autonomy – which can be corporations – 'Organs of the State'.

One of the purposes of Constitutions is to *prevent* Organs of the State from being excessively intrusive regarding the use of the fundamental rights protected by the Constitution. And it so happens that the right to property is among these fundamental rights. It is out of the reach of the political system, to some extent. Of course, the political system can regulate and reduce some of the uses of property. But it cannot change the fact that property is, to some degree, 'above the (legislative, executive or case[274]) law'. It is a constitutionally guaranteed competence 'as a matter of principle'. Laws can only come as limited derogations, 'as a matter of

---

[273] Although there are restrictions at times as to who the purchaser can be.

[274] Judges, as part of the judiciary, can no more intervene in the exercise of fundamental (property) rights than the other branches of government can. All they can do is protect these rights, i.e. protect the autonomy they entail. This is merely a consequence of the pluralistic nature of law: the legal order of the State is external to the legal orders of the despotisms which can be created via property rights, and State judges can only enforce State laws, which are always limited derogations to the principle of autonomy entailed by property rights. If they could interfere, that would be the end of the autonomy of owners, their decision-making power 'as a matter of principle', and it would be unconstitutional.

exception'. The modern liberal Constitution is first of all a Constitution providing for individual freedom. This is done by positing the individual's sphere of freedom as pre-existing the State. The individual's freedom is unlimited as a matter of principle while the State's ability to reduce this freedom is limited. And then, the State's authority is divided among authorities having their own specific set of competences. This allocation of competences is the result of the definition of a series of 'fundamental rights', on the one hand, and of a strict allocation of State prerogatives resulting from the separation of functions among executive, legislative and judiciary, on the other.[275] This fundamental structure of any modern constitution was firmly established in Article 16 of the 1789 French Declaration of Human Rights, which states that 'Any State which does not provide for fundamental rights and without separation of powers has no Constitution'.

In such a constitutional legal order, property being the right to be the decision-maker as a matter of principle over the private object of property, the protection of property rights by – and against – the State *prevents* the integration of owners as 'Organs of the State'. This is key to the institutionalization of the Power System as a liberal constitutional system of government in which owners will keep at least some of their prerogatives irrespective of political changes at the public governmental level. And in a globalized Power System, as we will see, this is even more fundamental.

In liberal constitutional systems of government, property is a key institution to structure the overall Power System.[276] Property decentralizes the decision-making power over assets as a matter of principle to the largest extent possible: down to the individual.[277]

The other side of the coin is that the individual decision-maker is potentially liable for any damage created by his or her property. With unlimited decision-making authority as a matter of principle comes also *unlimited liability* for the damages created by the object of property, and therefore for the decisions made in connection with the use of the

---

[275] Schmitt, *op cit*, note 199, pp. 264–265 & pp. 295–297.

[276] 'The political character of private rights becomes still more obvious as soon as one realizes that the conferring of private rights upon individuals is the specific legal technique of civil law, and that civil law is the specific legal technique of private capitalism, which is at the same time a political system.' Kelsen, *op cit*, note 12, p. 89. In this context, the expression '*private liberalism*' would be more appropriate.

[277] From the Medieval Latin *individualis*, from Latin *individuum* ('an indivisible thing'), neuter of *individuus* ('indivisible, undivided'), from in + *dividuus* ('divisible'), from *divido* ('divide').

property. With *property* comes *responsibility*, a point clearly seen by de Soto who underlined the social benefits of accountability.[278]

The right to property is therefore not necessarily a right over *something of value* if by value what is meant is 'positive economic value'. Property *enables* autonomous decision-making; but it also entails *liability for the decisions made* – or not made – in connection with the object of property or for the mere fact of being the owner. As a matter of example, one can take the case of the owner of a contaminated land. A tenant may have caused the contamination and the owner may have a contractual recourse against the tenant to obtain indemnification. But if the tenant is unable to clean the land (because he or she is bankrupt, for example), the owner, *because he is the owner*, must clean up the mess. And the cost may be more than the value of the land. Consequently, the land may have a *negative* value; property is not necessarily a right over something of (positive) value. Property is a right of autonomy but also a source of *liability* for the autonomous decisions made thanks to ownership. In the example used, leasing the land to a tenant conducting a polluting activity without securing an autonomous guarantee to be able to clean up the land in case the tenant can't is a serious mistake for which the property owner has to bear the consequences.

At the root of the overall Power System, one therefore finds property owners as the decision-/rule-makers as a matter of principle towards the objects of property. Via their rights over property, i.e. the right to make the rules in connection with what they own, owners are part of the Power System of society. But they also bear responsibilities for the existence of this power.

2.4 The Small-scale Despotisms

In constitutional systems of government, via property, at the lowest level in society's overall Power System, one finds myriads of what are or at least *can be*, as a matter of principle, *despotisms*. Irrespective of the democratic nature of what we usually understand as being 'the political system' (which is only the sub-part of the overall Power System routinely identified as 'political'), at the lowest level in the Power System, property rights allow the existence of micro-systems of governance created by property

---

[278] De Soto, *op cit*, note 20, p. 87.

owners – something Paolo Grossi calls 'legal absolutism'.[279] They are, as a matter of principle, micro-governments in which 'one person [the owner] makes all the rules and decisions without input from anyone else'. This is the definition of despotism. Without legal rules limiting the owners' subjective prerogatives, the despotic nature of organized production would be the one of a legal order freed from any notion of individual rights.[280] So much so that one of Lenin's objectives during the Bolshevik revolution was actually to make of the whole of society 'one single office, one single manufacture in which the masses obey to the will of those directing production'.[281] In a liberal Power System, it is a requirement to have institutions in a position to curb the despotism of property used in production. This is clearly lacking at the international level in our present World Power System, with limited exceptions such as, for example, the few rules provided for by the International Labour Organization.

Individual owners are, of course, free to organize differently the production and the operation of the rules governing the use of their property. They are fully entitled to structure the governance system over their property as they wish. And very often, they face the same legitimacy issue in the use of their autonomy as the one faced by holders of 'public' power during the phase of State consolidation. They can organize the decision-making process as a democracy, if they wish. And many business firms are not organized as despotisms. Their managerial autonomy derives from the autonomy granted by property rights. But property does not force owners to act as despots. Being more inclusive, however, is an *option* for the controllers of property rights, not an *obligation*. Liberal constitutionalism abstains consciously from constitutionalizing civil society.[282]

What we call 'democracies' are therefore only *marginally* democratic. *As a matter of principle*, the rules at the root of the Power System of liberal constitutional democracies are *despotic*. The democratic institutions of society are only a sub-part of the overall Power System. And they only operate *at the margin* of the Power System, the norms they create being applicable *as a matter of exception*.

---

[279] Grossi, *op cit*, note 179, pp. 128–130. On an analysis of firms as political entities, see Isabelle Ferreras, *Firms as Political Entities – Saving Democracy through Economic Bicameralism*, Cambridge: Cambridge University Press (2017).

[280] Anderson, *op cit*, note 270.

[281] Supiot, *op cit*, note 172, p. 210.

[282] *E.g.* Gunther Teubner, *Constitutional Fragments – Societal Constitutionalism and Globalization*, Oxford: Oxford University Press (2012), p. 15.

The operation of the despotisms can be modified via the political system understood in a restrictive manner, in limited, derogatory, 'as a matter of exception' way, via laws. In some jurisdictions, for example, employees and/or their representatives have been statutorily granted some rights over the management of the micro-governments (firms) to which they are subjected. There are wide differences in this respect among the various national polities.[283] It is well known, for example, that in Germany and in many Northern European countries, in certain large firms, employees have even been granted so-called 'co-determination' rights. But no matter the extent of the governmental rights given to employees or their representatives in these firms, these are still 'as a matter of exception' rights which *reduce* the autonomy of the owner but do not *reverse* the identity of the decision-maker as a matter of principle. One should remark that in the particular case of Germany, Article 14.2 of its Fundamental Statute (the equivalent of its Constitution) provides: 'Property entails obligations. Its use shall also serve the public good.' Germany's specific form of capitalism certainly derives from its peculiar rules regarding corporate governance. But at a deeper level, it also relies on a rather specific conception of property, which is certainly not a purely subjective right in the German constitutional order.[284]

2.5 Power in Times of Peace, Power in Times of War

The developments of this chapter have covered the operation of a constitutional system of government towards property in times of peace. People can pursue their own, private ends. In times of war, the situation is different. People and their resources must be mobilized for one goal: winning the war. Constitutions, as a consequence, often provide for different rules in times of peace and in times of war.

Interesting and numerous inferences could be drawn from a comparison of the operation of the Power System in times of war and in times of peace. The normal operation of a constitutional Power System I described

---

[283] *See*, in particular, Isabelle Ferreras, *Gouverner le capitalisme?*, Paris: Presses Universitaires de France (2012).

[284] *See* Gregory Alexander, for whom the core purpose of property under German constitutional law is not wealth maximization or the satisfaction of individual preferences, but self-realization, or self-development, in an objective, distinctively moral and civil sense; in Alexander, *op cit*, note 256. *See also* Grossi, *op cit*, note 179, pp. 248–253. On the specificities of the German situation, *see* Alexander, *op cit*, note 228, pp. 97–148.

requires the existence of an orderly situation. In case of internal or external disorder – of *social unrest* or *war* – the constitutional rules operate differently. This underlines in a different fashion how much property rights are intrinsically linked to the overall operation of the Power System. It also shows how the right to property and its operation very much depend on the overall mode of operation of society. It is not a right over goods but a right against people in connection with goods which varies depending on whether society is orderly or in a phase of turmoil.

In the remainder of this book, I will deal only with the operation of the Power System in times of peace.

3

Sovereignty and Property

The preceding chapters addressed the modern notion of property and its role in the liberal constitutional mode of government. In Chapter 1, the concept of property was explained as a right of decision-making as a matter of principle towards the object of property. In Chapter 2, private property was analysed as a constitutional prerogative protecting owners against excessive public governmental encroachments to their autonomy. It showed that as a right of decision-making as a matter of principle, property is part of a Power System which combines despotism and democracy in its governance.

  The present chapter deals with the relationship between the concepts of sovereignty and property. It first addresses the thesis developed by Douglass North, John Wallis and Barry Weingast on the role of organized violence in the development of a modern, open access society. Their intuition is that the present-day 'Western-type' society required a fundamental change from earlier societies. The 'limited access order' of the 'natural state', in which personal relationships form the basis of social organization, had to leave the way to an 'open access order' in which impersonal categories of individuals interact. In my own analysis, this is broadly correct. But North, Wallis and Weingast neglected the role of *law* in the process and, in particular, the role of the development of *constitutional* modes of government. Via modern international law, starting in Europe in the middle of the seventeenth century, sovereignty was allocated *among States*. Via liberal Constitutions, internal sovereignty *within States* was decentralized as a matter of principle to *owners*, who are the decision-makers as a matter of principle towards the objects of property they own. The operations of the political Organs of the State, of the administrative Organs of the State and of the legal rules protecting this autonomy can usefully be viewed in this perspective.

★★★

Constitutionally protected property rights are a decentralization of the power of rule- and decision-making towards the objects of property. Owners have authority towards the use of their objects of property, and therefore on those using them, 'as a matter of principle'. As written by Kingman Brewster in his article on economic federalism, 'the virtue of leaving considerable economic power in private hands is not too dissimilar from the virtue of leaving considerable political power in the federal States of a federation'.[285] Property diffuses power and is a very significant tool for the ordering of society. It is the keystone right because it makes individuals capable of self-government.[286]

It does not mean that the use of property cannot be curtailed via laws. On the contrary. Abuses of property, damaging use of property, inefficient use of property or any public interest sufficiently affected by the improper use of property may legitimate a reduction of the owners' autonomy, via generally applicable rules. This was constitutionally contemplated as early as 1789, Article 5 of the Declaration of the Rights of Man and Citizen providing that 'Statutes may only prohibit actions negative for society. Anything which is not prohibited by statute cannot be prevented, and none can be forced to do what it does not order'. The objectives which can be pursued by the adoption of statutes are limited: they must only prohibit actions *negative* to society. But the ability to adopt statutes to prohibit certain actions is contemplated: *it is part of the Rights of Man and Citizen*. The rise of the regulatory and welfare State which took place in several waves in the twentieth century was a reaction to issues created by large industrial firms, with poor working conditions, low wages, widespread contamination of the natural environment, the production of unsafe products and so on. These issues, which had to be addressed at the level of the macro-political institutions of the various national legal systems, resulted from an unrestrained use of private property as a right of decision-making as a matter of principle. With these issues arising, in great part due to industrialization, rules protecting the concurrent interests of employees, neighbours, tenants and owners, planning restrictions, zoning, environmental protection, the protection of values associated with cultural heritage and so on were adopted, limiting the autonomy of owners.[287]

---

[285] Kingman Jr. Brewster, 'The Corporation and Economic Federalism', in Edward S. Mason (ed.) *The Corporation in Modern Society*, Cambridge: Harvard University Press (1959), pp. 72–84, at p. 75.

[286] *E.g.* Rose, *op cit,* note 13, pp. 340–345.

[287] *See generally* Alain Wijffels, 'Rationalization and Derationalization of Legal Capacity in Historical Perspective: Some General Caveats', in Simon Deakin and Alain Supiot (eds), *Capacitas – Contract and the Institutional Preconditions of a Market Economy*, Oregon: Oxford and Portland (2009), pp. 49–62.

But the constitutional possibility of reducing the owners' autonomy was already contemplated in the 1789 Declaration of the Rights of Man and Citizen. There is a unity in the Power System of resource allocation which is usually misunderstood because of the improper understanding of the modern notion of property rights.[288] Property rights are *not rights over things*; they are *components of a system of constitutional government* and their extent varies with the evolving consciousness of the existence of interests insufficiently taken into account by private decisions, contracts and actions involving them.

To show this, I will confront my analysis with the one developed by North, Wallis and Weingast. They attempted and in part succeeded at demonstrating how economic and political developments are linked. But they missed several key issues and, in particular, the significance of the rule of law.[289]

North, Wallis and Weingast consider that the misunderstanding about how economic and political developments are connected is due to a lack of systematic thinking about the central problem of violence in human society.[290] Linking economics and politics via the control of violence, as they do, may seem far-fetched. But the link is extremely deep and powerful.[291] The main issue to deal with in society is *organized* violence: the use of violence or the threat of violence by organized groups to extract rents from the population subject to the violent organizations.

[288] On this unity, *see* Portalis, who considered that the drafting of the Civil Code required 'the ability of perceiving the whole of a State's constitution' ['*pénétrer, d'un coup de genie, toute la constitution d'un État*']; Xavier Martin, *Mythologie du Code Napoléon – Aux soubassements de la France Moderne*, Bouère: Editions Dominique Martin Morin (2003), p. 213. On Montesquieu's similar views, *see* Charles de Secondat, baron de La Brède et de Montesquieu, *De l'Esprit des loix, ou Du Rapport que les loix doivent avoir avec la Constitution de chaque gouvernement*, Genève: Barillot & Fils (1748).

[289] Fukuyama, on the contrary, insists on the importance of the rule of law, or lack thereof. *See* Fukuyama, *op cit*, note 128, p. 289. Often though, law is treated as a mere 'sub-discipline' (*e.g.* Claude Menard and Mary M. Shirley, 'The future of new institutional economics: from early intuitions to a new paradigm?', 10(4) *Journal of Institutional Economics*, pp. 541–565 (2014), p. 560) whereas it is not merely a 'discipline' of the social sciences but a key institutional development for the orderly structuring of society.

[290] North, Wallis and Weingast, *op cit*, note 6, p. xi. *See also* Karl Popper, for whom the essential political problem is to prevent physical violence, although he did not insist on the even more important issue of preventing *organized* violence: Karl Popper, *La société ouverte et ses ennemis*, tome 2, 'Hegel et Marx', Paris: Seuil (1979), pp. 84–86.

[291] In connection with globalization, *see* Anthony McGrew, 'Organized Violence in the Making (and Remaking) of Globalization', in Held and McGrew, *op cit*, note 3, pp. 15–40.

If these violent organizations are not held in check, property rights, as I have defined them, cannot exist: the right of decision-making as a matter of principle in connection with objects of property is protected neither by the State nor against the State. Protection by the State requires the building of an institution having the *monopoly* of legitimate violence over a territory. But for property rights to exist, this institution must then be subject to *mandatory rules limiting its own arbitrary tendencies*. The modern constitutional State is a formidable set of institutions to address these complex issues. It both monopolizes legitimate violence in the State and provides for effective rules to prevent the illegal use of the State monopoly over violence, including against owners.

In what may seem to be a paradox, to limit the existence of disorders in their various forms and to protect the population and its assets, an institutional system of organized violence is always required. This role today is played by the State. But unless and until those in control of society's police and armed forces – which today form part of the State – are effectively prevented from using their prerogatives in their own personal interests or those of their clients, the effective operation of a properly working Power System will be prevented. Subject to the risk of organized theft, or to unfair competition, those in a position to invest would do so in a limited manner or only by being part of the political coalition in charge.

In fact, the development of an economy free from disruptive political interference required the development of complex legal institutions combining, in particular, the protection and enforcement of property rights, as I have defined them – rights of decision-making as a matter of principle – with democratic political institutions subject to constitutional review.

3.1 North, Wallis and Weingast's Thesis

In connection with the central issue of violence, North, Wallis and Weingast divide human history into three 'social orders':

(1) In their view there is, first, the *foraging order,* composed of small groups characteristic of hunter-gatherer societies. I will not discuss this developmental stage – whatever its reality – as it is not particularly relevant for my purposes.
(2) There is then the *limited access order* or so-called '*natural state*' in which *personal* relationships form the basis of social organization. In a 'natural state', political entrepreneurs control violence on a territory via a

110

coalition dominating the population and potential competitors. The coalition can extract value from its control of violence. The members of the dominant coalition possess special privileges and, for the leader of the coalition (a king, for example), remaining in charge depends on maintaining a dominant coalition that can surpass all rivals. In such a 'natural state', persons are treated differently depending on their status, on whether or not they are part of the coalition – knights or nobles, for example – whether or not they form part of the clientele of a member of the coalition, whether or not the members of the coalition they are connected to are powerful within the coalition or not, the strength of their relationship with those members of the coalition and so on in endless combinations of the potential *personal* connections within the Power System created by the coalition. Members of the coalition have their clientele who can obtain favours and all large economic organizations are dependent on political favours – which rarely come for free.[292]

(3) Finally, there is the *open access order* in which personal relations still matter, but in which *impersonal* categories of individual persons interact over wide areas of 'social behaviour'.[293] In an 'open access order', impersonality grows out of the structure of institutions which keep their identity independent of the individual persons in charge. *Public offices* have become *impersonally defined* and distinct from the individual identity of the specific individual person occupying the office at any point in time.[294]

I will not discuss the details of these 'orders' nor the method employed in reducing complexity in this fashion. Rather, I will concentrate on the difference North, Wallis and Weingast make between the so-called 'natural state' and the 'open access order'. And, interestingly, the analysis made by North, Wallis and Weingast is somewhat resonant with the one of Karl Popper (who is not cited among their sources) who considered that the move from a tribal or *closed* society to an *open society* was one of the greatest revolutions in human history.[295] At one point in their book,

---

[292] North, Wallis and Weingast, *op cit*, note 6, p. 267. This mode of social organization is called 'the conglomerate State' by Harald Gustafsson. *See* Harald Gustafsson, 'The conglomerate state: A perspective on state formation in Early Modern Europe', 23(3–4) *Scandinavian Journal of History*, pp. 189–213 (1988), p. 195. In his view, this is the missing link between the medieval State and the unitary State: p. 212.

[293] *Ibid*, p. 2.

[294] *Ibid*, p. 156.

[295] Karl Popper, *La société ouverte et ses ennemis*, tome 1, 'L'ascendant de Platon', Paris: Seuil (1979), p. 143.

North, Wallis and Weingast put it in a simple way: 'natural states' cannot issue something as simple as a driver's licence on an impersonal basis.[296] This captures very well the fundamental issue raised by a so-called 'natural state'. But North, Wallis and Weingast fail to point at what the issue is with a 'natural state' and why it is deficient in comparison with an 'open access order': the 'natural state' is a political order which is not operating *as a State of law*.

North, Wallis and Weingast indicate that they have built their framework of analysis on the 'rich literature of history, political science, economics, anthropology and the social sciences'.[297] This is an impressive body of knowledge to build on. But law and legal theory are missing from the list. The same applies to North's earlier book, *Understanding the Process of Economic Change*,[298] which does not have a *single entry* for 'law'. North writes that 'the human environment is a human construct of rules, norms, conventions, and ways of doing things that define the framework of human interaction'.[299] But no mention is made of law. Later in his book, North mentions that 'the economic institutional structure was made possible by the evolution of polities that eventually provided a framework of law and its enforcement. Such a framework is an essential requirement for the impersonal exchange that is necessary for economic growth'.[300] But that is all. And these remarks are made in a short section differentiating confiscation and debt repudiation as an inefficient means of obtaining State revenue versus the trading of property rights and their enforcement. This certainly was a key development. But the role of law goes far beyond this and deserves much more extensive developments.

This neglect of law is quite unfortunate because it is via law that the institutions of an 'open access order' have been established. The notion of 'State' is not only a notion in *anthropology*, as North, Wallis and Weingast write.[301] In today's World Power System and in constitutional systems of

---

[296] North, Wallis and Weingast, *op cit*, note 6, p. 11.

[297] *Ibid*, p. 251.

[298] Douglass C. North, *Understanding the Process of Economic Change*, Princeton: Princeton University Press (2005).

[299] *Ibid*, p. 11.

[300] *Ibid*, pp. 133–134.

[301] They explain their understanding of what a State is with the following sentences: '*State* is a term of art with a specific meaning in anthropology, but less so in political science and economics.... For anthropologists, states do not appear until populations rise into the hundreds of thousands. In contrast, what we define as the natural state arises as societies reach populations of one thousand or more ...'; North, Wallis and Weingast, *op cit*, note 6, p. 53.

government, the notion of State is actually mostly *a legal one*.[302] The great achievement of building what North, Wallis and Weingast call an 'open order society' took place thanks to the invention of the notion of the State *in the legal sense*. Disregarding this historical reality leads to fundamental errors in the understanding (or lack thereof) of the combined operation of the 'economic' and 'political' systems which are sub-parts of the Power System in a constitutional system of government. Although North tries to address the issue that 'economists, typically, do not ask themselves about the structure that humans impose on themselves to order their environment, and therefore reduce uncertainty',[303] he totally missed the key invention of humankind in this respect: *the invention of the legal system*.

3.2 The Role of Organized Violence

Organized violence is rightly identified by North, Wallis and Weingast as the central issue in the institutional setting of any society. As written earlier by North, we tend to take order for granted. We should not. Understanding the underlying conditions of order and disorder is essential for coming to grips with the process of economic change and institutional evolution.[304] The modern State's relationship to violence is very important to understand. Having established a legal monopoly of violence over a given territory and the population on it, States *administer* violence. They exert violence. It is their primary role because this is how they maintain order, as a means of last resort. Behind any lawsuit addressed in State courts, for example, there is conflict, disagreement, quarrel and, in the background, there is the potential for physical violence. The role

---

[302] Grossi, *op cit*, note 179, p. 131. Sabino Cassese, 'The Rise and Decline of the Notion of State', 7(2) *International Political Science Review*, pp. 120–130 (1986). Michel Troper, *Pour une théorie juridique de l'État*, Paris: Presses Universitaires de France, collection 'Léviathan' (1994), p. 5.

[303] North, *op cit*, note 298, p. 13. North uses the fuzzy notion of 'institution', which he defines as 'the rules of the game in a society'. He stresses that they are 'hard to define because they include written laws, formal social conventions, informal norms of behavior, and shared beliefs about the world'; *see, e.g.*, Sebastien Galiani and Itai Sened (eds), *Institutions, Property Rights and Economic Growth – The Legacy of Douglass North*, Cambridge: Cambridge University Press (2014), pp. 5–6. Of course, there are many rules and 'institutions' beyond the legal realm. But methodically, I consider that it does make sense to start with the framework offered by the rules of law – and specifically the rules of constitutional law – and to then extend the complexity of the analysis once this key framework in a modern society is assimilated.

[304] *Ibid*, p. 7.

of the justice system is in part to provide an alternative to the use of violence among the litigants. In extreme cases, the enforcement of the decision may require the use of violence; but it will be *State* violence: the orderly administration of violence after the rights involved have been fairly adjudicated in a court of law. One can fully understand this choice against unrestrained violence in favour of law only if one realizes the extent of the problem raised by violence, which effective State institutions manage to prevent.[305] Even modern war is not undifferentiated violence, but is a mode of *legal relationship among States*, with a wealth of rules limiting the violent means available to the belligerents.[306]

States are by definition very dangerous organizations because there is no other organization on their territory in a position to keep them in check. The alternative is social unrest to protest against the abusive use of the means of the State. But it is a sign of an ineffective State, of a State which is not operating properly, since the way it uses its monopoly over legitimate violence is being challenged by social unrest, not via effective political action or judicial procedures. In an effective State, because it is in a monopoly position, procedures *internal* to the State should be available to prevent the State from abusing its monopoly position. And it is only procedures internal to the State which can prevent individual persons in charge of public offices from abusing their prerogatives. Creating these procedures has been quite a historical challenge. And in many parts of the world, the challenge has not yet been met with the setting up of appropriate and efficiently operating institutions. It is usually quite easy to identify States where this evolution has not taken place: when the head of the executive is also one of the richest – if not the richest – person in the State, the likelihood to have a modern State of law is limited. The State is typically still controlled by political entrepreneurs exploiting it to their benefit, directly or through side corporate organizations. In all the existing States of law, executives hold State offices for which they get a remuneration, generally quite reasonable given the extent of the duties of their offices.

The modern constitutional State is a relatively recent invention.[307] Max Weber defined the State as the organization having the monopoly of 'legitimate violence'. This is now a widely accepted definition. But in the beginning of the creation of the State, the question was not at all a question of *legitimacy*. The State did not arise suddenly, with an established legitimacy leading to the immediate acceptance of its role in

---

[305] *See also* Paul Riqueur, *Le juste*, Paris: Editions Esprit (1995), p. 189.

[306] *See generally* Michel Serres, *Le contrat naturel*, Paris: Editions F. Bourin (1990).

[307] Grossi, *op cit*, note 179, p. 28.

the administration of violence on a given territory. The embryo of what ultimately became modern States were originally violent enterprises led by 'political entrepreneurs'.[308] They did not provide much by way of services other than rudimental 'public order' and some form of justice.[309] They had numerous domestic and external competitors, and their 'legitimacy' was very questionable. State builders first had to create a monopoly in the administration of violence over a territory in which boundaries became relatively fixed only *gradually*; the question of the legitimacy of the power thus created arose later, although *invoking* legitimacy was always a powerful tool to extend the reach of the political enterprise.[310] Early on, invoking the King's divine right to rule, for example, was a very effective means to support the monarchies' legitimacy.[311] Later on, with the development of certain national histories and myths, 'the people' began to be viewed as the basis of State sovereignty. But it is clear that in the framework of the creation of the State System, the question of legitimacy comes second.[312] One must first go through the transformation of *violence* into *power*. The law and the legal system which produces and applies it play a critical role in this prior transformation. It is via law that *violence* is turned into *power* with a legitimate system of authority to wield power.[313]

International law makes no mistake: what matters for the existence of a State in international law is the *effectiveness* of a government over a territory and the population in it. It is not its *legitimacy* which matters. The lack of legitimacy may lead some States not to recognize the coming into existence of a new State. But this is an international political question, not a legal, structural one. In the process of creating a State, the issue is primarily to establish a monopoly position to provide order over a territory. States are the instruments of the transformation of *violence into power*, and of transformation of the administration of *force* into the

---

[308] 'William and his successors, Lilburne said, have made their companions of robbery, pillage and theft, dukes, barons and lords'; Michel Foucault, *Il faut défendre la société, Cours au Collège de France, 1976*, Paris: Gallimard-Seuil, collection 'Hautes Etudes' (1997), p. 93.

[309] Fukuyama, *op cit*, note 128, p. 330.

[310] In the modern context of State creation via secession, Megan Stewart provides relevant and useful data. They show that insurgents having the ambition of creating a new State tend to provide inclusive services to the population to build legitimacy, both internally and externally, which they will need when the time of international recognition will come; Megan A. Stewart, 'Civil War as State-Making: Strategic Governance in Civil War', 72 *International Organization*, pp. 205–226 (2018).

[311] Jackson, *op cit*, note 4, p. 78.

[312] *E.g.* Nonet and Selznick, *op cit*, note 32, pp. 55–58.

[313] Jackson, *op cit*, note 4, pp. 14–19.

administration of *law*. Legitimation comes next – one of the interests of legitimacy being that the administration of violence is much easier to achieve when it is perceived as legitimate. Wise rulers have an interest in building legitimacy, their power being made more secure in the process.[314] Legality does not require the machinery of democratic decision-making. But once the rule of law is established, no power, including a democratic majority, is immune from the duty to abide by superior rules.[315]

This transformation of the administration of *force* into the administration of *law* is what is behind the genius of modern law in the Power System as we know it. This is the great progress brought about by the existence of the constitutional legal system. It does not suppress violence. But by administering it via laws applied in an *impersonal manner*, the modern State transforms violence into a form of civilized *power*. Those in charge of an office within the State (the 'Organs of the State') must use their prerogatives not in their own interest but in the general interest. Those benefiting from it receive services. But the services are provided to them in an *impersonal manner*, to 'nationals', to 'citizens', to 'residents' and so on, i.e. to *categories* of individual persons. *Specific* individuals benefit from State services because they belong to *categories* of individuals, not because of their *personal* connections. This is one of the keys to modernity – probably one of the most important ones.

In a State of law, violence takes on a brand-new dimension. Internally, for example, police forces evicting a family from a house which rent is unpaid make use of force. But it is force administered by specialized administrative Organs of the State which apply it only after certain legal procedures have led to the recognition that the application for expulsion is legally grounded. The expulsion remains a very violent act. In its consequences for the family violently ousted from its home, it is hard to bear and to accept. But in cases where the procedures were adopted or approved by a democratically elected legislature, and they are effectively implemented impersonally in accordance with the rules set by law, we are dealing with an instance of *legitimate* violence. It is not applied in an indiscriminate fashion. It is applied after the rights of all those involved have been ascertained. If democratically elected majorities consider that families in need should be provided with subsidized housing, it is for taxpayers *as a whole* to pay the bill, not for the owner-landlord hosting a needy family against his or her will. The alternative is not to prevent the proper operation of property rights. Providing free or subsidized shelter

---

[314] Selznick, *op cit*, note 112, p. 11. *See also* Marcel Gauchet, *op cit*, note 7, p. 495.
[315] Selznick, *op cit*, note 112, pp. 11 & 18.

for families in need is the political alternative, using taxes raised to be able to provide the service.

It is this effective monopoly over *legitimate* violence which puts the State in a position to *protect property rights, enforce contracts* and *create predictability*. The State is thus in a position to create part of the conditions for a voluntary exchange economy to exist and develop. The flip side is that what are perceived as negative consequences of the autonomous operation of the private property rights system must be addressed by the political institutions of the Power System. The 'intervention' of the State in the autonomous operation of property rights and contracts via laws is the *necessary* counterpart to the substantial delegation of authority via property. When social issues appear in connection with the autonomous operation of society, they must be addressed via laws, by an effective political system to prevent the social demands from degenerating into violence. Hence, big government in open access orders is not an aberration but an integral feature of these societies when they follow their course towards economic development.[316] When the order in place is perceived as unfair and/or unresponsive to the demands of the population, the justice and police and other forces of the order and all those who appear to be the beneficiaries of the order appear as guarantors of injustice and the targets of the revolt against the established order for the establishment of a new order. No peaceful order can continue in the long run without a minimum of justice.

Those among us having the chance to live in a State of law take the existence of the State as we know it as a given. That is also the case for the mainstream schools of economic analysis which take for granted institutions (property, contracts, the State and so on) which have nothing 'natural' about them and are very much part of the overall institutional system leading to the production of goods and services. We fail to appreciate how difficult an enterprise it was to get to this stage of institutional development which makes it possible, for example, to differentiate possession and property. Consequently, we fail to understand how fragile it is, if we take it for granted. And we also fail to understand how law must be integrated into economic analysis if we want the analysis to be relevant to real-life economic activity. The whole regime of private property and contract, the whole system of enterprise by individuals, partners or corporations exists in a legal context and is inconceivable without it.[317]

---

[316] *E.g.* North, Wallis and Weingast, *op cit,* note 6, p. 122. *See also* Charles Perrow, 'A Society of Organizations', 20(6) *Theory and Society*, pp. 725–762 (1991).

[317] *See* Lippmann, *op cit*, note 83, p. 189.

The fact that mainstream economic analysis ignores all this is a major problem. There is some sort of underlying assumption that the laws of property, contract and corporation somehow exist as a natural set of rules originating from the nature of things. Economics provides no explanation of why and how the political system defines property rights, enforces contracts and creates the rule of law necessary for markets to function.[318] In fact, it presupposes the existence of an effectively operating State without even being aware of it. It presupposes, for example, that issues raised by 'market' imperfections, in the form of inequalities and negative externalities, will be addressed by a perfectly operating State, the financing of which is ignored or disregarded. This is in any case a very bold assumption to make about the efficiency of the political process.[319] But this assumption cannot be made in a globalized Power System in which global firms cohabit with decentralized States. No 'State' is in place at the global level to fulfil the functions States can (or at least could) fulfil at the local level; and local States are prevented from fulfilling these functions, alone or jointly, at the global level because they are competing organizations, for tax collection or job creations in particular. There are 'political market failures [and] like imperfect markets, world politics is characterized by institutional deficiencies that inhibit mutually advantageous cooperation'.[320] In such a setting, when there are non-separable activities, where profit and damage are inextricably connected for technological reasons, action at the firm level is a reasonable substitute, as we will see in more detail later on.[321]

3.3 Property Rights and Sovereignty

In their operation, property rights are very much connected to the notion of sovereignty. Both are a form of power over people, as acknowledged early on by Morris Cohen, as we have already seen. Or, for Léon Duguit:

> in the XVIIth and XVIIIth centuries, sovereignty is a right to command, held by the king. It is a right which has the same characteristic as the right to property. The king holds it like

---

[318] *E.g.* North, Wallis and Weingast, *op cit,* note 6, p. 110.

[319] Oliver D. Hart and Luigi Zingales, *Companies Should Maximize Shareholder Welfare Not Market Value,* ECGI Working Paper Series in Finance no 521/2017 (2017), p. 4.

[320] Robert O. Keohane, *After Hegemony – Cooperation and Discord in the World Political Economy,* Princeton: Princeton University Press (1984), p. 85.

[321] *E.g.* Hart and Zingales, *op cit,* note 319, also referring to Bénabou and Tirole, *op cit,* note 8.

he does for his patrimonial rights. Sovereignty is a property, but it is a unified and inalienable property.[322]

But although property and sovereignty are very much connected to each other, 'the exact mix of these two regimes is anything but simple or unidimensional'.[323]

The World Power System analysis I propose, integrating the analysis of the operations of micro- and macro-powers in any given Power System, allows addressing this relationship.[324] In the World Power System in place today, *external sovereignty* allocates power as a matter of principle to States. States are sovereign in international law and towards their territory and population. International law is theoretically neutral towards the mode of organization of the internal Power System of the various States composing the State System. They have constitutional autonomy.[325] As I have already mentioned, however, liberalism was embedded in the post-World War II institutions of the Bretton Woods system which structurally constrained States adhering to its institutions.[326] After having created the conditions for the development of market economies internally (*see generally* Chapter 4), States created the multilateral norms and institutions making it possible for markets to spread globally. Tariffs, quotas and non-tariff barriers were progressively reduced and, in some cases, eliminated. The commitment

---

[322] Duguit, *op cit*, note 172, pp. 10–11.

[323] Thomas W. Merrill, 'Property and Sovereignty, Information and Audience', 18 *Theoretical Inquiries in Law*, pp. 417–445 (2017), p. 444.

[324] World Power System analysis shares many concepts and conclusions with the world system analysis developed by Immanuel Wallerstein. There are major differences, however. Periodization is different, an issue which will not be addressed in detail in this book. On these periodization (and also geolocalization) issues, *see* André Gunder Frank, *ReORIENT; Global Economy in the Asian Age*, Berkeley, Los Angeles & London: University of California Press (1998). But the most significant difference with Wallerstein is the position on the role played by law in the creation and evolution of the systems. Wallerstein, in typical Marxian view of the world, considers that law is merely of secondary importance, an infra-structure. In World Power Analysis, on the contrary, law is a fundamental medium of structuring of the system found within and among all the components of the Power System. For a summary of Wallerstein's analysis, *see* Immanuel Wallerstein, *World-Systems Analysis – An Introduction*, Durham & London: Duke University Press (2004).

[325] Nguyen Quoc Dinh, Dailler and Pellet, *op cit*, note 236, p. 413.

[326] John Gerard Ruggie, 'International Regimes, Transactions, and Change: Embedded Liberalism in the Postwar Economic Order', 36(2) *International Organization*, pp. 379–415 (1982); and 'Taking Embedded Liberalism Global', in David Held and Mathias Koenig-Archibugi (eds), *Taming Globalization: Frontiers of Governance*, Cambridge: Polity Press (2003), pp. 93–129.

to international liberalization was institutionally coupled with norms and practices protecting national social communities. On the one hand, governments re-established a multilateral monetary and trade regime and progressively removed barriers to trade via a series of General Agreement on Tariffs and Trade (GATT) rounds; and, on the other hand, they made domestic social investments and provided for safety nets. New social rights were granted, to the extent that Charles Reich could write about the birth of the New Property[327] – which contributed to the confusion about what property rights are and further obstructed their understanding as rights of decision-making as a matter of principle. The 'New Property rights' are in fact entitlements to being protected against risks increased by the operation of property in an industrial, urbanized and individualistic society: unemployment, poor health, old age and so on. Given the autonomous operation of the market/property society leading to these increased risks, new social rights (the so-called 'New Property') were created, yet they are not property at all. But no matter the qualification of these new rights, one of the longest and most equitable periods of economic expansion in history ensued.[328] The institutions of a world economy encompassing States with compatible modes of operation were thus created.

States operating in accordance with the rules of a State of law are a minority. But it is in those States that property rights in the modern sense are the most effective. In liberal constitutional systems of government, constitutionally protected property rights operate as a decentralization of the State's sovereignty towards objects of property to owners. Owners are the decision-makers as a matter of principle towards the objects of property. One of the purposes of the democratic institutions is then to address the issues created and not properly addressed by the autonomous operation of the rights of autonomy, including property by owners.

In this regard, private and public property must be thought about *together*. As noted by Richard Ely more than a century ago, 'it is one of the great defects of current treatments of property that the concept of public property has been inadequately treated by economists and publicists generally'.[329] The necessity to understand that *private* and *public* property *require each other* derives from the content of property. Private property

---

[327] Charles A. Reich, 'The New Property', 73 *Yale Law Journal*, pp. 733–787 (1964).

[328] John Gerard Ruggie, 'The Social Construction of the UN Guiding Principles on Business and Human Rights', in Surya Deva and David Birchall (eds), *Research Handbook on Human Rights and Business*, London: Edward Elgar (2020) Art 4, ch 1.

[329] Ely, *op cit*, note 21, pp. 107–108. *See also* Amartya Sen, *Ethique et économie*, Paris: Presses Universitaires de France (1987, 1993), pp. 101–102.

being a decentralization of the decision-making power towards the object of property to the owner *as a matter of principle*, one must determine how the restrictions to the use of property, *as a matter of exception*, are defined and implemented. In a constitutional Power System, they are defined by the *political* Organs of the State. They are then implemented by the *administrative* Organs of the State, using the public property at the disposal of the various State's officials. This is how the prerogatives of sovereignty are being apportioned in liberal constitutional States. We get here confirmation of a point already made by Eirik Furubotn and Svetozar Pejovich that 'a theory of property rights cannot be truly complete without a theory of the State'.[330]

But in the legal system, there are two conceptions of the 'State'. One derives from *international public law* – the law of the legal relationships among States; and *constitutional law*, which provides the roots of the operation of the internal legal order of the various States. Both bodies of law deal with the operation of 'sovereignty'. But going deeper in the analysis requires paying attention to the fact that *the same word* 'sovereignty' is used to designate two very different legal concepts which need to be distinguished.[331]

3.4 International Sovereignty

First, the word 'sovereignty' designates 'international sovereignty'. It is a relationship of legal *equality* among States.[332] International sovereignty is, in a sense, the 'real estate' system of the modern World Power System.[333] Having 'international sovereignty', each State is left free, as a matter of principle, to deal with its internal affairs without interferences from other States or any other types of organizations. International sovereignty is a concept invented in Europe to create a new world order after the disruption brought about in Christendom by Protestantism.[334] It is usually considered that international sovereignty became the linchpin of the legal

---

[330] Furubotn and Pejovich, *op cit*, note 156, p. 1140.

[331] *See generally* Jackson, *op cit*, note 4; Jens Bartelson, *A Genealogy of Sovereignty*, Cambridge: Cambridge University Press (1995).

[332] In certain jurisdictions, the word 'nation' is used instead of 'State'. This is the case in the US. In this book, for all practical purposes, the word 'State' is used to mean what is called 'nation' in the US, as in the expression 'the law of nations', otherwise known as 'international law'.

[333] James Mayall, *Nationalism and International Society*, Cambridge: Cambridge University Press (1990), p. 20, and Jackson, *op cit*, note 4, p. 72.

[334] Jackson, *op cit*, note 4, p. ix.

structure of international society with the Westphalia treaties ending the religious, Thirty Years' War in Europe of 1618–48.[335] Around that time, international society became a society of States.[336]

For 'international sovereignty', we have a clear date and a clear explanation for its appearance.[337] It is a by-product of European history to address the institutional issues having arisen because of the institutional implosion of Christendom.[338] It was then exported with the process of colonization and, more importantly, decolonization which led to the creation of numerous new States.

Consequently, the number of States has substantially increased. After World War II and the process of decolonization, the number of sovereign States moved from about 50 to more than 150.[339] There are today about 200 sovereign States. The process of globalization is *also* a process of globalization of the State System.[340] Notwithstanding the political decolonization process, the 'colonization' of the global legal world by what was originally a 'European State System' remained. It is far from clear that the effectiveness of the State on societies which had originally structured power relations within them differently was and still is effective. In many areas of the world, the State is more the *form* of the local Power System, an appearance needed to participate in the State System rather than a deeply rooted reality. The State is often a façade institution in the service of an individual, a family, a tribe or a clan. Or the compatibility of the Islamic division of the world among the Islamic world (*Dar al-Islam*) and the non-Islamic one (*Dar al-Harb*) with the State System is still an open question.

After the process of political decolonization, however, to participate in international economic exchange, newly created political institutions had to join the existing international institutions. To do so, they had no other choice than to adopt the State form, at the macro-level in the local Power Systems and, in this regard, capitalism and communism were

---

[335] Although there are some discussions around the real significance of this date; *see* Derek Croxton, 'The Peace of Westphalia of 1648 and the Origins of Sovereignty', 21(3) *The International History Review*, pp. 569–591 (1999).

[336] Mayall, *op cit*, note 333, p. 2 & pp. 18–20.

[337] Although, as always, many authors deny the significance of this date; *see* Jackson, *op cit*, note 4, pp. 49–56.

[338] Schmitt, *op cit*, note 240, p. 127.

[339] Jackson, *op cit*, note 4, p. 13.

[340] Marcel Gauchet, *L'avènement de la démocratie – IV – Le nouveau monde*, Paris: Gallimard (2017), p. 215.

the twin forces of the Westernization of the globe.[341] And for those of the new States which did not belong to the competing world economy organized around the Soviet Union, they had to embrace the contract and property rights system of private government at the micro-level of their Power System.[342] The ideal of a free world economy implied as a prerequisite that each State had at least minimal constitutional provisions and procedures ensuring the existence of a public and a private sphere with the recognition of property rights and freedom of contracts.[343] International sovereignty led to a form of standardization of the legal shapes taken by the political organizations which are the linchpin of the World Power System: States.

Although they are sovereign, States were born in a group of States and live in a group of States. They are competing organizations, but they also exist thanks to each other. They can't exist alone without recognition from other States. For the first part of their history, States shared very limited common institutional arrangements. This changed dramatically after the two World Wars of the twentieth century, and especially after World War II. The level of devastation during the Second World War was such that the need was felt to completely change the international (inter-State) institutions created after the First World War and to build the foundations of a new international community. The representatives of 45 States met in San Francisco in 1945 and started building what was to become the United Nations system of institutions. The system hasn't proved to be as effective as many were hoping – in great part due to the practices generated by the Cold War – but the accomplishments of this system are still quite extraordinary. And since the disintegration of the Soviet Union in 1989, there is no competing institutional international arrangement. As David Held observed:

> economic globalization, and everything associated with it, was allowed to thrive and develop because it took place in a relatively open, relatively peaceful, relatively liberal institutionalized world order.[344]

---

[341] Alain Supiot, 'The public–private relation in the context of today's refeudalization', 11(1) *I-Con* 129–145 (2013), p. 134.

[342] Alain Supiot, 'The Dogmatic Foundations of the Market', 28(4) *Industrial Law Journal*, pp. 321–345 (2000).

[343] Schmitt, *op cit*, note 240, p. 233.

[344] David Held, 'Elements of A Theory of Global Governance', 42(9) *Philosophy and Social Criticism*, pp. 837–846 (2016), p. 839.

The successes of this system, however, have led to a form of gridlock.[345] The breadth and density of the World Wide Web of Contracts[346] made possible thanks to the institutions created after World War II has somehow led to institutional impotence, like Gulliver tied down by the countless threads of rope knit by the Lilliputians.

Four reasons have been identified for this blockage.[347]

The first one is *growing multipolarity*. There are simply many more States today than there were in 1945 in a position to express their sovereignty. In sheer numbers, we moved from 45 States to about 200. And many of these States derive their means of existence thanks to the loopholes created by a world economy without a world organization in a position to limit their ability to *abuse* their sovereignty. This is particularly acute in the field of international taxation (for more details, *see* Section 8.5).

The second reason for the gridlock is that we are facing *harder problems*. Dealing with the one which concentrates our attention in this book – climate change – implies addressing issues going deep into the daily life of inhabitants of all countries: our ways of eating, inhabiting, travelling, working; the will of the populations in developing countries to access a life of affluence via economic development; the will for others to benefit from the natural resources of their land in coal or oil, and so on. For David Held, 'the divergence of voice and interest within both the developed and developing worlds, along with the sheer complexity of the incentives needed to achieve a low carbon economy, have made a global deal extremely difficult to achieve and sustain'.[348] And, as we have seen in the General Introduction, the 2015 Paris Agreement – which is not even abided by – falls short of delivering what is required to avoid catastrophe.

A third reason for the gridlock is that the existing set of international organizations have not organically adapted to the evolutions of the World Power System. And it is very hard to change them, in part because of the increase in the number of their members and of those who work for them.

Finally, there is also gridlock because of the sheer fragmentation of the institutional system created after World War II.

International sovereignty is a key concept to understand today's predicament. It is, in some ways, the opposite of democracy since it is based on the legal premise that the international 'community' – assuming

---

[345] Thomas Hale, David Held and Kevin Young, *Gridlock: Why Global Cooperation is Failing When We Need It Most*, Oxford: Polity Press (2013). *See also* Thomas Hale and David Held et al., *Beyond Gridlock*, Oxford: Polity Press (2017).

[346] On the notion of World Wide Web of Contracts, *see* hereunder at Chapter 6.

[347] For a good summary, *see* Held, *op cit*, note 344, pp. 840–841.

[348] *Ibid*.

it even exists – has neither the power nor the authority to impose its will on individual States.[349] Which organizations have international sovereignty and can be qualified as 'States' under international law is determined by international law, via the recognition by 'a sufficiently large' number of existing States of the existence of a new State. The phenomenon of recognition is important because it leads to the treatment of a de facto organization as a *legal* person. It then enters the international legal system as a legal person able to have legal relationships with the other legal persons – the other States and the international organizations they have derivatively created – which are members of the legal order they create together.[350] Right now, there are only States and the organizations they created among themselves which exist as corporate organizations in international public law. Clans, tribes, business firms and so on have no *official* international legal existence. This could change given the fact that in many geographical areas of the world, the State has failed to become deeply embedded as an institution. This could also change given the increasing influence of multinational enterprises, which have no official legal existence but exercise considerable powers. As of now, the States are still the official linchpin institutions of the World Power System. But there were early suggestions that multinational enterprises could become persons under international law.[351] They do not need to be recognized as being States, which they are not. But they can still have a form of legal personality granted to them under international law.

More recently, it has been forcefully argued that multinational firms have acquired the power to create primary rules of international law. Without much notice, they have developed a capacity to author directly and formally their international legal rights via the international protection of their property, the international legal status of State contracts and the strategic use of corporate 'nationality', which firms can multiply within their corporate organization.[352] (This is addressed in more detail

---

[349] *E.g.* Joseph H.H. Weiler, 'The Geology of International Law – Governance, Democracy and Legitimacy', 64 *ZaöRV*, pp. 547–562 (2004), p. 548.

[350] See *op cit*, note 292, p. 190. On the fact that an unrecognized State still exists as a State, *see* Nguyen Quoc Dinh, Dailler and Pellet, *op cit*, note 236, pp. 526–527.

[351] *See* Arghyrios Fatouros, 'Problèmes et méthodes d'une réglementation des entreprises multinationales', *Journal du Droit International*, p. 456 (1974). *See also* D. Kokkini-Iatridou and P.J.I.M. De Waart, 'Foreign Investments in Developing Countries – Legal Personality of Multinationals in International Law', 14 *Netherlands Year Book of International Law*, p. 87 (1983), and Ignaz Seidl-Hohenveldern, *Corporations in and under International Law*, Cambridge: Cambridge University Press (1987).

[352] *See* Julian Arato, 'Corporations as Lawmakers', 56(2) *Harvard International Law Journal*, pp. 229–295 (2015).

in Section 9.1.) But this is a one-sided evolution, in which firms as global organizations manage to get *rights* without having *accountability* obligations in counterpart. A form of legal recognition of their existence would increase their accountability.

3.5 Internal Sovereignty

The word 'sovereignty' has a second meaning. It designates 'internal sovereignty', which is a relationship of *hierarchy*. It determines who has the ultimate power of decision-making *within* a State, within each particular combination of a territory, the population in it and an effective governmental authority over the other two components. The process of establishing *internal* sovereignties was both a European and a local one, with its idiosyncrasies in each and every State. It is anti-medieval and was a repudiation of the European Middle Ages.[353] In France, which played the role of the political and legal laboratory of modernity,[354] the process of establishing *factually* and *legally* the King's sovereignty took several centuries, involving a dynamic triangular relationship among power, law and what Michel Foucault named 'truth effects' (*effets de vérité*).[355] The legal and political system did not lead 'naturally' to the recognition of the King's sovereignty. Law was a command of the Kings, and legists provided them with the legal theories justifying their authority.[356] The *factual authority* of the King and his coalition led to the development of *legal theories* sustaining this authority which further supported it. Hence, the reinforcing triangular relationship between power, law and the 'truth effects'. Legal theories ordered by the King and delivered by jurists gave legal foundations to his factual authority, thereby reinforcing it, making of the King the 'sovereign'. A *factual* situation was therefore turned into a *legal one*. A factual state of order progressively became a State and then a State of law.

---

[353] Jackson, *op cit*, note 4, pp. 5–8. In the institutional arrangement which used to be known as the Holy Roman Germanic Empire, the situation was even more complex with more than a thousand political units, including some 15 dukes and counts, princes of the Church, more than 50 free cities with their own government, and 400 knights, directly linked to the emperor without the intermediation of any State; *see* Jean-Louis Halpérin, *Histoire des droits en Europe de 1750 à nos jours*, Paris: Flammarion (2004), p. 34.

[354] Grossi, *op cit*, note 179, p. 54.

[355] Foucault, *op cit*, note 308, pp. 21–22.

[356] Maine, *op cit*, note 130, pp. 79–81.

In all the competing institutional arrangements giving form to an effective Power System, developing a justice system in a position to issue somewhat impartial decisions *and* to enforce them was an essential part of the development of the political enterprise.[357] Faced with a situation of institutional pluralism leading to an entanglement of the various jurisdictions, political entrepreneurs attempted to rationalize the judicial system by the creation of standardized procedural rules.[358] Progressively, it led to the possibility to enact generally applicable laws. This process occurred relatively early in England where centralized royal courts established in London led to the creation of a Common Law, applicable to all the freemen of the Kingdom, under the King's authority.[359] The Norman Conquest resulted in a stronger central government in England than existed anywhere else in Europe at the time. The precedent was established that the King's Court had jurisdiction over freemen and, as manorial lords lost jurisdiction over freemen, they also lost control over their landholdings. And soon, the *rule of law* was developed, subjecting the State's operations to legal rules.[360]

In France, from the thirteenth to the sixteenth century, the nascent French State, like the English State, was essentially a State of Justice. The acts of the King in his Council were in the form of acts of justice, the Parliaments of Justice were key pieces of the royal administration, just as the King's officers – the Bailiffs of the North, the Seneschals in the South – were first of all officers of justice. The Parliaments of Justice represented an exceptional instrument of political centralization which made it possible to unify the Kingdom around justice by successively getting rid of the private wars – a system of generalized vendetta constituted the basis of medieval and feudal justice, then to avoid the dispersion and arbitrariness of the seigneurial courts, finally to secularize justice by tearing it away from the Officialities.[361] Subsequently, from 1661 onwards, when Colbert at the *Contrôle Général des Finances* gathered around his ministry the missions formerly belonging to the Chancery, the State of Justice evolved into a State of Finance. But due to the venality of the charges,

---

[357] For France, *see* Jean Picq, *Une histoire de l'État en Europe – Pouvoir, justice et droit du moyen âge à nos jours*, Paris: Les presses de Sciences Po (2009), in particular ch 9. *See also* Brian M. Downing, 'Medieval Origins of Constitutional Government in the West', 18 *Theory and Society*, pp. 213–247 (1989).

[358] Halpérin, *op cit*, note 353, p. 35.

[359] Grossi, *op cit*, note 179, p. 93.

[360] *Ibid*, p. 95. Douglass C. North and Robert Paul Thomas, *The Rise of the Western World – A New Economic History*, New York: W.W. Norton (1973), p. 64.

[361] Blandine Kriegel, 'La défaite de la justice', in *La Justice: L'obligation impossible*, Paris: collection 'Autrement, Série Morales' (1994), p. 137.

to the patrimoniality of public offices, firmly established by the Edict of Paulette under Henri IV (1604),[362] the Parliaments gradually entered into secession with the monarchy, against which they led the 'battle of three hundred years' that culminated in the eighteenth century with the revolt of the Parliaments of Britanny and Dauphiné, which resulted in the French Revolution.[363] Prior to the 1789 Revolution, despite centuries of efforts using a wealth of means against internal competitors (cities, lesser lords, officers, regional parliaments, guilds, corporations etc.) and external competitors, the *King* struggled to affirm his sovereignty.[364] It took the 1789 Revolution to eliminate all feudal rights and privileges acquired by the various intermediary orders of what was until then a corporatist State.[365] Soon after the French Revolution of 1789, the *nation* was declared to be the sovereign concomitantly with the 1791 Constitution and the King became the top civil servant of the State.[366] The French Revolution was the last episode of a long process of transfer of authority which led to absolutism. And, in fact, the Revolution led to the completion of what started as the consolidation of monarchical power into the creation of the internal sovereignty of the State.[367]

According to Hendrik Spruyt, the critical external change which set in motion the European process of institutional evolution took place in Europe with the extension of trade in the High Middle Ages.[368] From

---

[362] This voluntary yearly tax entitled the officers paying it to transfer their offices. It generated between 5% and 10% of the State's income.

[363] Kriegel, *op cit*, note 361, p. 136.

[364] Significantly, with regards to corporations, at the beginning of 1776, Turgot submitted to the King six edicts inspired by his doctrines. One provides for the 'suppression of jurandes and communities of commerce, art and crafts'. The Parliament of Paris, to whom the edict was sent for registration, made remonstrances. It was afraid that, as a consequence of the introduced freedom, there would be desertification of the countryside 'by the bait of small trade', poor manufacturing, difficulty for the police of the State to watch this crowd of workers henceforth able to create disorder, indifference with regard to the public good of isolated individuals; François Olivier-Martin, 'Le déclin et la suppression des corps en France au XVIIIe siècle', in 2 *Etudes présentées à la Commission Internationale pour l'Histoire des Assemblées d'États*, Louvain: Bureau du recueil, Université de Louvain (1937), pp. 149–163, at p. 158.

[365] Schmitt, *op cit*, note 199, p. 181.

[366] Halpérin, *op cit*, note 353, p. 39.

[367] Foucault, *op cit*, note 308, p. 207. On the importance of the 1789 French Revolution in this regard, *see* Gustafsson, *op cit*, note 292, at p. 197 & p. 201.

[368] Hendrik Spruyt, *The Sovereign State and its Competitors*, Princeton: Princeton University Press (1994), p. 25.

various perspectives, Henri Pirenne,[369] Fernand Braudel[370] and Karl Popper[371] insist on the importance of commerce for the development of institutions. The origin of this new economic expansion is still debated and the fact that the climate became milder seems to have played a key role. But whatever the origins of this economic upswing, the increase in economic production foreshadowed the return of local and long-distance trade. While economic exchange used to be largely local and often *in kind*, the division of labour and the growth of towns favoured the development of an expanding *monetary* economy. And, in turn, the monetarization of the economy had a profound impact on the existing political structure. Inevitably, it affected the system of in-kind transfers which was the linchpin of feudal organization.[372] Lords started to commute their military service obligations into monetary payments. Likewise, rather than receiving agricultural products, they preferred land rents from their peasants.[373] By entering a monetary economy, the warrior aristocracy eroded the very basis of its existence. In the Power System of the time, as in all Power Systems, the changes at the level of the micro-powers led to an evolution of the macro-powers. A rural, decentralized Power System built around the institutions of feudality progressively evolved into an urban, re-centralized Power System built around the institutions of the modern State.

Cities played a key role in this process. As explained by Fernand Braudel, there is no city without a necessary division of labour and no extended division of labour without the presence of a city. There is no city without a market and no regional or national markets without cities. And there is no city without both protective and coercive power, whatever the form of this power, regardless of the social group that embodies it.[374] Cities articulate the network of exchanges among cities to the network of exchanges between each city and its hinterland.[375]

---

[369] Henri Pirenne, *Medieval Cities: Their Origins and the Revival of Trade*, Princeton: Princeton University Press (1925).

[370] Fernand Braudel, *Civilisation matérielle, économie et capitalisme, XVe–XVIIIe siècles*, tome 1, 'Les structures du quotidien: le possible et l'impossible'; tome 2 'Les jeux de l'échange'; tome 3 'Le temps du monde', Paris: A. Colin (1979).

[371] Popper, *op cit*, note 295, p. 145.

[372] North and Thomas, *op cit*, note 360, p. 39.

[373] Spruyt, *op cit*, note 368, p. 61.

[374] Fernand Braudel, *Civilisation matérielle, économie et capitalisme, XVe–XVIIIe siècles*, *tome 1 'Les structures du quotidien: le possible et l'impossible'*, Paris: Armand Colin (1979), p. 423.

[375] Sassen, *op cit*, note 6, p. 41.

The growth of trade and the corresponding increase in the importance of urban centres gave rise to different forms of institutional arrangements among kings, aristocracy, burghers and church. As key players in this macro-change, developing cities had two competing preferences. They wanted the greatest amount of independence possible; but having a strong central power to protect them was also appealing. Protection from robbers, pirates, demanding competing feudal barons, feudal exactions and tolls would benefit long-distance trade.[376] There were originally alternatives to States as the key political organizations providing this kind of protection. The main institutional competing arrangements were city-leagues – like the Hansa,[377] city-States – like the Italian city-states,[378] and territorial States – like France.

In France, the impact of trade remained relatively low compared with what was taking place in future Italy and Germany. France was rather cut off from large-scale commerce, and cities were not strong enough to further their interests without a sovereign.[379] They could not be independent, as in future Italy, or form city-leagues, as in future Germany. The towns wanted first of all to be relieved from the onerous feudal burdens and they therefore sought royal protection.[380] In feudal theory, the king formed the top of the feudal hierarchy and could create new feudal relationships. Towns, as incorporated bodies, understood that they could be incorporated into the feudal system just like any vassal. The best possible situation for them was to be the direct vassal of the king, and not subject to any intermediary lord. In exchange, they agreed to pay the king for the service. And in the process, the tax known under the name of '*taille*', which used to be a direct, personal tax levied on commoners and irregularly levied by lords, changed in character. It was hated as a levy when it was raised by the local lords on whatever their subjects had put by and as often as they felt the need for it; under the new arrangement with the king, the *taille* became *fixed in amount*, and payable *on a set date*.[381] Being predictable, it became a cost of doing business like any other one, could be included in the computation of costs and *prices* and became much more acceptable. It significantly increased royal revenues.

---

[376] Spruyt, *op cit*, note 368, p. 63.

[377] *Ibid*, pp. 109–129.

[378] *Ibid*, pp. 130–150.

[379] Antonio Padoa-Schioppa, 'Conclusions: modèles, instruments, principes', in Antonio Padoa-Schioppa (ed.), *Justice et legislation*, Paris: Presses Universitaires de France (2000), pp. 394–434, at pp. 404–405.

[380] Spruyt, *op cit*, note 368, pp. 65–66.

[381] *See generally ibid*, pp. 89–94.

Fernand Braudel has devoted a lifetime to the study of early capitalism. In his view:

> in the West, capitalism and city was basically the same thing. The nascent capitalism, substituting for the power of 'feudal and bourgeois guilds' that of a new merchant aristocracy, has exploded the narrow framework of medieval cities, to bind itself eventually to the State, winner of the cities but heir of their institutions, their mentality and quite unable to do without them.[382]

Ultimately, territorial sovereign States took the centre stage for reasons of institutional isomorphism. For the State System to operate, States need to be able to negotiate with *peers*, i.e. organizations which, like them, can bind *the population* present on any given defined *territory*.[383] Otherwise, negotiations cannot be reciprocal.[384] Because of their territorial character, States are compatible with one another. Their respective jurisdictions can be precisely specified through agreement on fixed borders.[385]

These issues became particularly clear during the negotiations leading to the Treaties of Westphalia, which are widely acknowledged as a milestone in the creation of the State System. Non-State political actors and alternative institutional solutions survived the birth of the State System only for a limited period.

In other words, the evolution of the State, harnessing the monetary means created by trade and developing its territorial jurisdiction, and the development of a State System were mutually reinforcing processes.[386] States progressively appeared in Europe via many local paths but, ultimately, they settled as a *Power System*, existing with their shared

---

[382] Braudel, *op cit*, note 374, p. 453.

[383] Nguyen Quoc Dinh, Dailler and Pellet, *op cit*, note 236, p. 410.

[384] According to Paul J. DiMaggio and Walter W. Powell, 'Organizations in a structured field ... respond to an environment that consists of other organizations responding to their environment which consists of organizations responding to an environment of organizations' responses. ... The concept that best captures the process of homogenization is isomorphism. [It] is a constraining process that forces one unit in a population to resemble other units that face the same set of environmental conditions.' In Paul J. DiMaggio and Walter W. Powell, 'The Iron Cage Revisited: Institutional Isomorphism and Collective Rationality in Organizational Fields', 48 *American Sociological Review*, pp. 147–160 (1983), p. 149.

[385] Spruyt, *op cit*, note 368, p. 155.

[386] *Ibid*, p. 179.

characteristics (a territory, a population and an effective government over the two other components) because of their belonging to a *State System*.

★★★

We have seen that the organizations which have *international* sovereignty and can be qualified as 'States' under international law are determined by *international law*. The identification of who has *internal* sovereignty and the way internal sovereignty operates is determined by *constitutional law*.[387]

Under international law, each State is sovereign. A sovereign State is not under the obligation to adopt any particular form of Constitution.[388] It may opt not to have a written Constitution and, under domestic law, the identity of the sovereign varies with the domestic political system.

There are, of course, many options available to organize the political system understood in a restrictive sense: division of powers among legislative, executive and judicial branches of government; checks and balances; and so on. But in liberal States, the constitutional system of division of power goes beyond that. The Constitution of liberal States defines two types of prerogatives (it may not be written like this, but the effective organization of the liberal States can be analysed in this fashion). It is *constitutional provisions* which:

(a) define the *political* 'Organs of the State', i.e. a series of offices in which persons will act, make decisions, and order the use of public property *not* in their individual capacity but as *Organs of the State*, the State being understood as a separate and potentially eternal person to which their activities in the discharge of the duties of their offices are imputed;[389]

(b) limit the ability of laws to discriminate among individual persons, forcing laws to be made of *general provisions* applying to broad classes of individuals, law being applied in a consistent and non-discriminatory manner;[390] and

(c) protect private property rights which are also 'impersonal'. The physical characteristics of the objects of property vary. The prerogative they entail for the owner to be the decision-maker as a matter of principle does not.

---

[387] Xavier Bioy (sous la direction de), *La personnalité juridique*, Toulouse: Presses de l'Université Toulouse 1 Capitole (2013), p. 53.

[388] Jackson, *op cit,* note 4, p. 11.

[389] North, Wallis and Weingast, *op cit,* note 6, p. 166.

[390] *Ibid*, p. 143. *See also* Haggard, MacIntyre and Tiede, *op cit*, note 111, p. 211.

3.6 Political Organs of the State, Administrative Organs of the State and Law

From the internal point of view, as an organization, the modern State is a particular form of conglomerate, providing various services (police, army, justice, education, health services etc.) using public assets which often have specific characteristics due to their use for the performance of State functions. This is the case, for example, for the weapons used in the military such as fighter jets, army tanks or navy vessels which are objects of property usually reserved to the State. It also applies, to a lesser extent, to the assets used by the police. But beyond these fundamental functions of the State as a provider of physical order, a series of *public* property rights are also required for the *private* property rights to operate effectively. Without streets, highways, canals, railroads, navigable airspace and airports, ports, telephone lines, fibre-optic cables or public utility lines transporting electricity, water or natural gas, and so on, fundamental rights such as free movement or property rights would be made very difficult to exercise. *Private* property can only effectively operate if interlaced with *public* property.[391]

To provide the services via this organization structured to perform them we call 'the State', the State uses resources and collects taxes to be able to pay for them. Functions that are usually considered essential such as those of defence, security, justice and education have a common denominator that allows them to function: finances. Today, finance brings together money, taxes, the budget, credit, a banking system, a whole machinery to mobilize capital and so on. But in the centuries before the nineteenth century, *taxes* were the basic resources of States.[392]

As an organization, the State is *governed*. It is *governed* by the executive branch of the political Organs of the State. In liberal States, the general population (i.e. that segment of the population which is *not* comprised of civil servants) is *not* governed as a matter of principle. The general population must abide by mandatory laws and rules. But it is not subject to the *command* of the State as an organization. It is governed only when it accepts to participate in organizations, as an employee, for example, when the coordination of the division of labour requires that their activities be governed, organized. But with regards to the State, those of us who are *not* civil servants are *not* governed. Making the distinction is fundamental

---

[391] *See also* Merrill, *op cit*, note 105, p. 2091.

[392] Gabriel Ardant, 'Financial Policy and Economic Infrastructure of Modern States and Nations', in Charles Tilly (ed.), *The Formation of National States in Europe*, Princeton: Princeton University Press (1975), pp. 164–165.

to the understanding of the operation of a liberal Power System, including at the global level.

The Organs of the State effectively come in two kinds:

(1) There are rule- and political decision-making organs. They are the 'political institutions' of the democratic State, the composition of which may change at elections. The executive branch of the government is particularly in charge of foreign affairs, the military and so on. It is also in charge of the administrative, day-to-day operations of the State. Whether the top executive authority is a president, a prime minister, a chancellor and so on, this executive authority appoints ministers, secretaries of State and other officials who will each oversee one of the departments of the government in charge of providing a specific set of services, the combined operation of which is 'the State' in the administrative sense. A series of political appointees will head the ministries of education, defence, internal affairs, foreign affairs and so on. Only these political appointees change when majorities change at elections and they manage the various State services (schools, army, police, diplomatic services and so on) in accordance with the (usually indirect) wishes of the electorate.

(2) There are then the Organs of the State in charge of the administrative implementation of the various State's functions. The personnel of these governmental departments does not change at elections. That's the permanent side of the State, composed of military personnel and civil servants with potentially various legal status adapted to the fulfilment of their duties, in charge of implementing the law as it exists at any given point in time and as amended by the political institutions of the State's constitutional mode of operation. The specialized branches of government (schools, army, police, diplomatic services and so on) will provide specific services defined by law in an impersonal way to segments of the population defined in general terms by law as well. They will do it using the assets owned by, and in the name of, a special legal person called 'the State' which keeps its permanence irrespective of the changes which may occur in the identity of the political personnel at the head of the political organs of the State. This is what allows the continuity of the administrative and legal organization of the State, irrespective of changes due to the operation of democratic constitutional institutions.

An important role of the State is, via the political Organs of the State, to adopt the laws applicable to the activities of individual persons and other legal persons, which are *not* 'Organs of the State'. They are not *governed* in the sense that no *order* can be given to them to perform any given activity, as would be the case for members of the military or civil servants. When individual persons perform activities they must, when the legal system provides for relevant applicable rules, follow these rules. For example, if there is a statute providing that the maximum speed limit on highways is 60 miles per hour, the law does not order anyone to use their car or go to a particular location with it. But in case a person makes use of her freedom of movement and uses her car and drives on a highway to go where she wants, there is a restriction about *how* she can use the object of her property – the car. The owner of the car is not governed; she does what she wants with her car as a matter of principle and the activity she can entertain with the car is only limited as a matter of exception. Her autonomy is reduced, not eliminated. She can go where she wants with the car and can also decide not to go anywhere. But when she makes use of it on a highway, she must abide by the speed limit. Via the political system, it has been considered that driving faster than 60 miles per hour is too dangerous, or leads to an excessive consumption of petrol, or whatever. The potential uses of all cars are now impacted and the autonomy of all car users is affected in the public interest as defined at that point in time by the legislative power. But the car users are not *governed*. The new law does not make of them 'Organs of the State'. Those who are governed are the *law enforcers* who must now apply the law in a new fashion in an equal manner to all those who breach the new law and get caught. It is only in case of breach of the law that the law offender becomes governed: she must pay a fine or, for more serious offences, her freedom can be taken away. But a law-abiding person is not governed.

Louis Rougier provided an interesting metaphor on this issue:

> Manchester liberalism could be compared to a road traffic system in which cars could circulate as they wish without traffic rules: ensuing traffic jams, difficulties to circulate, accidents would be innumerous, unless larger cars would force the smaller ones to always get out of their way, which would end up in being the law of the jungle. The socialist State is like a road traffic system in which a central authority would set in an authoritative manner who has to use their car when, where to go and via which route. A really liberal State is the one in which car drivers are free to go wherever they want, while abiding by traffic rules.[393]

---

[393] Louis Rougier, *Les mystiques économiques: comment l'on passe des démocraties libérales aux États totalitaires*, Paris: Librairie de Médicis (1938), p. 88.

Of course, the situation is radically different if an Organ of the State – the commander-in-chief, for example – orders the army to attack a particular country. The use of property rights (public and private) can be *directed* and those effectively in charge of their operation are directed to use these assets in a particular fashion. They become governed. We arrive, via another route, at the previously identified point that the legal system operates differently in times of war and in times of peace.[394] But, again, I am concentrating on the operation of the legal system in times of peace, when individual persons who are not part of the Organs of the State are *not* governed and enjoy their rights of autonomy as limitedly (marginally) constrained by laws. It is important, however, to realize that the operation of such a system requires an effective control over the use of violence (internal and external) and that the operation of the constitutional system of government protecting property rights as rights of decision-making as a matter of principle is only possible in a relatively orderly society.

The consequence of the continued existence of rights of autonomy is that in a globalized World Power System, many of those who should normally be subject to newly adopted rules can avoid their application. They can opt out of any local, State political system by delocalizing all or part of their activities. The existence of the rights of autonomy is a serious hindrance to the effective operation of a political system whose operation is decentralized on a territorial basis.

---

[394] *See* Section 2.5.

4

From Political Enterprise
to the Modern State

So far in the first part of this book, I have addressed the notion of property as being primarily a legal notion, giving the owner a right of decision-making as a matter of principle towards the object of property. Modern property is part of a constitutional mode of government, being part of the rights of autonomy enabling private persons to autonomously conduct their lives. Public prerogatives are performed by Organs of the State, via procedures which are radically different from the rights of autonomy attached to private property. Private property rights are a specific mode of decentralization of sovereignty.

The present chapter explains how the State evolved from being merely a type of political enterprise to the institution it is today. It is an alternative explanation to the movement from a 'natural state' to an 'open order society' as it is explained by North, Wallis and Weingast. In its origins, the State was nothing more than a coalition of powerful individuals, mostly men controlling a territory via the use of physical violence if necessary. Property rights in the modern sense hardly existed at this stage of institutional development. Accessorily, violent coalitions of political entrepreneurs provided a service to the population: a form of order against defeated rivals, internal or external. With its successes, the political enterprise will augment this service, extending its jurisdiction and effective control over competing forces. It will both facilitate and benefit from the progressive development of market exchange. As we will see, the modern State is intrinsically linked to modern taxes, payable in *money* and not *in kind*. Via a very long process, the resources needed by States to provide the services they deliver will be extracted via taxation and not mere compulsion in the context of the development of a monetary economy developed in part thanks to State action. States developed an inherent interest in protecting property rights and facilitating monetary exchange as a means to gain access to more resources via the taxation of a monetary economy.

★★★

4.1 Coalitions

In its origins, what cannot yet be called the 'State' in the modern understanding of the word is nothing more than an organization controlling and exerting physical violence on a territory. At the primary stage of their development, future 'States' can hardly be differentiated from organizations of gangsters receiving payments in return for a 'protection' against a violence they otherwise would exert themselves. It is easy to see in this forced exchange relationship *outright extortion*. And the parallel between the State and an organization of criminals is very old.[395] But if in its origin the State can hardly be distinguished from an association of gangsters,[396] it is also clear that any stable organization of criminals having established a territorial jurisdiction, such as the Mafia, the 'Ndrangheta or Cosa Nostra, also provides, *incidentally*, a protection service against less well-organized criminals.[397] Even an extortionist State can represent a *progress* compared with disorganized violence. As Mancur Olson wrote, *stationary* bandits, continuously stealing from a given group of victims, are preferred by the victims over *roving* bandits. The reason for what may seem a mystery is that

---

[395] In *The City of God*, St Augustine tells the story of the reply given by a pirate seized by Alexander the Great: 'For when that king had asked the man what he meant by keeping hostile possession of the sea, he answered with bold pride, "What do you mean by seizing the whole earth; because I do it with a petty ship, I am called a robber, while you who do it with a great fleet are styled emperor"'. This story has subsequently reappeared under different formats and versions. *See also* Susan Strange, *States and Markets*, London: Pinter Publishers (1988, 2nd edition 1994), p. 49 and, *generally*, Anton Schutz, 'Saint Augustin, l'État et la "bande de brigands"', 16 *Droits*, pp. 71–82 (1992).

[396] Frederic C. Lane, 'Economic Consequences of Organized Violence', 18(4) *Journal of Economic History*, pp. 401–417 (1958) p. 403.

[397] *E.g.* North and Thomas, *op cit*, note 360, p. 87; Lane, *op cit*, note 396, p. 402; Fabrizio Hinna-Danesi, 'Mafia – Politique – Entreprise', *Les Petites Affiches*, 20 mars, n° 35, p. 19 (1996), at p. 20. *See generally* Lucien François, *Le cap des tempêtes – Essai de microscopie du droit*, 2e édition, Bruylant-LGDJ (2012), p. 315.

the rational stationary bandit will take only a part of income in taxes because he will be able to exact a larger total amount of income from his subjects if he leaves them with the incentive to generate income that he can tax. If the stationary bandit successfully monopolizes the theft in his domain, then his victims do not need to worry about theft by others. If he steals only through regular taxation, then his subjects know that they can keep whatever proportion of their output is left after they have paid their taxes. Since all of the settled bandit's victims are for him a source of tax payments, he also has an incentive to prohibit the murder or maiming of his subjects. Bandit rationality, accordingly, induces the bandit leader to seize a given domain, to make himself the ruler of that domain, and to provide peaceful order and other public goods for its inhabitants, thereby obtaining more in tax theft than he could have obtained from migratory plunder. There we have the first blessing of the 'invisible hand': the rational, self-interested leader of a band of roving bandits is led, as though by an invisible hand, to settle down, wear a crown, and replace anarchy with government. ... The violent entrepreneurs do not call themselves bandits but, on the contrary, give themselves and their descendants, exalted titles. They sometimes even claim to rule by divine right.[398]

It is hardly surprising that the Mafia has sometimes been described as an organization competing with the State for the provision of order.[399] But although the State is very similar in its origins to an organized band of robbers, it sometimes evolved into something more legitimate. Of course, we know of many States which are still in an early developmental stage. The operation of these States is usually a highly lucrative activity for those in charge. But the private economy to which the populations have access to in these States, except in some cases where they benefit from worthy natural resources in large quantities such as oil, is most of the time in a disastrous state.

---

[398] Olson, *op cit*, note 123, p. 568. This is the perfect answer to those who assert that 'someone powerful enough to create a system of property rights is powerful enough to violate them'; *e.g.* Galiani and Sened, *op cit*, note 303, p. 61. The authority in a position to create a system of property rights has an inherent interest in respecting it.

[399] *See*, *e.g.*, Fabrice Rizzoli, 'Pouvoirs et mafias italiennes. Contrôle du territoire contre État de droit', 132 *Pouvoirs*, pp. 41–55 (2010).

It is important to realize that States as we know them did not appear in a 'state of nature'. The idea, for example, that individual persons existed as *legal persons* and had *rights* – in particular, property rights – prior to the existence of the State and that they decided to create the State as an association which purpose was to protect these pre-existing rights is historically inaccurate.[400] This philosophical fable which is at the root of the political theories developed by Hobbes, Rousseau or Locke had the great advantage of creating narratives which were helpful in placing – intellectually and then institutionally – certain rights out of the reach of the State and its organs. These rights were deemed to have existed *prior* to the State. Their existence, in this intellectual construction, could not owe anything to the *subsequent* existence of the State and had to be respected by State rulers. But this is not at all how things happened, and it is impossible for institutional development to occur in this way. To have rights, one must exist as a *legal person* and being a legal person depends on having a legal personality granted by a *legal order* in a position to ensure the effective existence of the rights granted by the legal order.[401] Rights cannot predate the effective existence of the legal order granting legal personality and rights and enforcing them. Any talk of natural, fundamental, inalienable or inviolable rights has no theoretical value and is irrelevant.[402] Social contract theories were only clever strategies inverting the process of historical development to try to embed in institutions principles to prevent history from turning back.[403] They led to the institutional embedding of the notion that subjective rights come before objective right, both logically and chronologically. That the individual comes first, and the State second. This affirmation of human rights derived from a radical inversion of the political relationship between the State and the individual.[404] With the inverted perspective, the institutional building of society starts from its base and the individuals

---

[400] Saleilles, *op cit*, note 42, pp. 567–568.

[401] For Hans Kelsen, a juridical subject is not a person facing the legal order, different from it, but it is the legal order, either as the personification of the whole or as a part of it. Similarly, what is called a subjective right is not something different from objective right, but simply the same right appearing from a particular point of view; Kelsen, *op cit*, note 235, p. 30.

[402] *E.g.* Bobbio, *op cit*, note 11, p. xii.

[403] The immediate events which provoked Locke into writing his book were the attempts by the Stuarts to set up an absolute monarchy. Locke's 'fragment on property… is a skillful of dialectic aimed, not at the analysis of an institution, but to help along an argument against the divine pretensions of kings.' *E.g.* Walton H. Hamilton, 'Property – According to Locke', 41 *Yale Law Journal*, pp. 864–880 (1932), p. 867.

[404] Bobbio, *op cit*, note 11, pp. ix–x.

that make it up.[405] And this change was a key evolution for the progressive development of protective institutions: the individualistic conception of society has made progress from the recognition of human rights within a single State to the recognition of human rights at the World level. Thanks to the inversion of the perspective, human rights have evolved from the realm of each State's individual law to become part of the laws among States.

'State of nature' theories, however, remain fables built on the idea of an ahistorical development of society which is nothing more than a pure artificial creation of the mind.[406] Irrespective of the key role they played in historical institutional development, believing today in these fairy tales prevents a proper understanding of the origin and function of a Power System operating thanks to the existence of rights of autonomy – including property rights – and Organs of the States enforcing these rights.

In the 'state of nature' (whatever that means), the only ones who have effective prerogatives are those who have physical strength, usually well advised (if they want to sleep relatively peacefully at night) to form a coalition to exercise their authority. No one has 'property', autonomy or rights in the modern sense of the word. Property comes when the coalitions of violent entrepreneurs become civilized with a policed administration of violence and an effective decentralization of the capacity of decision-making as a matter of principle through property rights. An author like Mirabeau saw this connection very clearly:

> You know that the State and Society are only based on property. If there are countries where men have nothing of their own, they are not subject to anyone. These countries are deserts exposed to the races of some brigands. Nothing can attach men to a country as property or salary. Where the property is missing, where there is no pay, there is no State.[407]

---

[405] Kelsen, *op cit*, note 242, p. 103.

[406] Grossi, *op cit*, note 179, pp. 131–332.

[407] Mirabeau (Victor Riqueti, Marquis de), *Théorie de l'impôt*, sans lieu d'édition [Paris], ni nom d'éditeur [Chaubert et Hérissant] (1760), p. 103. 'Vous savez que l'État et la Société ne sont fondés que sur la propriété. S'il existe des pays où les hommes ne possèdent rien en propre, ils ne sont sujets de personne. Ces pays sont des déserts exposés aux courses de quelques brigands. Rien ne peut attacher les hommes à un pays que la propriété ou le salaire. Là ou manque la propriété, là ou manque le salaire, là il n'y a plus d'État.' And *see also*, p. 105: '... *sans propriété, point d'État, point de Sujets attachés au territoire, point de réunion d'hommes. En raison de ce qu'on assure & étend la propriété, on assure, étend & corrobore la Société & l'État, & ainsi en raison inverse.*' ['... without property, no State, no subjects attached to the territory, no association

Property rights have nothing 'natural' about them. They are dependent on the State's power and ability to enforce them in an impersonal manner, which requires a very complex administrative machinery.

4.2 The Provision of Services by the State and the Need for Market Exchange

The modern State is unique in its claim for sovereignty and territoriality.[408] As counter-intuitive as it may seem, the construction of modern States was a much more difficult exercise than the building of great empires. As it just so happens, great empires *preceded* the modern State. With the modern State, it is no longer enough to protect a few trade routes and collect part of the value created by long-distance trade at a few unavoidable tolls.[409] It is necessary to *create* the infrastructure required for a *market society* to develop and generate the economic resources required to finance public governmental institutions and a judicial system paid by the State and not by those administered, with an army paid by the State, with warehouses filled with purchases made on the market and not by requisitions, with public works carried out by specialized bodies and not by forced labour. All this was accomplished gradually – the development of the market requiring the development of the infrastructure itself requiring the development of the market – to the extent, and *only to the extent*, that a *monetary* exchange economy became anchored, affecting always more activities, and spreading over larger areas, from ports and trade centres.[410]

A key condition for building long-term, stable modern States was access to *money*, the ability to raise taxes paid in *money* providing the means to *pay*: *pay* civil servants and soldiers, also *pay* a multitude of suppliers of products and services of all kinds.[411]

We have seen that political theorists deny the importance of the State for the existence of *property rights*. They typically consider that property rights preceded the State.

Now it is the denial by most economists of the importance of the State for the existence of a '*market economy*' which must be tackled. As I have

---

of men. Because when one insures and extends property, one ensures, extends and corroborates Society and the State, and also in opposite reason'].

[408] Spruyt, *op cit*, note 368, pp. 34–35.

[409] Gabriel Ardant, *Histoire de l'impôt*, Livre I, 'De l'antiquité au XVIIᵉ siècle', Paris: Fayard (1971), p. 69.

[410] *See generally* Ardant, *op cit*, note 392, p. 192. *See also* Philippe Norel, *L'histoire économique globale*, Paris: Seuil (2009), especially pp. 229–230.

[411] Ardant, *op cit*, note 409, p. 214.

already mentioned, mainstream economists generally tend to overlook the role of the State, of institutions and of the law.[412] Douglass North (1993 economics Nobel prizewinner) acknowledged it: neo-classical economic theory provides an understanding of the operation of markets in developed economies but was never intended to explain how markets and overall economies *evolved*.[413] Mainstream economists start with the fable that in the beginning there was barter exchange. Then money is introduced as a convenience.[414] In the dominant, orthodox approach, social phenomena are explainable by the purely rational behaviour of agents pursuing the maximization of their personal advantage and the market is the institutional device ensuring an optimal coordination among the various ends pursued by the agents. The role played by the legal system in the creation of markets is simply ignored. But some implicit assumption that the legal system exists in the background is necessarily present. The existence of a legal system guaranteeing the existence of property rights and contract enforcement is taken for granted.

This type of approach is prescientific. It takes as a given institutions and concepts which have nothing 'natural' about them and are required for the existence of the phenomenon observed.[415] The fact is that modern market economies developed in parallel with the modern State, the existence of which is a requirement for the existence of a 'market' economy.[416] When Karl Polanyi wrote that internal trade was created in Western Europe by State intervention,[417] he was only half right. The relationship goes both ways: States are themselves partly a creation of internal trade, of the developments of internal markets. A co-construction process took place.

If we take property rights, we have seen that their value is dependent on the existence of an effective State in a position to enforce them.[418]

If we take the case of contracts, their economic value depends on the ability to enforce them against a potentially recalcitrant party.[419] To obtain non-voluntary compliance, it is necessary to have access to force to get the recalcitrant party to live up to his or her word. In an orderly society, the party suffering the breach of contract cannot use force herself;

---

[412] *See* Chapter 1.

[413] *E.g.* North, *op cit*, note 298, p. 65.

[414] *See* the Introduction to Part I.

[415] Audier, *op cit*, note 16, p. 80.

[416] *See* Jacques Rueff, for whom the market is a social institution and, in large part, a creation of the State; in Audier, *op cit*, note 16, p. 133, and Pistor, *op cit*, note 18, pp. 2–4

[417] Karl Polanyi, *La grande transformation*, Paris: Gallimard, Bibliothèque des sciences humaines (1944, 1983), p. 96.

[418] *See above* at Section 1.3.

[419] *See above* at Section 1.1.

otherwise nothing would stop violence from answering to violence and from spreading.[420] The aggrieved party must use the State's court system to obtain a legal title allowing her to have recourse to a bailiff and, if necessary, to the police for forced compliance of the contract or payment of an indemnity. Of course, the details of the procedures depend on local laws and differ substantially from one State to another. But wherever a State of law exists, that is how the Power System operates. *Violence* has been converted into *power*, and the adjudication of the parties' rights is not based either on their relative physical or on their personal strength in the Power System. It is impersonal. And here also, the effectiveness of State institutions is a prerequisite for a somewhat advanced exchange economy to exist.

Mainstream economic analyses adopt the paradoxical and untenable position of taking the State for granted while neglecting its essential role. Most mainstream economists see the State as a consumer of resources – which it is – forgetting that in return, the State provides services and infrastructure essential to the existence of a market exchange economy.[421] 'Ultra-liberal' economists even treat the State as if it were still in the developmental stage of being an extortionist.[422] But the State and the market economy have evolved *together*. States and markets are historically linked in their development by a relationship in which one is, at least partly, the reason for the existence of the other.[423] The market needs the physical order, the physical infrastructure (roads, ports, canals, all major communications networks[424] etc.) and the intellectual infrastructures (the

---

[420] Hodgson, *op cit*, note 222, p. 149. Supiot, *op cit*, note 249, p. 142.

[421] Many of them being so-called 'natural monopolies', since it is not feasible for multiple suppliers to provide the same infrastructure or services.

[422] An author like Pascal Salin, for example, who presided over the Mont Pèlerin Society between 1994 and 1996, writes that 'The state has no moral or scientific justification, but (…) constitutes the pure product of the emergence of violence in human societies'. And with regards to taxes, he states that: 'Taken according to a norm decided by the holders of State power, without respect of the personality of each person, the tax penalizes risk-taking and is fundamentally slavery, going against its intended aim, flouting the fundamental rights of human beings and the property of the individual': https://www.wikiberal.org/wiki/Pascal_Salin.

[423] On this issue, *see* Michel Beaud, *Le système national mondial hiérarchisé*, Paris: AGALMA, La Découverte (1987), pp. 41–44 and Graeber, *op cit*, note 74, p. 71.

[424] The French administration of all 'roads and bridges' (*ponts et chaussées*) was created in 1716.

language,[425] the legal system[426] or standardized weights and measures,[427] in particular) provided by the State which, in turn, requires private monetary exchange for the financing of the services it provides, via the taxes levied on exchange and on the incomes and goods it generates.[428] Both the modern State and the development of a market society are the result of an evolutionary process connecting the two which started many centuries ago. Irrespective of ideological positioning, the market, the State, freedom of contract, the individual and property rights form part of *the same complex institutional arrangement*. So much so that when the State disappears or gets corrupted, the illusion of individual sovereignty fades away rapidly.[429]

States are part of the institutions creating wealth, although it is a known issue that we lack the appropriate method of measuring the value of the

---

[425] Prior to the 1789 French Revolution, 'the kingdom of France was still divided into a number of territories speaking different languages. A particularly sharp cut separated the oil-speaking countries from those of langue d'oc. It was not patois, but real local languages. This variety of tongues did not facilitate inter-regional trade or the movement of men. Earlier, royalty seems to have been unfavourable to this linguistic diversity. The edict of Villers-Cotterets, taken under Francis I, orders that the drafting of official acts be done in French only. This was specifically directed against Latin. However, a first step towards the generalization of the French language was taken, which contributed to the development of the national economic area.' Pierre Dockès, *L'espace dans la pensée économique du XVIe au XVIIIe siècle*, Paris: Flammarion (1969), pp. 41–42. *See, generally*, Gustafsson, *op cit*, note 292, p. 192.

[426] Prior to the standardization of rules following the 1789 French Revolution, France was 'divided by various legal rules. North of the Loire were the countries of custom, in the South the countries of Roman law. In addition, each province in the North and Center had its own custom and within these provinces there remained a multitude of local customs.' Dockès, *op cit*, note 425, p. 42.

[427] Prior to the French Revolution, another significant 'obstacle to trade that will remain despite many attempts to reform until the Revolution was the variety of weights and measures. Each seigneury, each city had its own system and each type of goods corresponded to particular units. In addition, the same measure often had different names for different regions and the same name covered various realities.' Dockès, *op cit*, note 425, p. 42.

[428] Dockès, *op cit*, note 425.

[429] Alain Supiot, *L'esprit de Philadelphie – La justice sociale face au marché total*, Paris: Seuil (2010), p. 107. *See also* Norberto Bobbio, *Il futuro della democrazia*, Torino: Einaudi (1984, 1991), p. 7. For a personal account of the genesis of the modern State and of a monetary exchange economy, *see* Michel Foucault, *Sécurité, Territoire, Population, Cours au Collège de France, 1977–1978*, Paris: Gallimard-Seuil, collection 'Hautes Etudes' (2004).

goods and services they produce.[430] It is fundamental to understand the importance of the State for the existence of a thriving economy because when enterprises or individuals make profits using the infrastructure of economically advanced States, using the corporate system to pay taxes at low rates in States which do not provide the necessary infrastructure, they undermine the very basis of their existence and well-being.[431] An individualistic, 'market' view of the economic system disregards the institutional side of economic activity. It sees the State as a predator – which it can be – forgetting that without properly operating States, the overall liberal economic and Power System is unsustainable. Governments are among the producers of part of the total economic output even if they have no other function than the orderly use and control of violence.[432]

The historical process which led to the institutionalization of constitutional forms of government protecting property rights is not at all the history of a movement from a 'natural state' to an 'open order society' as written by North, Wallis and Weingast. There was nothing 'natural' in the society which preceded the current one. It was a system of government in which individual persons and property rights as we know them did not exist as such. For the historian Marc Bloch:

> the word 'ownership' as applied to landed property, would have been almost meaningless [in feudal society], for nearly all land and a great many human beings were burdened at this time with a multiplicity of obligations differing in their nature, but all apparently of equal importance.[433]

In feudal society, persons were part of numerous organizations and the prerogatives of modern property were usually shared in numerous complex ways. 'Market exchange' was a totally marginal medium of exchange.[434]

---

[430] Stiglitz, Sen and Fitoussi, *op cit*, note 66, p. 79.

[431] For a similar conclusion with regard to the welfare State, *see* Robert Gilpin, *The Political Economy of International Relations*, Princeton: Princeton University Press (1987), pp. 60–63.

[432] Lane, *op cit*, note 396, p. 402. *See also* Fried, *op cit*, note 197, p. 75.

[433] Marc Bloch, *Feudal Society*, Los Angeles: Manyon (1970), pp. 113–116.

[434] *See*, for example, Fernand Braudel, *La dynamique du capitalisme*, Paris: Arthaud (1985), pp. 21–23. Rafe Blaufarb insists that it is misleading to speak of ownership at all when describing property in the Old Regime. *See* Blaufarb, *op cit*, note 183, p. 3. Regarding this new property, which I call 'modern property', Blaufarb makes reference to a 28 September 1791 Statute proclaiming that 'the entire territory of France is free, just as the persons who inhabit it'. *See* p. 211.

Prior to its modern development, market exchange played a marginal role in many societies. The progressive development of the institutions of a market society – which go way beyond the mere existence of physical market places – required a myriad of institutional evolutions: standardization of the law, of language, of weights and measures, reduction of internal barriers to trade and so on.

One incentive for the development of monetary exchanges and the deep institutionalization of market exchange was the need to run an efficient tax system. The incentive came from the requirements of the development of the modern State.

A first requirement was the reduction of internal barriers to trade. As Necker wrote to Louis XVI just a few years before the French Revolution of 1789:

> Your Majesty has already made known to me via his Decree on tolls the desire he has to facilitate internal trade. ... But the complete suppression of all these tolls will only be ... an imperfect blessing, so long as the kingdom, independently of its divisions in different countries of the *gabelle* [a tax on salt], will contain others still absolutely distinct, known under the name of the Provinces of the Five large farms, Provinces deemed foreign, & foreign Provinces; all divisions which entail toll offices, in order to exact the rights established on all the goods which come out of some of these Provinces to enter into others. It must be admitted that this whole constitution is barbarous; but it remains the effect of the gradual constitution of the Kingdom, as well as the general projects undertaken, but which remained imperfect ...[435]

With regards to weights and measures, Necker was aware of the benefits their simplification would bring. But it required so much work that he was wondering whether it was worth the effort:

> I have been busy examining the means which should be employed to render the Weights and Measures uniform throughout the Kingdom; but I still doubt whether the usefulness which would result from it would be proportionate to the difficulties of every kind which this operation would entail, given the changes of evaluation which would have to

---

[435] Jacques Necker, *Compte-rendu au Roi*, Paris: Imprimerie Royale (1781), p. 95.

be made in a multitude of contracts, feudal dues, and other acts of all kinds.[436]

Only with the French Revolution would the metric system be implemented, suppressing thousands of medieval weights and measures of a mind-boggling variety.[437] This was, of course, made easier by the suppression of the *Ancien Régime* privileges providing for innumerous in-kind payments measured using the full variety of the old systems.[438]

4.3 Modern Taxes and Modern State

There are numerous relationships between economic exchange and political power. The most crucial link, however, from the outset, has been taxation. One may think that taxation is of interest for specialists only and of secondary importance. Or one may think about it only in its *macro*-political dimension. And there is no doubt that the notion that there should be 'no taxation without representation' – the *macro-political aspect* of taxation – played a key role in the development of *democratic* political institutions. It was one of the key ideas which led to the institutionalization of the political institutions of the Power System built around the State System and the development of democratic institutions.

Tax is a mode of legal appropriation of private property by the State. For modern taxes, it is property usually in the form of money. Since compulsory transfer of property must occur to finance the provision of the services made available by the State, then at least representatives of those who will be forced to pay should have a say in determining *what* must be provided by the State, *in which quantity* and for *how much*. The setting of the amount of taxes and determination of which categories of taxpayers should contribute in what proportion must be decided at least in part by those affected. The history of the evolution of political institutions is intrinsically linked to the institutionalization of this principle.

Some of the most significant historical events are directly connected to this issue.

---

[436] *Ibid*, p. 97.

[437] *See*, for example, the *Tables de comparaison entre les Mesures Anciennes et celles qui les remplacent dans le nouveau système métrique, avec leur explication et leur usage, pour le Département de la Haute-Garonne*, A Toulouse chez Veuve Douladoure, Imprimeur-Libraire, an XIII (1805) or Mercadier, *Tableaux des anciennes mesures du département de l'Ariège comparées à celles du nouveau système métrique*, Foix: Chez Pomiés l'ainé (1805).

[438] Spruyt, *op cit*, note 368, p. 159.

As is well known, in England, as early as 1215, following the 1214 defeat at the Battle of Bouvines, the barons obtained in the *Magna Carta* that:

> No 'scutage' or 'aid' may be levied in our kingdom without its general consent, unless it is for the ransom of our person, to make our eldest son a knight, and (once) to marry our eldest daughter. For these purposes only a reasonable 'aid' may be levied. 'Aids' from the city of London are to be treated similarly (Article 12).[439]

The principle was thus established that no tax could be levied without the barons' agreement. The need to obtain the Parliament's authorization to raise taxes was subsequently reaffirmed in the 1689 Bill of Rights.

In North America, as is also well known, tax issues led to the War of Independence. Protests against taxation without representation followed the *Stamp Act* and escalated into boycotts, which culminated in 1773 with the *Sons of Liberty* destroying a shipment of tea in Boston Harbour. Britain responded by closing the Boston Harbour and passing a series of punitive measures against the Massachusetts Bay Colony. Massachusetts colonists responded with the establishment of a shadow government which wrested control of the countryside from the Crown. Twelve colonies formed a Continental Congress to coordinate their resistance, and effectively seized power. The British attempts to disarm the Massachusetts militia led to open combat on 19 April 1775, which ended in September 1783, the Congress issuing in the meantime a Declaration of Independence on 4 July 1776.

In France, until the French Revolution, the nobility was tax exempted and, consequently, the general estates (*états généraux*) were content to abandon their tax prerogatives from 1439 onwards. This is one of the reasons why representation never became as important in France as in England. The tax exemption of the nobility was hated, and social unrest developed as the burden of taxation – bearing mostly on the third estate whose members were neither noble nor affiliated to the Catholic Church via the *taille*, the *gabelle*, the *aides* and *traits* – increased substantially throughout the sixteenth, seventeenth and eighteenth centuries. In

---

[439] On 16 May 1214, John Lackland ordered the raising of a new tax, from which only those who accompanied him in Poitou would be exempt. The amount, much higher than the customary rate, provoked the meeting of the barons and the request for a series of guarantees. After various events, in 1215, the Confederates marched on London. John Lackland had to give in, approve the petition of the barons, and grant the 'Great Charter'.

addition, the sale of public offices to private persons extended the tax privilege beyond the nobility and clergy to wealthy families. Because of this, the *Ancien Régime* never managed to establish a bright line between 'public' and 'private' – public offices being sold to private persons.[440] A reduced tax base and the inability to change the corporate structure of the economy led to the 1789 Revolution. The line between 'public' and 'private' was then drawn by expropriating without compensation the venal office holders. Professional corporations were dissolved in 1791 and a new tax, the *patente*, was introduced in the very same statute (and was eliminated in 1976 only). A new public system was progressively built in which the recruitment for positions of power in the administrative Organs of the State was to be impersonal and based on merit.[441] This is the origin of the French *grandes écoles*, still in existence today.

But this relates only to the political, public, macro-institutions of a 'market' society. One cannot understand the history of political institutions, their evolution and link with the development of a monetary economy, as well as some of the problems created by globalization, without understanding the challenges and difficulties of taxation not only *politically* but also, much more importantly, *practically*. In his book on the *Theory of Taxation*, Mirabeau made it very clear. Insisting on the need to have clear legal rules in society, furthermore he insisted on how this is particularly important with regards to taxation:

> Everything rolls on rules; but the exactitude and the clarity of these rules are indispensable depending on the importance of the topic to be established. There is not in all political science any object more important than the perception of finance, since from there depends, as we have shown, all the strength and harmony of a State. There is therefore no object that requires more exact and clear rules.[442]

In the last pages of his book, he insists on the importance of these rules and on their connection with the protection of property:

---

[440] Fukuyama, *op cit*, note 128, pp. 339 & 352. The 'Great Demarcation', as Rafe Blaufarb calls it, introduced by the 1789 French Revolution, laid the foundations of France's new constitutional order and crystallized modern ways of thinking about politics and societies. This led to radical distinctions between the political and the social, State and society, sovereignty and ownership, the public and the private. *See generally* Blaufarb, *op cit*, note 183, particularly pp. 1–2 & 11.

[441] *Ibid*, p. 371.

[442] Mirabeau, *op cit*, note 407, p. 117.

> If ... I do not know what the taxman will take from my harvest, I will never know if the land, and the seeds I am advancing, are mine, and if it is appropriate for me to risk for uncertain wealth that which I possess with certainty. But how can one know if the taxman is at every moment the master of increasing the size of the portion? This arbitrary right would exist only to annihilate itself.[443]

Mirabeau makes a clear connection between the certainty of tax rules and property rights: if the investor does not know for sure what amount of taxes will be payable in case of a successful investment, he does not know in fact what he will *own* and will not invest resources he knows are his for uncertain ones.

The procedures of appropriation via taxation are now usually very strict. But the macro-political dimension of taxation should not obscure the *practical* necessities of taxation and its difficulties. These difficulties explain in great part the incentives existing for States to participate in the development of a 'market economy'.

4.4 Practical Issues in Taxation

For our purposes, the key progress in the development of a State of law leading to the development of an exchange economy was the reduction of arbitrariness in the perception of taxes and the falling of taxation under the rule of law. The ignorance of the role of law in this area also leads to neglecting the role of the 'State of law' in economic development. For some, it remains a mystery why State officials are motivated to enforce laws.[444] The reason is simply that it is much easier to run a State and collect taxes in an effective State of law, although reaching that stage is a formidably complex enterprise.

In their analysis, North, Wallis and Weingast completely miss the importance of taxation in the creation of what they call an 'open access order' society. In the index to their book *Violence and Social Orders*, there is *not a single entry* for 'taxes' or 'taxation'. The extraction of taxes, however, is intrinsically linked to the violence-controlling institutions of *any* society – which is the central object of their study. It makes it hard to understand how they could miss such a key issue. Modern taxes as we know them are intrinsically linked to the operation of the modern State. States have the

---

[443] *Ibid*, p. 290.
[444] Hodgson, *op cit*, note 222, p. 159.

monopoly to tax their population and they established this monopoly via the monopolization of legitimate violence over their territory. Ignoring this fundamental fact in a book entitled *Violence and Social Orders* is more than a major blunder.

At a minimum, the modern State in fact has a *double monopoly*: legitimate violence *and* taxing power, each of the two monopolies reinforcing the other. Creating a State requires building a war-waging, internal order-producing and tax-collecting institution.[445] Taxation was the primary means through which European State builders in the sixteenth century and later supported their expanding armies. These, in turn, were their primary instrument for establishing control over their borders, pushing them outward, defending them against external incursions, and ensuring their own authority within these borders. Conversely, military needs were the main incentive for the creation of new taxes and the regularization of old ones. The need feeds itself: reversing the resistance to taxation imposed the maintenance of a military force. And so turned the narrow circle connecting State building, military and police institutions and the extraction of scarce resources from a resistant population.[446]

Here also, Mirabeau is very clear in his book on the 'Theory of taxation', addressed to the King and which, incidentally, led him to imprisonment:

> Everyone feels the necessity of an active force that defends him, in the interior, from intestine greed and, outside, of that of strangers. As a result, everyone agrees to contribute to this public force, which is really the produce of this consent. It is therefore his advantage that everyone considers in this contribution. ... In a word, this is a market like any other, nothing for nothing, it is the motto of men, and God himself wanted it. If you wanted forced contribution, exorbitant and destructive, you would be led to violence, you would come to the crime against freedom, to the injury of property & injustice, & you would break the links & the agreement constitutive of society and sovereignty.[447]

---

[445] *See generally* Norbert Elias, *La civilisation des mœurs*, Paris: Calmann-Lévy (1939, 1969, 1979, 1991). Halpérin, *op cit*, note 353, p. 37.

[446] Charles Tilly, 'Reflections on the History of European State-Making', in Charles Tilly (ed.), *The Formation of National States in Western Europe*, Princeton: Princeton University Press (1975), p. 23.

[447] Mirabeau, *op cit*, note 407, pp. 6–7.

In Mirabeau's view, the need for protection against internal and external violence is a given. Starting from this need, there is agreement that one must contribute to the existence of a 'public force'. And in this exchange relationship, one can identify '*a market like any other*'. Even more significantly, in the absence of this market, of this exchange, there is only forced contribution, destroying liberty, damaging property, creating injustice and breaking the bounds of society and sovereignty. Taxation is a *constitutive* exchange between the provision of order by the State to society and the provision by society to the State of the means required to develop the institutions bringing order.[448] Via taxes, the State collects the resources needed for its continued existence via the provision of services – the most important one being security. And being progressively understood as an autonomous legal person, the State was in a position to improve its credit and borrow to make collections and disbursements match through time.[449] The subjective personality of the State was asserted in connection with the issues raised by the public debt and the continuity of this debt was thus extended to perpetuity, allowing to establish, between successive generations, an impressive solidarity. This was reinforced by the process of State constitutionalization, often imposed by State bankers in search of security over capricious despots.[450] This ability to commit over the very long term opened the possibility for the State to use the enormous resources of credit.[451]

Importantly, for an 'open order society' – as North, Wallis and Weingast call it – to exist, the tax system must *also* be applied in an impersonal manner based on *rules* (tax laws) which must treat equally people in the same situation and not in an arbitrary fashion. This allows planning for those who are subject to tax payments and successful State builders understood this early on. Those who did not or who faced too much resistance implementing an efficient tax system – like the French kings who never managed to tax the nobility and had great difficulties taxing the priests – ended up losing their power (and eventually their heads) via a revolution generated by the dramatic financial situation of the French State at the end of the eighteenth century. To change the system, the King had to convene the General Estates – which had not been done

---

[448] *See also* North and Thomas, who state 'We can, as a first approximation, view government simply as an organization which provides protection and justice in return for revenue. That is, we pay government to establish and enforce property rights'; North and Thomas, *op cit*, note 360, p. 6.

[449] Charles Tilly, *Contrainte et capital dans la formation de l'Europe – 990–1990*, Paris: Aubier (1990, 1992), pp. 146–147.

[450] Polanyi, *op cit*, note 417, pp. 24 & 34.

[451] Hauriou, *op cit*, note 177, p. 118.

since 1614. Once in meeting, the Third Estate called itself the National Assembly which marked the beginning of the end for Louis XVI. In France, prior to the Revolution, stability for investors was obtained via privileges[452] – paid for on an individual basis – not via generally applicable laws. These expedients further contributed to the problem: privileges, not the rule of law, were the basis of prerogatives. Combined with other issues, this led to the French Revolution.

There are hundreds of examples of poor taxing practices, because taxing is a very difficult exercise and often, out of necessity – because their mere survival is at stake – States had (and still have) to resort to expedients violating this principle. Confiscation, coinage debasement, office selling and the like were often used to collect resources to address short-term problems.[453] But they created long-term negative effects and were avoided by wise rulers. So much so that arbitrariness in taxation was seen by explorers during the sixteenth, seventeenth and eighteenth centuries as one of the reasons for the lack of technical progress in the 'Oriental world' as opposed to the evolution which started being felt in Europe.[454] In the creation and existence of modern States, unending runaway fiscal crises are more the norm than the exception.[455] But to be successful in the long term and have access to the increased resources only a developed economy can provide, States had to develop tax systems effective at collecting resources *and* at providing incentives to invest – or at least not to discourage investment, as was the case for most of history.

This could only happen via the adoption and enforcement of generally applicable, impersonal tax laws.

4.5 From Compulsion to Modern Taxation

With regards to compulsory transfers, apart from some mood swings at those times of the year when the tax bills find their way to our mailboxes, we now clearly differentiate rapine, robbery, looting, extortion and taxation. Originally, however, the differentiation among the various modes of compulsory (and often violent) transfers was not so obvious.[456]

---

[452] North and Thomas, *op cit*, note 360, pp. 122–127.

[453] Sassen, *op cit*, note 6, p. 49.

[454] North and Thomas, *op cit*, note 360, pp. 122–127.

[455] Ardant, *op cit*, note 409, p. 12. *See also* North, *op cit*, note 156, p. 139.

[456] Carlo M. Cipolla, *Before the Industrial Revolution – European Society and Economy, 1000–1700*, London: Routledge (1976), p. 20.

The differentiation became possible only when the production and procurement of goods and services came to exist without threats and without the use of physical force.[457] It is only when the use of physical force became a centralized monopoly over vast territories – State territories – that a double differentiation took place. One could then start differentiating the domain of *voluntary* transfers (goods or services are voluntarily exchanged by the seller against the *voluntary* payment of a *price* by the buyer) and the area of *compulsory* transfers (services – and first of all protection services) provided by the State thanks to the *mandatory* payment of *taxes*.[458]

In a fundamental way, via the various services they procure, States are part of the institutional setting required to produce wealth. It is inappropriate to see them *only* as organizations *consuming* resources. Like any organization producing services, States make *use* of and consume resources. To have the means to pay for these resources, they raise taxes. But in exchange, they *provide services*. The provision of these services is not paid via the payment of a *price*; it is paid, in a collective manner, using an apportionment among those who pay and those who get the services which is not necessarily proportional to their contribution, via the perception of *taxes*. Some States are certainly more effective and efficient than others in fulfilling this mission. And the geographical structure of certain States certainly facilitates the taxation exercise over less well-positioned States. In States in which foreign trade was a significant part of the economy, the costs of measurement and of collection of the taxes was typically low. This was even more the case for States with important sea trade, the number of ports being limited. In contradistinction, where exchange was primarily local, internal to closed economies isolated one from another, the cost of measurement and collection of taxes was much higher.[459]

But whether they are effective or not at taxing, States have as a minimum the role of providing several services to the population located on a given territory: those services which *only* a monopolistic organization can provide.[460] This is specifically the case for the provision of justice or order through the military and police forces, which is at the root of the existence of States in the first place. Only a monopolist can provide effective justice because at the end of the day, there should be only one

---

[457] Norbert Elias, *La dynamique de l'Occident*, Paris: Calmann-Lévy (1939, 1969, 1975), p. 84.

[458] Primarily, but also through various services such as compulsory military service.

[459] North and Thomas, *op cit*, note 360, p. 99.

[460] Lane, *op cit*, note 396, p. 414.

decision ascertaining the rights of litigants in any particular dispute. Only a monopolist can exert legitimate violence over a territory and the population located on it because otherwise the competition among enforcers would rapidly degenerate into civil war. And as we have seen, only a public governmental monopolist over the means of coercion can create and enforce property rights.[461] A monopolist is required to hold everyone within the limits of peaceful competition.[462]

Many of the State-provided services reduce what has been called by some 'transaction costs' without noticing, often, the fundamental role played by the State in the development of a market economy.[463]

In reality, we have to conduct our analysis of the modern Power System by integrating the required existence of the State as a monopolist, which is a complex task. So much so that certain 'ultra-liberal' economists or political scientists deny the need for a State. Their ignorance of the role of the State leads them to develop analyses in which all services are provided by 'the market' while 'the market' cannot exist without the State ... And one can clearly identify the need for the services the State provides in areas of the world where failed States do *not* provide the protection service or in places experiencing civil war: the local economies are always in a disastrous state and life opportunities existing there are very limited. The ultra-liberals' paradises of stateless societies do in fact exist: they are called, for example, the *Democratic Republic of Congo*, the 227th country by GDP per capita (800 dollars per year), with its non-performing institutions and militias; or the *Central African Republic* (228th country with a GDP per capita of 700 dollars), with its fighting factions and ethnic and religious cleansing. The advocates of ultra-liberalism yearning for a society free of any State should spend some time in these wonderlands to see what the real-life consequences of the implementation of their theories would be, i.e. the disappearance of an effective State.[464] No doubt that if they survive the experience, they will rush to their tax-supported consulate to seek repatriation to the orderly comfort of their home State.

Without certain organizations specializing in violence and able to acquire and maintain a monopoly of violence over a given territory, the

---

[461] North and Thomas, *op cit*, note 360, p. 69. *See also* Supiot, *op cit*, note 249, pp. 159–161.

[462] *See* Macpherson, *op cit*, note 116, p. 95.

[463] North and Thomas, *op cit*, note 360, hint at this issue in a limited way, noticing that 'as trade was expanding a need was created for larger political units to define, protect and enforce property rights... The provision of governmental services was also subject over some range of output to economies of scale', p. 94.

[464] 'Where the libertarian paradise on Earth should flourish, we actually find ourselves in the antechamber of hell'; Supiot, *op cit*, note 249, p. 288.

pacification of the territory and of exchange, and thus the differentiation between 'political' and 'economic' activities, would never have happened.[465] It is only once violence over the State territory becomes monopolized into the State that local competition for the appropriation of goods will take place without resorting to physical violence[466] using means *legally available to the whole population as a matter of principle* via the institutions of private law, such as property rights and contracts. Two separate spheres of power – public and private – developed with different rules applicable to them. Without the differentiation, which is relatively new and established on a firm basis only under a constitutional mode of government, markets and economic organizations could *not* have developed to the extent they have.

This differentiation was the result, first, of the levy of taxes without the use of force, except in marginal cases. This has been a very slow process and one much easier to achieve over *monetary exchanges*. The taxation of the peasantry in cash, difficult because the peasantry was initially very limitedly involved in *monetary exchanges*, has been a constant source of revolts and uprisings.[467] At the same time, in economies which were mostly agricultural, it was simply impossible for the nascent State to raise significant resources without taxing the peasantry. Modern political institutions did develop *only* when a series of organizational and technical advances freed a growing proportion of the population from working in the fields, grapevines or forests. Before this, feudalism was the only tax system available, the collection of resources being local and taking place *in kind* or *in services* rather than through the collection of money.[468] And the fact of the matter is that the difficulties of taxing the peasantry were such that it gave strong incentives to State builders to develop *monetary exchange*, fairs and markets. Before that, there was no single actor with a monopoly over the means of coercive force and the distinction between public and private had yet to be articulated.[469]

Necker, writing a report to Louis XVI on the fulfilment of the duties of his office, underlined the great advantages of monetary taxation over taxation in services:

> A man without faculties, a laborer, who is required to work every year for seven or eight days of forced labor, would have

---

[465] Elias, *op cit*, note 457, p. 97.

[466] *Ibid*, p. 84.

[467] Ardant, *op cit*, note 392, p. 167.

[468] North and Thomas, *op cit*, note 360, pp. 28–32.

[469] Spruyt, *op cit*, note 368, p. 12.

to pay only twelve to fifteen sols for his part to the imposition
of the roads; and he would find much more compensation for
this small contribution, by the introduction of new works for
money, for the benefit of which he would participate by his
work. No doubt, then, that forced labor is obviously contrary
to the interests of this class of your subjects, to which the
benevolent hand of your Majesty must constantly be extended,
in order to temper, as far as possible, the imperious yoke of
the propertied and wealthy. ... Moreover, the distribution
and collection of a tax in money are subject to certain rules,
whereas the distribution of forced labor and the supervision
over its execution multiply arbitrary decisions and punishments
and oblige to hand over a great power in subordinate hands.[470]

Necker makes it clear: monetary taxation is a form of *justice* as it takes
away those who are subjected to payments in kind from the arbitrariness
of holders of property rights, *from the yoke of the propertied*. But the taxpayer
needs to be put in a position to *sell* his products or services on a *market*
to be able to have the money needed to pay in *cash*.[471] To develop market
exchanges, State builders tried, when possible, to take control over cities
– those physical locations where most of the monetary exchanges were
taking place. This was easier to achieve in areas where 'city-States' and
'city-leagues' did not dominate within the Power System, as was the
case in future Italy or Germany.[472] In Vauban's view, for example, *creating*
monetary flows was required to build the State in France. He analysed
the economic circuits and their special location, the 'body politic' being
comparable in his mind to the human body which existence depends on
the flow of fluids. The architect of modern French borders and of the '*pré
carré*' doctrine – a regularly shaped territory being easier to defend than a
fragmented one – argued that trade in a country is useful 'to facilitate the
traffic and the movement of money no less necessary to the body politic
than the blood for the human body'.[473]

Money can circulate; locally provided compulsory services *cannot*. And the
development of the modern State required the progressive conversion of
an economy in which exchanges *in kind* dominated to an economy with

---

[470] Necker, *op cit*, note 435, p. 70.

[471] Ardant, *op cit*, note 409, p. 69.

[472] *See* above at Section 3.5.

[473] Dockès, *op cit*, note 425, p. 159. *See also* Braudel, *op cit*, note 434, p. 49; Catherine
Larrere, *L'invention de l'économie au XVIIIe siècle – Du droit naturel à la physiocratie*, Paris:
Presses Universitaires de France (1992), pp. 107–108.

exchanges *mediated via money*. Via industry and movable property, objects of exchange are multiplied, great wealth is easily transported, all distances are reduced, a continual circulation is established between all parts of a kingdom, the capital accumulates, and the State can, by means of taxation, acquire the means of paying for a civil government and an army which belong, not to each section which furnishes it, but to the whole society.[474]

Of course, the level of taxation must be such that it does not discourage economic activity. As Mirabeau puts it:

> The more the Prince grows his income, the more he alters the
> property in his State, the more he really impoverishes himself,
> the more he increases his embarrassment, the more he works
> to put himself in the arms of deception and brigandage.[475]

Beyond the level of taxation, it is then the *regularity of the tax* which will be fundamental. Taxation, in the early Middle Ages, was *extraordinary* and *ad hoc*, taxes being due *not* on the return of a given *date*, but in relation to particular *events*.[476] Feudal aids were due to pay the ransom of the lord, the dubbing of the eldest son, the dowry of the eldest daughter and, irregularly, for the defence of the realm in cases of public emergency, the *casus necessitates*. The first three cases depended on the personal life of the lord and his family, while the fourth was referring mainly to the *regnum* and *patria*. Gradually, the state of emergency became a permanent state. Taxation, once linked to particular *events*, started to intervene at regular *dates*. The State, as a service provider organization, had become *permanent* and so were its needs.[477] In 1515, France had 7,000–8,000 office holders working for the king, which gives an idea of the relatively small size of the political enterprise at the time. By 1665, the royal administration had 80,000 administrative office holders. (As a matter of comparison, in 2015, France had 5,451,000 civil servants.) Or, similarly, the Bavarian government had 162 officials in 1508; they were 866 in 1571.[478] The notion of *necessitas* acquired a new meaning. Initially linked to an *emergency* situation – a hostile incursion, the war against religious or political

---

[474] Barnave, 'Introduction à la révolution française, texte présenté par Fernand Rudé', Paris: Armand Colin, *Cahiers des Annales* n° 15 (1960), p. 20.

[475] Mirabeau, *op cit*, note 407, p. 113.

[476] On the provisions of the Magna Carta, *see* above in Section 4.3.

[477] Ernst H. Kantorowicz, *The King's Two Bodies – Study in Medieval Political Theology*, Princton: Princeton University Press (1957), pp. 284–286.

[478] Fukuyama, *op cit*, note 128, p. 329.

enemies or against rebels – it began to be linked to the *regular, budgetary* needs, of the *government*.[479]

A long tradition has accustomed us to place absolute monarchic power on the side of lawlessness, arbitrariness, abuse, caprice, privilege and exceptions. It led to disregarding this fundamental historical trait that Western monarchies were built as *legal systems*, have constructed themselves through *theories of law* and have made their power mechanisms operate under the forms of law, progressively reducing arbitrariness.[480] Arbitrariness no doubt existed in early monarchies; but to the extent possible – and often, necessity knows no law – the architects of the State tried to restrict it as much as possible. This is true particularly *with regard to economic exchange and its rules*. With regards to taxation, Mirabeau made it very clear:

> From the proscription of the unlimited and isolated right to impose arbitrarily, results that of arbitrarily distributing impositions, even if legal and agreed to. It would be exercising over the individual, the tyranny we have just proscribed as to the universality.[481]

The *regularity* of taxation is of considerable importance. With regularity, taxes become a cost of doing business like any other one. If they are not regular, levies or taxes are not included in the calculation of costs. For someone having committed to sell a product at a given price, an unexpected tax increasing production costs comes as a disaster disrupting his forecasts. For any given sum to be taxed, occasional taxation bears much more on economic activity than taxes levied regularly. An *inevitable* consequence of the lack of regularity in taxation and arbitrariness is hoarding and lack of investment in medium- or long-term projects. The absence of stable, predictable tax rules has for consequence that the resources of the most active men are devoted to speculative trade, quickly made, and quickly settled, leaving few traces to the detriment of land improvements, the construction of factories and the acquisition of capital goods.[482] Activity and, even more important, *investment* – a key to economic development – depends on what potential investors think lies

---

[479] Kantorowicz, *op cit*, note 477, p. 209.

[480] Foucault, *op cit*, note 308, p. 115. On the difference between Western and Eastern societies in this regard, according to Gabriel Ardant, *see* Ardant, *op cit*, note 409, pp. 302–309.

[481] Mirabeau, *op cit*, note 407, p. 115.

[482] Ardant, *op cit*, note 409, pp. 300–301.

ahead for their projects; *after* tax.[483] In societies in which violence is not monopolized and disciplined by the existence of a legal system binding the sovereign *itself*, including with regards to the imposition of taxes, the chains of actions binding members of society to each other can only be short. Once the monopoly of violence consolidated within States, however, the division of functions was able to develop and exchange chains could extend, expending the breadth and density of the World Wide Web of Contracts.[484] It is to the extent that European States have sought not only to replace requisitions by taxes, but *also* to restrict *arbitrariness* by *law*, that they triggered *technological progress and the evolution of the economy.*

This view about a European dynamic leading the way to a World Power System is heavily criticized by authors like André Gunder Frank. He considers that the Eurocentrism of Marx, Weber, Toynbee, Polanyi, Braudel, Wallerstein and most other contemporary social scientists[485] is anti-historical and, in fact, ideological.[486] Gunder Frank agrees that we need a holistic global world perspective to grasp the past, present and future history of the world – and any part of it.[487] But Gunder Frank denies any advance of the Europeans in science, technology, rationality and reason and considers that the Europeans did not in any sense 'create' the world economic system itself nor develop world 'capitalism'. Gunder Frank, however, has a bias which is a handicap to perceive what was unique about the European story. Gunder Frank indicates that:

> ... a major thesis of this book is ... that institutions are not so much determinant of, as they are derivative from, the economic process and its exigencies, which are only institutionally instrumentalized rather than determined. That is, the situations are the derivative and adaptive instruments and not the cause ... of the economic process.[488]

There is no question that anyone writing from any particular location, training and culture always runs the risk of being something-centric. But

---

[483] *Ibid*, p. 299.
[484] On the notion of World Wide Web of Contracts, *see* hereunder at Chapter 6. Elias, *op cit*, note 457, p. 189.
[485] *See also* the interesting developments by Michel Foucault in *Dits et écrits – 1954–1988*, tome III (1976–1979), Paris: Éditions Gallimard, Bibliothèque des sciences humaines (1994), starting at p. 370.
[486] Gunder Frank, *op cit*, note 324, pp. xv–xvi.
[487] *Ibid*, p. 29.
[488] *Ibid*, p. 206.

even taking this fact into account, and being agreed that many social theories and historic discourses are Eurocentric, one can still identify an institutional dynamic in which State and market were linked in their development via the need for States to get access to taxes paid in cash and for participants to market exchange to benefit from the justice, security and other services provided by States. Non-commercial, intra-community exchanges were elusive and could not give rise to modern taxation. The development of the modern State was intrinsically linked to the development of the market economy and the reduction of non-market exchanges. Political ambitions and the fiscal needs attached to their achievement combined to tie the State development to the spreading of the market.[489] For a wealth of reasons, this dynamic was particularly effective in Europe. *Contra* Gunter Frank, I find that in this particular dynamic, *legal* institutions were the real determinants.

---

[489] For a description of the early exchanges among Kings and merchants in late medieval England, *see* Gary Richardson, 'Guilds, laws, and markets for manufactured merchandise in late-medieval England', 41 *Explorations in Economic History*, pp. 1–25 (2004), especially at pp. 18–20. *See also* Pierre Rosanvallon, *Le capitalisme utopique – Critique de l'idéologie économique*, Paris: Seuil (1979), p. 118.

5

The Mixing of Democracy and Despotism

So far in the first part of this book, I have analysed property as a constitutional prerogative decentralizing to owners the right of decision-making as a matter of principle towards objects of property. As such, property is a building block in the Power System, laws coming as derogations to this principle. Laws are reducing the owners' decision-making autonomy as a matter of exception. Public and private prerogatives, although operating via different rules, operate in combination. The public prerogatives of the Organs of the State exist, on the one hand, to provide services which can only be provided by a monopolist in the provision of order over a territory and population and, on the other hand, in agreement with Pigou's teaching, to correct negative externalities and reduce inequality. The liberal constitutional mode of government in effect combines a principle of autonomy in economic affairs, via property and freedom of contracts, and of democracy in collective decision-making to reduce this autonomy when required. This combination of private and public prerogatives in a 'market economy', far from being incidental, is *constitutive* of a specific Power System. It is a system in which monetary, market exchange requires the existence of State property, and State institutions, to exist. And public prerogatives could not exist without the resources provided by the taxation of private monetary exchanges taking place in their jurisdiction.

One can clearly see how globalization – with *globalized* firms and markets, on the one hand, and *local* States, on the other – can be a powerful disruptor of this Power System.

In this chapter, I will show that constitutional systems of government promoting the protection of property rights necessarily lead to a pluralistic Power System mixing democracy and despotism. This is because property, with its absolute prerogatives and the decentralization of sovereignty it represents, was designed to protect individuals' autonomy. But with the advent of a *corporate* economy, these prerogatives have been concentrated within business firms. A new form of legal pluralism developed, in an unofficial manner, outside the official, positive legal system. Although they have no formal existence, firms play a role in the effective operation of the Power System. They are relays, organizations coordinating the operation of large sectors of the economy. After each of the major crises of the twentieth century – the two World Wars and the Great Depression, in particular – radical evolutions occurred in the State legal systems to re-equilibrate the imbalanced operation of the private side of the Power System. Protective laws were adopted; social rights were granted. Via the Constitutional Revolutions of the twentieth century, the liberal, nightwatchman State moved to become the welfare and regulatory State. Western democracies, following the trauma of the Great Depression and the sacrifices imposed on their citizens during the two World Wars, sought to achieve inclusive economic growth and full employment. Decades after Bismarck's adoption of the first social security laws in Germany, the Beveridge Plan in Great Britain, the Plan Commission in France, Roosevelt's 'New Deal' and the adoption of the 1946 Full Employment Act in the US were symbols of this commitment to government interventionism and the welfare State.[490] They undermined the idealized notion of a self-regulating economy without government intervention. These Constitutional Revolutions, however, are now being slowly eroded and challenged by globalization.

★★★

The earlier developments in this book have shown, in particular, that property is a right of autonomy allowing the creation by owners of decentralized, autonomous rules applicable to those making use of their property. These systems of rules generate heteronomy for those who are subject to owners or their agents. They must abide by the rules created by others. They contractually trade their autonomy by accepting private heteronomy for a compensation. The existence of the rules autonomously created by owners and imposed upon others is made possible by State law, but the exercise of the prerogatives property entails is not attributed to the State. The State is confined to a passive role; the one of an arbitrator of private disputes, and the guardian of rules it has not laid down.[491] Property grants an ability to make decisions and rules in connection with the use

---

[490] Gilpin, *op cit*, note 431, p. 131.

[491] *E.g.* Nonet and Selznick, *op cit*, note 32, p. 46.

of property *as a matter of principle* which are *autonomous* from the State governmental apparatus, from the Organs of the State. Owners are not public officials,[492] civil servants or Organs of the State. They do not hold an office. When laws reduce the autonomy of owners, their flexibility to adopt decentralized rules is being reduced. But the owners do not become *governed*. They are still the rule-makers as a matter of principle; they are still *owners*. Property *is still the same concept*: the right of decision-making *as a matter of principle* in connection with the object of property. Owners simply face an increased set of constraints, *as a matter of exception* to their prerogatives as owner as a matter of principle. Those who are governed are those who are making use of the property rights of owners who are *organizing* their activities, such as employees. They may benefit from new rights that they can now oppose to owners who have less autonomy. But they are still *governed* by owners.

Property rights are *not* a *delegation* of authority by the State, something which can be taken back. The prerogatives entailed by property rights are protected by constitutional provisions of a hierarchical level equal to those providing for the operation of the political Organs of the State. This is what is so specific about property as a method of allocation of governmental authority:

(a) Particular objects of property can obviously be expropriated by the State. As we have seen, objects of property can mandatorily be appropriated by the State – i.e. without the owner's approval – *when the public interest requires it*. If a new road or railway track or an airport must be built in the public interest, private property rights may have to be transferred following a decision-making procedure involving one or several of the political 'Organs of the State', even against the owner's will. Indemnification must usually be paid in such circumstances. In relatively exceptional circumstances, property can thus be taken away from private owners against their will and become public property in this fashion. Without this possibility, 'property would become a curse of society'.[493]

(b) The extent of the autonomy of the owner can be reduced. Laws and regulations adopted via the democratic political process can have as a consequence that the owner of a home may not burn trash in his backyard; or the owner of a car may not drive it beyond speed

---

[492] Katz, *op cit*, note 186, p. 243.

[493] *E.g.* von Ihering, as cited by Ely, *op cit*, note 21, p. 496. On takings, *see generally* Alexander, *op cit*, note 228, who provides detailed accounts of the issue in various jurisdictions around the globe.

limits; or the owner of a factory cannot use a production process contaminating the natural environment and so on. Values protected via the democratic process of norm creation, in order to have an environment free of smoke, safe roads, reduced pollution etc. may lead to a *reduction* of the autonomy of the owner, to a *reduction* of the potential uses of property.

(c) However, the fundamental *content* of what property is *cannot* be reversed. Property is still a right of decision-making *as a matter of principle* towards the object of property, no matter the increased constraints created. If the constraints created are excessive, they can be requalified as being equivalent to a *taking*, which may lead to a right to be indemnified. But generally, property remains a right as a matter of principle and if this principle would be reversed, it would be the end of the rights of autonomy. It would mean that, as a matter of principle, every disposition, use or transfer in connection with the objects of property is prohibited unless there is a specific derogation to this principle. A right of autonomy is the exact opposite: owners have a constitutional right to be the rule-makers as a matter of principle in connection with the use of their rights and, with regards to property, with what they own.

Because of the recognition of property rights, law in a constitutional system of government protecting private property is, by definition, *pluralistic*. The constitutionally guaranteed right to property allows the creation of what I have called the small-scale despotisms.[494] A constitutional legal system protecting property rights is a system of legal pluralism comprising innumerous legal orders. This has nothing to do with 'customs';[495] this has a lot to do with State constitutional law's enabling dimension, in particular via property.

5.1 Property and Legal Pluralism

Because enforced constitutional rules protect property rights and property rights enable rule-making, the rules created by owners are part of the constitutional *legal system*. Rules of the house, factory rules, students' rules[496]

---

[494] *See* Section 2.4.

[495] Hodgson, *op cit*, note 222, p. 153.

[496] Simon Whittaker, 'Public and Private Law-Making: Subordinate Legislation, Contracts and the Status of "Student Rules"', 21(1) *Oxford Journal of Legal Studies*, pp. 103–128 (2001).

and so on are *law proper*, *mandatory* and *enforceable* rules created by owners because of their constitutionally protected property right over the factory or the house or any other object of property. At its roots, each and every constitutional legal system protecting property rights is necessarily *pluralistic*. Beyond the law of the State, the law in the law books, the official law, the law taught in law schools, there are myriads of small-scale legal orders creating law as a result of constitutionally protected rights of autonomy, including property rights. These legal orders exist as such and some have even succeeded at conquering their autonomy with regard to both national and international laws.[497]

It is important to be aware that property rights are not the only means through which the State provides for enabling powers to create autonomous legal orders. In this book, I am concentrating on legal pluralism in modern legal orders, based on property rights, and on a *specific type* of legal order: the business firm. But legal pluralism in a State of law protecting property rights and other rights of autonomy goes way beyond the existence of business firms as legal orders.[498] Large-scale law (State law created by the Parliament or the executive power) and the large-scale political system (the executive and the other political Organs of the State) depend for their existence on *relays* in the administration of order and the setting of the micro-rules required by day-to-day life in a myriad of different institutional environments.[499] Property is only one of the means to decentralize the rule-making capacity and the implementing procedures needed. The authority of parents over their children, for example, also entitles parents to create rules 'of the family'. Laws and judges only marginally amend these rules. They do it, for example, in cases of child abuse. But no judge will decide whether Timmy must be in bed at 7 pm rather than 8 pm. Depending on local laws, it is for the parents or one of the parents to decide. State family laws create a

---

[497] Pierre Gothot, 'François Rigaux ou la chute des masques', in *Nouveaux itinéraires en droit. Hommages à François Rigaux*, Bruxelles: Bruylant (1996), pp. 3–27, at p. 13.

[498] *See generally* Jean-Guy Belley, 'L'État et la régulation juridique des sociétés globales – Pour une problématique du pluralisme juridique', 18(1) *Sociologie et sociétés*, pp. 11–32 (1986), Burdeau, *op cit*, note 249, pp. 87–88, Santi Romano, *op cit*, note 257, Georges Gurvitch, *Le temps présent et l'idée du droit social*, Paris: Vrin (1931), Georges Gurvitch, *Eléments de sociologie juridique*, Paris: Aubier (1940), Maurice Hauriou, *Principes de droit public*, Paris: Dalloz (1910, 2010), Maurice Hauriou, *Aux sources du droit – Le pouvoir, l'ordre et la liberté*, Caen: Bibliothèque de Philosophie Politique et Juridique, Textes et documents, Université de Caen (1933, 1986), Georges Renard, *La philosophie de l'institution*, Paris: Sirey (1939), Gidon Gottlieb, 'Relationism: Legal Theory for a Relational Society', 50 *University of Chicago Law Review*, pp. 567–612 (1983).

[499] Foucault, *op cit*, note 485, p. 406.

framework of enabling rules within which the rule-makers, as a matter of principle, are the parents and, for most of the issues, the final legislators, judges and enforcers of the rules they make.[500]

But in connection with the institutional structure of the economy, property is *the* key concept. The foundations of today's Power System lie in property, not at all because it is an 'original' or 'natural' right. It is a *constitutional* prerogative which grants powers of decision-making as a matter of principle in the continuum of allocation of prerogatives going from individuals up to the Organs of the State. And, in fact, the normative produce of the Organs of the State is constitutionally subordinated to the primacy of private property. The use of property can be regulated, oriented, constrained. But it remains as the right of decision-making as a matter of principle. So much so that François Rigaux could write (about Belgium) that 'our true Constitution is the Civil Code'[501] or, as Charles Demolombe or Jean Carbonnier put it for France, the Civil Code is the civil constitution of the French people.

5.2 From Official to Unofficial Legal Pluralism

What is at stake in a proper understanding of property was clearly expressed by Hans Kelsen:

> Property is the right *in rem* par excellence and is the starting point of the whole construction. It is defined as the exclusive domination of a person over a thing and it is opposed to the claim creating a legal relationship of a purely personal (*in personam*) nature. This distinction, which plays an important role in the theory of private law, is also ideologically charged. It is maintained in spite of the constantly renewed objection that the legal domination of a person over a thing consists solely of a relation between a subject of law and other subjects of law, or more exactly a relation between the conduct of an individual and that of one or more other individuals, namely the legal possibility for the owner to prevent all other subjects

---

[500] On the governmental role of families and of the father in the French Civil Code, *see*, in particular, Martin, *op cit*, note 288, pp. 216–286. *See also* Montesquieu, who sees fathers as accessories to police forces, whose power is necessary to limit the burden of magistrates and reduce the tribunals' workload; Montesquieu, *op cit*, note 288, letter CXXIX, vol. III, p. 258.

[501] Gothot, *op cit*, note 497, p. 10.

from enjoying the property and the obligation of the latter not to infringe the right he has to dispose of it.

In defining property as a relationship between a person and a thing, one conceals its important social and economic function, which according to socialist theories consists of 'exploitation'. In fact, ownership is a relationship between the owner and all other law subjects, who are bound by the objective right to respect the owner's exclusive power over his thing. But traditional legal science refuses to admit that the subjective right of the owner is only a secondary aspect of the obligation of other subjects of law. It insists on the primary character of subjective rights and goes so far as to identify them with the right itself.[502]

The almost universal denial of the pluralistic legal structure of society is important to understand because the pluralistic legal structure of society does not derive from globalization. Globalization only makes it more *visible*. But legal pluralism has always been there, even in modern, supposedly positivist State law. Historically, the *ancient regime* macro-legal orders of pre-modern States were *officially* pluralistic legal orders.[503] Society was understood as a body made of bodies. With the modern dissolution of most intermediary groupings, official legal pluralism has left the stage to be replaced by a monistic legal order *officially based*, on the one hand, on the rights of autonomy of *individual* persons free from the restraints of the old corporate institutions of society and, on the other hand, the organs of the sovereign State as the sole official producers of legal rules over the whole territory and population. State law became an object of idolatry.[504] But irrespective of the stance taken by legal positivists that law proper is State law and that there are no intermediate legal orders any more, even in a society having *officially* destroyed all intermediary groupings, such as the French one,[505] there is still legal pluralism. It

---

[502] Kelsen, *op cit*, note 242, p. 107.

[503] François Olivier-Martin, 'La France d'ancien régime, État corporatif', 5 *Annales de droit et de sciences politiques*, pp. 690–702 (1937) and Olivier-Martin, *op cit*, note 364.

[504] Grossi, *op cit*, note 179, p. 127.

[505] It was the great Frederic Maitland who wrote in 1905: 'No longer can we see the body politic as *communitas communitatum*, a system of groups, each of which is a system of groups. All that stands between the State and the individual has but a derivative and precarious existence. Do not let us at once think of England. English history can never be an elementary subject; we are not logical enough to be elementary. ... it is always best to begin with France, and there, I take it, we may see the pulverizing, macadamizing tendency in all its glory, working from century to century, reducing to

is *unofficial* because it is hidden behind, in particular, the concept of *property right* usually understood as a direct right over a thing. As we know now, property is a right of decision-making as a matter of principle which partially translates into a right of rule-making to which third-party users of property must abide. The 'private' legal orders may not be 'intermediary' in the sense that they have no *official* existence and do not *officially* mediate between individual persons and the State. They are not intermediary also in the sense that they are not territorial and may very well operate in the infra- or supra-State level. And private legal orders do not benefit from a *delegation* of power or a positive recognition of the rule-making power they have. In this respect, it is inappropriate to consider that the reason why corporations exist is that they disperse collective power from government to civil society, as David Sciuli does.[506] It is the *opposite* which occurred: collective power was dispersed from government to *individuals* (not 'civil society'), via property rights and liberties. Their *concentration* into the ownership of large *corporate organizations* led to a new form of *concentration* of power, with a great degree of autonomy from governmental powers, and not at all to a dispersion of (private) power.[507]

The legal orders built on the basis of property rights are not part of the *official* system of allocation of power in society. But the autonomy they have in this legal system is actually *higher* than in officially pluralistic legal orders because they derive their autonomy from property, a right as a matter of principle, *a constitutional right*, and *not a delegation of authority* which could be taken back. In this regard, corporate powers are certainly not 'public'; but at the same time, they are hardly 'private'.[508] They belong to a *different category* whose fundamental rules are yet to be identified. Because of the property rights they concentrate under their management structure, corporations can issue commands, regulate the activities of those making use of their assets, adjudicate disputes, impose rules of behaviour, delegate the use of resources, train individuals to abide by their rules, discipline and punish. They are 'quasi-public'; which also means that they are still 'quasi-private'.

Traditional doctrine about property is clearly embarrassed about the inferences of this analysis, as Hans Kelsen wrote two generations ago. It

---

impotence, and then to nullity, all that intervenes between Man and State'; Frederic W. Maitland, 'Moral Personality and Legal Personality', 6(2) *Journal of the Society of Comparative Legislation*, pp. 192–200 (1905), pp. 195–196.

[506] David Sciuli, *Corporate Power in Civil Society – An Application of Societal Constitutionalism*, New York: New York University Press (2001), p. 26.

[507] *See* Chapter 8.

[508] David Ciepley, 'Beyond Public and Private: Toward a Political Theory of the Corporation', 107(1) *American Political Science Review*, pp. 139–158 (2013), p. 140.

is eager not to acknowledge theories of exploitation based on property. The production of intra-organizational rule is still seen either as non-law or as delegated lawmaking that must be recognized by the official legal order to exist. Rule-making by 'private governments' is presented as subjugated under the hierarchical frame of the national constitution that deemed to represent the historical unity of law and State.[509] This is, of course, a prudent position if one wants to avoid dealing with the complex issues of the proper rules applying to non-public and yet not private governmental institutions. But with globalization, we must go beyond this comfortable position. The legal structure of the World Power System must be understood *as it is* if we want to have a chance to adjust its operation to today's predicament. Remember: we are facing climate change, unbearable inequalities and deadly challenges to democratic political institutions. My key point is that we have to take seriously the fact that historical developments in the practice of law have been breaking frames and the recurrent challenges about law's hierarchy so easily silenced in the nation-State's past can be silenced no more.[510]

5.3 Relays in the Power System

Many small-scale despotisms – political systems made possible by the modern notion of property – are in existence, underneath the official political system. They are in effect part of the overall political and legal system thanks to the liberal constitutional structure of government. But this is not official. Liberal Constitutions actually provide for the means of the legal existence of complex pluralistic legal and political systems which are comprised, on the one hand, of the many autonomous sub-systems of everyday life we deem to be 'private' (families, business firms, churches etc.) and, on the other hand, of the macro-political and legal systems (understood in the restrictive sense) we deem to be 'public'. The part of the constitutional rights – the rights of autonomy – out of the reach of the democratic institutions created via the Constitution allows the construction of this myriad of despotisms. They are affected by the laws adopted through the democratic system of government and macro-institutions, but only at the margin of their operations because of the *content* of the concept of property. It may be hard to accept it, but we only *marginally* live in democracies: of all the rules applicable to us in our

---

[509] Gunther Teubner, 'The King's Many Bodies: The Self-Deconstruction of Law's Hierarchy', 31(4) *Law & Society Review*, pp. 763–788 (1997), pp. 768–769.

[510] Gunther Teubner (ed.), *Global Law Without a State*, Dartmouth: Aldershot (1997).

daily lives, only a marginal number is created via democratic political institutions.[511]

Norms created via the public, official, political system, higher in the hierarchy of norms, always come as *limited derogations* to the autonomy of owners. Political regulation via law in effect is merely a reduction of the sovereignty of the owners. The owners remain the rule-makers as a matter of principle towards the object of property they own. They can create organizations whose existence is enabled by State constitutional rules; but these organizations are *not* part of the State. State constitutional law provides for the possibility of their existence; but they are not Organs of the State.

It is even more so in a globalizing world because of the competition among States to attract productive activities, or (as we will see in more detail later on) at least the accounting acknowledgement of value creation in their jurisdiction.[512] There are today large 'private' powerful organizations benefiting from the enabling laws of numerous States allowing them to exist on a global scale. They are clearly not 'Organs of the State'. But, like other autonomous institutions present in society (families, churches and so on), their existence is made possible by State laws. They do exist as a consequence of the inner constitutional structure of States in our Power System.

In their analysis, North, Wallis and Weingast note that most organizations have their own internal institutional structure: the rules, norms and shared beliefs that influence the way people behave within the organization.[513] But their analysis of what they call 'rules' and 'norms' stops there, which necessarily considerably limits their ability of understanding the way in which organizations are inserted within the Power System in a constitutional mode of government. A proper understanding of property rights leads to a more fundamental conclusion that it is the modern constitutional system and property rights which are at the origin of the autonomy which most organizations enjoy to develop and adapt their own internal institutional structure. Constitutional systems of government protecting property make it possible to create autonomous small-scale *legal orders* – systems of rules creation and enforcement – by *owners*. Of course, this is not very important in connection with the property rights over pens, eggs or apples. But it is fundamental when it comes to the understating of the operations of the enormous masses of productive assets controlled by the managerial structures of large business firms. An

---

[511] *See generally* Bobbio, *op cit*, note 429.

[512] *See* Section 8.5.

[513] North, Wallis and Weingast, *op cit*, note 6, p. 16.

enterprise is a government because the law entitles the enterprise to organize itself to make rules for the conduct of its affairs, which those who are subject to its rule-making capacity have to abide by. In the official legal system, it is a *private* government because the rules it makes with the licence provided by property are final and are not reviewable by any public authority.[514] The consequence is that the private governments of business firms

> impose a far more minute, exacting and sweeping regulation of employees than democratic States do in any domain outside prisons and the military. Private governments impose controls on workers that are unconstitutional for democratic States to impose on citizens who are not convicts or in the military.[515]

Those in control of these large organizations decide to hire and fire, they create the rules applicable within the firm, make decisions about what will be produced with the assets controlled, how production will be organized, with what consequences for the natural environment, the neighbours, what R&D policy will be implemented, where production will take place, the level of compensation of the workforce, on-job training programmes, to what extent the payment of taxes will be 'optimized' through various legal means making it possible to shift profits and so on. These large firms are large legal and political orders; pure and simple. Interestingly, in many countries, including the US, firms enjoy these prerogatives thanks to the fact that they benefit from the rights extended under the Bill of Rights to *individuals* – although they are *not* individuals. And simultaneously, the rights of individuals, who are supposed to be the primary beneficiaries of the Bill of Rights, have no 'horizontal effect' against the 'private' governments employing them, unless it can be demonstrated that these 'private' governments are acting on behalf of the State (i.e. that they are performing a so-called 'State action'). This is, of course, a US domestic issue to be addressed by the US people. But at the global level, refusing to consider the existence of 'private governments' and to draw the consequences for the analysis of politics, law and economics in today's world amounts to ignoring the fundamental rules of operation of today's society at its grassroots level, in day-to-day life.

---

[514] Selznick, *op cit*, note 112, p. 269.

[515] Anderson, *op cit*, note 270, p. 63. *See also* Dan-Cohen, *op cit*, note 23, p. 174; Pierre-Yves Gomez and Harry Korine, *Entrepreneurs and Democracy – A Political Theory of Corporate Governance*, Cambridge: Cambridge University Press (2008), p. 20.

5.4 Acceptability

Strangely, this mode of operation of the Power System meets almost general acceptance. This is surprising because the liberal constitutional mode of government de facto organizes the coexistence of a myriad of small-scale, everyday-life despotisms, with democratic rule applying *only* to the operations of certain of the Organs of the State (those I have called the 'political Organs of the State'; *see* Section 3.6). The fact that competition is open in both the economic sphere and political one may be a powerful explanation for the widespread acceptance of this peculiar mode of operation of the Power System. Or at least the widely shared *belief* that competition is open may explain the sustainability of this Power System. It was not brought upside down by an extension of those having a right to vote via a reduction of census suffrage.[516] This evolution merely led to an extension of the State's role – what I call the Second Constitutional Revolutions (in Section 5.6 and in the Introduction to Part II) – which did not challenge the right to property and only led to an extension of the rules created via the political system to reduce the sphere of the prerogatives exercised freely as a matter of principle. The Power System appears – and to some extent is – open: people are free to try to get more property and to try to get access to more prerogatives via ownership. And they are free to try to get elected and get access to political power via the electoral process. They can thus access the institutions via which part of the rules of the game can be changed which will affect, as a matter of derogation, how the small-scale despotisms will operate. And democratic political institutions allow a certain degree of correction of the issues generated by the micro-governments created thanks to the ownership of property rights. In this fashion, economic and political spheres in the Power System are deeply connected.[517] Political responsiveness in open access orders leads political officials to provide a range of public goods and services that respond to political demands generated in case the operation of the private side of the Power System leads to dissatisfaction.

---

[516] Burdeau, *op cit*, note 249, p. 120. In France, nearly 7 million electors were summoned in 1792 for the election to the National Convention, as against 30 million today; but more importantly, there were only 110,000 electors in 1817, 241,000 in 1847, 9.5 million in 1848 and 6 million in 1851; Alain Renaut, 'État de droit et sujet de droit', 24 *Cahiers de philosophie politique et juridique*, p. 51, Caen: Presses Universitaires de Caen (1993), p. 63.

[517] North, Wallis and Weingast, *op cit*, note 6, p. 145.

And it is a fact that via this system, the official law – the law of the State – has been adapted to answer to at least part of the demands generated through time within society.

Early on in the creation of the State legal order, the focus of State builders in connection with economic exchange was on creating institutions and delivering services in order to enhance the access to markets, the development of the rule of law and the impersonal administration of justice.[518] Then the emphasis was on infrastructure building (roads, canals, railroads and so on) enabling a further extension of the market economy and of its fiscal potential.[519] By 1900, the focus of lawmakers shifted markedly from the promotion of economic growth to its regulation.[520] Due to economic development and the rise of negative externalities and hard living conditions for the unpropertied – negative consequences of economic development not taken into account in the price system – the State had to adapt further to internalize part of the negative externalities generated and to tax part of the wealth created to redistribute it.

5.5 Correcting Unbalances

In the US, the unbalancing of the constitutional arrangements following the surge of private corporations to structure business enterprises took place primarily in the local State constitutional orders. The concentration of property rights over productive assets in large enterprises led to the rise of private powers operated with almost complete disregard for those negatively affected. Twelve-hour shifts were legitimated by the 'freedom of contract' enjoyed by the contracting parties. Termination at will of employment agreements was a direct consequence of the right to property. Polluting the environment was not an issue as long as no one suffered enough damage and had enough resources to sue. Accidents in the workplace were interpreted as resulting from the fault of careless employees who had to bear the consequence of their lack of caution. Or sue their fellow workers who had hurt them.[521] And so

---

[518] North, Wallis and Weingast, *op cit*, note 6, p. 145. *See also* North, *op cit*, note 298, p. 141.

[519] *Ibid*, p. 145; Larrere, *op cit*, note 473, pp. 107–108.

[520] Ely, *op cit*, note 134, p. 8.

[521] This was the so-called 'fellow servant' rule pursuant to which an employee injured on the job could not sue his employer if the injury was caused by the negligent act of another employee. Since the employer was usually a distant legal figure, this meant no recovery for industrial accidents in factories, railroads and mines. Friedman, *op cit*, note 40, p. 55.

on. Political and union struggle led to an adaptation of the missions of the State which modified *qualitatively* the *protection services* offered. From the role of 'nightwatchman State', concentrating on the provision of *physical* order, the protection of property rights and the enforcement of contracts, the State had to take on the role of a 'welfare State' to correct some of the consequences of an unbalanced contracting world in a world of inequality in property ownership. In the parlance of Bénabou and Tirole, the State internalized negative externalities and reallocated income.[522] Democratization of political life led to an extension of the State's protection services. From a mere protector of property rights and a provider of formal commutative justice and infrastructure, the Organs of the State were further developed and started protecting a range of interests affected by economic exchange. Social insurance laws, labour laws, environmental laws, consumption laws and so on were implemented to provide more redistributive justice and internalize negative externalities. In short, a set of laws of territorial application was adopted through time to correct the negative effects of a monetary exchange economy left to itself. A series of interests other than a mere protection of property and the enforcement of contracts became protected via the adoption of mandatory norms and the creation of new, specialized, administrative agencies.

Legislators sought to redress unbalanced social and economic outcomes by 'mandating a redistribution of property' in favour of those viewed as being disadvantaged. This redistribution could take two forms: either a restriction of the autonomy of the decision-makers as a matter of principle (owners) or taxation and subsidization. Legislators did both, adopting statutes improving working conditions, setting minimum wages and taxing the income and assets of the wealthy.[523]

This relatively recent role led to Constitutional Revolutions, which can be called the *Second Constitutional Revolutions*, in almost all States, with the rise of the 'social State' in Europe or the 'New Deal' in the US.

5.6 The Constitutional Revolutions of the Twentieth Century

Using the institutions of the State to make the law evolve in reaction to economic issues created by industrialization and economic crises was not easy. Henry Sumner Maine's view of the historical evolution as being from status to contract moved full circle – free contracts leading the way to

---

[522] Bénabou and Tirole, *op cit*, note 8, pp. 1–19.
[523] Ely, *op cit*, note 134, p. 8.

new forms of status.[524] Here, again, the routes taken varied from country to country. In the US, the first institutions to react to new demands were certain State legislatures. By 1900, the US had become an industrial nation. A broad-based reform movement, known as Progressivism, emerged. Its primary concern was to correct the imbalance of economic power associated with the new industrial order. Progressives enjoyed considerable success at the State level in persuading legislators to enact a wide range of statutes protecting employees in the workplace. These measures curtailed contractual freedom and the rights of owners to use their property.[525] At first, there was a strong resistance of the judiciary against this evolution.

As summarized by Robert Cox:

> the first phase of liberating the market from social control undermined social cohesion and produced conflict. In a second phase, society, bit by bit, reasserted control over the economy, attempting to moderate the socially disruptive effects of the market and to bring the economy back under social control. The medium for doing this was politics, in which there came about a measure of agreement between traditionalist conservatives and social reformers against the 'extreme middle' of pure market liberals. The movement began with regulation of factory conditions, continued with social insurance and the institutionalizing of labour-employer bargaining and the rise of socialist and social democratic political parties to culminate during the mid-twentieth century in welfare States and the acceptance of full employment as a primary goal of State policy. This second phase of the double movement went hand in hand with the extension of the vote to all adults and with the expansion of the State's scope to cover most issues of concern to people. Liberal democracy acquired a social dimension and social ills became a primary concern of politics.[526]

As we have seen, in the views of the Framers of the US Constitution as translated into the Bill of Rights, property and personal rights were

---

[524] Ardant, *op cit*, note 409, p. 14.

[525] Ely, *op cit*, note 134, pp. 101–102.

[526] Robert W. Cox, 'Democracy in Hard Times: Economic Globalization and the Limits to Liberal Democracy', in Anthony McGrew (ed.), *The Transformation of Democracy? – Globalization and Territorial Democracy*, pp. 49–72, Cambridge: Polity Press (1997), p. 52.

united. The Fifth and Fourteenth Amendments protect both liberty and property. With the new protective laws, the issue was to find how the competing interests of liberty and property could be reconciled and which branch of government should strike the balance.[527]

The issue crystallized around the interpretation of the due process clause of the Fifth and Fourteenth Amendments. The origin of the due process clause can be traced back to the language of the expression 'by the law of the land' found initially in the English *Magna Carta* of 1215.[528] This old wording actually appeared in many of the State Constitutions of the US.[529] Historically, the guarantee of due process was defined mostly in procedural terms, requiring that customary legal procedures be followed before a person could be punished for criminal offences. The initial purpose of due process was to protect individual persons against arbitrary punishments or the taking of property. But by the late eighteenth century, courts began to develop *substantive* interpretations of the clause. Early cases protected against the outright attempts by legislatures to transfer private property from one party to another, which was a rather straightforward interpretation of the constitutional provision. But progressively courts went further. They started to consider that regulations could have the same practical effect as a taking of property. In 1856, for example, the New York Court of Appeals found that a statute outlawing the sale of liquor was a deprivation of property without due process as applied to liquor owned when the law took effect.[530] For the Court, 'the legislature cannot totally annihilate commerce in any species of property, and so condemn the property itself to extinction'.[531] Following this emerging doctrine of substantive due process, courts broadly reviewed legislation and struck down laws deemed unreasonable 'deprivations of property' without due process. Any excessive encroachment to the use of property could be equated with an unconstitutional deprivation of property. Of course, such an interpretation was due to an understanding of property as a right over things and led to an extensive restriction of public governmental powers to regulate the private uses of property.

The principles of what has been called *laissez-faire constitutionalism* gained currency among the US Supreme Court Justices in the 1880s. Economic

---

[527] Ely, *op cit*, note 134, p. 9.

[528] 'No freeman shall be taken, or imprisoned, or be disseized of his freehold, or liberties, or free customs, or be outlawed or exiled, or any otherwise destroyed, nor will we pass upon him nor condemn him, but by lawful judgment of his peers and by the law of the land.'

[529] Ely, *op cit*, note 134, p. 78.

[530] *Ibid*, p. 79.

[531] *Ibid*.

due process soon became the most important judicial instrument used to safeguard property rights as they were understood at the time. Simultaneously, the Supreme Court developed an important corollary doctrine: the principle of 'liberty of contract'. The liberty of contract doctrine proceeded on the assumption that both parties to a contract enjoyed equal bargaining power and should be allowed to determine freely contractual terms. Justice Harlan wrote it in clear words:

> The right of a person to sell his labor upon such terms as he deems proper is in its essence the same as the right of the purchaser of labor to prescribe the conditions upon which he will accept such labor from the person offering to sell it. So the right of the employee to quit the service of the employer, for whatever reason, is the same as the right of the employer, for whatever reason, to dispense with the services of such employee. ... In all such particulars the employer and the employee have equality of right, and any legislation that disturbs that equality is an arbitrary interference with the liberty of contract, which no government can legally justify in a free land.[532]

It is hard to find a clearer denial of the inequality in negotiation deriving from the control of property right by one party and its absence by the other. Roscoe Pound could legitimately ask: 'Why is the legal conception of the relation of employer and employee so at variance with the common knowledge of mankind?'[533] For him, the law of contracts was surcharged with fallacy. And no one, apparently, had the wisdom of raising the fact that protective laws were *always* challenged by employers, and *never* by employees. Unsurprisingly, employees never thought about complaining that their liberty was unjustifiably hampered by protective laws.

There were instances in which the Court recognized that States could lawfully restrict property and the principle of liberty of contracts in appropriate situations under the so-called police power.[534] In 1898 for example, the Supreme Court upheld a statute limiting the period of employment in mines to eight hours a day.[535] Rejecting a challenge based on the liberty of contracts doctrine, the Court stressed the unhealthy conditions of mine work and realistically noted that mine owners and

---

[532] *Adair v. United States*, 208 U.S. 11, 175.
[533] Fisher, Horwitz and Reed, *op cit*, note 41, p. 27.
[534] Ely, *op cit*, note 134, pp. 88–90.
[535] *Ibid*, pp. 90–91. *Holden v. Hardy*, 169 U.S. 366 (1898).

their employees 'do not stand upon an equality, and that their interests are, to a certain extent, conflicting'.[536]

But the seminal case is the famous *Lochner v. New York* decision of 1905.[537] In 1896, the New York State Legislature unanimously passed a statute on bakeries. This statute prohibited working more than 10 hours per day or more than 60 hours a week in bakeries. A certain Joseph Lochner, owner of the 'Lochner's Home Bakery' in Utica was fined twice and decided to bring his case up to the US Supreme Court. Lochner's lawyer argued that the Bakeries Act could not be interpreted as a measure necessary to protect health since the 'average bakery today is airy, comfortable, summer and winter, and always [fragrant]'. If such laws were to be maintained, he argued, 'the precious freedom of the individual ... will be swept under the guise of State police power'.

The US Supreme Court agreed. Writing on behalf of the majority (5 to 4), Justice Peckham held that the statute violated the liberty of contract protected by the Fourteenth Amendment. He acknowledged that a State may enact laws to protect the health of workers but could find no direct relationship between the number of hours worked and health. For Peckham, bakers were perfectly able to defend their interests and there was no reason to treat them as 'wards of the State'. For him, the statutes limiting the working hours were nothing but a 'restriction on the rights of the individual'.[538] In Justice Oliver Wendell Holmes' dissenting opinion, this case was 'decided upon an economic theory which a large part of the country does not entertain'. In his view, the Court should exercise judicial restraint and defer to 'the right of a majority to embody their opinions in law'. But his powerful dissident opinion did not convince the majority and, for the next 30 years, the Court closely scrutinized the 'reasonableness' of numerous statutes affecting property rights.[539]

In *Adkins v. Children's Hospital* (1923),[540] for example, the Supreme Court ruled again on a similar case setting minimum wage and annulled a statute of the District of Columbia setting a minimum wage for women. Again, for the Supreme Court, it was an unacceptable violation of the liberty of contract.

The Supreme Court changed its position only after the Great Depression and the spectacular re-election of Roosevelt in 1936 during what is called

---

[536] *Ibid*, p. 91.

[537] 198 U.S. 45 (1905): 102–3. *See generally* James W. Ely Jr., *The Guardian of Every Other Right – A Constitutional History of Property Rights* (2nd edition), Oxford: Oxford University Press (1998), pp. 101–118.

[538] Ely, *op cit*, note 134, p. 102.

[539] *Ibid*, p. 103.

[540] 261 U.S. 525 (1923): 106–7, 125.

in the US the '1937 Constitutional Revolution'.[541] In *West Coast Hotel Co. v. Parrish* (1937),[542] Chief Justice Hughes (writing for a majority of 5 against 4) overruled the *Adkins* case. Decrying the 'exploitation of one class of workers who are in an unequal position in terms of bargaining power', he recognized a wide discretion to State legislatures to protect employees' health and safety and ensure 'freedom against oppression'. He was effectively invalidating the liberty of contract doctrine. In his dissenting opinion, Justice Sutherland continued to consider that the minimum wage law at stake was not only an arbitrary interference with the right to negotiate wages but also amounted to discrimination *against* women by reducing their ability to compete with men.[543]

Since 1937, the States and the federal government of the US are now constitutionally free to adopt laws that limit liberty of contract by prohibiting certain contractual clauses to protect certain values (health, wages for a decent life, the natural environment etc). And when they do, their laws supersede contractual agreements. The Supreme Court opened the door to the rise of the regulatory and welfare State. As a result, Congress enacted increasingly intrusive control over the use of private property and business activity.[544] In contrast with the limited role of government under the laissez-faire philosophy, the doctrine of liberal constitutionalism affirmed public governmental power to redress social ills, regulate business and intervene in the economy.[545] An *integral feature* of the modern Power System is the growth of public government. This is not an aberration, an abnormal operation of the political system.

Very similar developments took place in other political systems also (*see* the introduction to this chapter).[546] As a consequence of these changes, numerous contracts falling under the jurisdictions of regulatory States were modified. Prices were affected because of the internalizing and equalizing interferences of the political components of the Power System. Revolutions took place in a constitutional way in the sense that without even amending the written Constitution, evolving constitutional

---

[541] Ely, *op cit*, note 134, p. 127.

[542] 300 U.S. 379 (1937).

[543] Ely, *op cit*, note 134, p. 127.

[544] *Ibid*, p. 129.

[545] *Ibid*, p. 133.

[546] *See* Jean-Philippe Robé, *L'entreprise et le droit*, Paris: Presses Universitaires de France (1999); reprinted in *Le temps du monde de l'entreprise – Globalisation et mutation du système juridique*, Paris: Dalloz (2015), starting at p. 100, and Julie E. Cohen, *Between Truth and Power – The Legal Construction of Informational Capitalism*, Oxford: Oxford University Press (2019), p. 2.

interpretations accompanied, often through crises, a fundamental evolution of the Administrative Organs of the State and of regulatory law.

It is these Constitutional Revolutions which are being challenged by the globalization of firms. It brings States into a new competitive game affecting their ability to play their role in protecting the interests insufficiently taken into account by the price system or in rules of corporate governance.[547]

The governmental challenge in today's World Power System is similar to the difficult situation in which American politics was in the first decades of the twentieth century. At the time, industrialization had changed the scale of economic organization in the US and created enormous new concentrations of power. A significant disjunction existed between the 'nationalization' of economic activity, i.e. its spreading over a whole continent, and the ability of local (State) democratic political institutions to regulate it. The answer to this issue was found in a centralization of political power within the (national) *federal* government, creating a strong *national* federal State, and fostering a strong sense of identity and national solidarity. Courts, and in particular the American Supreme Court, eventually agreed to let this revolutionary process occur. Transposed to the difficulties liberal democracy is facing today, this would suggest that a solution lies in a global government. But a world government is neither desirable nor possible in any foreseeable future. Instead, we need to realize that contemporary conditions call for new thinking about what form democracy and effective government can take in today's predicament by facing the surge of global firms in a world without a global State.

This is the object of the second part of this book.

---

[547] Anthony McGrew, 'Globalization Beyond Borders? Globalization and the Reconstruction of Democratic Theory and Politics', in McGrew, *op cit*, note 526, p. 240.

Firms in the World Power System

Introduction to Part II

The second part of this book explains the position of global firms in the World Power System and how a renewed understanding of the effective structure of the Power System can lead to an adjustment of their role. Today's World Power System is facing obvious difficulties to address potentially deadly issues such as climate change. This is in part due to the globalization of firms and of value chains which make it almost impossible for States to fulfil their internalizing and redistributive functions. States are now in the uncomfortable position of having to behave both as the whole and as the part, as the container and the content, as the inclusive instance of power and as a mere component included in a larger Power System.[548] States provide the infrastructure and rules required for the operation of a market economy but they are also participants in the competitive game to attract under their jurisdiction the localization of part of the economic process, which negatively affects their ability to fulfil their constitutional role. A key proposal of this book is that a renewed understanding of the real operation of the World Power System must integrate the role played by global business firms and markets. A proper understanding of the Power System could lead to an amended mandate for firm governance, internalizing the negative externalities they otherwise generate.

This second part stresses the importance of *corporate* property. The only type of corporation which has been discussed to some extent in the first part of this book is the State. We have seen how central this development has been for the creation of a market economy and, more generally, for the institutionalization of an open access society. But we now live in a world of corporations and the fact that, for most significant economic activities, individual persons act via separate legal, corporate persons has completely changed the economic, legal and political landscape. When liberal Constitutions were first put in place starting at the end of the eighteenth century, it was not envisioned that the rights of autonomy granted to individuals would be extended to corporate vehicles. Corporations were feared and perceived as incompatible with

---

[548] Riqueur, *op cit*, note 305, p. 141.

liberal democracy. But the introduction of the business corporation into the legal system proved irresistible; and it led to a move from liberalism to a form of capitalism whose governance structure is much more complex than the State/individual, political/economic, public/private dichotomies of the liberal system would make us believe.

★★★

In the first part of this book, I have addressed the importance of the existence of the State as a separate legal person owning public property, operated by 'Organs of the State' whose activities are imputed to 'the State'. The Organs of the State must make use of their prerogatives in specific, objective and impersonal ways – in the pursuit of the 'general interest' – for the State to operate as a State of law and give rise to the operation of an 'open access society'.

Opposite to the State, I addressed the existence of constitutionally guaranteed private prerogatives – rights of autonomy – enjoyed by individual persons. I did put the emphasis on a specific right of autonomy – the right to property – to analyse the combined operation of the 'private sphere' of the Power System with the 'public sphere', the one operated by Organs of the State. A constitutional system of government guaranteeing rights of autonomy decentralizes the authority to make decisions in connection with the use of the objects of private property to the largest extent possible. It empowers individual persons to make effective use of their rights of autonomy and entitles them to benefit from the positive consequences. But it also makes them accountable for the negative ones.

So far, the importance of corporate property has been disregarded.

As we have seen, the State is a particular form of corporate person to which the actions of the 'Organs of the State' are being attributed. It is a corporate person in the sense that the State is a legal person which is not an individual. Its existence as a legal person is separated from the existence of any natural individual person in particular. The State – when it is a State of law – provides a series of services in an impersonal manner. It is operated by individual persons holding offices. Their functions and the rules applicable to them are important for the existence of a State of law. Certain individual persons are, of course, better at fulfilling these functions than others. But in a properly operating State of law, the specific characteristics of the individuals are less important than the fact that the duties of their offices must be fulfilled via impersonal rule- and decision-making. The birth of the modern constitutional State occurred by subsuming the personal identity of all rulers in the durable

186

and perpetual corporate organization of 'the State'.[549] This is the process through which particular individuals with privileges – kings in particular – became replaced by offices, Organs of the State, keeping their permanence irrespective of the changes in the identity of the individuals in charge of these offices.

A World of Corporations

There are now many more forms of corporate persons than the State. Some are public, some are private.

The existence of numerous corporations in the 'private' sector of the Power System has important consequences. The fact that for a number of activities, individual persons actually act via separate legal persons to whom certain of their actions are attributed completely changed the operation of the Power System. We have glanced at some of these evolutions when we looked at how the boundary between *private-made law* and *public-made law* was moved because of industrialization. The liberty of contract and the autonomy granted by property were reduced. State and federal laws impacting on economic exchange developed. This is what I have called the Second Constitutional Revolutions in Sections 5.5 and 5.6. It led to the birth of the welfare and of the regulatory State.

I will now go deeper into the analysis of how the Power System evolved because of the rise of the corporate system of firm organization. Because of the development of a corporate economy, the Power System is now global with an imbalance in favour of 'private'-made law. The liberal Constitutions established in the late eighteenth century addressed the issue of the relationship between the *individual* person and the *State* on a *territorial* basis. This was done in the context of an economy which was overwhelmingly agricultural. At the time of their drafting, the creation of business corporations was either prohibited or strictly controlled. Business corporations were not contemplated in the constitutional, liberal, individualistic structures of government and they did not have to be: they hardly existed at the time.[550] Adjusting the operation of the legal system to their introduction as instruments available to organize business activity has proved to be extraordinarily challenging. And it is now even more so in a World Power System without political unity to address major global issues

---

[549] North, Wallis and Weingast, *op cit*, note 6, p. 249.

[550] On the twists and turns to manage – or fail – to apply the protective constitutional provisions of the US Constitution to corporations, *see* A. Conrad, 'Constitutional Rights of the Corporate Person', 91 *Yale Law Journal*, pp. 1641–1658 (1981–1982).

such as climate change created in part by the globalization of production, of economic exchange and of business firms.

On top of the world agenda of global issues lies the environmental crisis. It is not the only one and there are a number of converging crises due to the inadequacy of the existing institutional structure of the existing World Power System. I have briefly presented the issues created by the reaching of several of the Planetary Boundaries in the General Introduction at pp 20-23. But I will concentrate on the climate change crisis which is the most severe one since it threatens the survival of the human species.

The Corporate Danger

When the voices to expand 'freedom of incorporation' were first heard during the nineteenth century, the risks associated with the creation of these legal instruments were perceived by many. Adam Smith, for a start, believed that in a fully free market, the commercial and manufacturing sectors would be populated by small-scale enterprises, run by independent artisans and merchants, with just a few employees.[551] In his pin factory – his model of the enterprise with an efficient division of labour – there are only *ten* workers. The world of Smith is that of trades at the craft level, shopkeepers, transporters, woodcutters and shepherds.[552] In Smith's view, the large-scale enterprises existing at the time were a product of State-licensed monopolies, tariffs and other mercantilist protections.[553] Joint-stock corporations were needed only to raise the large concentrations of capital needed for banking, insurance, canals and water utilities.[554] For anything else, Adam Smith wanted to do away with corporations. In his view, if corporations were to be used for other activities, fraud and speculation would occur. There was also the perception that business corporations could lead to the formation of private powers in a position to compete with the State.

In fact, while the corporation is at the heart of the legal structure of the large modern enterprise, the history of its introduction into the liberal legal system is at the heart of the historical development of industrial

---

[551] Anderson, *op cit*, note 270, p. 21.

[552] Sassen, *op cit*, note 6, p. 101.

[553] It is surprising that many of those who present Adam Smith as the Founding Father of economics forget about his absolute disdain for corporations. *See*, for example, Bénabou and Tirole, *op cit*, note 8, who write that: 'The invisible hand of the market, described in Adam Smith, harnesses consumers' and corporations' pursuit of self-interest to the pursuit of efficiency'.

[554] Anderson, *op cit*, note 270, p. 21.

and then financial capitalism and of their induced effect on the changing role of the State in the economy; in a world far away from the one of Adam Smith.

From Liberalism to Capitalism

The progressive introduction of business corporations has fundamentally changed the operation of the Power System. Echoing the warnings issued at the time of their introduction into the legal system, Justice Louis Brandeis, one of the most famous Justices of the US Supreme Court ever, wrote in the 1933 case *Liggett v. Lee* that the public corporation is a 'Frankenstein monster which States have created by their corporation laws'.[555] This is something to remember when our children ask us what we are doing to correct our dysfunctional Power System: the Frankenstein monsters have been set in motion by our forebears.

There was a very interesting debate on the role of business corporations in the concentration of property rights and on their impact on the role of the State at the so-called 'Lippmann Colloquium' held in Paris in August 1938. Among the numerous liberal intellectuals who participated, one finds Raymond Aron, Friedrich Hayek, Robert Marjolin, Ludwig von Mises, Michael Polanyi, Wilhelm Röpke, Louis Rougier, Jacques Rueff, Alexander Rüstow and Alfred Schütz. The colloquium led to the creation, a few years later, of the Mont Pelerin Society, which still exists. At the colloquium and during the first years of the Society's activity, two strands of neo-liberalism expressed themselves. One of them was the ordo-liberalism of Röpke and Rüstow; the other was advocated by von Mises and Hayek.[556] As is well known, the second strand eliminated the first, 'neo-liberalism' meaning today *only* the second strand.[557] What is interesting for our purposes is that the ordo-liberals, whose legacy is unfortunately vastly ignored, had a clear understanding of the role of law in the effective operation of a liberal society. For someone like Louis Rougier, only the 'liberal mystic' misses the importance of:

---

[555] *Louis K. Liggett Co. et al. v. Lee, Comptroller et al.*, 288 U.S. 517 (1933) 548, 567.

[556] Audier, *op cit*, note 16, p. 180. *See also* Philip Mirowski and Dieter Plehwe (eds.), *The Road from Mont Pelerin – The Making of the Neoliberal Thought Collective*, Cambridge: Harvard University Press (2009), especially pp. 46–51, Foucault, *op cit*, note 131, pp. 165–190 and Slobodian, *op cit*, note 240, especially pp. 7–13.

[557] Audier, *op cit*, note 16, pp. 207–209.

property, inheritance, contracts, the various types of business partnerships and corporations, the currency, the banking organization, weights and measures which do exist via a series of rights, guarantees and obligations sanctioned by the authority of the State.[558]

Or for someone like Wilhelm Röpke, it is utopian to present a competitive market economy as a 'natural order' while it is 'the artificial and fragile produce' of a particular civilization.[559] For Walter Eucken, the central problem of economic thought was that it has lost all connection with social and political reality. Adam Smith and other classical economists had recognized the fact that the economy is embedded in the legal and political system. Although this is often forgotten, Adam Smith listed 'three duties of the sovereign':

> according to the system of natural liberty, the sovereign has only three duties to attend to: ... first, the duty of protecting the society from the violence and invasion of other independent societies; secondly ... the duty of protecting, as far as possible, every member of the society from the injustice or oppression of every other member of it, or the duty of establishing an exact administration of justice; and thirdly, the duty of erecting and maintaining certain public institutions and certain public works.[560]

This definition of what the State ought to do in Adam Smith's work is rather elastic. The second and third duties would exhaust the possibilities of even the most interventionist of States. And Jacob Viner has drawn a list of *additional* governmental functions to be found in other sections of *The Wealth of Nations*.[561] It is rather long. But because these tasks were not listed in one place, and because Smith's emphasis in his book was constantly on the superior performance of the 'system of natural liberty', he left the impression of circumscribing the role of government much more than he in fact proposed.[562] The most important mistake Smith

---

[558] *Ibid*, p. 80.

[559] *Ibid*, p. 187.

[560] Adam Smith, *The Wealth of Nations*, New York: The Modern Library (1994), p. 745.

[561] Jacob Viner, 'Adam Smith and Laissez Faire', in *Adam Smith, 1776–1926*, Chicago: University of Chicago Press (1928), pp. 116–155.

[562] Joseph J. Spengler, 'The problem of Order in Economic Affairs', in J.J. Spengler and W.R. Allen (eds.), *Essays in Economic Thought: Aristotle to Marshall*, Chicago: Rand McNally and Co. (1960), pp. 6–34, at p. 18.

and his followers made, however, was to overlook the fact that, in the absence of appropriate rules and of a coercive agent to enforce these rules, if necessary, the actions of autonomous agents will not be so coordinated as to produce harmony.[563] And it is this somewhat misleading impression which has set the tone for subsequent writers. Economic thought became isolated from these issues in the nineteenth century, and economists lost sight of both the political and legal contexts of economic problems and the influence of law and political institutions on economic phenomena.[564]

Aware of the role of law in the effective operation of the economic system, Wilhelm Röpke clearly saw the difference between liberalism and capitalism. For him, 'capitalism is nothing else than this soiled, adulterated form which liberalism has taken in the economic history of the last hundred years'.[565]

In this move from liberalism to capitalism, business corporations have played a major role. But for today's 'neo-liberals' – the heirs of the *second* strand of thought expressed at the Lippmann Colloquium – there is no issue in treating them like individuals, and this topic was quickly dismissed in the debates.[566] And it still is.

The fact is, however, that the development of the freedom to incorporate limited liability business corporations led to a concentration of property – of the rights of decision-making as a matter of principle. It led to a reduction of the autonomy of (most of) the individuals and to a redefinition of the roles of the State. In last instance, it led to a globalization of issues raised by the rise of 'private' powers and the globalization of the Power System. Business corporations have been injected into the legal system with much reluctance. But the competition among States led to this outcome which proved irresistible. This has rapidly led to dramatic changes in the legal and Power Systems. There is no doubt that there were immense benefits from the mass production and distribution they made possible. They are marvellous instruments to concentrate capital, assets, labour and all the other factors of production and to give continuity to these concentrations. But an unbalanced evolution of the Power System in which private interests came to dominate collective ones is now creating serious and potentially devastating global issues.

---

[563] *Ibid*, p. 23.

[564] *E.g.* Gerber, *op cit*, note 89, p. 33.

[565] Audier, *op cit*, note 16, p. 199. On the distinction between liberalism and capitalism, see also Giovanni Arrighi, *The Long Twentieth Century – Money, Power and the Origins of our Times*, London, New York: Verso (1994, 2006).

[566] Audier, *op cit*, note 16, pp. 282–286.

To understand how we came to this situation, we must start by distinguishing the concept of 'firm' from the one of 'corporation'. There is widespread confusion between the two terms at present and this prevents a proper understanding of the structuring of the economy, of the World Power System and of its evolution with globalization.

The concept of firm is detailed in **Chapter 6**. The chapter starts by making a sharp distinction between the concept of firm and the concept of corporation. The two words are often used as synonyms, in many different languages, but they correspond to radically different notions. The firm is an organization performing an economic activity. The corporation is a type of legal person, most firms of some significance being legally organized using business corporations. The chapter goes on to present the notion of the World Wide Web of Contracts which today connects almost everyone to almost everyone. But the nature of the contracts in this web varies significantly, pure market sale and purchase contracts being at one end of the contractual spectrum. At the other end, one finds relatively stable *clusters* of contracts. Some are the contractual substratum of business firms. The chapter goes on to analyse the legal structure of the unincorporated business firm, its position in the World Wide Web of Contracts and the notion of the firm's limits. It then explains the incorporation process and what changes when a corporation is used to legally structure a firm. The importance of the fact that the corporation is treated as a legal person having legal personality is stressed and the fact that the incorporation leads to two separate forms of property rights linked to the same assets – the property right over the *productive assets* of the corporation and the property right over the *shares of stock* issued by the corporation – is underlined. Finally, the additional fundamental features of corporations are presented: the fact that shares exist as autonomous objects of property, that the listing of shares leads to the existence of the primary and secondary markets for shares, that incorporation allows investments in illiquid assets while giving liquidity to financial investors via shares, that the incorporation leads to assets and liability partitioning, and that via the incorporation process, capital is locked in which entitles long-term investments. Finally, the shareholders' economic and political rights are reviewed, and the role of corporate officers in charge of the pursuit of the company's interests is presented.

In **Chapter 7**, we will explore further some fundamental features of business corporations. One of their key features is that business corporations have what is called 'legal personality': they are treated by the legal system as 'persons' in a position to own assets, contract and be liable for the torts which are imputed to them. Corporations can issue shares of stock which entitles them to raise equity capital. Businesses can then be developed through them. The shares are autonomous objects of property and with the development of capital markets, two separate forms of property have gained in importance: the ones owned by corporations over productive assets; and the ones owned by shareholders over shares. Both categories of *owners* are the decision-makers as a matter of principle *over what they own*: the productive assets for the corporation and the shares for the shareholders. And contrary to current folklore, shareholders do not own firms, nor corporations, nor their assets. The asset and liability partitioning deriving from the existence of the corporation as a separate legal person is a *fundamental* feature of modern capitalism. Combined with the locking in of productive assets in the ownership of the corporation, this legal structuring of businesses has concentrated residual control rights – property rights – over productive assets into the ownership of corporations. This concentration of power into the hands of firm managers raises the issue of the proper rules of governance applicable to global firms as significant participants in the World Power System. Agents of the owners of assets, they are the ones making the decisions as a matter of principle towards the use of these assets.

In **Chapter 8**, we will analyse how business corporations developed in the industrializing world in a legal environment which was initially hostile to them. Competing firms have led competing States to amend initially restrictive corporate laws to transform incorporation from a *privilege* into a *right*. Freedom of incorporation is now widely accepted. The development of corporate law has led to the advent of financial capitalism, i.e. a form of capitalism in which two forms of capital exist in connection with any given bundle of assets and contracts concentrated into any given firm structured using a corporation having issued shares of capital. There is first the capital and contracts required by the productive activity; and there is then the financial capital represented by the financial instruments issued by the corporation used to legally structure the firm. To understand the role played by financial markets, I will present the evolving relation between firms and States in a globalized economy. To do this, I will use the simple model of a firm adapting its corporate structure to the opportunities offered by the evolving legal rules in an international economy. This will lead me to further insist on the necessity to differentiate firms from corporations and to underline the importance of the rules of corporate governance in a globalized world.

In **Chapter 9**, I will address the need to cope with firms as participants to the World Power System. I will look at the issues raised by the fact that in an open economy, the competition among large firms derivatively leads to a competition among States to offer firms accommodating legal environments. This limits the States' ability to internalize negative externalities and to redistribute income. Given the defects of the State System, it is at the firm level that governmental rules must be developed so that firms consider the consequences of their activities. This issue raised by the rise of private government has been spotted early on in both the US and Europe. But the development of these schools of thought was hampered by the spread of the simplistic 'agency theory' which has led to biased firm government worldwide. Firm managers are deemed to be under a duty to maximize profits which leads to an erosion of all the States' functions in the provision of infrastructure, wealth redistribution and regulation. The bias extends to accounting rules which do not provide a fair presentation of the impact of a firm's operations over its economic and natural environment and prevents firms from adapting their practices to the requirements of today's predicament.

In **Chapter 10**, I will first present the issue of climate change and the daunting task of dealing with it in our divided World Power System within a relatively short time frame. To address this issue, created in part by our divided Power System, we must take seriously the real structure of the Power System and find the way to re-engineer multinational enterprises in a way that they consider climate change issues in their day-to-day operations. A flawed agency theory has led to improper firm governance, the maximization of shareholder short-term interests leading to a massive production of negative externalities and to accounting rules which reinforce the pressure of this inadequate mandate. The price system isn't sufficient to lead to a proper accounting of the operations of producing firms. The depletion of some forms of capital – like nature's CO_2 absorption capacity – is not accounted for because no one owns it or can sell it, and consequently there is no price for it appearing in the accounts. This can be corrected via an improvement of *accounting* rules, leading to the possibility for equity markets to properly value the shares of the corporations used to structure productive activities. We need to move to true/full-cost accounting by integrating into the accounts of reporting entities (public or private) the replacement cost of the CO_2 used in their value chains, via a life-cycle approach encompassing the impacts of products and services from their design to the sourcing of the materials used, the production, transportation, sale and then recycling and waste management. Using the notion of replacement cost prevents any attempt at *pricing* environmental services which would be subjective and/or artificial. The move allows to go beyond the sole measurement of the *financial* sustainability of firms. Firms also need to show that they are compatible with the preservation of natural resources; they need to be *environmentally* sustainable. It is the only way to preserve autonomous firms and our constitutional systems of government.

6

Firms

The concept of firm is explained in this chapter, which starts by making a sharp distinction between the concepts of 'firm' and 'corporation'. The two words are often used as synonyms, but they correspond to radically different notions. A firm is an *organization* performing an economic activity. A corporation is a type of *legal person* — most firms of some significance being organized using business corporations.

   Making the confusion between 'firm' and 'corporation' in ordinary, everyday language is not a major issue. But when one addresses issues of governance, it becomes highly problematic. In the analysis of the World Power System, the confusion prevents any proper reasoning.

6.1 The Need to Differentiate Firms from Corporations

Multinational firms have played, and most likely will continue to play, a fundamental role in the evolution of the World Power System. The very existence of large, formally *private* organizations having concentrated property rights means that the State does not monopolize collective power in society, be it at the national or international level.[567] Property rights being rights of decision-making as a matter of principle, their concentration under firm management has brought vast amounts of decision-making power into these organizations. What these organizations are, however, is vastly misunderstood. This prevents understanding the operation of the World Power System: as explained by John Gerard

---

[567] Sciuli, *op cit*, note 506, p. 16.

Ruggie, a current and systematic political analysis of the multinational enterprise in the context of global governance is missing.[568]

A first issue to understand precisely the position of firms in the World Power System is that there is a widespread confusion in the literature on economic organizations between the concepts of 'corporation' and 'firm'. The two words are often used interchangeably, 'company' or 'enterprise' being also sometimes used as synonyms. Before her untimely death, Lynn Stout made me the great honour of agreeing that 'the careless but unfortunately common habit of treating them as synonyms confuses and misleads'.[569] And the fact is that the consequences of this linguistic and conceptual confusion are extraordinary.[570] They are a major hindrance for

---

[568] John Gerard Ruggie, 'The Multinational as Global Institution: Power, Authority and Relative Autonomy', *Regulation & Governance*, pp. 1–17 (2017).

[569] Lynn A. Stout, *Corporate Entities: Their Ownership, Control, and Purpose*, Cornell Law School Research Paper No 16–38 (2017), referring to my insistence to differentiate both. *See also* Stephen Bottomley, *The Constitutional Corporation – Rethinking Corporate Governance*, Aldershot: Ashgate (2007), p. 27.

[570] On the difficulty of convincing authors that it is fruitful to differentiate the two terms, *see* Deakin, Gindis, Hodgson, Huang and Pistor, *op cit*, note 80, pp. 194–198. They prefer the word 'firm' to 'apply to individuals or organizations with the legally recognized capacity to produce goods or services for sale'. As a consequence, with their definition, an individual person can be 'a firm'. But it also means, as a consequence, that, the firm being 'a singular legal entity', there can be no 'multinational firms' since a multinational firm is not a 'legal entity'. And also, since they take the firm as being synonymous with the concept of 'legal entity', employees are not part of 'firms'. They just contract with 'the firm'. This is quite a strange consequence of this definition, and one can then question its wisdom. I do not see any interest in using this terminology, which just adds to the confusion. In their parlance, 'a firm' is a legal person (individual, partnership, corporation, etc). It is a misleading use of the word. A firm certainly needs one or several legal persons to exist as an organization; it needs to be legally structured using either the legal personality of an individual or of a partnership or of a corporation, or several of these legal persons in combination. The firm is the 'organized economic activity' (not just the 'activity' as indicated in their footnote #6 discussing my own work, where they do not mention my reference to the concept of '*organized* economic activity' which is the one I am using and which should be discussed) which will exist as a consequence of the structuring of exchange relationships around these legal persons. There can then be multinational firms, and employees are, of course, members of firms. And the main issues deriving from the fact that the firm does not have legal personality (while it can operate via the legal personality of individuals or partnerships or corporations) are left to be resolved, whereas the terminology proposed by Deakin *et al.* makes them disappear *from the vocabulary*. But they are still with us, *in reality*. Deakin *et al.*, on the contrary, think that the 'puzzles concerning the nature and identity of the firm are solved once we recognize it as a legal entity' (*see* p. 197). But the puzzles are only apparently solved

an understanding of the modern Power System and of the institutional structure of economic activity generally. This may also explain why the economic theory of the firm has not made much progress over the last 30 years or so. Economists, disregarding the *legal* structure of the firm, are unable to agree on what a firm is.[571] Ignoring the legal structure of the firm leads them to confuse the notions of 'firm' and 'corporation' and to develop their analyses using concepts which are not suited to the economic system as it effectively exists. What we experience is a bit like witnessing apprentice biologists discussing the functioning of a living organism, saying that it is made of 'atoms', by which sometimes they really mean 'atoms', and sometimes they mean 'cells', even sometimes 'organs'. My point is that they would be better off differentiating atoms, organs and cells. They may want to disregard the advice and continue the confusion, sometimes calling a cell an atom, sometimes calling an atom an atom or an organ, sometimes calling an atom a cell, and so on. Or they can say that at the end of the day, it's all really just atoms. In doing so, our biologists/economists will keep on having a hard time bringing anything useful to the understanding of *life* (or the *real-life economy*) – which they are entirely free to accept and go on with their amusing discussion.[572] But the brain surgeon in the operating room is still facing an organ, made of cells, and has little immediate interest in being reminded that the whole thing is really just atoms. And the patient cares even less.

There is no doubt that the legal language is technical and not easily accessible by non-specialists.[573] But real-life business people make the effort and must do so if they want to survive in the real-life economy. Why should those who make it a profession to study and, presumably, improve

---

because the firm as an economic organization goes way beyond its legal structure, including the legal person(s) used to legally structure it in legal reality. But the firm is still there as a reality to be understood ... Interestingly, in Hodgson's otherwise excellent book on *Conceptualizing Capitalism*, the index has no entry for 'groups of companies' or 'groups of corporations' or 'multinationals'. But of course, these key concepts of present-day capitalism can't be addressed if one makes the confusion between the firm and the legal persons (of various kinds – individuals, partnerships, corporations, etc.) used to structure them; Hodgson, *op cit*, note 80, pp. 477, 481 & 487. And Hodgson insists on treating the firm as a legal person; *ibid*, pp. 204–206.

[571] Hodgson, *op cit*, note 33, p. 10.

[572] Put slightly differently, it is as if physicists denied the usefulness of chemists studying atoms, the importance of biologists studying cells and organs and the relevance of having medicine. Which would be fine if they remained in their field as physicists and did not pretend to be doctors.

[573] Simon Deakin, 'Tony Lawson's Theory of the Corporation: Towards a Social Ontology of Law', 41 *Cambridge Journal of Economics*, pp. 1505–1523 (2017), p. 1515.

the operation of the economy be exempted from making the same effort? Of course, 'no single discipline has a monopoly of terms used in general language'.[574] But the issue is not to correct the *general language* which is full of confusion and imprecisions. In their everyday discussions, people can do whatever they want and can confuse firms and corporations, cells and atoms. It is of limited consequence. The issue we must deal with is to address the way *professional* economists and other social scientists use the words 'firm' and 'corporation' as synonyms in their *specialized language*. One of the proper functions of science is to take concepts from our everyday language and clarify them in such a way that they become suitable instruments of scientific communication. And confusing 'firm' and 'corporation' is a killer for anyone having the ambition to develop a scientific analysis of the phenomenon (firm or corporation) observed. Business people, of course, also often make use of the ordinary language and say that they are selling *their* company or that they own *their* firm. But when they hire professionals to accompany them in the process, what they are offered to review are draft 'Share Sale and Purchase Agreements'. No one has ever seen a '*Company* Sale and Purchase Agreement' nor a '*Firm* Sale and Purchase Agreement' because neither the firm nor the corporation (or company) are objects of property. They therefore can't be purchased or sold, or leased or given, i.e. they do not *exist* in real *economic life* as objects of property which can be bought or sold for a price. I do contend that *this* is a major obstacle for any social scientist, including *professional economists*, to understand and explain the operation of economic reality. Many issues met in the understanding of the real-life economic system are in part due to this lack of clarity in the use of the *specialized* language describing the objects of real-life economic and legal transactions. With a more accurate use of the *specialized language* applicable to property rights, contracts, corporations and firms, in particular, a good part of what is taken for granted today by most mainstream economists would lose value. But TINA: There Is No Alternative. It is impossible to build a *science* on the basis of the *general language*. And the specialized language of real-life economic transactions is the legal language. As the 1991 economics Nobel prizewinner Ronald Coase wrote:

> The degree to which economics is isolated from the ordinary business life is extraordinary and unfortunate. ...
> It requires an intricate web of social institutions to coordinate the working of market and firms across various boundaries. At a time when the modern economy is becoming increasingly

---

[574] *Ibid*, p. 1510.

institutions-intensive, the reduction of economics to price theory is troubling enough. ...

Knowledge will come only if economics can be reoriented to ... the economic system as it actually exists.[575]

In a first approximation, the *firm* is an *organization performing an economic activity*: the firm is the process of coordinating various resource providers via the firm management through which goods are produced or services are delivered. The *corporation* is a form of *legal person* which can be used to legally structure firms. As a legal vehicle, the corporation has very peculiar features which we will review later, but a firm can be created without having recourse to a corporation.

A firm can be created by a single individual person. It is then a 'proprietorship' in which an individual legal person contracts with suppliers of raw materials, of machines and employees – supplying labour – for example, and will organize the manufacturing of products or the delivery of services to be sold to clients. This organized activity is 'a firm'. The individual organizing the operation of this economic activity is not 'the firm'. The organized economic activity is.[576] To operate, the firm *needs* to be organized via a legal person. There is no alternative. Otherwise, property rights can't be owned, and enforceable contracts can't be signed. Employees can't be hired, supplies can't be purchased, and nothing can be sold to prospective clients. But the *legal person* to be used as the counterparty to the suppliers of inputs and purchasers of outputs can be an *individual* person. It does not necessarily have to be a partnership or a corporation. The firm is an *economic organization*; the partnership or corporation is only one of the numerous *legal tools* which can be used to legally structure firms, to make them exist in the real-life legal and economic systems. Traditional economic analysis, obsessed with its view of 'the market' as the main medium of economic exchange, has prevented a proper understanding of firms as an alternative arrangement to the market. This alternative to market exchange – intrafirm exchange – is legally built using property rights, contracts and legal persons who can be individuals, partnerships or corporations.

When corporations are used, however, the impact on the firm management and on the firm's social and natural environments can

---

[575] Ronald H. Coase, 'Saving Economics from the Economists', *Harvard Business Review* (December) p. 36 (2012).

[576] On this, *see also* Romano, *op cit*, note 257, and Massimo Severo Giannini, 'Gli elementi degli ordinamenti giuridici', 8 *Rivista trimestriale di diritto pubblico*, pp. 219–240 (1958), pp. 230–231.

be very significant. This is particularly the case now that their use is widespread in firms operating on a worldwide basis. The combined effect of their mode of operation has fundamentally changed the operation of the World Power System.

The reader will note that my starting point is not the 'transaction', as is the case in most institutional economics. Like Alfred Chandler, the great business economic historian, I am convinced that the unit of analysis must be the firm.[577] And so agreed Ronald Coase, who was surprised by the lack of importance given to the firm in mainstream economics:

> The firm in mainstream economic theory has often been described as a 'black box'. And so it is. This is very extraordinary given that most resources in a modern economic system are employed within firms, with how these resources are used depend on administrative decisions and not directly on the operation of a market. Consequently, the efficiency of the economic system depends to a very considerable extent on how these organizations conduct their affairs, particularly, of course, the modern corporation.[578]

But to proceed with this analysis, it is an absolute requirement to make the difference between the firm and the corporation – a distinction Coase clearly was not making since he is using both terms as synonyms in the above citation. Firms can exist without having recourse to corporations. By combining the understanding of the firm as an economic organization and of the corporation as a type of legal person used to own key property rights used in its operations, one can explain why the firm has been the instrument in capitalist economies for carrying and propelling economic growth and transformation. As I will progressively show, with the issues presented by globalization, an understanding of the firm is a prerequisite for developing the policies, procedures and accounting rules required to address them.

To understand the role of firms in the World Power System, a good starting point is to perceive the legal structure of the global economy as a World Wide Web of Contracts. We have seen what property rights are. Now we must understand how property rights owners are connected with other legal persons not only via property rights but also via contracts. Then we will see what the introduction of the business corporation changes.

---

[577] Alfred D. Chandler, 'Organizational Capabilities and the Economic History of the Industrial Enterprise', 6(3) *Journal of Economic Perspectives*, pp. 79–100 (1992), p. 99.
[578] Coase, *op cit*, note 81, p. 714.

6.2 The World Wide Web of Contracts

For Henry Sumner Maine, writing in 1861, the movement from ancient to modern society was a movement from 'status' to 'contracts'.[579] Historically, the law of persons was the law of status: the notions of slave, serf, servant, ward, infant, wife, cleric, king and so on all corresponded to *statuses* recognized by law. They each clothed the individual with salient disabilities or privileges.[580] Each one was connected via his or her birth, his or her place of abode or profession to *groups* which determined his or her place in society.

With modernity, the hierarchical and status-based organization of society was erased and gave way to the notion of equal status of all individual persons. The remaining categories of incapacity (affecting minors, women and the physically and psychologically unable, in particular) were not viewed as types of *statuses* but as *exceptions* to the general rule of general capacity.[581]

The preamble of the French Constitution of 1791 presented to the King by the National Assembly on 3 September 1791, immediately follows the reiteration of the 1789 Declaration of the Rights of Man and Citizen.[582] It states:

> The National Assembly, wishing to establish the French Constitution upon the principles that it has just recognized and declared [those of the 1789 Declaration of the Rights of Man and Citizen], abolishes irrevocably the institutions that have injured liberty and the equality of rights.
>
> There is no longer nobility, nor peerage, nor hereditary distinctions, nor distinction of orders, nor feudal régime, nor patrimonial jurisdictions, nor any titles, denominations or prerogatives derived therefrom, nor any order of chivalry, nor any corporations or decorations which demanded proofs of nobility or that were grounded upon distinctions of birth, nor any superiority other than that of public officials in the exercise of their functions.
>
> There is no longer either sale or inheritance of any public office.

---

[579] Maine, *op cit*, note 130.

[580] *E.g.* Selznick, *op cit*, note 112, p. 62.

[581] Deakin and Supiot, *op cit*, note 182, p. 3.

[582] *See* Assemblée Nationale, *Constitution française, présentée au Roi par l'Assemblée Nationale le 3 septembre 1791*, Dijon: Imprimerie P. Causse (1791).

> There is no longer for any part of the nation nor for any individual any privilege or exception to the law that is common to all Frenchmen.[583]

All the differences of the *Ancien Régime* statuses were thus ironed out by these new constitutional provisions which further stated the equality in rights of all in society. And, furthermore, the last sentence of the Title I of the 1791 Constitution (providing for the *Fundamental Provisions Guaranteed by the Constitution*) ends with the sentence: 'A code of civil laws common to all the kingdom shall be made.'[584] It is the announcement of the Civil Code which will eventually be enacted in 1804.[585] According to the most astute commentators, it is nothing less than 'the civil constitution of the French people'.[586] But beyond any comment, this is what the text of the 1791 Constitution states in plain words: a body of civil laws common to all is one of the *Fundamental Provisions Guaranteed by the Constitution*.

By abolishing all 'the institutions that have injured liberty and the equality of rights', France implemented the movement identified by Maine from 'status to contracts' in the most radical manner. But, as we know now, the move was also a move from 'status' to '*property* and contracts'. It was a move from a heteronomous organization of society via innumerous corpuses with countless collective properties to an autonomous creation of society via the use of property and contracts by individuals. The two changes are interlinked: it is because we, as legally equal individuals, have rights (including this specific right of autonomy we call *property*) that we are all *contracting* individual persons.

In the traditional liberal view, property created relationships between individuals and the things they owned. Contracts, in turn, created voluntary relationships between otherwise equal legal persons. Both sets of relationships clearly belonged to the private sphere.[587] For others, property is really a relationship among people, and property rights bestow on owners powers over others with respect to the objects of property. For early socialists, 'property' was simply 'power' and had to be restricted. But for many commentators, like Bentham, for example, although the existing scheme of private property and contracts effectively constrained liberty for

---

[583] *Ibid*, p. 6.

[584] *Ibid*, p. 9.

[585] On the history of the Civil Code, *see generally* Jean-Louis Halpérin, *Histoire du droit privé français depuis 1804*, Paris: Presses Universitaires de France (1996, 2001).

[586] *See* Section 5.1.

[587] Supiot, *op cit*, note 342, p. 326.

non–owners, any attempt by the State to rearrange rights would merely substitute one form of constraint for another.[588]

Notwithstanding the differences in interpretation, society became contractualized when the proportion of *prescribed* bonds within society declined in favour of *agreed* bonds; when *heteronomy* gave way to *autonomy*.[589] And thanks to the principle of freedom of contracts, we began to be, and are still to a large extent, inserted within society via a cluster of contracts surrounding us and connecting us to our contracting parties.

The move from status to contract (and property) took different paths in different jurisdictions. In France, it took a revolution, the 1789 Declaration of the Rights of Man and Citizen, the assertion of the freedom of commerce and industry by the Statute of 2–17 March 1791 and the adoption of the Civil Code in 1804 to create a unified private legal system over the whole of France. Not only did the legislator declare broad principles; mandatory intermediary groupings were all destroyed. Free associations were also banned just three months later. A corporate social order, with a long history, was erased by the full power of the law. The free and sacred right to individual property, and the free contract having the status of private statutes among private parties, came to be the two legal instruments granted to make it possible to create a new order. It was based on individual autonomy, freedom of contracts and property rights. Henceforth, the equal individual disposes of whatever capital he has accumulated or borrowed; he trades as he pleases, produces as he pleases and sells the products freely; and he can procure himself by contract the work of others.[590]

In England, it was via the Common Law that the country became individualistic by progressively abolishing a body of institutions that stood in the way of economic change. In 1800, the law of contracts was a relatively minor field of law. Most of the relationships we would now characterize as contractual were governed by specialized bodies of law in which compulsory, status-based terms figured prominently. The assertion of freedom of contract and of the law of property in the modern sense were the best instruments at hand to change the mode of organization of society, to move from heteronomy to autonomy.

By 1900, English contract law had moved from a position of obscurity to become the centrepiece of private law. Employment relations which had long been regulated by the law of 'master and servant' were now

---

[588] *See generally* Fried, *op cit*, note 197, in particular pp. 50–53.

[589] *See ibid*, p. 50.

[590] *Ibid. See generally*, Blaufarb, *op cit*, note 14.

governed by the same principles as those used to rule the sale of goods.[591] But when the liberal ideals of contract and equality swept the old common law of 'master and servant', they also diminished law's ability to grasp the reality of power inequality in the wage relationship. Contractual freedom affirmed *equality* but laid the foundation for unregulated *subordination*. With the advent of the liberal contract among formally equal parties, the legal control over property actually became the control of other human beings by human beings. Property rights assumed a new social function. Without any change in the norms applicable to it, below the threshold of collective consciousness, a de facto right was added to the absolute personal domination over things. This right was not founded in any special legal provision any more. It was not a privilege. It came from the power to control, issue commands and implement them which the owner has in connection with the use of his property.[592]

Via the means provided by contract law and the subsequent globalization of the economy, we are now all participants to what can be called the World Wide Web of Contracts. When we buy a piece of bread at the bakery, the bread we purchase is the outcome of actions performed within the bakery and outside it by its suppliers because of the contractual interactions among numerous parties. The owner/operator of the bakery is legally connected to the employees working in the bakery pursuant to employment contracts. The same owner/operator is contractually linked to the suppliers of flour, water, salt, sugar, butter, electricity and so on, needed to produce the goods offered for sale at the bakery. For many of the inputs used in the production of the bakery, they arrive at the bakery at the end of long chains of contracts among other owners, employees and suppliers, and so on.

The set of contracts leading to the possibility to buy a piece of bread at the bakery is nothing in comparison with the networks of contracts leading to the production and distribution of complex products such as computers or cars. But what unites us all is that all these sets of contracts connecting legal persons (individuals, partnerships and corporations) are part of the World Wide Web of Contracts. This World Wide Web of Contracts is like the skeleton of a gigantic and living network, constantly evolving, used to serve as the conduit of the production and distribution of products and services and of the compensations paid for them. And via the World Wide Web of Contracts, the impoverishment of a neighbourhood in Pittsburgh can be connected to the growing prosperity of an urban area in Singapore or the decisions made in the boardroom of

---

[591] *E.g.* Fisher, Horwitz and Reed, *op cit*, note 41, p. 76.

[592] *E.g.* Nonet and Selznick, *op cit*, note 32, p. 44.

a Korean electronics company in Seoul can be vital to the prosperity of communities in the Neath Valley in South Wales.[593] Globalization is very much connected to the development and increased density of this web of contracts and those operating in it, i.e. all of us, although at different scales depending upon our means. As the Group of Lisbon put it in 1995, globalization is the result of the many links and interconnections that unite States and societies and help shape the present global system.[594] The World Wide Web of Contracts describes all the exchanges and processes via which events, decisions and activities that occur in one part of the world end up having significant repercussions on individuals and communities living far away.

But the World Wide Web of Contracts is not a seamless network of horizontal, equal, contractual relationships. It is a legal structure built by legal persons resulting from their contracting activity to put in place the legal conduits of economic exchanges. But the various conduits can vary significantly one from another.

6.3 Contracts and Stable Exchange

The contracts in the World Wide Web of Contracts vary considerably in content. Some are pure sale and purchase contracts: a product is sold and purchased instantaneously for a price. A property right is exchanged immediately against payment of a price – money. There is no ongoing relationship deriving from this kind of contracts. And most of the people on the planet do not even realize that these operations are contracts. We have what resembles most a pure market transaction. Or, as Philip Selznick puts it, the purposive contract is the characteristic legal institution of a market economy. It is made to complete a specific transaction, or to further a discrete objective. Only a tenuous and temporary association is created; open-ended obligations are alien to its nature.[595]

These contracts are numerous – probably the most numerous ones. All of us, in our daily lives, are parties to several such contracts: when we buy bread at the bakery, petrol at the station, our newspaper at the stand. It means *billions* of these contracts are concluded daily in the world economy.

---

[593] Giddens, *op cit*, note 169; Anthony McGrew, 'Globalization beyond borders? Globalization and the reconstruction of democratic theory and politics', in McGrew, *op cit*, note 526, pp. 231–266.

[594] Groupe de Lisbonne, *Limites à la concurrence – pour un nouveau contrat mondial*, Lisbonne: Fondation Gulbenkian; Paris: La découverte (1995), p. 60.

[595] Selznick, *op cit*, note 112, p. 54.

But the pure market transaction is just one extreme of the spectrum of economic exchange. It can only play a very limited role and a very specialized function in any economy, even in a so-called 'market economy'.[596] There are many other types of contracts in the economy. The most interesting contracts serving as a conduit for economic exchange are probably those having *duration*. They connect contracting parties *through time*. A lease connects a landlord and a tenant *through time*; a distribution contract connects a manufacturer and a distributor *through time*; an employment contract connects an employer and an employee *through time*; and so on. In the bakery, the baker is connected to the owner of the premises via a lease. He is connected to the suppliers whose inputs are needed to operate the bakery by long-term supply contracts providing for preferential pricing clauses if he buys significant quantities of input. He is contractually linked to employees operating the equipment in the bakery via employment contracts; and so on. The baker can then sell bread and his other products thanks to the series of contracts he negotiated, having duration, somehow interconnected and having a relative stability enhancing the baker's ability to predict his costs of production and to set his prices to make a profit.

Whereas the pure market sale and purchase transaction is one extreme of economic exchange in the World Wide Web of Contracts given its lack of duration, at the other extreme, there are what can be described as *clusters of contracts* having duration, *interconnected*, serving as the legal conduits of *continuous economic exchanges* among *numerous parties* participating to the organizations existing because of the performance of these contracts.[597]

These clusters of contracts and their interconnectedness is what explains the relative stability of our society. Of course, the clusters of contracts change and evolve. We sometimes change job, move to a different location which means that the cluster of contracts in which we are inserted will be evolving. But people change jobs and homes seldom and the sub-part in the overall World Wide Web of Contracts made up of contracts having duration is relatively stable.[598]

---

[596] Ian R. MacNeil, 'Relational Contracts: What We Do and Do Not Know', *Wisconsin Law Review*, pp. 483–526 (1985), pp. 485–487.

[597] For a detailed study based on a real-life analysis of the contracts used to legally structure Alcan in Canada, *see* Jean-Guy Belley, *Le contrat entre droit, économie et société*, Québec: Les éditions Yvon Blais Inc. (1998). On the specificities of relational contracts, *see* notably Ian R. MacNeil, 'Economic Analysis of Contractual Relations', in P. Burrows and C.G. Veljanowski (eds.) *The Economic Approach to Law*, London: Butterworths (1981).

[598] Niklas Luhmann, *Observations on Modernity*, Stanford: Stanford University Press (1998), p. 20.

The relative stable existence of clusters of contracts allows the operation of *organizations*. Some of the clusters of contracts allow the existence of 'households'.[599] Others allow the existence of 'firms'. The reader should note immediately that the households and firms are *not* clusters of contracts. The clusters of contracts are only part of what they require to exist, to *sustain* them in a society in which the medium of exchange relationships is defined by the legal system.

In this book, I concentrate on these organizations we call firms.[600]

6.4 Firms

As we have seen, it is very important to differentiate the concept of 'firm' from that of 'corporation'. It is *impossible* to organize a firm without having recourse to at least one *legal person*. A legal vehicle is needed to *own* at least some of the assets used in the operation of the firm and to *conclude* the contracts with suppliers (providers of inputs) and clients (purchasers of outputs). But the legal vehicle can be an *individual*. It does not need to be a corporation. Firms and corporations are *therefore necessarily different concepts*, unless one refuses to qualify as being a 'firm' the business created by an individual entrepreneur not using a separate legal vehicle to structure his business. To measure the legal complexities created by the introduction of business corporations into the legal system, into firm management and into the Power System, one must start by analysing the relationship between an individual entrepreneur and the firm he creates and operates, in case *no* corporate legal person is being used to legally structure the firm. Starting with the legal structure of a firm created and operated by an individual person *without* having recourse to a partnership, a limited liability partnership or a corporation will help us

---

[599] 'The household is a nonmarket coordinator surrounded by market coordination'; Charles E. Lindblom, *The Market System – What It Is, How It Works, and What to Make of It*, New Haven and London: Yale University Press (2001), p. 102. Sub-parts of some households happen to also be businesses and, actually, 90% of the world's businesses are family businesses. Most of them are very small: e.g. the shop around the corner. But there are some very large family enterprises. In Hong Kong, the top 15 families control assets worth 84% of the country's GDP; in Malaysia, it is 76%, 48% in Singapore and 47% in the Philippines. *See The Economist*, 18 April 2015, Special Report, p. 4.

[600] A close version of this argument can be found in Jean-Philippe Robé, 'Conflicting Sovereignties in the World Wide Web of Contracts – Property Rights and the Globalization of the Power System', in Graf-Peter Calliess, Andreas Fischer-Lescano, Dan Wielsch and Peer Zumbansen (eds.), *Soziologische Jurisprudenz, Festschrift für Gunther Teubner*, Berlin: De Gruyter Recht (2009), pp. 691–703.

appreciate what happens when a corporation is used to legally structure the firm.

In conducting this analysis, I will do *exactly* what Milton Friedman (1976 economics Nobel prizewinner) did *not* do in his famous 1970 article titled 'The Social Responsibility of Business is to Increase its Profits'.[601] This short article is very important because it triggered the development of a school of thought named 'agency theory'.[602] This theory is flawed beyond repair because it disregards the reality of the legal structure of real-life business firms while pretending that it is built on it. And it was the case from the start. Milton Friedman completely disregarded the legal structure of the firm, dealing with it as if it were a *proprietorship*, while taking care to write that he was dealing in his article with the duties of the directors of large *corporations*.[603] This was a fundamental error and has led to dramatic misunderstandings about the proper rules of governance of business firms legally structured using *corporations*.[604] Most contemporary issues raised by improper rules of firm management, especially at the global level, can be traced to this erroneous idea – the idea that firms are managed well when they are managed to maximize short-term profits.[605]

6.5 The Unincorporated Business

As a starting point, we will look at the case of an individual entrepreneur owning a factory. To operate the factory, she executes a series of bilateral contracts with other owners owning the assets she needs for production to take place. It can be, for example, pieces of machinery or materials or supplies to be used in the production process. She will also need a workforce to operate the factory and, to be able to organize the activities of the workforce, she executes employment contracts with employees. Then, at some point, the pieces of machinery are installed in the factory and the materials and supplies are delivered. The employees arrive at the factory and production starts. From now on, the *firm* does exist. The entrepreneur pays the price of the materials purchased and the salaries of

---

[601] Milton Friedman, 'The Social Responsibility of Business is to Increase its Profits', *The New York Times*, 13 September 1970, pp. 32–33, 122 & 126.

[602] Hart and Zingales, *op cit*, note 319, p. 2.

[603] *See* Robé, *op cit*, note 158.

[604] *See* Lynn A. Stout, *The Shareholder Value Myth – How Putting Shareholders First Harms Investors, Corporations and the Public*, BK Business Books (2012); Jean-Philippe Robé, 'Science v. Ideology: A Comment on Lynn Stout's New Thinking on "Shareholder Primacy"', *Accounting, Economics, and Law: A Convivium*, Vol. 2, Issue 2, Article 7 (2012).

[605] *E.g.* Lynn A. Stout, *op cit*, note 604, p. 11.

the employees producing the goods using these materials in the factory under her direction. She will sell the goods for a price. She will make profits or losses.

The firm is *not* a bundle of assets.[606] How would these assets be 'bundled' together without something in addition to the assets? Adolph Berle expressed it clearly: without the entire organization of personnel 'the physical plant would be junk'.[607] And this organization is made possible via the content of property rights and of contracts.

The firm is *not* a nexus of contracts.[608] How would the contracts work together without being indirectly connected *via a legal person* – an individual, a partnership or a corporation – having concluded them? A contract cannot be a party to another contract: only legal persons can contract. Treating the firm as a 'nexus of contracts' eliminates the complex issue of what changes when the *legal person* concluding the contracts *is not* an *individual* entrepreneur any more but a fiction of the law: *a corporation*.

And the firm is *not* merely a team.[609] What would any team do without the assets required for the production and the contracts determining who does what in the team and for what consideration? Plus, the notion of team takes away the superior position of the owner of the productive assets in the organization of the team's work. And as we know, this superior position derives from his right of decision- and rule-making as a matter of principle.

---

[606] *See* Grossman and Hart, *op cit*, note 219 (they 'define a firm to consist of those assets that it owns and over which it has control'; *see* p. 693), and Hart and Moore, *op cit*, note 219.

[607] Berle, *op cit*, note 24, p. 6.

[608] For Fama, '[t]he firm is just the set of contracts covering the way inputs are joined to create outputs and the way receipts from outputs are shared among inputs'; Eugene F. Fama, 'Agency Problems and the Theory of the Firm', 88(2) *Journal of Political Economy*, pp. 288–307 (1980), p. 290; for Fama and Jensen, 'an organization is the nexus of contracts, written and unwritten, among owners of factors of production and customers'; Eugene F. Fama and Michael C. Jensen, 'Separation of Ownership and Control', 26(2) *Journal of Law & Economics*, pp. 301–325 (1983), p. 302. *See also* Harold Demsetz, 'The Theory of the Firm Revisited', 4(1) *Journal of Law, Economics and Organization*, pp. 141–161 (1988). As noted by Zingales, one of the major shortcomings of this approach is that it is unable to explain why firms merge at all. If the firm is simply a collection of contracts, the results achieved through a merger could be more simply obtained by writing a contract combining the two separate firms. *See* Luigi Zingales, 'In Search of New Foundations', 55(4) *Journal of Finance*, pp. 1623–1653 (2000), p. 1637.

[609] *See* Alchian and Demsetz, *op cit*, note 173.

The firm is the organized economic activity existing because of the cluster of contracts executed to operate the factory, connecting via the entrepreneur the resources providers needed to produce the goods or services and the purchasers of the goods or services. There is a widespread temptation to view it as an 'entity' comprising the assets and the individuals using them in the pursuit of the firm's activity. It is a convenience; but this convenience is to be avoided. This 'entity' has no legal personality, we do not know where to put its limits and the use of the word is misleading in making believe that the 'entity' has a legal existence of its own in the legal system. It is better to do without it.[610]

The firm is *not* a legal person. 'Legal personality' is a creation of the law and the firm has no legal personality under the law. The legal person owning the property rights over the key assets used for the operation of the firm, having concluded all the contracts required for the operation of these assets and bearing the consequences (positive or negative) of the operation of the firm is – in our example so far – the individual entrepreneur who has legal personality and owns the factory. The organized economic activity – the firm – is not a legal person and will not bear any of these consequences in a legal sense. The firm can be successful and grow; or it can be a failure and disappear. But the legal consequences in terms of profits or losses will be borne by the individual entrepreneur.

As a matter of illustration, if the products produced by those who work in the firm are defective, the individual entrepreneur is the legal person who will be sued by the purchasers of the products. As the legal person having executed the sales' contracts, owning the assets and selling the production, she will be the legal person potentially liable for any defective product or accident taking place in connection with the firm's activities. If the business is unsuccessful to a point that the individual entrepreneur cannot sustain the losses, she is the one who will become bankrupt, with her assets sold to compensate the affected parties in compliance with the rules of bankruptcy law. If the business is successful, she is the one who will pocket the profits, pay the corresponding taxes and enjoy the remainder. As the owner of the key assets used in the operation of the firms and of the production sold, she has the authority to decide, as a matter of principle, what to produce, the quality level of the production and she will bear the consequences, positive or negative, of her decisions. She has unlimited liability for her mistakes, errors, lack of judgement,

---

[610] On this issue, *see also* Deakin, *op cit*, note 573. One exception to the inexistence of this entity in positive law is in antitrust law which, to address its specific remit, treats the group of companies as a single economic actor.

faults, lack of luck and so on – and she will profit without limits from her chance, intelligence, shrewdness, hard work and so on.

6.6 The Firm in the World Wide Web of Contracts

Some economists deny that the concept of firm has any meaning. Steven Cheung, for example, considers that 'the truth is that according to one's view, a "firm" may well be as small as a contractual relationship between two input owners or, if the chain of contracts is allowed to spread, as big as the whole economy. ... Thus, it is futile to press the issue of what is or is not a firm'.[611]

The 'chain of contracts' is indeed as large as the world economy. As we have seen, all economic exchanges in the whole world economy can be analysed as a web of contracts relating to the allocation and use of resources. This is what I call the World Wide Web of Contracts.[612] But the World Wide Web of Contracts is not a 'firm'. Many of the contracts in the World Wide Web of Contracts are pure quid pro quo, purchase and sale contracts connecting property rights owners in the world economy for an instant only. When there is an isolated act of purchase and sale, no continuing association, where buyer and seller accept no obligation with respect to their future conduct, we probably have what approximates most to the pure market transaction of the classical economists.[613] No relationship is involved.

But the pure market transaction is just one *extreme* of the spectrum of economic exchange: ownership of something is instantaneously exchanged against immediate payment of a price. Two property rights are instantaneously exchanged.

At the other extreme in the structure of the World Wide Web of Contracts, there are *clusters* of contracts having duration connected in such a way as to give *power* to those in control of these clusters over the organization created thanks to the cluster. As a matter of example, one such cluster allows operating the firm we call 'Microsoft'; and another one allows operating the firm called 'Toyota'. All the firms in the world are all interconnected via the World Wide Web of Contracts – something

---

[611] Steven N. Cheung, 'The Contractual Nature of the Firm', 26(1) *Journal of Law and Economics*, pp. 1–21 (1983), pp. 17–18.

[612] *See* Robé, *op cit*, note 600. For Charles Lindblom, 'The market system is not a place but a web'; in Lindblom, *op cit*, note 599, p. 40.

[613] *See* G.B. Richardson, *The Organization of Industry*, 82 Economic Journal, pp. 883–896 (1972), p. 886.

many would call 'the market'. But their interconnection does not make of all of them *one single firm* as Cheung would have it. The world economy is not a firm. It is made of pure sale and purchase contracts *and* of an evolving set of firms which are legally structured using semi-autonomous clusters of contracts having duration and allowing the exercise of *power* – via these contracts and the property rights owned – over the participants in these firms. The source of their power lies in what property is: a right of decision- and rule-making in connection with the objects of property as a matter of principle. The owner of the productive assets decides how they are to be used, by who, for how much, where and so on – as a matter of principle. The sets of property rights controlled in this fashion by the organizations coordinating the production of goods or the delivery of services are autonomous. One *bundle* of contracts connecting a series of contributors to the corporate structure of one specific firm allows the operation of 'Microsoft'; and another one allows the operation of 'Toyota' as a separate organization from Microsoft and any other firm. These semi-autonomous sub-parts of the World Wide Web of Contracts and of the World Power System have loose boundaries. The cluster of contracts connecting the property rights over which the authority of the firm is being exercised does not end abruptly like the limits of a State's territory. Authority is stronger over, say, the employees than over franchisees, for example. But if the limits to the effectiveness of the authority exercised within a firm and allowing it to operate as an organization are not always clear cut, at their *core*, firms operate via legal instruments allowing them to issue *orders* and exercise *authority*. Instantaneous 'horizontal' market transactions among equals are at the opposite end of the spectrum of economic transactions and do not create 'firms'.[614]

Ronald Coase already acknowledged in his 1937 article 'The Nature of the Firm' that this 'nature' is the ability to give orders. He later acknowledged that his 1937 study was incomplete and should have been extended to include all 'the contracts that enable the organizers of the firms to *direct* the use of capital (equipment or money) by acquiring, leasing, or borrowing' [emphasis added].[615] In Coase's mind, what is important in a firm is the ability to *direct* resources: be it employees

---

[614] *See also* Yuri Biondi, *The Firm as an Entity: Management, Organization, Accounting*, Università degli Studi di Bescia, Dipartimento di Economia Aziendale, Paper no 46, August (2005), p. 33, available at http://ssrn.com/abstract=774764.

[615] *See* Ronald H. Coase, 'The Nature of the Firm – Influence', in Oliver E. Williamson and Sidney G. Winter (eds.), *The Nature of the Firm – Origins, Evolution, and Development*, Oxford: Oxford University Press (1993), pp. 61–74, at p. 65. Coase considers the main weakness of his groundbreaking article as giving an incomplete picture of the nature of the firm by using the employer–employee relationship as the

or capital. This is unfortunately often ignored although it shades an interesting light on what Coase was after in 'The Nature of the Firm'. What Coase called the ability to 'direct the use of capital' is what I call the ability to make decisions as a matter of principle thanks to the ownership of property rights over objects of property or to the contracts transferring part of this authority over employees. The firm is an organization in which the ability to give orders to employees is very important for its existence. Or, in Elizabeth Anderson's words, the boundary of the firm is defined as the point at which markets end and authoritarian direction begins inside a firm.[616] But the organizational dimension of the business firm goes well beyond this.

One can take as examples three very different real-life global firms:[617]

Total is a conventional integrated multinational firm operating in the oil and gas industry. It has activities in 130 countries via a corporate group which comprises nearly 900 subsidiaries. It means that Total S.A., the mother company of the Total group of companies, directly or indirectly owns the shares issued by 900 corporations through which part of its business activity is being conducted. Via these hundreds of corporations, about 100,000 employees are being employed and conduct the activities of the firm named 'Total'. It means the business of Total is partly structured via 100,000 employment contracts. But the reach of the enterprise 'Total' goes further. As part of its marketing business, for example, Total services 16,000 stations worldwide, some of which it owns, some of which are owned by franchisees with which certain subsidiaries of the Total group of companies have contracts. 'Total' is the outcome of the activities of all the participants to its operations via the various contracts concluded with parts of the group of corporations used to legally structure Total.

Starbucks is an example of an enterprise structured as a buyer-led supply chain. The Starbucks group of corporations employs 150,000 people. It means that 150,000 individuals have an employment contract with one of the legal entities used to legally structure Starbucks. The Starbucks enterprise sources coffee from thousands of traders, agents and contract farmers across the developing world. This means that coffee enters into Starbucks' organization via thousands of contracts with suppliers, which themselves have tens or hundreds of employees and potentially structure themselves via tens or hundreds of other contracts with vendors of agricultural products or machines. Starbucks processes

---

archetype of the firm. He points, however, to a footnote (no 3) where he warned that the firm may imply control over another person's property as well as over their labour.
[616] Anderson, *op cit*, note 270, p. 39.
[617] For more details, *see* Ruggie, *op cit*, note 568, pp. 1–17.

coffee in over 30 countries. That means it owns coffee roasters via tens of subsidiaries, which themselves have contracts with hundreds of employees and other suppliers. Starbucks distributes coffee to retail outlets through over 50 major distribution centres which it owns through yet other corporations. And it operates some 17,000 retail stores in over 50 countries globally, which means Starbucks has massive numbers of lease contracts in its contractual structure.

Apple is an illustration of an enterprise structured as a producer-led network. The components of its iPhone 6 are manufactured by 785 suppliers in 31 countries. The product is designed in the US and assembled in China. Some 60 suppliers are US-based, several themselves multinationals, some headquartered in other countries. Many US suppliers also outsource the production of components to companies in Japan, South Korea and Taiwan, which in turn source from yet other enterprises in South East Asia. The corporate and contractual structure via which its property rights are being put to use has, of course, a formidable degree of complexity.

One can thus identify sub-parts of the World Wide Web of Contracts which are being *organized* via miscellaneous legal means. These organized networks of exchanges are what I call firms. Where are their limits?

6.7 The Firm's Limits

Interestingly, in our example with Microsoft and Toyota as two firms cohabiting in the World Wide Web of Contracts, Microsoft's and Toyota's clusters of contracts are probably *directly* in contact with each other. It is likely that Toyota benefits from Microsoft licences to operate at least some of the computers used in the conduct of its business and it is quite possible that many of the Microsoft company cars are Toyotas, for example. But none of the contractual arrangements pursuant to which Toyota uses Microsoft's software or Microsoft uses cars manufactured by Toyota gives any *authority* to the managers of any of the two firms to *command* those of the other. Like any other firms, 'Microsoft' and 'Toyota' both operate in the World Wide Web of Contracts. The chain of contracts in which they are inserted is as big as the whole economy, to use Cheung's expression. But 'Microsoft' and 'Toyota' exist as separate *firms* in the World Wide Web of Contracts; they are separate productive *organizations* in the World Power System. Their planning systems are coordinated with one another not via a central plan but by the market system.[618]

---

[618] Lindblom, *op cit*, note 599, p. 79.

Cheung's mistake is to consider that the firm is a 'chain of contracts'. To start with, the contracts used to legally structure the firm are not in 'chains', with one contract linked to the next, itself linked to the next, etc. The contracts are in *clusters*, concluded by the various contributors with one or several legal *persons* used to legally structure the firm. And then, the cluster of contracts and corporations which serves as a firm's legal structure are *only* its legal structure. Each firm's legal structure is the set of legal arrangements pursuant to which the use of a series of specific economic resources are *organized* by the firm's management and are not merely sold and purchased. The content of the contracts determines the firm's boundaries. Pure sale and purchase contracts are at the *limit* of the firm. Inputs and outputs are merely purchased or sold. This is *market exchange*. What is not merely purchased or sold is produced by the firm's organization and is at the heart of a firm's activity and takes place within the firm.

In the World Wide Web of Contracts, the boundaries between two firms are determined by answering one question: does one legal party in a contractual relationship have some form of control over the activities of the other? If the answer is yes, the contracting parties are integrated, in whole or in part. If the answer is no, the contracting parties are independent. They have a market relationship. Many times, the answer to the question will be 'it depends on the issue' and a contracting party may be deemed integrated for some purposes but not for others. Certain suppliers are fully integrated. Other suppliers can be contractually controlled and be de facto integrated into the firm's value chain for all or just part of their activities. This is the case, for example, for franchisees, which are very much integrated for some purposes (the look of the shop, opening hours, products sold etc.) but, usually, less so for others (hiring and firing policies, employee compensation etc.). Within the World Wide Web of contracts, there are sub-networks which mix internalization within the multinational firm and linkage to independent suppliers in complex systems of sourcing, producing and distributing. Some lead firms have the ability to drive the organization of international production networks, even when they are not fully controlled via corporate means. This derives from numerous sources of power, including the ability to choose and switch between suppliers. The sheer volume of the purchases made by some firms gives them great power over suppliers.[619]

---

[619] On these issues, *see*, in particular, Mark P. Dallas, Stefano Ponte and Timothy J. Sturgeon, 'Power in Global Value Chains', 26(4) *Review of International Political Economy*, pp. 666–694 (2019), and Stefano Ponte and Timothy Sturgeon, *Explaining Governance in Global Value Chains: A Modular* 'Theory-Building Effort', 21(1) *Review of International*

As an organization built thanks to property rights and the contracts concluded with contributors of resources, the firm must, for its continued success, at least cover its expenses with earnings. The firm, via its legal structure, must make profits. Assuming all costs are being accounted for (i.e. that there are no negative externalities, in particular), a profitable firm creates value. If losses are made or there are negative externalities (not accounted for), the firm may destroy value. This is a very complex topic in which the legal structure of the firm and the accounting system must be taken into account, which is not the case today due to the generalized lack of understanding of what firms really are. We will return to this very important question later.[620]

6.8 The Importance of Firms

This view of the role of the firm as acting within the World Wide Web of Contracts echoes the visual metaphor given by Herbert Simon (1978 economics Nobel prizewinner) which significantly reduces the importance of markets in the real economy:

> ... Any creature floating to our Earth from Mars would perceive the developed regions to be covered mostly by firms, these firms connected by a network of communications and transactions we know as markets. But the firms would be much more salient than the markets, sometimes growing, sometimes shrinking, sometimes dividing or even swallowing one another. Surely, they would appear to be the active elements in the scene.[621]

The truth of the matter is that in the World Wide Web of Contracts, markets are *at the margins of firms* and are *marginal* to the overall system of governance of society – they are marginal to the Power System. The productive organizations created by owners because of their right

---

Political Economy, pp. 195–223 (2014). *See also* Gunther Teubner, 'The Many-Headed Hydra: Networks as Higher-Order Collective Actors', in Joseph McCathery, Sol Picciotto and Colin Scott (eds.), *Corporate Control and Accountability – Changing Structures and the Dynamics of Regulation*, Oxford: Oxford University Press, pp. 41–60 (1993), at p. 56. *See also* John Gerard Ruggie, *The Paradox of Corporate Globalization*, M-RCBG Faculty Working Paper Series 2020-01 (2020), p. 5.

[620] *See* Section 10.4.

[621] Herbert A. Simon, *An Empirically Based Microeconomics*, Cambridge: Cambridge University Press (1997), p. 35.

of decision- and rule-making as a matter of principle are at the *centre* of the productive system. Markets are the means through which firms (productive organizations) either get access to some of the resources they use in their own production processes or dispose of the goods or services they produce. Markets provide an essential incentive to produce efficiently goods potential purchasers (other firms or end users) will want to buy. But 'the market', as an institutional tool, is marginal in the overall production system. The economy in which we live, far from being a 'market economy', is a combination of markets and of firms, of autonomous exchange among separate parties and of organized exchange among related parties. This was true in a world without corporations. But firms were small, and it was expected – as we have seen in the case of Adam Smith – that they would remain small. With the extension of corporate law and industrialization, some firms have grown enormously, and their operations have changed the operation of the Power System. State contract law is marginal in the strict sense of the word. It operates *at the margin, at the border,* of the private legal orders of firms. Its relevance progressively decreases when we reach the core of the internal operation of any organization. On the contrary, its relevance increases when one approaches the limits of the enterprise.[622]

To understand this, it is necessary to understand the consequences of the incorporation of a business.

6.9 The Incorporation Process

There are many ways to 'incorporate' a business. The details vary in the various State jurisdictions of the world, but the following description is accurate in most corporate laws.

Let us assume that Mr Smith owns a factory and the business operated with it. The organization via which the factory is operated, via which the inputs are being purchased and the outputs are being sold, is a firm (or an enterprise, a word I use as a synonym). Let's call this firm 'Steel Production'. Let us further assume that the factory and the business are worth 10,000,000 dollars and that Mr Smith wants to incorporate his business. Mr Smith can create a corporation (let us call it 'Steel Production Inc.'), contribute the factory and the business being run using the factory to Steel Production Inc. and get shares of stock in exchange. After the incorporation process, the 10,000,000-dollar factory and business are

---

[622] Jean-Guy Belley, 'L'entreprise, l'approvisionnement et le droit. Vers une théorie pluraliste du contrat', 32(2) *Les Cahiers de Droit*, pp. 253–299 (1991).

owned by Steel Production Inc. and Mr Smith now owns shares issued by Steel Production Inc. (e.g. 1,000,000 shares worth 10 dollars each on the date of incorporation).

Via the incorporation process, a new class of property rights, very distinct but connected to the factory and the business, has been created. All the productive assets originally owned by Mr Smith to operate the factory are now owned by Steel Production Inc. and all the contracts he concluded to operate the business have been transferred to Steel Production Inc. Steel Production Inc. is now the contracting party opposite the contributors of resources or the purchasers of output, not Mr Smith. Via the incorporation process, the identity of the owner of the assets Mr Smith used to run his business has changed: it is *not* Mr Smith any more; it is Steel Production Inc., a potentially eternal and separate legal person. Steel Production Inc. owns the complex bundle of property rights and is party to the contracts originally used to operate Steel Production. Mr Smith now owns a totally separate and distinct form of property: shares, issued by Steel Production Inc. These two forms of property are connected; *but they convey radically different rights and duties*. They are *both* property rights, i.e. rights of decision- and rule-making as a matter of principle, but not towards the same assets.

As I have already mentioned, whether organized via the legal personality of a single entrepreneur, or via the legal personality of a partnership or via the legal personality of a corporation (like Steel Production Inc.), the firm is different from the legal person(s) used to legally structure it. The various legal devices having legal personality which can be used to legally structure the firm offer different sets of advantages and disadvantages. The firm will be managed differently depending on its legal structure. The management of the firm will be different whether the firm is organized, for example, by an individual entrepreneur bearing personally all the consequences, positive or negative, of the operation of the firm or through a multinational group of corporations. But the firm *cannot* be equated with the legal vehicle(s) having legal personality used to make it come into existence.

6.10 The Consequences of Incorporation

After contribution of the factory and the business created by Mr Smith to Steel Production Inc., on Day 1, Steel Production appears to be the same organization, the same firm, the same enterprise. The factory is the same, although it is now owned by the corporation. The employees are the same, although their employment contracts are now with the corporation. They may not be aware of this, but they now obey the boss (Mr Smith) not because he owns the factory but because he is an agent (the CEO) of the corporation owning the factory. The suppliers are the same, although their supply contracts are now with the corporation. The clients are the same, but their purchase contracts are now with the corporation; and so on.

It may not be immediate, but the new legal structure of the firm will soon affect the operation of the firm. In most large firms, the legal persons serving as the contracting party opposite the contributors of resources to the firm are corporations. The fact that a corporation is used to legally structure firms is disregarded by most economists because corporations are deemed to be mere 'legal fictions' of no importance because only individuals are deemed to be 'real'.[623] The corporation is reduced to a set of 'contracts' among shareholders and managers. With this construction, 'firms' and 'corporations' are equally treated as being 'legal fictions' and are deemed to be operating like markets.[624] This is very convenient because in this fashion, one can disregard the importance of business firms and corporations in economic analysis: everything comes down to contracts and prices.

The existence of corporations, however, deeply affects the operation of firms and of the economy. Because a corporation has legal personality, *real* rights and liabilities are allocated by the legal system to these 'legal fictions'. Corporations – and more appropriately groups of corporations for large firms – around the globe are the tools used for the creation of the relatively stable clusters of contracts connecting property rights owners in the World Wide Web of Contracts allowing firms to operate on a global, quasi-eternal, private and, to a large extent, secret way. Their shareholders own property rights which are totally separate – shares – and are only remotely connected to the operations of large firms.

---

[623] *See* Michael C. Jensen and William H. Meckling, 'Theory of the Firm: Managerial Behavior, Agency Costs and Ownership Structure', 3(4) *Journal of Financial Economics*, pp. 305–360 (1976).

[624] *See* the efforts by Alchian and Demsetz to demonstrate that 'the firm and the ordinary market [are] competing types of markets' (Alchian and Demsetz, *op cit*, note 173, p. 795), and those of Jensen and Meckling for whom 'the "behavior" of the firm is like the behavior of a market' (Jensen and Meckling, *op cit*, note 623). Or *see also* Cheung for whom 'it is futile to press the issue of what is or is not a firm'; *see* Cheung, *op cit*, note 611, pp. 17–18.

6.11 Corporations

Corporations are treated by the State legal systems as legal persons, i.e. they can participate in the legal systems because they have 'legal personality'. They can own property, have debts, contract, sue and be sued in courts, get bankrupt and so on. They can 'function' in the economy like human beings of age can.

The importance of legal personality has been disregarded by many. Some actually dismissed its significance by calling it a 'legal fiction' – essentially because only people, humans made of flesh and blood, are deemed to be 'real'.

It is, of course, true in some sense that corporations are 'fictions'. But the same applies to the US, the EU or the UN. All these 'legal persons' are 'fictions' in the sense that they do not have physical existence and are a creation of the mind to serve as legal vehicles operating in the legal system to fulfil various purposes. But 'legal fictions' are not 'fictions' in the sense that a novel is a 'fiction'. It is hard to deny that the existence of the US, the UN, Germany or NATO as 'legal fictions' has a real-life impact. We have seen that the 'State' is precisely the legal person to which the actions of the 'Organs of the State' are being imputed. In a society in which the relations among individual persons and institutionalized groups are in great part structured by *law*, it is of high importance to take into account which are the 'fictions' habilitated by the *legal system* to own property, have debts, contract, sue and be sued in courts, get bankrupt or accumulate assets and live an infinite life. And it is of equal importance to be aware of which groups or institutions or notions *do not* have legal personality and therefore cannot own property, have debts, contract and so on. As we have seen, the State is that legal person to which the actions of the 'Organs of the State' are being legally imputed (*see* Section 2.1). This invention has been a key progress for the development of a Power System operating in an impersonal manner, as a State of law, thus opening the door to economic, social and political modernity. It was a fundamental progress for the institutionalization of an 'open access order'.[625] The development of the State's legal personality allowed the creation of an organization with a potentially eternal existence, remaining the same irrespective of innumerable changes in the State personnel at all levels. It gave the State political unity and institutional continuity. This invention of English and French lawyers from the twelfth until the fifteenth century played an instrumental role in the structuring of the State System as the backbone of

---

[625] *See generally* Chapter 3.

the modern Power System.[626] The State's properties, contracts, obligations and duties remain unaffected notwithstanding political changes due to the continuity of its actions made possible thanks to the continuity of its legal personality.

Not understanding that *the same applies to business corporations* is a failure of gigantic proportions because it is preventing the understanding of the operation of firms and of the economic system more generally. Corporations are the legal persons to which some of the actions of firm managers are being imputed. Their operations via corporations deeply affect the operation of the economy and of the legal and Power Systems.

6.12 Corporate Personality versus Notions it Should Not be Confused with

To understand the concept of corporate personality, one must be very precise in the language used and distinguish this notion from related concepts.

A very different notion is that of *individual*. An individual is a physical person, a human being taken as such in his or her biological existence making of him or her a specific living being. A slave is an individual; a child is an individual; an old man is an individual; a woman is an individual; a king is an individual. Every human being is an individual, intrinsically, whatever his complexion or her position in the legal or social systems.

The concept of *person* is different. A *person* is a creation of the legal and political systems. Individuals are all *different*; legal persons are *equal*. It took centuries for Occidental culture to develop this notion.[627] The person is, from the legal point of view, a subject of rights and duties and, as a rights- and duties-bearing person in the State legal order, she is a creation of the State's legal order.[628] As a legal person, she may own property rights, enter into contracts, be prosecuted or sue in court. Every human being, every individual, is *not* necessarily a person and there are persons who are not human beings. For example, when slavery existed, individuals, people of flesh and blood, could exist as *individuals* without being *persons*; they had no existence as persons from a legal perspective. These individuals were

---

[626] Olivier Beaud, 'La notion d''État', 35 *Archives de Philosophie du Droit*, pp. 119–141 (1990), p. 134.

[627] Alain Supiot, *Homo Juridicus – Essai sur la fonction anthropologique du droit*, Paris: Editions du Seuil (2005), p. 46.

[628] Schmitt, *op cit*, note 199, p. 57; Supiot, *op cit*, note 627, pp. 10–11.

not treated as *subjects* of rights, but as *objects* of rights – as *things* (with often a slightly different status from inanimate objects or animals). As to those legal persons who are not individuals, such as the State, a municipality or a business corporation, they are subjects of rights and obligations without being individuals.

The concept of person is fundamental for our analysis. Without the concept of person, which is the single most important invention of Western legal culture,[629] modern markets and economic organizations are inconceivable. The existence of markets postulates the existence of contracts, which can only exist between 'contracting entities' which must be 'persons' in our legal systems. Like property rights, contracts require the existence of legal persons to hold the prerogatives they entail. And this existence depends on the operation of a specific type of legal system which operations are based on the concept of legal person. In this sense, the concept of individual legal person is no less 'fictional' than the concept of corporation understood as a legal person.[630]

Then comes the concept of *citizen*. Only individual legal persons may be citizens. One must be a subject of rights, an individual rights-bearing person, to be a citizen. One must be an individual person to have these *special rights* that make an individual person a citizen. But what the citizen has in addition compared with the legal person is the opportunity to participate in the political system of the State of which he is a citizen. This usually results in the fact that the citizen can vote and be a candidate at elections. The citizen is a restrictive category from that of legal person. With the progress of democracy, the number of citizens of the various national polities has increased. During the nineteenth century, there were three sorts of franchise restrictions: the regime *censitaire*, basing suffrage on the possession of wealth or the payment of taxes; the regime *capacitaire*, restricting suffrage on the basis of literacy or formal education; and household responsibility criteria, which limited political participation to heads of households occupying a dwelling of a minimum size or rent.[631] And until recently, access to citizenship was restricted to males.

With regards to citizenship, there is a big difference between natural persons and legal entities. If there are natural persons who are not citizens (children, for example, are not citizens), in modern democracies many natural persons are also citizens. Corporations, however, are never citizens.

---

[629] Supiot, *op cit*, note 341.

[630] Deakin, *op cit*, note 573, p. 1512.

[631] *E.g.* Samuel Bowles and Herbert Gintis, *Democracy and Capitalism – Property, Community and the Contradictions of Modern Social Thought*, New York: Routledge (1986), p. 42.

It has not always been the case. At certain points in history, certain societies had a corporate form of social organization. They were *officially* pluralistic legal systems, officially comprising a wealth of intermediary groupings between individual persons and the State, officially participating in legal and political life. Corporations were part of the constitutional system of government. They had a political role, were part of the official Power System and sometimes could even vote. It was the case in Ancient France, as we have seen at Section 3.5.[632] In individualistic regimes of constitutional government, this is never the case.

Finally, one can mention the concept of *national*. A national is a person holding the nationality of a State. It is a concept close to, but different from that of citizen. It is possible to be a national of a State without being a citizen. This is the case, for example, for minors who have a nationality but do not vote. Or all or part of the rights of citizenship may be granted by a State to persons who are not its nationals. In some States, foreign residents are sometimes allowed to cast their vote at local elections although they are not nationals.

It is the concept of *person* — with the precise meaning given to this term — which is of interest for us in this book, and particularly that of *juristic person*, that is to say, human institutions which are *not* individual persons but that the legal system treats as legal entities, as subjects of rights and obligations, as points of imputations of responsibilities and liabilities: as persons.

6.13 The Importance of Being a Legal Person

Legal persons receive from the legal system the ability to have recourse to the State legal system to get their rights — and in particular their property and contractual rights — enforced. They are also subject to the legal and enforcement systems and can have obligations imposed on them. That's the flip side of the coin and it is a very significant consequence of having legal personality: the enforcement of the contracts they conclude can be imposed upon them; and they are subject to laws and regulations. And they can have liabilities, as already seen by De Soto.[633] They can be made accountable for the decisions and actions imputed to them.

As for the groups or institutions which do *not* have legal personality — like *firms* — they do *not* exist in contemplation of the law as persons; they do *not* have *rights* and, conversely, they *cannot incur liabilities*. They are not

---

[632] *See* Olivier-Martin, *op cit*, note 503, pp. 690–702.

[633] De Soto, *op cit*, note 20, p. 87.

points of imputation. Via corporations, they are everywhere they want to be; but thanks to their inexistence as a legal person, they are nowhere in the legal system, as such, as the overall encompassing organization they practically are.

This is a *key issue* to understand the operation of the present World Power System: firm managers can operate firms, as organizations, as if they had *rights* – which they exercise through the corporations used to legally structure the firm – without incurring the *liabilities* firms create as organizations existing beyond their corporate structure. In the legal world, top firm managers are 'organs of the corporation(s)', not organs of the firm(s). In a globalizing world, this is certainly one of the most complex issues to address. Multinational firms are legally structured around groups of corporations established in the jurisdictions of many States. The rights and duties generated via the firm's operations are attributed to the various corporations used to structure them, and not to the worldwide economic organization existing as a consequence.

6.14 Incorporation and the Multiplication of Property Rights

Via the introduction and the development of corporate law, capitalism as we know it appeared. Two separate but interrelated property systems came to life: the property over *productive assets* owned by corporations and the property over the financial assets (shares in particular) issued by corporations and which can be owned by other corporations or other legal persons.

Productive assets, whether they are tangible (buildings, machines etc.) or intangible (patents, trademarks, algorithms etc.), now tend to be concentrated in the ownership of corporations, artificial legal persons which concentrate the power of decision- and rule-making as a matter of principle granted by these property rights. Concentrating property rights, they concentrate *sovereign* rights, rights of decision- and rule-making as a matter of principle.

In this system, shareholders only own the securities issued by corporations. The bundle of property rights owned by the corporation and of contracts executed by it in connection with the operation of its assets (the firm) is legally totally isolated from the shareholders. Shareholders are not even among the constituents of the firm as an organized economic activity.

Businesses (composed of real assets, real people etc.) are managed by corporations or, more precisely, by agents of the corporations in the name of corporations. Shareholders manage shares, exercise the rights they have thanks to the shares they own, which are not direct rights over the business of the corporation. There is, on the one hand, the so-called 'real' economy, and, on the other, the financial system. The two are somewhat related, but not in a direct way. It is impossible to understand capitalism without understanding the dual type of property rights in existence in connection with the operation of a corporate economy. Rights over *things* are structured within firms via the corporations owning them. Rights over *shares* can be exchanged, sold, given, inherited without any impact on the structuring of firms via corporations. Vast and relatively stable organizations have been created thanks to corporations. But this has inherently affected the Power System, which was not designed to cope with the surge of these autonomous corporate powers having concentrated the prerogatives of decision-making granted by property, which were originally designed to protect *individual* persons against the State and have turned against them in their confrontation with firms.

The fact is that if one does not develop a legally grounded analysis of the firm which requires a legally grounded analysis of property rights and of their reconfiguration via corporate structures, *it is impossible to understand the effective operation of modern capitalism* and of the World Power System. Modern capitalism relies on the existence of artificial legal persons to own, directly or indirectly, real assets, enabling the development of organizations existing in the long term, and leaving to mortal individuals only *derivative rights* via the securities issued by these 'artificial' legal persons. These derivative rights, and in particular shares of stock, are traded, generate income and have value as *separate* assets connected to, but at the same time isolated from, the activities of business firms. They are the assets subject to the vagaries of human life such as death, inheritance and divorce.

There is, however, another important side to the existence of financial markets due to the existence of the share as a specific form of property right. The management of shares as assets separated from the underlying business activities – a process some have called the 'financialization' of the economy, otherwise seen as the process of transforming future income streams into marketable securities[634] – deeply affects the operation of business firms and of society in general.

To understand why, we will now look more deeply at the features of business corporations.

---

[634] Ying Zhang and Jane Andrew, 'Financialization and the Conceptual Framework', 25 *Critical Perspectives on Accounting*, pp. 17–26 (2014), p. 19.

7

The Features of Business Corporations

In the first chapter of the second part of this book, I have shown the importance of differentiating firms from corporations. Firms are economic organizations operating in the World Wide Web of Contracts via nexuses of contracts. These contracts are executed by legal persons which can be individuals or partnerships or corporations or any other legal entity entitled to have a business activity. The firm is the economic organization and the corporation is a particular category of legal person used to legally structure firms. Corporations are key legal tools for the structuring of large firms because they have extraordinary capabilities, in particular with regard to the concentration of capital and the continuity of their existence.

Now we will look deeper into the features of business corporations.

★★★

Business corporations have very peculiar characteristics which explain their widespread use in the structuring of business activities.

The head paragraphs of what follows have been written with the late Lynn Stout, and with Paddy Ireland, in *The Modern Corporation Statement on Company Law* and have been endorsed by legal scholars worldwide, each one being knowledgeable about corporate law in a large number of State legal systems.[635] This project arose from our shared conclusion

[635] Lynn A. Stout et al., *The Modern Corporation Statement on Company Law* (2016), available at https://papers.ssrn.com/sol3/papers.cfm?abstract_id=2848833. The endorsers include: Lynn A. Stout, Cornell Law School, Jack G. Clarke Business Law Institute; Jean-Philippe Robé, SciencesPo Law School; Paddy Ireland, Kent Law School; Simon Deakin, University of Cambridge; Andrew Johnston, University of Sheffield Law School; Margaret M. Blair, Vanderbilt University Law School; Lorraine E. Talbot, University of York, York Law School; Janet Dine, Queen Mary, University

that certain beliefs about corporations and corporate law, which are widely held and relied upon by business experts, the financial press and economists who study the firm, are unfounded. The most serious error is the assertion in law schools, business schools and the financial press that shareholders 'own' the firm or the corporation or the company.[636] This fundamental mistake is the cornerstone of intellectual constructions in which corporate issues, and particularly issues of governance, are all reducible to private property and private contractual issues, and thus can be addressed via liberal market economics. Some of these widely held constructions, such as 'agency theory' or the purported duty to 'maximize shareholder value' are severely mistaken and lead to numerous shared errors in the way corporate law concepts are understood.[637] We thus decided to draft and make available a summary of certain fundamentals

---

of London, (CCLS); Beate Sjåfjell, University of Oslo Faculty of Law; Cynthia A. Williams, York University – Osgoode Hall Law School; Marios Koutsias, University of Essex School of Law; Andrew Pendleton, University of York (UK); Gerald F. Davis, University of Michigan, Stephen M. Ross School of Business; David Chandler, The Business School, University of Colorado Denver; Jean Du Plessis, Deakin University, Geelong, Australia – Deakin Law School; Andrea J Bather, University of Waikato Management School; Beau Linton Lefler, The University of Hong Kong School of Business; Christopher M. Bruner, University of Georgia School of Law; Thomas Wuil Joo, UC Davis School of Law; Daniel J.H. Greenwood, Hofstra University College of Law; Thomas Clarke, University of Technology, Sydney; Martin Lipton, Wachtell, Lipton, Rosen and Katz; Rebecca Johnson, University of Victoria Faculty of Law; Irene-Marie Esser, University of South Africa School of Law; Roman Tomasic, University of South Australia; Hugh Christopher Willmott, City University London – Sir John Cass Business School, Cardiff Business School; Jeroen Veldman, City University London Faculty of Management; Paige Morrow, New York University (NYU).

[636] Andrew G. Haldane, Chief Economist, Bank of England, states that it 'is corporate finance 101 [that] at least for publicly listed companies, its owners are its shareholders. ... It is the centrepiece of most corporate finance textbooks. It is the centrepiece of company law. It is the centrepiece of most public policy discussions of corporate governance'. But after having explained that in effect, shareholders do not possess the incidents of ownership, Haldane goes on to explain that '"ownership" is really a misnomer when applied to shareholders. Associating "shareholding" with "ownership" thus makes little substantive sense, despite its widespread use in popular discourse'. In Andrew G. Haldane, *Who Owns A Company?*, Speech given by Andrew G. Haldane, Chief Economist, Bank of England, University of Edinburgh Corporate Finance Conference, 22 May 2015, pp. 2 & 14.

[637] *See, e.g.,* the point made by Martin Shkreli, the former CEO of Turing, who claimed that it was his duty to the shareholders to raise fifty-fold the price of Daraprim, a life-saving drug, a step which was endorsed by most of the press reporting the story.

of corporate law, applicable in almost all jurisdictions. The intent was to help prevent analytical errors which can have severe and damaging effects on corporate governance and the social and natural environments in which it operates.

The following paragraphs are a more detailed account of this joint effort.

7.1 Legal Personality

Corporations are universally treated by State legal systems as 'legal persons' existing separately and independently of their directors, officers, shareholders or other individual persons with whom the legal entity interacts. Legal separateness or 'personhood' is a powerful legal tool. It ensures that corporations have rights, including especially the right to own property rights and enter into contracts. As legal persons, corporations can commit torts. Having 'legal personality', business corporations can operate in the legal system. They have legal standing. Treated as legal persons they are, like any other legal person, the decision-makers as a matter of principle in connection with what they own, in particular productive capital.

Legal personality is something very peculiar despite its widespread use in today's world. What is it about? The legal system treats some institutions which have no physical existence as if they were *persons*. This is equally true of the State and of a business corporation.

The State owns roads, schools, military aircraft, submarines, employs civil servants, entertains international relations with other States and so on. The State contracts, signs treaties and has a budget. It can borrow, and its legal personality immensely increased its credit.[638] It can sue, and it is possible to sue it. The State *is a legal person*.

It is the same for a business corporation: it owns assets which it can use to develop a business, it can execute contracts with suppliers and clients, it can employ staff. The business corporation *is a legal person*. Corporations are treated by the legal system as if they had a real life of their own. The actions of individual persons acting on their behalf – the *organs of the corporation* – are imputed to the corporation, not to the individuals acting on behalf of the corporation. And in so doing, the legal system *indeed* gives them a *reality* since the world *is* in fact structured using them. The concept of legal *fiction*, because it is used to structure the *real* world, gave birth to a *reality* which cannot be overlooked. So much so that if, by some magical trick, all the legal entities which exist today were instantly

---

[638] Tilly, *op cit*, note 449, p. 147.

eliminated, our World Power System would collapse instantly. There would be no more States; the concepts of nationality, citizenship and even legal person would lose their meaning. There would be no more public international organizations, no more municipalities, no more commercial companies. Widespread confusion would follow: we would not know who owns what, who has what authority to decide in the name of whom via which procedure, who can sign which type of contract, in the name of whom, who is responsible for what and so on. We would find ourselves instantaneously in absolute chaos.

And if we tried to structure anew our complex world *without* resorting to legal personality, it would simply be impossible: we would not know how to operate a sophisticated world without the concepts of State, of international organization and of business corporation. Corporate personhood – be it the one of the State or of the business corporation – provides stability and persistence in time which the fragile legal personality of mortal individual persons simply cannot offer. Corporate persons are potentially immortal. No unavoidable death will lead to the transfer of their property at the end of their physical life, as is the case for mortals.[639] Of course, they can fail and become bankrupt. But they are never sick. They never sleep. They have specialized activities. They operate through known procedures and agents. Corporate personality, whether it is the one of States, of international organizations or of business corporations, is a fundamental tool for the structuring of a complex, now global society. One cannot overestimate the importance of this notion: it is simply the single most important invention in human history. As we have seen, it played a key role in the development of the modern State and of the State System and of its globalization. It has been equally important for the development of large firms and of a modern, now global economy.[640] It

---

[639] *See* Ely, *op cit*, note 21, pp. 452–453. *Also* Saleilles, *op cit*, note 42, p. 25.

[640] Quite surprisingly, it is, first of all, case law and not legislation which declared that corporations are legal persons. In France, neither the original Civil Code nor the Commercial Code mention the legal personality of partnerships or of corporations. *See* Saleilles, *op cit*, note 42, pp. 10 & 299. In the US, the US Supreme Court decided that corporations have legal personality without hearing arguments. In the 1886 case *Santa Clara v. Southern Pacific* (118 U.S. 394 (1886)), Chief Justice Waite orally directed the lawyers that the Fourteenth Amendment equal protection clause guarantees constitutional protections to corporations in addition to natural persons, and that the oral argument should focus on other issues in the case. The court reporter noted, in the headnote to the opinion, that the Chief Justice began oral argument by stating, 'The court does not wish to hear argument on the question whether the provision in the Fourteenth Amendment to the Constitution, which forbids a State to deny to any person within its jurisdiction the equal protection of the laws, applies to these

is certain that industrial revolutions and technological progresses were key in this process. But the quantum leap in legal engineering made possible by the invention of legal personality was key.

Regarding the type of micro-power one calls a firm, we have seen that some economists have tried to analyse the corporation, which serves as its legal support, as a mere 'nexus of contracts' among shareholders, directors and managers. They believe it is possible to reduce legal personality to a set of *individual* relationships and thus to escape the singularity it represents. It is simply impossible.[641] This serious mistake has tragic consequences because it is at the origin of many of the existing shortcomings in the current operation of the World Power System. We will see that it is essential to correct this mistake if we are to meet the challenges presented by globalization.

7.2 Shares as Autonomous Objects of Property

Business corporations are very efficient legal devices to raise and concentrate capital. We have already looked at this issue in the General Introduction (at pp. 24–26), when we saw that despite its perceived incompatibility with the operation of a liberal society, the growth of the business corporation was unstoppable. Business corporations were needed to concentrate financial and, indirectly, productive capital.

Business corporations can raise capital by issuing various types of securities. One type of security that many but not all corporations issue is shares of stock, which are owned by shareholders. For example, a firm needing 1,000,000 dollars to finance a project can do it by using a corporation issuing 100,000 shares with a face value of 10 dollars. A shareholder contributing 420,000 dollars to the corporation will get 42,000 shares, i.e. 42 per cent of the issued and paid capital stock of the company. From the date of contribution, the company is the owner of the 420,000 dollars initially owned by the shareholder and can use them to purchase productive assets, hire employees and so on to legally build the firm; and the shareholder owns 42,000 shares of capital issued by the company. He owns 42,000 times one share issued by the company, each share being owned independently from the others. If and when dividends will be distributed, the shareholder will get 42 per cent of the distribution.

---

corporations. We are all of the opinion that it does.' (118 U.S. 394 (1886) – Official Court Syllabus in the *United States Reports*).

[641] *See also* Edward M. Iacobucci and George G. Triantis, 'Economic and Legal Boundaries of Firms', 93 *Virginia Law Review*, pp. 515–570 (2007).

And at shareholders' assembly meetings, the shareholder will have 42 per cent of the votes. And if 100 per cent of the share capital of the company is being sold in one transaction, the shareholder will get 42 per cent of the purchase price.

Contrary to a widely held 'common–sense' idea, shareholders do not own *corporations*; nor do they own the *assets* of corporations.[642] Harold Demsetz wrote more than 50 years ago that 'what shareholders really own are their shares and not the corporation'.[643] The shareholder in our example does not own 42 per cent of the company or 42 per cent of its assets. He owns 42 per cent of the shares issued by the company, i.e. 42,000 shares. The *conversion of property rights* via the process of incorporation is a *fundamental feature of incorporated businesses*. It is often neglected, and authors sometimes consider that shareholders 'own' firms and, indirectly, therefore 'own' the assets owned by corporations used to legally structure firms. Nothing could be further from the truth, legally speaking. And one misses one of the fundamental features of capitalism if one makes this error. From the incorporation moment, the assets owned by the corporation and the shares issued by the corporation and owned by the shareholders *will live separate lives*.

Given the importance of property rights in the Power System, it is fundamental to strictly identify who owns what in a corporate enterprise. Remember: the owner is the legal person having the authority to make decisions as a matter of principle in connection with what he or she owns. The owner of shares has this authority *over the shares*. The owner of the assets of the corporation – the corporation itself, which is not owned by anyone and is represented by its agents – has this authority *over these assets*. Not making the distinction and considering that shareholders own the business, the assets, the firm, the corporation and so on leads to endless confusions and reasoning errors. Harold Demsetz, for example, who does not distinguish between the firm and the corporation, writes that 'While we can describe with fair clarity who owns which rights under which circumstances, we cannot stipulate with equal clarity which party owns the assets of the corporation'.[644]

---

[642] As early as 1897, Ernst Freund wrote that '… a shareholder of a railroad company has no direct right of property in the rolling stock, the roadbed, the station houses, etc. of the road; he cannot use the cars at his pleasure, he can give no orders to the employees, and *if he performs acts of ownerships, he is a trespasser*' (emphasis added); Ernst Freund, *op cit*, note 160, p. 34. *See also* Stout, *op cit*, note 604, pp. 37–38.

[643] Harold Demsetz, 'Toward a Theory of Property Rights', 57(2) *American Economic Review*, pp. 347–359 (1967), p. 357. *See also* Ciepley, *op cit*, note 508, pp. 145–147.

[644] Demsetz, *op cit*, note 220, p. 450.

Fortunately for real-life businessmen and women, it is quite the *opposite*: the corporation owns the productive assets and the shareholders own the shares issued by the corporation. Demsetz's confusion is due to the classical confusion between *ownership* and *possession* and the classical disregard of the importance of legal personality and property as legal institutions allowing complex combinations of prerogatives, direct and indirect, over assets. If this clarity as to who owns the assets of the corporation – i.e. the corporation itself – did not exist, the worlds of collateralization, structured finance, private equity, leveraged buy-out, securitization and so on would simply not exist. And for better or worse, they do. If the shareholders were owners of anything else than the shares, the whole complex economic, financial and legal system in which we live would simply collapse.

This clarity as to who has legal title to what exists because the corporation has a strong form of separate legal personality which allows partitioning assets and therefore allows breaking *any* property right connection between the shareholders and the firm's assets and activity conducted via the corporation. The corporation fully owns its assets; and the shareholders fully own their shares. As a matter of principle, the shareholders can do as they please with their shares: give them, sell them, loan them and so on. They *own* them: they are the decision-makers as a matter of principle towards them. But they *cannot* do as they please with the corporation and its assets. They *do not own* the corporation and they *do not own* its assets.[645] They are *not* the decision-makers as a matter of principle towards them. The only thing they can do with regards to the corporation is exercising the rights they have because of their ownership of the shares, i.e. mostly vote in shareholders' assembly meetings and collect dividends when they are distributed. These are quite significant rights, but they are not akin to a property right over the corporation or its assets. It is the neglect of this fundamental characteristic of the corporation as a totally separate legal person which leads to a lack of clarity in mainstream economists' understanding as to who owns what; not some uncertainty in the law, as Demsetz seems to think, or some mind-boggling complex phenomenon.

It is important to note that, strictly speaking, no one owns the corporation.[646] It is only according to current folklore that a corporation is said to be owned by its shareholders. Shareholders own the shares issued

---

[645] Stout, *op cit*, note 604, pp. 36–38.

[646] Lynn Stout originally thought that corporations own themselves. *Ibid*, p. 37. She later changed her mind. *See also* John Kay, 'Is it meaningful to talk about the ownership of companies?', *Financial Times*, 11 October 2015. But it does not make much of a difference. What does matter is that shareholders do not own the corporation.

by the corporation; and the corporation owns the assets. But no one owns the 'corporation in itself'. A useful intellectual exercise to understand this is to imagine the case of a successful corporation with a lot of cash which would repurchase all the shares it issued. It is usually prohibited for corporations to own a substantial proportion of their share capital. But if it were not the case, a corporation could buy all the shares it issued.[647] The corporation would simply own 100 per cent of its issued share capital and exercise the rights attached to the shares, i.e. vote in the shareholders' assembly (it would be the sole shareholder) and collect dividends (in fact, keep all the profits made by not declaring a dividend). If the corporation were to sell some of its shares later on, as it could do with any of its other assets, someone else other than the corporation would own these shares; but no one would own the corporation more than heretofore.

Certainly, the shareholder owning a majority of the shares in a corporation can appoint the directors and indirectly *control* the corporate affairs. But even the ultimate control over the corporate affairs must be exercised within the constraints set by corporate law. In most legal systems, a shareholder who would directly interfere in the management of the corporate affairs would become a de facto manager and lose the benefit of his limited liability as a shareholder. And the control over shareholders' assembly meetings can be a source of duties towards minority shareholders limiting the autonomy of the controlling shareholder. A controlling shareholder has, of course, very significant powers and prerogatives and this is possibly necessary for corporations and the businesses they legally structure to be operated efficiently. But a controlling shareholder does not own the corporation's assets, nor does he own the corporation, which is not a 'thing'.

7.3 Assets and Liability Partitioning

A key feature of corporate personhood is that corporations – as separate, property-owning legal persons – own their own assets and incur their own liabilities. Corporate assets and liabilities are separate from shareholder assets and liabilities.

This strict *partitioning of assets and liabilities* has key economizing consequences. The corporation's assets are protected from the shareholders: if shareholders face misfortunes in their personal lives, their creditors can only go after what they own – their shares (and their other assets). The

---

[647] *See also* Dan-Cohen, *op cit*, note 23, pp. 46–47.

shareholders' creditors cannot collect against the assets which are owned by the corporation.

The *autonomy and integrity of the business* is therefore protected. The corporation's assets, creditors, contracting parties etc. are all protected. This strong entity shielding plays a key role in the development of large firms: the assets used and the clusters of contracts with providers of resources to the firm *are not affected by events occurring at the shareholders' level*.

The strong form of legal personality of a corporation therefore *protects the corporation's welfare* from the shareholders' misfortunes. Large businesses whose well-being will not be threatened by the incidents of human life can then be built. As I have shown, this aspect of corporate personality has been fundamental for the development of the modern, impersonal *State*. The *same* applies to large business corporations which make it possible to legally structure large firms having potentially an *eternal life*.

Conversely, the shareholders' welfare is protected from the misfortunes of the business. As a result of the 'limited liability' of shareholders, the creditors of corporations can only enforce their claims against the corporation's assets, not against those of the shareholders. Shareholders are affected by the corporation's failures only indirectly and their losses are limited to any decline in the *value* of the shares they own.

This autonomy leads to the need to have reliable accounting information audited by independent auditors.[648] The issue is how to properly account for the operations of the business. In the past, there was a clear understanding that creditors had to be protected and, therefore, a principle of precaution prevailed. Then, in this area like in many other ones, agency theory had a strong impact and led to a change in the rules of accounting to make them more suitable to the needs of shareholders. I will address this important issue in more detail in Sections 9.5 and 9.6.

7.4 Locking in Capital

Another critical consequence of corporate personhood is that the assets of the corporation are 'locked in' and protected against shareholder claims. Shareholders have no direct claim over the assets of the corporation, which they do not own. Shareholders cannot force the corporation to disgorge its assets. Capital lock-in is a fundamental feature of the corporate form which makes it possible for corporations to pursue long-term, large-scale

---

[648] On the different stages of accounting methods, *see* Jacques Richard, 'The Dangerous Dynamics of Modern Capitalism (from Static to IFRS' Futuristic Accounting)', 30 *Critical Perspectives on Accounting*, pp. 9–34 (2015).

economic projects. If the shareholders want liquidity – money instead of their shares – they must sell what they own: their shares. And shares as a shareholder's asset offer the great advantage – when they are listed on a liquid market – to give shareholders *liquidity*. In addition, shareholders have liquidity for whole or part of their investment: they can decide to sell just part of their shares. This is quite a significant advantage when the underlying assets are illiquid. As a matter of illustration, it is not an easy transaction to sell a nuclear power plant or a portion of a nuclear power plant; selling one share of a company owning a nuclear power plant is trivial.

Assets partitioning and locking in also have the advantage that the sale of shares in the secondary market or the transfer of shares through inheritance do not directly affect the business of the corporation: the corporation's assets, contracts and liabilities are left unchanged. This is a key factor of corporate ownership giving stability to large business firms irrespective of the shareholders' wilful or accidental exit from their investment.

7.5 The Elimination of the Haggling over Residual Control Rights

As I have already mentioned in Section 1.10, Oliver Hart has developed an analysis pursuant to which the incompleteness of contracts leads to a theory of ownership: if a contract concluded by parties is incomplete (which will always be the case in a world of positive transaction costs), ownership of the assets involved will be an important source of power enhancing the owner's bargaining position during renegotiations. The owner is in a strong position because of the residual rights of control characterizing ownership. The owner of an asset may bind himself or herself and the asset he or she owns via a contract; but for anything which is not specifically provided for in the contract, the owner has the residual control rights and therefore has a strong ex-post bargaining position. This is because the owner, as an owner, has the right of decision-making as a matter of principle in connection with the asset owned.

Hart's fundamental insight, as we have seen, is in line with my definition of property as a prerogative of the owner in connection with an object of property 'as a matter of principle'. The owner has the 'residual control rights', in Hart's parlance.

But Hart's insight also leads to *another* conclusion he did not draw. It leads to understanding one of the key advantages of using a *separate legal person* to legally structure a business. Creating an 'artificial' legal person owning or controlling the assets used in the business avoids having to agree in advance in detailed contracts among the shareholders to specify who will do what in what circumstances and get what in return. With the contribution or the purchase of an asset to or by a corporation, *all the residual control rights over the asset are now owned by the 'artificial' legal person, not by any of the shareholders*. There is no issue of '*residual control rights*' over the *corporation's* assets among the shareholders: *full title* to the assets is owned by the corporation. After contribution of the assets to the corporation, decisions about their use will *not* be made by *contracting parties* negotiating to revise their contract (the statutes of incorporation and/or by-laws of the corporation) with some shareholder having residual control rights over all or part of the real assets while others have none. The decisions will be made by the *officers or directors or shareholders*, in accordance with the company's *articles of association and the applicable default corporate law rules*, which provide for procedural rules, quorum and majorities governing how decisions will be made through time in connection with the business. Issues about the residual control right are fundamentally affected by the contribution of the asset to a corporation. There is much more predictability about what will happen in unexpected situations because the residual control rights are in the ownership of the corporation and decisions will be made according to the procedures of corporate law.

The fact that we do *not* live in a comprehensive contracting world provides *another* incentive for creating separate legal *persons* to own the assets used in businesses and contract with suppliers and, as a consequence, deal with future issues as they arise by exercising the rights of decision-making as a matter of principle in accordance with the by-laws and corporate law and not through ex-post haggling.

The incompleteness of contracts, therefore, leads to an understanding of ownership *beyond* what Hart thought: it leads to an understanding of ownership by separate 'artificial' legal persons.

The so-called '*legal fiction*' of the corporation, far from being negligible in economic analysis, *is in fact central to it* in our present, corporate economy.[649]

Without the creation of a 'legal fiction' to serve as contracting counterparty to the contributors of resources to the business, the structuring of the business would be very complex and would be much more open to opportunistic behaviour. Claiming that the corporation is

---

[649] Jean-Philippe Robé, 'The Legal Structure of the Firm', *Accounting, Economics, and Law: A Convivium*, Vol. 1, Issue 1, Article 5, available at: http://www.bepress.com/ael/vol1/iss1/5 (2011). This point is seconded by Deakin, Gindis, Hodgson, Huang and Pistor, *op cit*, note 80, p. 197.

nothing more than a 'nexus of contracts', as Eugene Fama and Michael Jensen do,[650] is fundamentally wrong. The contracts are not bound to each other in a 'nexus'. This representation makes the corporation disappear as a legal person, although it is party to all the contracts thanks to the assets it owns as a legal person. This is one of the two fallacies about corporations: treating them as dense sites of market activity and not as legal entities (the other one being to forget that they are *legal persons*, and not *individuals*[651] – as discussed in Section 7.1). Neglecting the existence of the corporation in economic analysis is a killer. It would be like neglecting the existence of the State as a legal person in political analysis. The permanence of the State is ensured via its legal personality, and the existence of numerous rules for the use of its assets and personnel. If the corporation were nothing more than a 'nexus of contracts' – assuming this could exist in reality – the business created based on this would be extremely fragile since each and every contract would be subject to the opportunistic behaviour of contracting parties owning assets key for the business. Understanding the corporation as a 'nexus of contracts' misses one of its key characteristics as an autonomous legal person owning assets which are not affected by ex-post contracting opportunism.

7.6 The Concentration of Property and the Nature of Corporate Prerogatives

Due to the characteristics of the shares, markets on which this type of securities are being traded have grown considerably in the economy. Business enterprises were able to develop and concentrate property rights over productive assets. They made use of the autonomy provided by the definition of property rights and of the freedom of contract granted to legal persons in a liberal society. And they did so enjoying the *subjective* prerogatives initially constitutionally provided for *individual* persons only, not for *organizations* such as business firms.

Firms have no legal existence as such. Firms operate in the legal system via corporations to which the actions performed in the operations of the firm are imputed. Business firms can therefore take full advantage of liberal *individual* rights (freedom of contract and property rights) via corporations enabling them to exercise their prerogatives without the constraints that normally accompany the exercise of *power*, including the

---

[650] *See* in Section 6.5.

[651] *See generally* Pettit, *op cit*, note 68, pp. 379–394.

exercise of the prerogatives it confers in the interests of those affected by their use.

As a reminder (*see* Section 2.2), **private** prerogatives are generally *unqualified, autonomous, optional,* in the *private interest* and *transferable.*

When one looks at their characteristics, **corporate** prerogatives are much closer to public prerogatives than to private ones. As we have seen in Section 2.1, **public** prerogatives are *qualified, heteronomous, mandatory, non-transferable* and in the *public interest.* Corporate prerogatives are very similar, with one exception. They are:

- *qualified*: they are powers which are not for everyone but only attach to certain qualified persons, directors and officers;
- *heteronomous*: they entail a capacity to create rules that bind others (this clearly applies within firms);
- *mandatory*: the persons having these prerogatives are not entitled to use them freely at their convenience. They have a legal duty to exercise their prerogatives (that is their mandate as corporate officers and directors);
- *non-transferable*: these prerogatives are not part of a right and are never transferable. At most, they can be delegated to other persons, which leaves untouched the holder's own power (this is also applicable in the corporate context);
- BUT these prerogatives certainly do not have to be used in the *public interest.* Otherwise, corporations would be Organs of the State, which they clearly are not. The acts performed, and faults committed in the performance of these prerogatives, are not attributed to the State but to the corporation. Although some argue that corporations/firms should be run in the public interest, I do disagree because that would make of them public institutions, Organs of the State, which they are clearly not. But they are not purely private either.

As we know, shareholders do not own corporations. And contrary to a widespread belief, they are not residual claimants in the ordinary life of the corporation.[652] They are not entitled to everything left over after the corporation's legal obligations have been met. The corporation is its own residual claimant and it is the board which decides what to do with the

---

[652] Jean-Philippe Robé, 'L'actionnaire est-il un créancier résiduel?' in Philippe Batifoulier, Franck Bessis, Ariane Ghirardello, Guillemette de Larquier and Delphine Remillon (eds.), *Dictionnaire des conventions – Autour des travaux d'Olivier Favereau,* pp. 24–29, Villeneuve d'Ascq, Presses Universitaires Septentrion (2016).

corporation's residual.[653] And even in a case of liquidation, which means that the corporation does not exist any more and that the issue of who is the residual claimant in corporate *life* is moot, the shareholders have more the position of *heirs* than *owners*.[654] And heirs inheriting a corpse did not have any right over the way their pre-deceased family member conducted her life.

As discussed in the next chapters, firms and the corporations used to structure them should be managed in the interests of those directly affected, which includes, but goes beyond, shareholders.

---

[653] Stout, *op cit*, note 604, pp. 39–41.

[654] Ciepley, *op cit*, note 508, p. 146.

8

The Spreading of the Corporate System and its Consequences

In Chapter 7, we have looked at the fundamental features of business corporations.

I will now analyse how business corporations developed in the industrializing world in a legal environment which was initially hostile to them. Competing firms have led competing States to amend corporate laws which were initially restrictive. Incorporation was transformed and turned from a *privilege* into a *right*. Freedom of incorporation is now widely accepted. The development of corporate law has now led to the advent of financial capitalism, i.e. a form of capitalism in which two forms of capital exist in connection with any given bundle of assets and contracts concentrated into any given large firm. There is first the capital and contracts required by the productive activity; and there is then the financial capital represented by the financial instruments issued by the corporation used to legally structure the firm. To understand the role played by financial markets, I will present the evolving relationship between firms and States in a globalized economy. To do this, I will use the simple model of a firm adapting its corporate structure to the opportunities offered by the evolving legal rules in an international economy. This will lead us to a reassessment of the necessity to differentiate firms from corporations and to insist on the importance of the rules of corporate governance and of accounting in a globalized world.

★★★

Although the legal features of business corporations are hardly considered in classical economics, the use of business corporations to legally structure real-life large firms is universal. By taking the view that corporations are merely *'legal fictions'*,[655] that 'the firm and the ordinary market [are] competing types of markets',[656] and that 'the "behavior" of the firm is like the behavior of a market',[657] the dominant analysis is condemning itself to irrelevance for the analysis of the real-life global economy. The use of business corporations is universal, and the architects of large firms go through the pain of using them for solid reasons. Some of them have been reviewed in the prior chapter. Now we must analyse how business corporations came to play their role in the operation of the World Power System. The control over a corporation's affairs allows the control over the operations of a firm for which the corporation, or a group of corporations, serves as the owner of key property rights. And to operate the productive assets, the corporation is the centralizing contracting party to the cluster of contracts through which the other resources required for the activity are organized.

It is on these foundations that world-class businesses exist today, with hundreds of thousands of employees and income higher than the gross domestic product of many States. How can one understand the relationship these organizations entertain with the official legal and political systems? How is it possible to analyse the economy within a conceptual system ignoring this reality?

Business corporations were almost non-existent when the liberal Constitutions of the late eighteenth and nineteenth centuries were adopted. In the liberal States, Constitutions addressed, on the one hand, the creation of Political Organs of the State and, on the other, the recognition of the existence of autonomous owning and contracting *individual* persons. The local Power Systems had a relatively simple legal structure having *officially* eliminated intermediary corpuses. The only corporate bodies the US Constitution mentions are the constituent State governments, and then the local jurisdictions of government that State legislatures incorporate (counties, cities or townships).[658] At the time, the few business corporations in existence were treated as an anomaly. They were rare, and their creation was accepted under exceptional circumstances only. Their existence and impact were of course completely disregarded in the allocation of power in the liberal constitutional mode of government. Only the individual person and public governmental authorities – Political Organs of the State – were considered.

---

[655] Jensen and Meckling, *op cit*, note 623.

[656] Alchian and Demsetz, *op cit*, note 173, p. 795.

[657] Jensen and Meckling, *op cit*, note 623.

[658] Sciuli, *op cit*, note 506, pp. 190–191.

The same applied in France where the 1789 Revolution led to the destruction of all intermediary bodies.

8.1 State Affairs

Everywhere, in the early nineteenth century, the formation of business corporations was a State affair. Whether in France, in England – even in the States of the US – the creation of business corporations was initially authorized on a case-by-case basis by the *government* for *public* purposes only.[659] Originally, this technique to concentrate capital was seen as a substitute for public borrowing,[660] allowing the construction of *public* equipment (roads, bridges, canals) in the *public* interest.[661] At the 1896 meeting of the American Economic Association, Henry Carter Adams summarized his President's address by saying that:

---

[659] For France, *see* André Amiaud, 'L'évolution du droit des sociétés par actions', in *Le droit privé au milieu du XXème siècle – Etudes offertes à G. Ripert*, Paris: Librairie Générale de Droit et de Jurisprudence (1950), tome 2, pp. 287–295; Claude Champaud, *Le pouvoir de concentration de la société par action*, Paris: Sirey (1962), p. 4; Paul Durant, 'L'évolution de la condition juridique des personnes morales de droit privé', in *Le droit privé français au milieu du XXème siècle – Etudes offertes à G. Ripert*, Paris: Librairie Générale de Droit et de Jurisprudence (1950), tome 1, pp. 138–159; C.E. Freedeman, 'Joint-Stock Business Organizations in France, 1807–1867', 39(2) *Business History Review*, pp. 184–204; C.E. Freedeman, *Joint-Stock Enterprises in France 1807–1867: From Privileged Company to Modern Corporation*, Chapel Hill: University of North Carolina Press (1979); *generally* Ripert, *op cit*, note 43; for England, *see* B.C. Hunt, *The Development of the Business Corporation in England, 1800–1867*, New York: Russell & Russell (1969, 1st edition 1936); for the United States, *see* Merrick E. Dodd, 'American Business Association Law a Hundred Years Ago and Today', in A. Reppy (ed.), *Law: A Century of Progress – 1835–1935*, New York: New York University Press, (1937), vol. 3. pp. 254–293; L.M. Friedman, *A History of American Law*, New York, Simon & Schuster (1973); R.E. Seavoy, *The Origins of the American Business Corporation (1784–1855) – Broadening the Concept of Public Service during Industrialization*, Westport: Greenwood Press (1982).

[660] Anne Lefebvre-Teillard, 'L'intervention de l'État dans la constitution des S.A.', 59 *Revue Historique de Droit Français et Etranger*, pp. 383–418 (1981), p. 393; Adams, *op cit*, note 28, pp. 117–118 & 145–147.

[661] As a consequence, it was mainly the *société en commandite* which was the legal instrument used to concentrate capital at the time of the first industrial revolution; Fohlen, *op cit*, note 46, and 'Société anonyme et développement capitaliste sous le Second Empire', *Histoire des Entreprises*, pp. 65–79 (1961).

> A corporation … may be defined in the light of history as a body created by law for the purpose of attaining public ends through an appeal to private interests.[662]

A major trigger everywhere for the evolution which ensued was the construction of railroads.[663] After 1845, the rapid growth of rail transport was crucial in accelerating economic growth. The railways encouraged investment in larger production units that could take advantage of the increased size of the markets[664] and stimulated the development of production technologies that supported overall economic growth. In the US, the railways also accelerated the expansion of regional markets to the point of creating a *national* market.[665] They were much more efficient than canals or steamers in the face of the enormous dimensions of the US territory, and they served much larger areas that the lack of waterways prevented from fully participating in the commercial economy.[666]

None of this could have occurred without recourse to the limited liability corporation. Corporations were used to create objects of property required for the development of the market economy. To do this, objects of private property – such as the private plots of land which combination was required to create the tracks of land necessary for the creation of canals or railroads – had to be forcefully appropriated via expropriation. And the

---

[662] Ciepley, *op cit*, note 508, p. 142.

[663] Alfred Chandler concludes that the spread of the factory system depended on the 'reliability and spread of the new communication and transportation. Without a steady, all-weather flow of goods into and out of their establishments, manufacturers would have had difficulty in maintaining a permanent working-force, and in keeping their expensive machinery and equipment operating profitably'; Alfred Chandler, *The Visible Hand – The Managerial Revolution in American Business*, Cambridge: Belknap Press (1979), p. 245. Similarly, Oliver Williamson notes that 'the incentive to integrate forward from manufacturing into distribution would have been much less without the low-cost, reliable, all weather transportation afforded by the railroad'; Oliver Williamson, 'The Modern Corporation: Origins, Evolutions, Attributes', 19(4) *Journal of Economic Literature*, pp. 1537–1568 (1981), p. 1551. Additionally, Williamson notices that 'forward integration by manufacturers into distribution was one of the significant consequences of the appearance of the railroads. Low-cost transportation combined with the telegraph and telephone communication permitted manufacturers efficiently to service a larger market and, as a consequence, realize greater economies of scale in production'; *ibid*, p. 1553. For France, *see generally* Fohlen, *op cit*, note 46 and Fohlen, *op cit*, note 661.

[664] Alfred D. Chandler, *Scale and Scope – The Dynamics of Industrial Capitalism*, Cambridge: Belknap (1994).

[665] But this is true in many other jurisdictions as well; Gauchet, *op cit*, note 340, p. 454.

[666] Seavoy, *op cit*, note 659, pp. 268–269.

legal instrument used to gather the financial resources to proceed with the creation of these exceptional assets was itself in derogation of the traditional private 'rules of the game'. By derogation to the principle of unlimited liability, weak assets partitioning via unlimited liability partnerships and so on, solid legal persons owning these assets and isolating the shareholders from their potential misfortunes and the assets from the shareholders' misfortunes, were introduced, via special laws, into the legal system.

The risks to the individual person and society created by corporations were very visible at the time of the 'Copernican revolution' that the American and French revolutions – the First Constitutional Revolutions – operated.[667] Opponents to the introduction of this type of legal instrument into the liberal legal system saw in them the seeds of the creation of a new feudalism, in total contradiction with liberal principles. They saw great dangers in them.[668] Discussions about them were often inflamed. Those who demanded the right to be able to freely create these 'wonderful instruments of capitalism'[669] in the name of free enterprise confronted those who emphasized that these instruments would be precisely the cause of the disappearance of the freedoms of the individual person. The idea that shareholders could see their liability limited to their contribution was perceived as a source of serious dangers. Equally, the idea of granting management rights to agents who did not own the assets themselves was perceived as a serious risk of generating irresponsibility. By concentrating property rights, limited liability corporations were concentrating the decision-making power as a matter of principle into organizations which, consequently, were losing some of their 'private' character. It is not *individual owners* who were going to make decisions over their own assets and be potentially liable as a consequence. It is *agents*, acting on behalf of potentially eternal and powerful organizations, who were going to make decisions about somebody else's property.

Yet in the second half of the nineteenth century, the liberalization of corporation law would be almost complete.[670] The dual phenomenon of industrialization, nationalization of the market in the US and internationalization of trade in other parts of the world, and especially Europe, was instrumental in overcoming the States' resistance to the introduction of this legal technique. This 'liberalization movement' came

---

[667] Levy-Bruhl, *op cit*, note 44, pp. 40–52.

[668] Saleilles, *op cit*, note 42, pp. 4–5. Lefebvre-Teillard, *op cit*, note 660, p. 389.

[669] As expressed in Ripert, *op cit*, note 43, starting at p. 109.

[670] Abram Chayes, 'The Modern Corporation and the Rule of Law', in Edward S. Mason (ed.), *The Corporation in Modern Society*, Cambridge: Harvard University Press, (1959), pp. 25–45, at p. 35.

because of a mix of competition among firms and, derivatively, among States to facilitate firms' activities. States were led to abandon their initial resistance to letting private parties create limited liability corporations. As we have seen in the General Introduction (at pp. 14–20), this relaxation of corporate law has been nicknamed in the US the 'race-to-the-bottom' by its opponents and the 'race-to-efficiency' (or 'to-the-top') by its proponents.[671] Similar developments took place in Europe, in the wake of the expansion of free trade *via* treaties in the last third of the nineteenth century.[672]

8.2 Modern Capitalism

The introduction of the business corporation into the liberal legal system will lead to the advent of modern capitalism and, ultimately, to its financial form.

Capitalism, although it is very hard to define, is of course older. Fernand Braudel linked its rise to the growth of cities and then to the State (*see* Section 3.5). But modern *financial* capitalism is different. It leads to the simultaneous existence of two forms of capital in connection with the same bundle of assets and contracts used to structure firms.

Corporations own the assets used in the business operations and contract about their use. Capital here refers to an aggregation of economic goods and/or services used in the *production* of other goods and/or services. Corporations concentrate the prerogatives of decision-making as a matter of principle into potentially eternal artificial legal persons; shareholders own the shares issued by these corporations; and the management teams use the prerogatives over the productive assets to organize production into stable organizations.

Shares are also understood as a form of capital. But they are not *productive* goods. The value of this form of capital will depend on the expected *financial* performance of the operations of the corporation having issued the shares. The property rights and contracts concentrated into

---

[671] *See generally* Mark J. Roe, 'Delaware's Competition', 117 *Harvard Law Review* (2003). *See also* Seavoy, *op cit,* note 659.

[672] Jean-Philippe Robé, *L'entreprise et le droit*, Paris: Presses Universitaires de France (1999), pp. 60–61; reprinted in *Le temps du monde de l'entreprise – Globalisation et mutation du système juridique*, Paris: Dalloz (2015), pp. 100–139. For France, *see, e.g.,* C.E. Freedeman, *Joint-Stock Enterprises in France 1807–1867: From Privileged Company to Modern Corporation*, Chapel Hill: University of North Carolina Press (1979). For England, *see, e.g.,* B.C. Hunt, *The Development of the Business Corporation in England, 1800–1867*, New York: Russell & Russell (1969, 1st edition 1936).

business corporations, and the securities they have issued, can actually see their evaluation move in *opposite* directions because they are priced in different markets. Financial capital is valued autonomously from the value of the underlying productive assets, its value being mostly based on expectations regarding future financial returns, the creation of so-called 'shareholder value'. This is possible because the property over the assets of the corporation and the property over the financial instruments issued by the corporation represent separate property rights which do exist autonomously and are priced in different markets. But, contrary to an error shared by Marxists[673] and many mainstream economists, the financial capital is not *fictitious*. This shared mistake is again the outcome of confusing property with things and their possession. Shareholders own assets (shares) which provide prerogatives and have a value as a consequence. Conceivably, the market value of a corporation's shares could drop indefinitely without hurting the corporation.[674] The reduction in the value of its share capital does not impact directly the content of its assets or the contracts it executed. Of course, however, failing stock prices shake a corporation's suppliers and customers. They will cut off its access to equity financing, certain loans may be called. It can open the market for corporate control, the devalued stock of the corporation making it easier to purchase it and change management. The financial markets do indeed impact on the operations of corporations and on the management of real assets.

With the development of financial markets and the elaboration of complex Financial Structures (more on this notion later, at Section 8.4) the shareholders operating in the financial markets will use their prerogatives over corporations in ways which will affect their operations. Many active – and indirect – shareholders are more and more removed from the effective business operations. This is what leads to the opposition between what can be called the *real capital* (tools, machines, buildings, patents, trademarks etc.) and *financial capital* (shares, bonds, derivatives, structured securities). The existence of the two in combination and relative independence has led to the so-called 'financialization' of the economy, i.e. the pursuit of short-term 'shareholder value' in the management of business firms.

To understand how this came about, the firm must be differentiated from its Financial Structure which lies on top of it when shareholders are professional investors. The transactions among the legal entities in the Financial Structure of the firm are separate from the firm as an economic

---

[673] Cédric Durand, *Le capital fictif*, Paris: Les Prairies Ordinaires (2014), p. 67.

[674] Paul P. Harbrecht, 'The Modern Corporation Revisited', 64 *Columbia Law Review*, pp. 1410–1428 (1964), p. 1419.

organization because they do not contribute to the production of the goods or the services the firm delivers. Buying the shares issued by the corporation in the *secondary* market is an 'investment' only for the purchaser: the price paid for the shares does *not* go into the treasury of the corporation whose stock is bought.[675] The wealth flows from one purchasing shareholder to a selling one without significantly furthering the function of capital formation, capital application, capital use or risk bearing. Despite the constantly repeated assertions made by mainstream economists, a purchaser of stock on the *secondary* market does not contribute his savings to any enterprise, thus enabling it to invest in plants and operations.[676] He does not take *any risk* for any new *productive* investment: he merely estimates the chances of the corporation's shares increasing in value. His only contribution to the economic system is the provision of *liquidity* to pre-existing shareholders. This is a very important function, because it justifies in part – but in part only – why shareholders invest in the *primary* market for shares. In other words, contrary to widespread belief, for the most part (i.e. transactions on the secondary market), 'stock exchanges neither allocate capital, nor serve their classical function of directing savings into productive use'.[677] The financial markets are a parallel system of wealth investment which has grown alongside the productive system but in relative isolation.

The Financial Structure, however, because of the feedback effect of the investors' expectations, has a strong impact on the way the firm's operations are organized.

But prior to addressing the impact of the Financial Structure of the firm, we first need to understand the interaction between the firm and the State.

The assets owned by corporations are property rights. They are therefore rights of decision-making as a matter of principle in connection with the objects of property. The State's widely recognized role in connection with economic activity is to internalize negative externalities and to reduce inequality, in accordance with the democratically expressed wishes of the population.

Consequently, the legal environment offered by any State may be more or less attractive for any given activity. But in a globalized world, the firms' Financial Structures lead to a global race to the bottom which prevents the Power System from properly operating.

---

[675] *Ibid.*

[676] Berle, *op cit*, note 24, p. 16.

[677] Harbrecht, *op cit*, note 674, pp. 1415–1416.

8.3 The Interaction Between Firms and States

To understand the interaction between firms and States, we can use a simple model: a firm is created in Country A. It faces the evolution of the legal landscape, adapts to it and uses the opportunities it offers.

One can start with a firm structured using one single corporation. The corporation, as a separate legal person, is used to legally structure the firm. Agents of the corporation, acting in its name, execute a series of contracts enabling the corporation to have access to the resources required for the operation of the business. The supply contracts are the conduits used to convey the productive resources needed by the organization to perform its activities. The firm replaces market relationships by organizational ones to produce goods or services. The production process is not a market process: it is a process controlled by the firm's organization.

The supply contracts pursuant to which inputs are being integrated into the firm's organization can be pure sale and purchase agreements, or loans, or employment contracts. Upstream in the value chain, there may be other firms or individuals. Downstream, the outputs can be purchased and used by other firms or consumers.

There is then what the firm does: creating or destroying value using the inputs it is coordinating. To survive, the organization needs to create value: it needs to be financially sustainable. Accounting rules are fundamental in determining whether value has been created or not by the firm. It is the *accounting system* which determines which firms are creating value and should survive and which are destroying value and should disappear. Or at least, this is how the system should be working and, for many reasons which I will explain in more detail later on, the accounting rules are quite deficient in differentiating which firms are value producing from those which are value destroying. Accounting rules are not neutral. If certain costs in the process leading to the production of goods or services are neglected, the accounting of the firm's operations can lead to the conclusion that the firm is creating value when it is not the case. It is a very serious issue in our present world in which, for example, environmental costs are in great part neglected and not accounted for. This is what is leading to the dramatic destruction of our natural environment.

To understand how firms and States interact in an open, globalized economy, I will develop a simple model showing how firms adapt and adjust to regulatory changes and opportunities.

In this scenario, to facilitate understanding the operation of the model, the turnover and the assets used in the production **remain constant**. The firm produces **the same** widgets, in **the same** quantity and quality with the same inputs and they are sold to clients for **the same** price. All other things remain equal at each step apart from the specific change identified, the consequences of which are shown in the model.

In our starting position, Corporation A Inc. in Country A owns intellectual property ('IP'), some cash and a factory. It has three individual shareholders: X, Y and Z. It purchases raw materials, employs workers transforming these materials into widgets and has contracted a loan with a bank to have access to funds to pay for the raw materials and salaries while the production takes place and clients are found to purchase the production.

The initial structure of the enterprise is as follows in Figure 8.1:

Figure 8.1: The initial structure of the enterprise

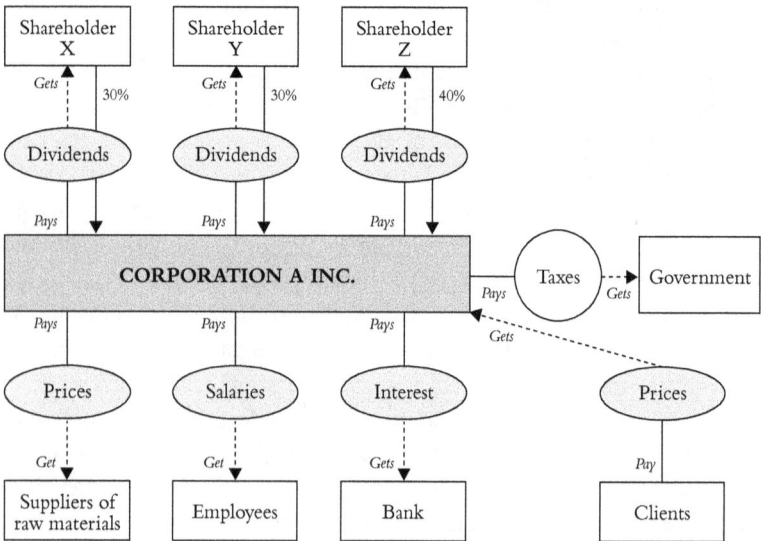

Step 1 – I start with the following assumptions. Over a period, the prices of the inputs and of the output, the turnover and the tax rate are as follows in Table 8.1.

[In this model, there is no line for the cost of facilities, machinery and maintenance, for example, because they would not affect the outcome and omitting them allows to keep things simpler and clear.]

Table 8.1: The simplified presentation of profits and losses at the starting position

Raw materials cost (input)	100
Labour cost (input)	100
Interest cost (input)	30
Sales (output)	500
Profits	270
Tax (30%) cost	81
After-tax profits	**189**

Step 2 – A new law is introduced which increases labour costs by 20 per cent.

The result of the firm's operations over the same period with the same assumptions apart from the rise in labour costs are now as follows in Table 8.2:

Table 8.2: The impact of labour costs increases at Step 2

Raw materials cost (input)	100	
Labour cost (input)	120	(+20)
Interest cost (input)	30	
Sales (output)	500	
Profits	250	(–20)
Tax (30%) cost	75	(–6)
After-tax profits	**175**	(–14)

All things otherwise remaining equal, after-tax profits (and taxes) are reduced as a result of a local political decision to reallocate part of the value created to labour. Assuming the statute has been democratically adopted, the State played its redistributive role, as accepted, inter alia, by Bénabou and Tirole.

Step 3 – As a result of the new statute and the increased labour costs, Corporation A Inc. decides to move half of its producing operations to Country B where labour costs are two-thirds cheaper.

The results of the firm's operations are now as follows in Table 8.3, again, everything else remaining equal.

This reorganization of the producing activities leads to an increase in after-tax profits of 28 units (and of taxes by 12) compared with the situation in Step 2 and of 14 (and 6) units compared with the original situation in Step 1.

Table 8.3: The impact of the production delocalization in Country B at Step 3

	Total	Country A	Country B	
Raw materials cost (input)	100	50	50	
Labour cost (input)	80	60	20	(−40)
Interest cost (input)	30	15	15	
Sales (output)	500			
Profits	290			(+40)
Tax (30%) cost	87			(+12)
After-tax profit	203			(+28)

Both Corporation A Inc. and the State of Country A benefit from the move. But unemployment in Country A has increased.

Step 4 – A new environmental law increases the cost of raw materials in Country A by 20 per cent.
The results of the operations of the firm are now as follows in Table 8.4:

Table 8.4: The impact of the new environmental law at Step 4

	Total	Country A	Country B	
Raw materials cost (input)	110	60	50	(+10)
Labour cost (input)	80	60	20	
Interest cost (input)	30	15	15	
Sales (output)	500			
Profits	280			(−10)
Tax (30%) cost	84			(−3)
After-tax profit	196			(−7)

After-tax profits are decreased by 7 units and taxes by 3. Here also, the new statute is a manifestation of the State's role accepted by Bénabou and Tirole: negative externalities (here environmental damage) are being internalized, leading to reduced profits and taxes (given our assumption that everything else remains equal).

Step 5 – The management of Corporation A Inc. decides to reorganize the operations by creating a holding company. Corporation A Inc. will remain in existence as a subsidiary operating company, but will only distribute the widgets. A new subsidiary will be created in Country B to host all the production. Apart from management employees, the others

are terminated, and new employees are hired in Country B by Corporation B Inc.

The legal structure of the firm is now as follows in Figure 8.2:

Figure 8.2: The legal structure of the firm at Step 5

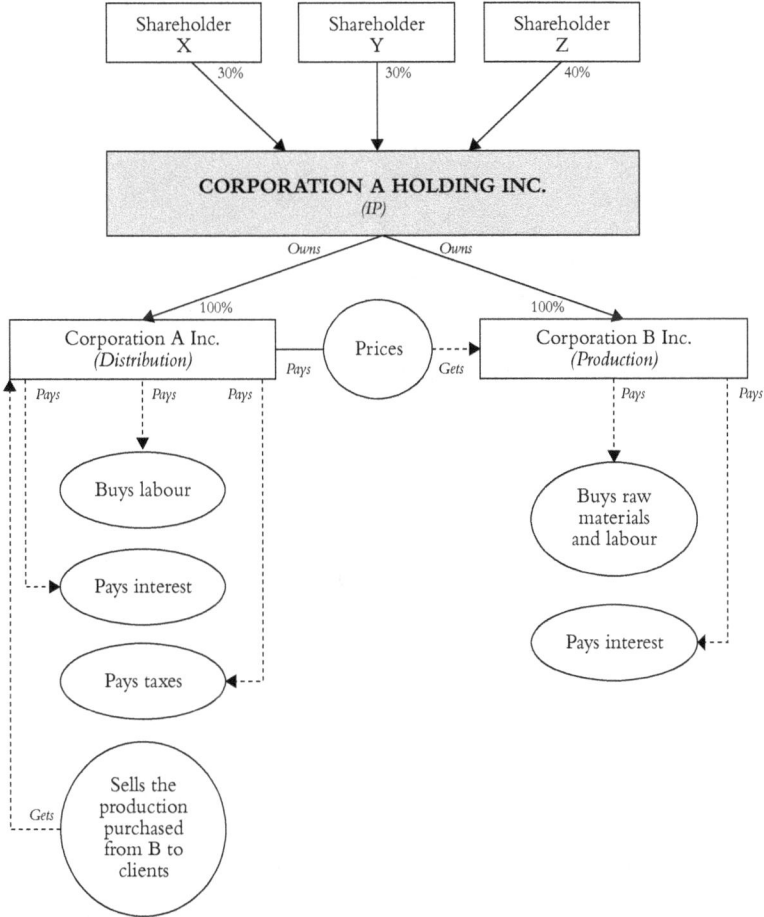

The results of the firm's operations are now as follows in Table 8.5.

Consolidated after-tax profit is increased by 27 units and consolidated tax is increased by 3. Corporation A Holding Inc. clearly benefits from the move. But, of course, the negative externality (environmental damage) has been moved to Country B and there is even less employment in Country A. And Country A will collect fewer taxes: 76 units instead of 84. Country B, now hosting the polluting activity, collects 11 units in taxes and has attracted investments and jobs.

Table 8.5: The impact of the increased production delocalization in Country B at Step 5

	Total	Country A	Country B	
Raw materials cost (input)	100	0	100	(−10)
Labour cost (input)	60	30	30	(−10)
Interest cost (input)	30	15	15	
Sales B to A			200	
Profits made by B			55	
Tax (20%) cost for B			11	
After-tax profit for B			44	**(+44)**
Sales A to clients		500		
Price paid to B		200		
Profits made by A		255		
Tax (30%) cost for A		76		
After-tax profit for A		179		**(−17)**
Consolidated after-tax profit		**223**		**(+27)**

Step 6 – In this step, the management of Corporation A Holding Inc. decides to locate the IP initially owned by Corporation A Inc. in a subsidiary (Corporation C Inc.) directly owned by the shareholders.

A 5 per cent royalty will be paid on the turnover of the entities making use of the IP.

No tax is payable on royalties in the jurisdiction chosen to incorporate the new subsidiary.

The legal structure of the firm is now as follows in Figure 8.3:

Figure 8.3: The legal structure of the firm at Step 6

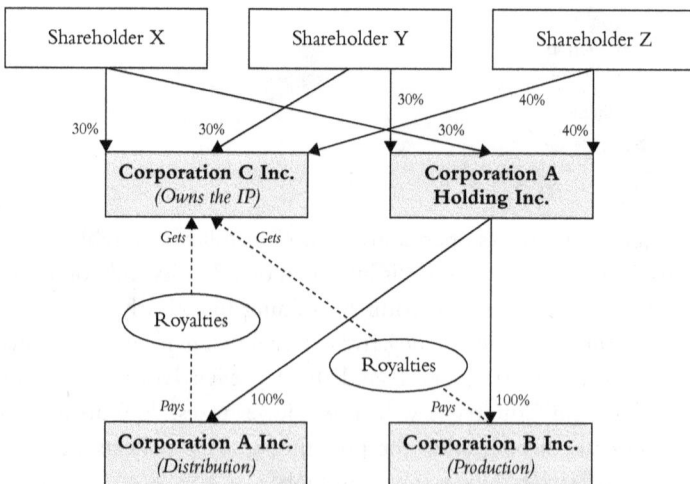

The results of the operations of the firm are now as follows in Table 8.6:

Table 8.6: The impact of the offshoring of the IP in Country C at Step 6

	Total	Country A	Country B	Country C	
Raw materials cost (input)	100	0	100	0	
Labour cost (input)	60	30	30	0	
Interest cost (input)	30	15	15	0	
Royalties paid to C	35	25	10	0	(+35)
Sales B to A			200		
Profits made by B			45		
Tax (20%) cost for B			9		
After-tax profit for B			**36**		**(−8)**
Sales A to clients		500			
Price paid to B		200			
Profits made by A		230			
Tax (30%) cost for A		69			
After-tax profit for A		**161**			**(−18)**
Royalties collected by C				35	
Tax (0%) cost for C				0	
After-tax profit for C				**35**	
Consolidated after-tax profit		**232**			**(+9)**

Consolidated after-tax profit is increased by 9 and consolidated tax is reduced by 9. In this move, Corporation A Holding Inc. increases its profits, but the State in Country A collects lower taxes (69 instead of 76) and the same applies to the State in Country B, which collects 9 instead of 11.

Step 7 – In the final step, a management services company is created in a jurisdiction which taxes the income derived from such services at a rate of 5 per cent.

This company will provide management assistance to all the operating subsidiaries of the group (Corporation A Inc. (distribution) and Corporation B Inc.).

All these companies in the group will pay a 3 per cent service charge on their turnover to this entity.

The legal structure of the firm is now as follows in Figure 8.4.

The results of the operations of the firm are now as follows in Table 8.7.

Here again, after-tax profits are increased (by 1 unit) and taxes are reduced (by 1). The two States in both Countries A and B lose 3 units and 1 unit, respectively.

Figure 8.4: The legal structure of the firm at Step 7

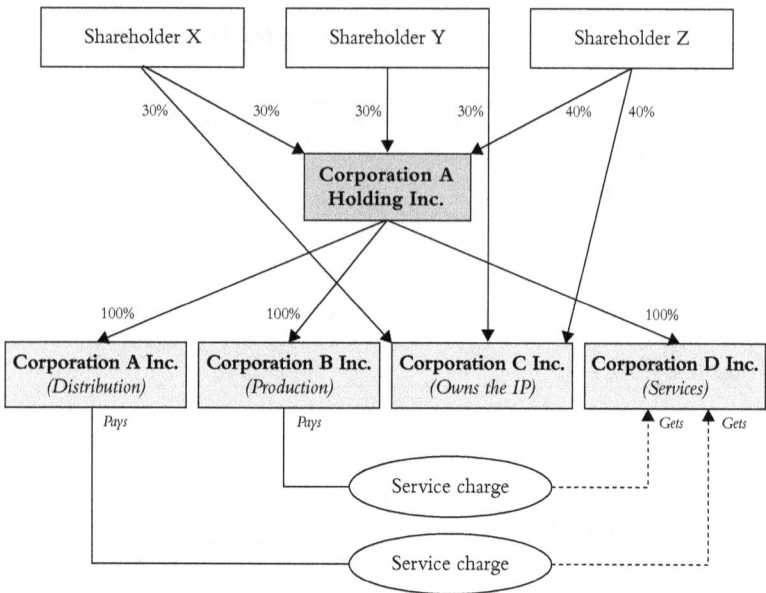

Table 8.7: The impact of the offshoring of management services in Country D at Step 7

	Total	Country A	Country B	Country C	Country D	
Raw materials cost (input)	100	0	100	0	0	
Labour cost (input)	60	20	30	0	10	
Interest cost (input)	30	15	15	0	0	
Royalties paid to C	35	25	10	0	0	
Royalties paid to D	21	15	6	0	0	(+21)
Sales B to A			200			
Profits made by B			39			
Tax (20%) cost for B			8			
After-tax profit for B			31			(−5)
Sales A to clients		500				
Price paid to B		200				
Profits made by A		225				
Tax (30%) cost for A		68				
After-tax profit for A		157				(−4)

(continued)

THE SPREADING OF THE CORPORATE SYSTEM

Table 8.7: The impact of the offshoring of management services in Country D at Step 7 (continued)

	Total	Country A	Country B	Country C	Country D	
Royalties collected by C				35		
Tax (30%) cost for C				0		
After-tax profit for C				**35**		**(+0)**
Service charge collected by D					21	
Profits made by D					11	
Tax (5%) cost for D					1	
After-tax profit for D					**10**	**(+10)**
Consolidated after-tax profit	**233**					**(+1)**

Several comments can be made based on this model:

- The model is very simple, and many firms use much more sophisticated legal structuring devices to optimize their operations – from their own perspectives. They arbitrage the byzantine legal and fiscal structures of the State System in a way that benefits them, but not necessarily the societies in which they are embedded.[678]
- Of course, the model presented is only a model and the 'accounting' of the operations is kept very simple by only looking at cash movements and disregarding the cost of asset transfers, their tax treatment, amortization and so on.
- The measuring of the impact of any change depends on the numbers chosen, which could be higher or lower. But this does not change the overall *direction* of the impact of the changes, in terms of reduction or increase in costs, profits, taxes and net profits.
- In the model, labour costs are first increased due to the newly adopted statute in Country A at Step 2 but it leads to a reorganization of the enterprise which leads to an overall reduction of labour costs. Salaries and social charges paid in Country A move from 120 to 60 while the replacement cost of the required labour in jurisdiction B is only 20. After-tax profits increase by 28. Corporation A Inc., but also the State

---

[678] Richard Phillips, Hannah Petersen and Ronen Palan, *Estimating the Share of Corporate Income and Profits Controlled by OFC-Based Subsidiaries*, forthcoming, *in fine*.

in Country A and the State in Country B benefit. The only losers are employees in Country A.

- The cost of materials is increased at Step 4, reducing after-tax profits by 7. But this cost is also reduced thanks to an internal reorganization. After-tax profits increase by 27, a net gain for Corporation A Inc. of 17. The State in Country A collects less taxes (a reduction of 8), while the State in Country B collects more taxes. But the pollution of the environment increases in Country B.

- Then the tax organization of the group is optimized, at Steps 6 and 7, by the creation of two subsidiaries in low or zero tax jurisdictions to host the IP and management services. Overall, profits increase again by 9 and 1 thanks to these two moves, a cost directly borne by the States in Countries A and B.

- The after-tax profits of the corporation in Country A are significantly reduced over the period (−32). Its consolidated after-tax profits, however, are significantly increased (+44).

The main observation is that in an open globalized world, firms have at their disposal legal instruments which they can use to adjust their *internal* organization to reduce their costs, the negative consequences (for them) of certain statutes, and increase their net profits.

This phenomenon is totally ignored by those who do not recognize the difference between 'the firm' and 'the corporation'. In the original structuring of the firm in our model, there is only one corporation, with producing activities in one country, one workforce and one government involved. At the end of the various reorganizations detailed, the firm which is still producing the *same* quantity of widgets for consumption and collects the *same* turnover − as a result of our assumptions − is now organized using *five* corporations with two in the original State jurisdiction (Country A), production being organized by another corporation in another country (Country B), another entity in another country (Country C) owning the intellectual property and yet another corporation providing services for the rest of the group from another State jurisdiction (Country D).

The opportunities offered by the internal corporate reorganizations are particularly hard to resist in a world in which the dominant mantra is that corporate officers have a legal *duty* to maximize 'shareholder value'. In our model, the sums which can be distributed to Shareholders X, Y and Z have increased significantly (from 189 to 233). Shareholder value *has* been created. But *not a single additional widget* has been created for consumption. The turnover is the same. 'Value' is created because the original employees have been terminated and replaced by less expensive ones; because the natural environment is damaged and because the overall tax cost has been reduced. *Shareholder value* has increased; but no *real value* has been added. This corruption of the language regarding 'value' is typical of the dominant Newspeak which prevents the understanding that the so-called creation of 'shareholder value' often means 'real value' destruction.[679] As written by Rob Gray, '*organizational income has been grossly overstated for some considerable time*'.[680] This is one of the single most important issues of our time: dominant economic theory advocates corporate governance rules based on a principal/agent theory which is highly deficient because of its ignorance of the legal and accounting systems. Today's productive organizations proclaim the creation of 'value' when in fact they are destroying State institutions and forms of capital (social and environmental) other than financial.

We will now see how the mandate to 'maximize shareholder value' is imposed on firms by looking at their Financial Structure and how it is also being 'optimized' in a globalized world.

This part of the organization of the World Power System lies on top of enterprises. It is *not* part of enterprises, of firms, because it does *not* contribute to the production of real-life products or services. It is purely financial. I call this aspect of the structuring of ownership relationships in a firm the 'Financial Structure'.

8.4 The Financial Structure of Firms

We can take as a starting point the same Corporation A Inc. we started with when we looked at the firm's structure in the World Wide Web of Contracts.

As a reminder, the starting position is as set out in Figure 8.5.

In the starting position, Shareholders X, Y and Z are shareholders because of their contribution to Corporation A Inc. At the incorporation stage, X and Y contributed the factory they originally jointly owned. Z got shares because he contributed the intellectual property ('IP') and cash. As a result, X received 30 per cent of the shares in Corporation A Inc., Y also received 30 per cent and Z 40 per cent.

---

[679] Supiot, *op cit*, note 429, p. 134. *See also* Margaret M. Blair, *Ownership and Control – Rethinking Corporate Governance for the Twenty-First Century*, Washington, D.C.: The Brookings Institution (1995), p. 241.

[680] Rob Gray, 'Accounting and Environmentalism: An Exploration of the Challenge of Gently Accounting for Accountability, Transparency and Sustainability', 17(5) *Accounting, Organization and Society*, pp. 399–425 (1992), p. 419.

Figure 8.5: The financial structure of the firm at the starting position

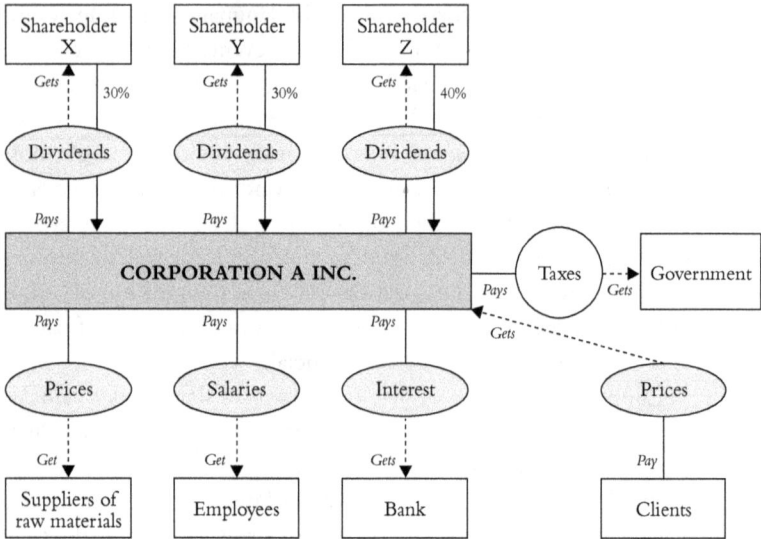

The steps I described so far in the legal adaptation of the firm's legal organization to the opportunities offered by a globalized economy are *independent* from the ones I will analyse now. These following steps relate to the evolution of the Financial Structure, i.e. to the structuring of the ownership of the *share* capital. Of course, very different ownership structures can be created to optimize the tax treatment of the flows of income and capital gains derived from the ownership of the shares issued by the corporations used to structure business firms.

Initially, in our model, Corporation A Inc. was created by three entrepreneurs who contributed assets and developed a business via Corporation A Inc. They progressively developed a group of corporations – for the reasons we have seen – and in the process, Corporation A Holding Inc. became the holding company of a group of companies to serve as the legal backbone of an evolving enterprise. Our entrepreneurs were successful, and investors are interested in buying the business from them. Three investors decide to combine their forces. They offer three billion dollars to Shareholders X, Y and Z who decide to sell their shares. Shareholders X and Y make 900 million dollars each. Shareholder Z makes 1.2 billion.

It is relevant to note that Corporation A Holding Inc. earns *nothing* in this transaction: when shareholders sell their shares, they make a capital gain (or losses) and collect the proceeds. The underlying corporation collects *nothing*. It is quite important to notice this because the notion that shareholders invest 'in companies' is right only when they invest in the *primary* market for shares, i.e. when they contribute something to the company and get shares in exchange. This is what Shareholders X, Y and Z did when they created their business. The shareholders acquiring their shares, however, do not make *any* investment in Corporation A Holding Inc., which is not richer or poorer following the transaction. The selling shareholders are.

For reasons I will explain hereunder, the acquisition structure is as set out in Figure 8.6.

This acquisition structure may seem excessively complex. In fact, it is quite simple, and many real-life structures are much more sophisticated and refined. In addition, the Financial Structure described hereunder is not particularly aggressive and is created for a wealth of *legitimate* reasons. But appreciating the reasons underlying the creation of this Financial Structure is useful to understand how the use of the legal system may be legitimate or may lead to abuses.

We will now look at the reasons for the apparent complexity of this acquisition structure.

- Corporation A Holding Inc., the 'target' of the acquisition, is at the bottom of the structure. It is the same legal entity as the one on top of the group of corporations used to structure the business, as shown in the beginning of Section 8.3. It is easy to understand that anyone purchasing 100 per cent of the shares issued by Corporation A Holding Inc. will control the outcome of its shareholder assembly meetings and therefore will be able to appoint the Board members – the directors – who will be in a position to appoint the CEO. A new holding company (Holdco SAS (France)) has been created to serve as the immediate vehicle for the acquisition. The reason for this is that in many countries a company owning 100 per cent of the share capital of another one can create a so-called 'tax integration'. For overall purposes, the companies are separate legal entities; but for tax purposes, they are treated as a single entity. It means that if the acquisition company – in our case Holdco SAS (France) – borrows to finance part of the acquisition cost of the shares issued by the target company (Corporation A Holding Inc.), the interest cost will come as a deduction of the income made by Corporation A Holding Inc. Consequently, Corporation A Holding Inc. will bear part of the cost of the acquisition of its own shares. This possibility is of course heavily employed.
- The three (indirect) investors, at the top of the structure, are three different legal entities: (1) Investor ONE Holding Inc., (2) a US Pension Trust and (3) Investor TWO Holding Inc. They themselves have their own Financial Structure (not visible in our chart) on top of them,

Figure 8.6: The acquisition structure

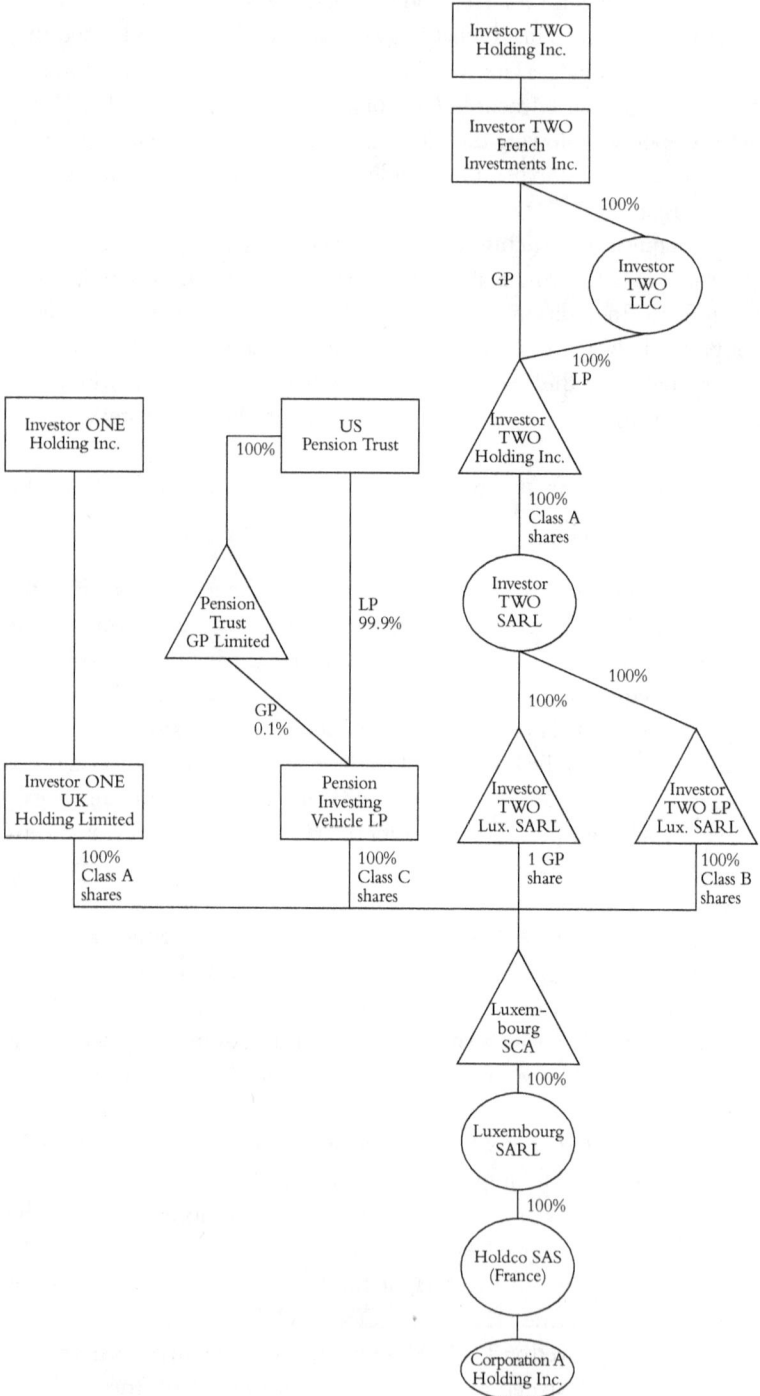

which can be made up of individuals or of other companies, up to individuals. The chain of corporations between 'real productive assets' and the ultimate individual beneficiaries (sometimes called 'beneficial owners') can be extremely long depending on the circumstances and, very often, the 'tax planning' of the beneficial owners. Increasingly, with the concentration of wealth we are experiencing, this planning and the investment strategies are conducted via so-called 'Family Offices', which are a type of specific business organization professionalizing much of the investments and administrative burdens of wealthy families.

In our example, the three financial investors have invested via separate structures until we reach Luxembourg SCA in the chart. This is their sole joint investment vehicle.

I will now explain each of the three shareholders' investment structures. Each acquirer's acquisition structure, which will form part of the Financial Structure of the firm, has its own rationale.

- Investor ONE Holding Inc. invested via a company called Investor ONE UK Holding Limited. One reason for this can be that it has other investments made via this specific structure. One cannot tell by just looking at the structure. The investment in Luxembourg SCA has been made via the purchase of 100 per cent of the class A shares issued by Luxembourg SCA. This is one way to structure equity investments: three investors investing 25 per cent, 35 per cent and 40 per cent of the purchase price of an acquisition can purchase 25 per cent, 35 per cent and 40 per cent of the same class of shares. Or they can purchase 100 per cent of each of three categories ('classes') of shares, the first representing 25 per cent, the second 35 per cent and the third 40 per cent of the investment. These different categories of shares give different rights and obligations to the different shareholders.
- The US Pension Trust invested by purchasing indirectly 100 per cent of the class C shares. The beneficiaries of a pension trust are usually present and future retirees, the purpose of the pension trust being to convert retirement savings into investments to put the pension trust in a position to pay pensions to retirees from the day they stop working. Like many investors, they are risk averse. The reader should note that along the line of investment from Corporation A Holding Inc. to the top of the investors identified in the corporate chain, all the entities are limited liability companies or partnerships. It means that normally, liabilities in one company cannot move up the corporate chain. But despite this structural, and usually efficient protection, there is still a remote risk of 'piercing the corporate veil'. In some

unusual circumstances and in some jurisdictions, it can be sometimes considered that shareholders exceeded their role as shareholders, that they participated to the management of the operations, and that they should be held liable for this in case of mismanagement. To prevent this from happening, several devices have been invented.

One of them is the use of one or several limited partnerships in the corporate chain. This is what the US Pension Trust did when it decided to invest via Pension Investing Vehicle LP. This vehicle is a limited partnership in which all the decisions are made by a so-called 'General Partner', the Limited Partner having a purely passive role. The General Partner in Pension Investing Vehicle LP is Pension Trust GP Limited. The Limited Partner is US Pension Trust. US Pension Trust owns 99.9 per cent of the shares of Pension Investing Vehicle LP. But because it is a passive investor, it cannot be held to be a de facto manager: it makes *no* decisions. Pension Trust GP Limited makes *all* the decisions. But it will typically own only one share in Pension Investing Vehicle LP, and this one share is the extent of what is at risk in case it were deemed to be a de facto manager. And it is itself a limited liability structure protecting the US Pension Trust from liabilities moving upstream. One easy way to designate these structures is to call them a 'fuse'. If anything goes wrong downstream in the corporate chain, the 'fuse' goes bankrupt which protects the assets upstream. In this fashion, they are 'bankruptcy remote'.

- Investor TWO Inc. is even more risk averse than US Pension Trust: it has installed two 'fuses', one on top of the other. One reason for this is that it is closer to the real business than the other investors: via Investor TWO Lux. SARL, it is the *general* partner in Luxembourg SCA, the vehicle used by the three investors to make their joint (indirect) investment in Corporation A Holding Inc. As the general partner, it is the one in charge of making the day-to-day decisions in the management of the partnership and therefore bears managerial risks the other partners do not normally have.

- Now looking downstream from Luxembourg SCA onwards, we see another Luxembourg entity and Holdco SAS (France). We know why Holdco SAS (France) has been created: to be able to create a tax integration in France. But what is the use of a second Luxemburg entity (Luxembourg SARL) between Luxembourg SCA and Holdco SAS (France)? There are several reasons to create a 'double Luxco' structure. One of them is to improve the security package given to the banks which are financing the acquisition. This is not very relevant for our purposes. Another one is that it gives an additional option to the investors at the time of the exit of their investment. Depending on the circumstances at this future point in time, when the laws may have changed, it may be better to sell shares in Holdco SAS (France), or shares in Luxembourg SARL or shares in Luxembourg SCA. In each case, the new investor will get control over the operations of the underlying business; but the capital gains (or losses) made by the selling shareholder will be located at a different level in the corporate chain and, potentially, in a different jurisdiction (France or Luxembourg). This increases the opportunities to optimize the tax treatment of the exit from the investment.

In all these acquisition structures, two major considerations dominate: the isolation of risks, to protect the other investments from potential issues arising from a new investment; and the tax treatment of the transaction, at the time the investment is being made, during the time period the investment is held and at the time of the exit from the investment. It does not mean that investors are not interested in the underlying business: they are. They are of course always hoping that they are (indirectly) investing in a business in which there are growth perspectives. But that part of the legal engineering which corresponds to the legal structuring of their investment depends on considerations which have nothing to do with the operations of the underlying business. After risk partitioning, tax optimization is the key concern. And at this level of legal optimization, because we are only dealing with incorporeal assets (shares, loans, bonds, trademarks, patents, algorithms etc.) there is much more flexibility in the design of optimization schemes. Many of the tax-optimizing schemes have exotic names, usually mixing humour and cynicism, such as the '*Dutch Sandwich*' [to avoid EU withholding taxes on untaxed profits moved to non-EU tax havens], the '*Double Irish*' [to avoid US corporate taxation on most non-US profits], the '*Single Malt*' [which directs profits to countries with which Ireland has a double taxation agreement but that do not have any corporation tax], the '*Round Trip*' [through which Mauritius – the 124th economy in the world – is (facially) the largest foreign investor in India – the 6th economy, Indians themselves making the 'Round Trip'], the '*Singapore Sling*', the '*Bermuda black hole*', the '*K2*' (now extinct), the '*Laundromat*' [dear to Russians investing in the UK, the capital of which is now nicknamed Londongrad[681]], the '*inversion*' [meaning the reincorporation of merging companies in a low-tax haven] and so on.

---

[681] Tourist agencies can organize what they call 'Kleptotours' for those who want to see part of the 44,000 properties owned by foreign corporations, 91 per cent of them being registered in tax havens; *e.g.* https://www.letemps.ch/economie/londres-paradis-blanchiment-largent-sale-nigerian

This separate kind of legal engineering in the legal structuring of investments is the reason why what I call the Financial Structure of firms is not part of *firms* as *business organizations*: the members of the firm, including its top management, often have very limited or no knowledge about it nor do they need to know anything about it to be able to operate the business. And those who know about it are usually under strict confidentiality obligations and do not deal with the firm's operations. It is the world of the HNWI (or '*henwees*' for the *cognoscenti*),[682] family offices,[683] hedge funds,[684] private equity funds, trusts, *Anstalten* and other legal devices used to structure wealth, to safeguard it from the various risks it can be exposed to (political, tax, divorce, death, insolvency etc.), maintain its value through diversification and increase it via tax optimization (also known as 'tax planning'). An in-depth analysis of this side of the re-structuring of property rights would require a lengthy treatise. It would be extremely hard to prepare because there are many blind corners in this area. And here, classical legal notions tend to lose their meaning. Each segment in these structures is usually legal. It is the overall structures which are, in a sense, *extralegal*. By this notion, I mean that they make it possible to *legally violate* the fundamental constitutional rules of our societies to accumulate wealth in order to exist in the small high-life social world.

But these structures and the issues they create are not immediately related to my main themes.[685] My main analysis of the World Power

---

[682] High Net Worth Individuals, much sought after by private bankers, having so-called 'family offices' composed of professionals dedicated to them to optimize their personal and financial position worldwide. The 2013 World Wealth Report was jointly produced by Cap Gemini and RBC Wealth Management. It represented one of the largest and most in-depth surveys of HNWIs ever conducted. Worldwide, of course depending on the definition used for the acronym, there were 12 million HNWIs, with a combined wealth of $46.2 trillion.

[683] Since 1980, the share of the world's wealth owned by the top 0.01 per cent has risen from 3 per cent to 8 per cent. The wealth controlled by billionaires worldwide is estimated at close to US$9 trillion [that's US$ 9,000,000,000,000], out of which 3 to 4 US$ trillion are professionally invested via Family Offices; *The Economist*, December 15, 2018.

[684] The ten top-earning hedge-fund managers made between $1.6 billion and $410 million in 2017; https://www.cnbc.com/2017/05/17/the-top-earning-hedge-fund-managers-raked-in-11-billion-last-year.html.

[685] Among the good sources to consult are: Palan, *op cit*, note 54; Ronen Palan, Richard Murphy and Christian Chavagneux, *Tax Havens – How Globalization Really Works*, Ithaca: Cornell University Press (2010); Nicholas Shaxson, *Treasure Islands – Tax Havens and the Men who Stole the World*, London: The Bodley Head (2011).

System via an understanding of the concepts of property rights and of legal person, a differentiation of the notions of firm and corporation and of the institutional structure of the productive economy needs to be mastered before we can even start addressing the complex issues of the Financial Structures. But it is important to understand that via hundreds of thousands – if not millions – of financial structures on top of firms, a considerable proportion of the control over the world economy has migrated out of the States' jurisdiction. State laws are being used to build these Financial Structures, but in a way which prevents any particular State from having a clear vision of who has which interest in what.

What is key to our subject is the issue of firm management. As I have already mentioned in Section 6.14, the corporate officers in Corporation A Holding Inc. manage assets they do not own. These assets belong to Corporation A Holding Inc. and to the subsidiaries of the group. Legally speaking, these officers must manage these assets in Corporation A Holding Inc.'s interest – and, incidentally, in the corporate interest of each of the subsidiaries. But all these legal entities are legal fictions. What is their 'interest'? An individual owning assets manages them in his or her interest as determined by him or her. Being the decision-maker as a matter of principle towards what he or she owns, the owner is the one deciding autonomously what his own interest is. It is one of the purposes of having property rights in the first place. But for corporations, it is individuals who are *not* owners who are going to make the decisions in the name of the owner – usually a corporation, which is a legal fiction. In the furtherance of which interest are they going to make these decisions?

Today's mantra is that firm managers must maximize 'shareholder value'. As we have already seen, however, the creation of shareholder value doesn't necessarily require the creation of *real* value. In our example in Section 8.3, the same quantity of widgets with the same quality is being produced at every step with the same quantity of inputs. But profits, 'shareholder value', are increased. With modern corporate governance, a good part of the so-called 'shareholder value' which is created is in fact the result of the transfer of costs outside the accounting of the operations of the business firm. This is a consequence of the fact that corporations are legal persons while firms are not, as we have seen in Section 6.1. Corporations are instrumentalized within the firm as an organization to the sole benefit of shareholders. Firms can organize themselves using corporations in such a way that they can externalize risks, costs and tax payments onto others which maximizes their profits ('shareholder value') without necessarily creating any real value.

What all this shows is that with the extension of freedom of incorporation, the liberal constitutional scheme which was intrinsically based on an allocation of rights among the State and the individual person has allowed the concentration of subjective prerogatives originally defined to preserve the autonomy of *individual* persons into *organizations*. But firms are not individual persons. They are organizations.[686] The point can be made that the right to property can keep its purely *subjective* dimension only when it remains decentralized at the *individual* level. Once it is concentrated and administered by *organizations*, property takes on a more *objective* dimension of prerogatives to be used by the organization in the interests of those directly affected.[687] But the lack of treatment of 'corporations' in the Constitutions of the late eighteenth century and the development of enterprises in the 'public lawlessness' of private law[688] made it possible to build them as organizations de facto exercising power without reaching official legal life. We still view them as 'private', as owners-being-owned, under a duty to manage what they own in the interests of those 'owning' them. This has prevented understanding them as being part and parcel of the Power System. And it is a major hindrance to an understanding of the process of globalization as the institutionalization of a World Power System in which firms (and their Financial Structures), which do not have any official legal existence, play a major role by preventing the State System from fulfilling its internalizing and redistribution roles.

8.5 Firms versus Corporations

The consequences of the de facto existence of the enterprise (for our purposes, of the 'multinational' enterprise) as an organization and of its inexistence as a legal institution are endless. For instance:

(a) Contracting parties having a contract with a subsidiary corporation of the group enter into an agreement with this legal person only and do not have, in principle, any right against the other companies of the group. It is the case for all contractual parties including employees, who only deal with the subsidiary's local management and assets; they only benefit from local laws. Subordinates are in fact subordinated to other subordinates, while the ultimate decision-makers remain usually

---

[686] *See generally* Dan-Cohen, *op cit*, note 23.

[687] *See generally* Emmanuel Gaillard, *Le pouvoir en droit privé*, Paris: Masson (1985).

[688] *See also* Marcel Gauchet, *L'avènement de la démocratie – II – La crise du libéralisme*, Paris: Gallimard (2007), starting at p. 82; and Isabelle Ferreras, *Critique politique du travail – Travailler à l'heure de la société des services*, Paris: Les Presses de SciencesPo (2007), p. 29.

unreachable locally. And creditors of the local company do not have any right against any other company of the group.

(b) The law applicable to each subsidiary is, as a matter of principle, the one of the State where the subsidiary is incorporated or conducts business. Thus, a single organization (the multinational enterprise) may choose to establish part of its activities in specific legal environments suited to specific activities but not to others. Such an opportunity explains the relocation of businesses: an activity existing in an 'expensive' legal environment (i.e. with imperative norms imposing the internalization of negative externalities into production costs or taxes to redistribute income or which simply offers better schooling, infrastructure and the like to the local population at a higher tax cost) can be relocated in a less 'expensive' legal environment (in which negative externalities are supported wherever they fall or are internalized to a lesser extent, where inequality is less addressed and in which the State provides fewer services to the population – for less tax). Nevertheless, the activity is still carried out by the *same enterprise*, within one *single power structure*, one *single organization*. The multinational enterprise's ability to relocate its business activities throughout the world and the resulting – positive or negative – consequences introduces competition among States for the creation of local legal environments favourable to enterprises (and those who control them via their Financial Structure). States become *market players* and take part in the economic competitive game because their *legal systems* have become a *product* – or even a *service* – that multinational enterprises use to their best advantage.[689] In the process, the States lost the monopoly position a creator of property rights must have to address negative externalities and inequalities. Otherwise, the rights of decision-making as a matter of principle (property rights) are not counterbalanced by the norm-creation capacities of democratic institutions. The States System proves inefficient as a substitute for a properly operating State.

(c) *Intra-enterprise* exchanges are perceived as *inter-national* ones when crossing State borders. But the analysis of States statistics should be reinterpreted in order to take into consideration the reality of economic exchanges. The 'globalization of the economy' corresponds in fact mostly to a phenomenon of 'globalization of enterprises' and

---

[689] Alain Plantey, *De la politique entre les États – Principes de diplomatie*, Paris: Pédone (2nd édition, 1991), pp. 112–113.

of coordinated value chains.[690] For each enterprise, what appears to the external world as 'international trade' is, in fact, trade *internal* to enterprises. It takes place *outside the market*. Contracts are effectively concluded between the various subsidiaries involved to document the economic exchanges among them. Although legally speaking the contracts are entered into between distinct legal entities, it is the *same economic organization* which is *at both ends* of each contract internal to the firm. The fact that a corporation (an autonomous legal person) can control the management of myriads of other corporations (other 'autonomous' legal persons) via share ownership means that organizations can be created within which *planning* and *administration* supplant the market. The constituent units in the corporate group deliver goods and services to each other *not* at the price which would be set in a free market, but at a price set by the top management of the organization.[691] Corporate law lays out constraints on what can be done with the contracts and prices, as corporate officers usually have a duty to manage the company (and thus to enter into contracts) in compliance with the 'corporate interest' of the entity on behalf of which they act. And yet one knows that they can hardly resist their superiors' orders. The terms of the contracts (such as a licence providing for the payment of royalties against the right to use intellectual property, sales providing for the payment of prices in exchange for the delivery of goods or services, loan agreements providing for the payment of interest in connection with an intra-group loan, etc.) are not the same as those negotiated by two distinct parties defending their own interests with no other consideration in mind. Therefore, a large part of international trade takes place *within* organizations, is *organized trade* and is *not market exchange*. The amount of the royalties, the interest rates or the prices paid do not result from market competition. They are not the outcome of negotiations between autonomous market participants. They are set by the organization, the enterprise itself. They are *administered*. For the main part, international economic exchanges are *administered* by 'private organizations'. They are *not* the outcome of market competition. The firm is a *counter market*. The firm is a 'nonmarket or even antimarket institution, though lodged within a market system. ... corporate

---

[690] *See* Section 6.7 and DeAnne Julius, *Global companies and public policy – The growing challenge of foreign direct investment*, London: Pinter Publishers, Royal Institute of International Affairs (1991).

[691] *See* Lippmann, *op cit*, note 83, p. 216.

coordination is a rival to rather than an instrument of market-system coordination'.[692]

There is nothing 'wrong' about this. Early on, Ronald Coase made it clear that:

> in a competitive system there is an optimum amount of planning, and ... an optimum quantity of market operations.[693]

But it is essential to master this fact to understand globalization, which is far from being a globalization of 'markets'. It is the globalization of a complex Power System within which planned enterprises play a key role – and markets play a lesser one. The key market in the present World Economy is the market for State norms which allows global enterprises to tinker with costs and prices. The bulk of international trade does not occur between actors defending each their specific interests, and therefore *indirectly* those of their country of origin, paying or receiving a fiercely negotiated price to agree to buy or sell the object of the exchange. International trade occurs *within organizations*. This phenomenon is so significant that about 80 per cent of cross-border trade is in fact *intra-firm* trade:

> global exports today are dominated by very large companies, most of them transnational corporations [sic: firms]. Large firms [yes: firms] have become the most relevant actors in international trade, although their dominance is hard to quantify precisely, because of data limitations and obstacles to combining country-level trade data with transnational firm–level data.[694]

It is a fact of enormous importance, that the classical economic analysis, obsessed as it is by 'the market', prevents us from perceiving:[695] international trade is *organized* by multinational firms, which derive profits from the pros and cons of localizing this or that part of their activities in a specific location. Prices paid are the result of

---

[692] Lindblom, *op cit*, note 599, p. 75.

[693] Coase, *op cit*, note 198, pp. 12–13.

[694] UNCTAD, *Trade and Development Report 2018 – Power, Platforms and the Free Trade Delusion*, https://unctad.org/en/PublicationsLibrary/tdr2018_en.pdf, p. 53.

[695] *See also* Robert Gilpin, *Global Political Economy – Understanding the International Economic Order*, Princeton: Princeton University Press (2001), pp. 278–304.

organizational decisions; decisions taken within the organizations within which the exchanges take place. The same economic transaction is thus perceived in two ways: for those who perceive it from the outside of the organization within which it occurs, it appears as a *contractual exchange* between two separate legal persons; it looks like 'market exchange'. For those who see the business transaction from the perspective of the inside of the organization within which the exchange transaction takes place, it is a decision taken by the business organization and imposed on two subsidiaries within the organization. The two sides at each end of the exchange relationship are mere instruments of the organization and the price paid is the result of a *decision* within the organization, not a 'market price' arrived at after negotiation.

When two unrelated companies trade with each other, they have opposing interests. The paying party wants to pay as little as possible for a given quantity and quality of products or services and the selling party wants the exact opposite. The result is the payment of a 'market price', often referred to as an 'arm's length price'.[696] But, of course, this does not work for trades among companies within the same *organization*, within the same *firm*.[697] One of the most dramatic illusions of our time is the widespread belief that we live in a market economy. It leads to an ignorance of the micro-institutional reality of the Power System and of its pluralistic Constitution which mixes 'public' macro-powers and micro-powers which remain understood as being 'private' although they are *organized components* of the Power System. The delusion that we live in a market society when we in fact live in a corporate organizational society leads to a gross mismatch between our corporate world and the liberal individualist concepts we use to interpret and address this world. Painting the corporation/firm in private and contractual terms, as a 'nexus of contracts' in particular, hides an organizational reality behind the liberal imagery of a society composed of contracting individuals.[698]

(d) The competition among States' legal systems reaches a climax with tax laws. Each State has a sovereign authority over its tax system; but none

---

[696] *See* ICRICT (Independent Commission for the Reform of International Corporate Taxation), *Declaration of the Independent Commission for the Reform of International Corporate Taxation*, June (2015), p. 7.

[697] For a detailed analysis, *see* Yuri Biondi, 'The Firm as an Enterprise Entity and the Tax Avoidance Conundrum: Perspectives from Accounting Theory and Policy', *Accounting, Economics, and Law* (2017).

[698] *See also* Ciepley, *op cit*, note 508, pp. 139–140.

is unaffected by the tax system of others.[699] At the enterprise level, this is mainly due to the widespread practices of intra-group interest payments (which are tax-deductible), the payment of management services (also tax-deductible), the strategic location of intangibles (Step 6 in our example in Section 8.3) and 'transfer prices'. The prices of the products or services exchanged among the group subsidiaries do not correspond to 'market prices' and can therefore be increased or decreased compared with production costs depending on the advantages or disadvantages resulting from localizing gains or losses under any specific jurisdiction. This is a consequence of the phenomenon described above in paragraph (c). A multinational enterprise can quite easily locate its profits and capital gains in low-tax jurisdictions: it merely needs to acknowledge the profits or gains generated by the enterprise within the accounts of the subsidiaries located in these 'favourable' States' jurisdiction. It is possible to show how this can be done with a simple example.

Let's assume product X is manufactured by Subsidiary A in Country A and sold to Subsidiary C located in Country C. The corporate tax rate is 40 per cent in both Countries A and C. Producing product X in Country A costs 20€ and it can be sold for 100€ to consumers in Country C. Whatever the price paid (from 20 to 100€) by Subsidiary C to Subsidiary A for product X, the overall tax cost will be the same: $(100–20) \times 40$ per cent $= 32€$.

Now let's assume Subsidiary A does not sell product X to Subsidiary C, but instead sells it to Subsidiary B located in Country B. In Country B, the local corporate tax rate is 10 per cent. If Subsidiary A sells product X for 30€ to Subsidiary B which then sells it for 90€ to Subsidiary C, the total corporate tax paid will be $((30–20) \times 40$ per cent$) + ((90–30) \times 10$ per cent$) + ((100–90) \times 40$ per cent$) = 4 + 6 + 4 = 14€$.

Therefore, the effective corporate tax rate borne by the group of corporations/the enterprise in our example is 17.5 per cent $(14/(100–20))$ (as opposed to 40 per cent without involving Subsidiary B); and the State collecting the *highest* amount of tax is the only one having *no* initial involvement in this trade *and* having the *lowest* corporate tax rate. Country B collects 6€ while both Countries A and C now collect only 4€. And Country B collecting 6€ is costing Countries A and C a combined 24€ … Of course, this is the result of the assumptions made; but they show the type of outcomes the administration of prices by firms can lead to. Also, one needs to understand that there

---

[699] *See* ICRICT *op cit*, note 696, p. 12.

is no need for product X to go through Country B: it just needs to be sold via Subsidiary B, delivery being made directly from Subsidiary A to Subsidiary C, the final purchaser within the group. Of course, because of such tricks, most of the statistics relating to international trade are simply irrelevant and classical notions about 'comparative advantage' are also totally irrelevant…

Another important consequence of this is that the artificial introduction of Subsidiary B in the organization of intra-firm trade leads to an increase of 'shareholder value'. The group of corporations increases its profits by paying less tax. More profits are available for distribution to the shareholders. The corporate financials evidence the creation of more 'shareholder value'. But no real *value* has been created. The budgetary needs of Countries A and C remaining the same, other tax payers will have to bear the tax costs; or Countries A and C will increase their deficits and debts; or they will have to reduce the services provided to their local population. It is *essential* to master this phenomenon to understand globalization: it is possible to create 'shareholder value' *while not creating any real value at all*. It is even possible to create 'shareholder value' by *destroying* 'real value', as we have seen in our comments after Step 7 in our example given in Section 8.3. This is so because negative externalities are absent from corporate profit and loss accounts. This has led certain specialists of accounting to conclude that 'the pursuit of shareholder value generates the distribution of fictitious dividends'.[700] This is not always the case; but it can be so.

Moreover, as shown in our example in Section 8.3, intellectual property assets – trademarks, patents and so on – used by the enterprise can be located among the assets of a subsidiary established in a low-tax State (such as Country B of our example). The subsidiary owning these incorporeal rights will then receive royalties from all the other subsidiaries making use of these rights. These payments will decrease the local profits (royalties are treated as expenses): profits are then 'relocated' in a jurisdiction with lower or no taxes. More so-called 'shareholder value' has yet again been created with, yet again, no 'real value' created at all …

And the same can be done again with 'management services' provided by a subsidiary which will just happen to be located in a low-tax jurisdiction as shown in our example in Section 8.3 at Step 7. *Ad libitem* …

---

[700] Jacques Richard, *Comptabilité et développement durable*, Paris: Economica (2012), p. 8.

In a recent study, Thomas Tørslø, Ludvig Wier and Gabriel Zucman have been searching the 'Missing Profits of Nations'.[701] They provide a very useful and telling evaluation of the macro-impact of these profit-shifting strategies. To start with, they dismiss the common idea that globalization leads to a competition among States to attract *real capital* (what I call 'productive capital') which would lead to a race to the bottom in terms of marginal tax rate. In fact, what happens is a shifting of *accounting* profits using the methods I have briefly described above to jurisdictions with low or zero corporate tax rate. 'Productive capital' hardly moves; paper profits do. A first issue they encountered in their analysis is the unsurprising fact that there is limited reporting in tax havens. Consequently, most of the profits shifted are not visible in financial accounts. In their analysis, only 17 per cent of the multinationals' profits appear in these accounts. But what can be 'seen' is that firms in tax havens are abnormally profitable: the pre-tax corporate profits of the local subsidiaries of international firms in Luxembourg, Ireland or Puerto Rico represent about 250 per cent of the compensation of employees, when the worldwide average in non-tax havens is 36 per cent. But when one looks at the pre-tax corporate profits of *local firms* in Luxembourg, Ireland or Puerto Rico they are close to the worldwide average of 36 per cent ... And at the same time, in non-tax havens, foreign firms are always *less* profitable than local firms. The difference is that 'foreign firms', i.e. firms using a corporate group of corporations as the backbone of their legal organization, have at their disposal the optimizing tools described in our example which purely 'national firms' do not have access to. As a consequence, the EU countries lose about 20 per cent of their corporate tax revenue while in the US that number is about 15 per cent. And by applying a very low tax rate to the huge artificial tax base they attract, countries like Malta collect *more than 90 per cent of their total revenue* from profits shifted. For Puerto Rico, the number is 80 per cent. In Ireland, it is close to 60 per cent.[702] And 50 per cent in Luxembourg, Cyprus, Hong-Kong, Singapore and so on. And, like

---

[701] Thomas Tørslø, Ludvig Wier and Gabriel Zucman, *The Missing Profits of Nations*, 5 June 2018, available at: https://gabriel-zucman.eu/files/TWZ2018.pdf.

[702] Ireland is a particularly gifted country. Between 2009 and 2018, its GDP has increased by 64 per cent while the increase for the rest of the Eurozone was a meagre 10 per cent. From 2014 to 2016, foreign direct investment increased 129 per cent. In 2017, the country exported goods and services valued €343 billion, i.e. 166,102€ per employee, while Germany only managed 38,513€ per employee. Strangely, the largest port in Ireland ranks 29th in Europe. The reason for the miracle? Create a subsidiary in Ireland, have it buy your production cheaply and sell it dear to the final customer,

in our above example, the lower the rate, the higher the revenue. Of course, for enterprises, the outcome is that they have more cash at their disposal to distribute to shareholders: through profits shifting, they have – again – created 'shareholder value'. For each US$1 paid in a tax haven, close to US$5 is avoided in countries with a regular tax regime. Profits shifting has therefore two effects: it redistributes the tax base across countries in a manner disconnected from 'real value' producing activities. But, maybe more importantly, it redistributes *income* to the shareholders of multinational companies, in compliance with the prevailing mantra of maximizing 'shareholder value'.[703] The Organization for Economic Cooperation and Development (OECD) conservatively considers that between US$100 billion and US$240 billion is lost yearly in corporate tax revenue due to base erosion and profit shifting ('BEPS').[704] For the International Monetary Fund (IMF), the worldwide losses of corporate tax base erosion and profit shifting amounts to approximately US$600 billion.[705] There are of course difficult methodological issues leading to this divergence in the estimates. But there is no question that the numbers are of titanic magnitude and that they have a considerable impact on the governance of the World Power System: classical States are deprived from a large proportion of their means of action; negative externalities cannot be properly internalized and inequality is propelled to stratospheric levels.[706]

So far, I have presented how the legal structure of the World Power System can be used to 'optimize' shareholder value creation at the enterprise level. But the possibilities offered at the level of the Financial Structure are *even more* extensive due to the fact that at this level of the structuring of exchange relationships, there are *no physical assets* involved (like the plant to be closed at Step 5 of our example

---

and the difference appears in Irish – public and private – accounts. *See* https://www.xerficanal.com/economie/emission/Alexandre-Mirlicourtois-Le-PIB-irlandais-un-hold-up-fiscal_3746544.html.

[703] In their study, Tørslø, Wier and Zucman (*op cit*, note 701) propose as a solution apportioning profits proportionally to where sales are made. The important conclusion for us is that it is an amendment of accounting rules which is suggested. *See* more on this later in Chapter 10.

[704] OECD, *2017 Background Brief – Inclusive Framework* on BEPS, https://www.oecd.org/ctp/background-brief-inclusive-framework-for-beps-implementation.pdf.

[705] https://www.imf.org/en/Publications/WP/Issues/2016/12/31/Base-Erosion-Profit-Shifting-and-Developing-Countries-42973.

[706] For France alone, the loss in corporate income tax only is estimated between 15 and 20 US$ billion. And this is only for corporate income tax …

in Section 8.3), (almost) no employees (like those to be dismissed at Steps 3 and 5) and very few constraints limiting the use of the various 'havens' offered by accommodating States. The assets involved are all intangibles, such as shares, loans, patents, trademarks, logos, algorithms and so on. The opportunities for 'optimization' are endless. So much so that as per an UNCTAD 2018 Report:[707]

> Intellectual property charges are merely one of the many forms of more widespread profit shifting within companies or groups, that weigh negatively on public finances and collective wage bargaining in many countries. Indeed, the largest recipient country (the United States) is simultaneously the victim of the most massive intellectual property-related corporate tax avoidance by transnational corporations [sic: firms] 'trading' intangibles. Far from promoting innovation or competition, such schemes illustrate how corporate cost-saving strategies (especially in relation to wages and taxes) rely on international arbitrage and free-riding; and while they may be successful for creating monopolistic rents and crushing competition effectively, they do so at the cost of public welfare.

This unsatisfactory state of affairs explains the long-term debate in the international tax field between those who defend the existing 'arm's length' approach and those who propose to move to a 'unitary taxation and formulary apportionment' approach.[708] The first group does realize that although the corporations used to legally structure a firm are separate legal entities, the prices, royalties, interests and other payments formally agreed to among subsidiaries of the same group may be manipulated. They can be used to reduce profits in one location and increase them in another one. A first approach to this issue is to try to *reconstruct* each local entity's accounts by applying to the contractually agreed prices an 'arm's length' principle: what would the price have been had the two companies been autonomous entities not belonging to the same group of companies? The idea is to 'reconstruct' what market prices would have been if the firm had been inexistent and replaced by the market, i.e. if the prices would *not* have been *administered*? Of course, this leads to serious methodological issues, the key ones being that there are often no comparable market

---

[707] *Op cit*, note 694, p. 55.

[708] *See* Biondi, *op cit*, note 697.

prices for the goods exchanged which are often *intermediary goods* –
unfinished goods at any particular stage of the production process
splattered worldwide – for which there is no *market*; and, in any case,
the firm management has much more knowledge about the reality
of prices than outsiders – even tax authorities – who have to prove
their case with less information. This type of approach is very much in
line with the traditional view of the firm as a mere alternative to the
market, as an organization whose existence can be disregarded. The
reality of this approach is that it leads to what has been appropriately
termed *The Missing Profits of Nations.*[709]

As we have seen above in this section, a huge industry is busy
at profits shifting from high tax jurisdictions to low tax ones. The
alternative which has been imagined is that of 'unitary taxation and
formulary apportionment'. It is very much in line with the analysis
developed in this book. The firm is taken as the real economic
enterprise, and the corporations used to legally structure it are
understood as being mere legal instruments. But although the books
of each of the corporate entities used to structure the firm can be
cooked, the overall activity cannot. When the firm, as an economic
organization, meets the market, be it for inputs or outputs, the prices
paid *are* market prices. Independent sellers of inputs want the highest
price and independent buyers of output want the lowest one, at any
given level of quality and quantity of goods or services. The most
logical approach is to look at the income generated at the level of
the *firm*, and to apportion it among the various jurisdictions involved
based on a combination of criteria such as headcounts, value of the
local assets, and so on. Of course, moving from one approach – no
matter its lack of realism – to another one would affect innumerable
partial interests which would be negatively affected, including those
of tax havens and of the professionals who make a living running the
'arm's length assessment' industry. But if, to address the three State
functions required at the global level, there are solutions with regards
to negative externalities by internalizing via accounting the *cost* (if not
the *price*) of environmental damage, States are needed to provide the
infrastructure and to correct inequalities. And to do this they need
tax revenue.

The loss of tax sovereignty means that States are deprived from
part of their means of existence and action. As we have seen, States
have been built over history as dual monopolists concentrating the

---

[709] *E.g.* Tørslø, Wier and Zucman, *op cit*, note 701, pp. 25–26.

278

monopoly of legitimate violence and the monopoly to tax. One requires the other and a properly operating State fulfilling its functions is needed for a market economy to exists. The hundreds of billions of dollars lost by some States for much smaller gains by other States are a consequence of a globalization of firms and their Financial Structures, combined with the abuse of their sovereignty by an increasingly large number of States. But it goes beyond pure tax issues. The constitutional foundations of our society are challenged.

(e) The World Wide Web of Contracts can end up being completely distorted due to certain States' opportunistic positioning on the *world market for legal norms*. Certain States in fact *trade their sovereignty*.[710] They use their sovereignty to adopt norms which have *no other purpose* than *distorting* international economic exchange *to their advantage*. Some even sell passports for a price,[711] which allows reducing the effectiveness of the exchange of information among States to reduce tax evasion. This will be the next global game: Mr Durand, a French national, appearing as a different person than the same Mr Durand having a Maltese passport, and entitled to the protection afforded by Maltese law.[712] As a result, the same *individual* can be two *legal persons*, two citizens protected by two States and who do not appear as the same person in the system of information exchange.

As summarized by Anthony van Fossen:

> small island countries prosper to the degree that they implement effective organizational strategies to take advantage of unusual niche opportunities offered by the international political economic environment. ... Island microstates succeed to the extent they supply what people and organizations in continental countries want.

---

[710] Ronen Palan, 'Tax Havens and the Commercialization of State Sovereignty', 56(1) *International Organization*, pp. 151–176 (2002).

[711] Prices vary significantly depending on the value of the citizenship acquired in this fashion: €800,000 in Malta, $1,500,000 in the UK, $2,000,000 in Singapore and Cyprus, €500,000 in Mauritius, €250,000 in Greece, etc.

[712] For a report describing the investor citizenship and residence schemes created by Cyprus and Malta and the risks they create for the Member States and the Union as a whole, including in terms of security, money laundering, corruption, circumvention of EU rules and tax evasion, *see* https://ec.europa.eu/info/sites/info/files/com_2019_12_final_report.pdf.

> Island microstates develop innovative forms of
> sovereignty ... using local rules to attract non-local
> resources.[713]

The localization of whole segments of economic exchange is now often motivated by purely artificial considerations. It leads to a significant distortion of economic indicators such as GDP, corporate profits and trade balances. As a matter of example, after accounting for profit shifting, Japan, the UK, France and Greece turn out to have trade *surpluses* in 2015, in contrast to published data that record trade *deficits*. As far as the US is concerned, a *quarter* of the recorded trade deficit is an *illusion* due to multinational corporate tax avoidance.[714]

It is completely absurd – and fundamentally false – for statistics to 'evidence' that the Cayman Islands are the fifth largest financial centre in the world. This is true in a virtual world only, where one single building (*Ugland House, Church St, George Town KY1-1104, Cayman Islands*) is the home to 18,857 companies' headquarters (as of March 2008).[715] It just happens to be the address of the head office of the largest law firm in the Cayman Islands.[716] Delaware does even better, with one single office building being the legal address of 285,000 different corporations – which makes it a pretty crowded legal space in which even appearances are not protected.[717] It is also because of legal distortions that Luxembourg 'hosts' more banks than Switzerland, which itself counts more banks than dentists.[718] It is also absurd that there are 34 corporations per inhabitant in the British Virgin Islands (BVI); that Jersey is the European leader in banana trading; that Barbuda, the BVI and Bermuda received more foreign direct investments in 2010 than Germany; that the largest investors in China are Hong Kong (45 per cent) and the BVI (14 per cent) – only 4 per cent coming from the US; and so on.

The activities of all these seemingly exotic companies, banks and funds are not at all conducted *offshore* in these accommodating

---

[713] Anthony van Fossen, 'Passport Sales: How Island Microstates Use Strategic Management to Organize the New Economic Citizenship Industry', 13(1) *Island Studies Journal*, pp. 285–300 (2018), p. 285.

[714] *E.g.* Tørslø, Wier and Zucman, *op cit*, note 701, pp. 25–26.

[715] Palan, *op cit*, note 54, p. 241.

[716] Which just happens to also have offices in Dubai, Hong Kong, London, Singapore, the BVI, Dublin, Jersey and Luxembourg, which just happen to all be tax havens.

[717] Leslie Wayne, 'How Delaware Thrives as a Corporate Tax Haven', *NY Times*, 20 June 2012.

[718] Palan, *op cit*, note 54, pp. 3–4.

jurisdictions. They are conducted *onshore*, in the main real-life financial centres of the world. Only a few low value-added formalities are conducted locally. Along the same lines, the Cayman Islands, the BVI, Bermuda and Bahamas together shelter more than 52 per cent of the world's hedge funds (thanks to numerous common law 'efficiencies' applicable to the legal hub they compose with the City of London). Some argue that this percentage 'only' reaches 35 per cent, while others claim that it amounts to 80 per cent.[719] No one really knows, and this is part of the problem. In addition, with such opacity, interconnections with organized crime are guaranteed. As a result of this State competition and the 'offshoring' of wealth, wealthy individuals hold between 21 and 32 trillion US dollars of financial assets in offshore tax havens.[720]

All this shows that multinational enterprises, along with the funds on top of their Financial Structure owning an increasingly larger part of their shares of capital, benefit from a large degree of organizational autonomy and can choose from a large menu of legal devices offered by States willing to do what it takes to benefit from a global economy. Combined with the great variety of resources multinational enterprises control, which is due to the fact that their corporate structures are potentially eternal and can concentrate both real and financial capital with no other limit than their efficiency at doing so, such autonomy unsettles the official Power System centred on the 'State System'. The internal law of any given State is the result of a compromise among the various interests affected having expressed themselves in local representative political bodies.[721] Once a point of equilibrium is reached, the adopted laws apply equally to all those who are subject to them. But with 'globalization' it is possible for firms and for some individuals, the so-called HNWI, not to accept the outcome reached and to relocate all or part of their activities (or relocate themselves). They can choose not to be 'takers', 'buyers' of a legal system and to delocalize their activities in one or several competing State legal systems. This possibility calls into question the functioning of political

---

[719] Palan, Murphy and Chavagneux, *op cit*, note 685, p. 6. Hedge funds detained, in the first trimester of 2011, 2,000 billion dollars; see http://www.hedgefundresearch.com/index.php?fuse=press&1301697974.

[720] The research leading to this conclusion was carried out by James Henry, former chief economist at consultants McKinsey & Co. He used data from the World Bank, the International Monetary Fund, United Nations and central banks. As a result of the practices he exposes, governments worldwide suffer a lack of income taxes of up to US$280 billion. 'Super rich hold $32 trillion in offshore havens', *Reuters*, 22 July 2012.

[721] *See* Lippmann, *op cit*, note 83, p. 342.

institutions: it deprives those States which are exited from of at least part of their means of action since they lose the opportunity to tax the departing organizations or individuals.

States' sovereignty, which guaranteed States' autonomy *among them*, now turns *against them* because of the spreading of a competitive game that *both* opposes and links States to enterprises.[722] The States' capacity to produce international law to rebalance the system is completely undermined as they face a problem of collective action which has never been faced at such a level before. A great part of States' resources – even for powerful States – comes from their 'offer' on the global market for legal norms. The very possibility for States to pursue the policies favoured by their electorate in the context of classical analyses of law is challenged. This explains attempts to develop '*soft law*'[723] on a voluntary basis; or, on an even more voluntary basis, to get the largest enterprises to adhere to the 'Global Compact',[724] under the aegis of the UN Secretary General.[725] Whatever their effectiveness (and they have some), these theoretical and practical attempts highlight the inability of the classical legal and political systems to answer the questions raised by the globalization of the economy.

8.6 Corporate Governance in a Globalized World

When one analyses the impact of the globalization of enterprises on the Power System, 'corporate governance' rules take on a new dimension. Far from triggering purely 'private' questions, in the sense that the interests at stake would be only those of private 'stakeholders', *the entire constitution of the World Power System* is in fact challenged by the globalization of enterprises and the way they are being managed. The *delusion* that we

---

[722] Stopford, Strange and Henley, *op cit*, note 48.

[723] The literature on soft law is voluminous. For references, *see* Larry Cata Backer, 'Polycentric Governance in the Transnational Sphere: Private Governance, Soft Law, and the Construction of Public-Private Regulatory Networks for States and Transnational Corporations', 17(1) *Indiana Journal of Global Legal Studies*, pp. 101–166 (2011).

[724] Georg Kell and John Gerard Ruggie, 'Global Markets and Social Legitimacy: The Case for the Global Compact', 8(3) *Transnational Corporations*, pp. 101–120 (1999). John Gerard Ruggie was the UN Secretary-General's Special Representative for Business and Human Rights.

[725] T. Berns, P.-F. Docquir, B. Frydman, L. Hennebel and G. Lewkowicz, *Responsabilité des entreprises et corégulation*, Bruxelles: Bruylant (2007), and particularly, Benoît Frydman, 'Stratégies de responsabilisation des entreprises à l'ère de la mondialisation', at pp. 1–50.

are living in *market economies*[726] contributes to neglecting intra-enterprise global trade (which is *organized* trade), the resulting changes in power allocation by the shifting of wealth allocation and their impact on States, the State System, the political system, society at large and the natural environment. It is one of the consequences of the insufficient analysis of 'private' powers as constituents of the Power System and of their insufficient submission to constitutional norms.

In effect, States are still perceived as being in the position of *sovereign* 'public' powers when they are confronted with these 'private' powers. Control over a territory remains the basis of State authority and locating a business activity on a territory results in granting jurisdiction to the State over this activity. And yet, the de-territorialization of enterprises reduces States' leeway towards these organizations, which have the capacity to escape from States' (territorial) jurisdiction. There are other sources of authority than the control over a territory (for instance the control over numerous 'property rights' and their organized use in large business firms) which result in the creation of powerful organizations leading States to compete among themselves and forcing them to produce legal norms serving these interests. And simultaneously the territory and the population living on it, far from being only sources of power, are also the sources of heavy constraints for State Organs because of the greater demands for protection of the interests adversely affected by globalization. States must both serve the demands of firms and the contradictory demands of those people left behind due to reduced employability on the global employment market which expels them from their jobs; those of the natural environment destroyed by the increased competition among States to host polluting activities; and those of unstable and out-of-control financial markets due to financial black holes resulting from offshore finance, a general process of securitization of financial flows and tax havens and so on.[727] And while protective demands from the population remain at high levels, public budgets are the victims of the race to the bottom in terms of taxation to attract locally the accounting acknowledgement of revenues and profits.

The legal structure of enterprises combined with the structure of the State System and a mandate given to corporate executives to maximize

---

[726] John Kenneth Galbraith, *The Economics of Innocent Fraud – Truth for our Time*, Boston, New York: Houghton Mifflin Company, (2004), for whom it is a *fraud* to describe our economy as a 'market economy'.

[727] *See* comprehensive research by Palan, *op cit*, note 54, and Palan, Murphy and Chavagneux, *op cit*, note 685. *See also* Palan, *op cit*, note 710 and Shaxson, *op cit*, note 685.

short-term 'shareholder value' contribute to avoiding taxing a large proportion of the wealth generated. As a result, the wealth produced is concentrated in increasingly fewer hands.[728] In 2010, for example, 93 per cent of the *additional* income generated during that year in the US – US$288 billion – went to the top of 1 per cent of taxpayers, and 37 per cent to the top 0.1 per cent.[729] And whereas there is a growing need for greater public action to internalize the costs generated and to compensate the left-behind, the substitution of debt for income leads to a public debt crisis which becomes a structural problem significantly reducing the States' ability to address issues.[730]

States' sovereignty is being challenged by enterprises and those mastering their Financial Structures which are now able to introduce competition among the judicial, social and tax systems implemented throughout history to ensure the cohesion of the various interests present in society – as long as society was organized on a local, State basis, in relative autonomy from the internal mode of organizations in other States. The Westphalian State System is now giving way to a hybrid order, the World Power System.[731]

---

[728] Joseph E. Stiglitz, 'Of the 1 per cent, by the 1 per cent, for the 1 per cent', *Vanity Fair*, May 2011.

[729] Wolfgang Streeck, *Buying Time – The Delayed Crisis of Democratic Capitalism*, London & New York: Verso (2014), p. 53.

[730] The total amount of debt as of 2018 is estimated at $25 trillion (*Le Temps*, 14 January 2019). Gross borrowings of OECD *governments* from the markets, which peaked at US$10.9 trillion in 2010 in the wake of the financial crisis, are set to reach a new record level in 2019 by exceeding US$11 trillion; http://www.oecd.org/finance/oecdsovereignborrowingoutlook.htm. Global outstanding debt in the form of *corporate* bonds issued by non-financial companies has hit record levels, reaching almost $13 trillion at the end of 2018; http://www.oecd.org/newsroom/risks-rising-in-corporate-debt-market.htm. On the debt phenomenon, *see* Streeck, *op cit*, note 729 and Graeber, *op cit*, note 74.

[731] On the historical role of taxation to ensure cohesion, *see* Gabriel Ardant, *Histoire de l'impôt*, Livre I, '*De l'antiquité au XVIIe siècle*' & Livre II, '*Du XVIIIe au XXe siècles*', Paris: Fayard (1971 and 1972); and Ardant, *op cit*, note 392. On the creation of a hybrid Power System, *see* Cohen, *op cit*, note 546, p. 234.

8.7 The Recent Dynamic of the Power System

Understanding the current predicament of the World Power System requires a better understanding of the history of our shared Power System. In a nutshell:[732]

(a) The Power System focused on the 'State System' has been institutionalized since the mid-seventeenth century. Under this system, first formalized by the Westphalia treaties of 1648, States are equal in the international legal order and recognize each other as masters of the organization of their own *internal* affairs.[733] With the eighteenth- and nineteenth-century liberal revolutions, these internal affairs were progressively structured around the institutions of a market society which main instruments are property rights, contractual freedom and the right of free enterprise. On the international level, States reached the greatest sovereignty they could obtain; on the internal level, individuals have been granted a high degree of autonomy. The internal order shifted from a hierarchical, holistic, corporatist and organized society[734] to a society of autonomous individuals, free and equal (in rights), free to build the society they yearned for thanks to their property rights and the contracts they entered into among themselves.[735] There was a constitutional decentralization of the right of decision-making as a matter of principle to individuals, via the definition of modern property rights and the recognition of the ability to conclude the contractual agreements they wanted with other individuals.[736] The individual right-holder was thus turned into a 'small-scale sovereign'.[737]

And as Mirabeau wrote, should the Prince be the sole owner, he would have to look for others to share with him the possession of this property. Decentralization of authority would have to go down through some other means:

---

[732] For a summarized presentation, *see* Robé, *op cit*, note 600.

[733] Mayall, *op cit*, note 333, p. 23.

[734] Olivier-Martin, *op cit*, note 503; Olivier-Martin, *op cit*, note 364, and his *Histoire du droit français des origines à la Révolution*, C.N.R.S. (1992) (reprint of the 1948 edition).

[735] Alain Supiot, 'État, entreprise et démocratie', in Pierre Musso (ed.), *L'entreprise contre l'État*, Paris: Editions Manucius (2017), pp. 13–31, at p. 15; Ewald, *op cit*, note 104; Martin, *op cit*, note 288, p. 75; Burdeau, *op cit*, note 249, p. 119.

[736] Duguit, *op cit*, note 172, pp. xv & 5.

[737] Ripstein, *op cit*, note 253.

The Prince is the head of the State, but he is not the State, nor can he be. He has a kind of tutelary power, a right of protection & participation on all properties; but he is not the sole owner: & if he were, he should by all means look for Subjects, call men to share this expensive and sterile possession.[738]

In liberal States, the absolute sovereignty granted to the States in the international legal order was decentralized in favour of the 'private' sector in the internal order, allowing for almost absolute individual autonomy. As a matter of principle, property rights and contractual freedom[739] pull all agreements entered into among autonomous individuals out of the State's scope of action.[740] In a liberal society, with property as a right of decision-making as a matter of principle and the principle of freedom of contract, a State's absolute sovereignty on the *international* level turns out to be no more than a competence of *exception* in the *internal* order: everything which is not prohibited or regulated being de jure authorized.[741] Individuals' liberties are in principle *unlimited*, whereas State powers are *limited*.[742] Such a system arose from European history,[743] and from centuries of social, political, economic and legal evolutions that took place in this small region of the world. Born in Europe, adapted to the US,[744] this structure of social relations was exported through the process of colonization and decolonization;[745] and then by international institutions created after the Second World War.[746] Political decolonization led European powers to leave South America, Africa and Asia. But the *legal colonization of the world by the State System* remained. New political movements taking the place of expelled colonialists had to take the legal form of a 'State' to join the existing international organizations

[738] Mirabeau, *op cit*, note 407, p. 106.
[739] Morris R. Cohen, 'Property and Sovereignty', 13 *Cornell Law Quarterly*, pp. 8–30 (1927), Hale, *op cit*, note 168, and 'Force and the State: A Comparison of 'Political' and 'Economic' Compulsion', 35 *Columbia Law Review*, pp. 149–201 (1935).
[740] De Vareilles-Sommières, 'La définition et la notion juridique de propriété', *Revue Trimestrielle de Droit Civil*, pp. 443–495 (1905).
[741] Schmitt, *op cit*, note 199, p. 286.
[742] *Ibid*, p. 296.
[743] Schmitt, *op cit*, note 240.
[744] Schmitt, *op cit*, note 199, pp. 171 & 182–183.
[745] Bertrand Badie, *L'État importé – L'occidentalisation de l'ordre politique*, Paris: Fayard (1992).
[746] Ruggie, *op cit*, note 326 (1982), pp. 379–415.

and participate to the international economic system, often forcing them to adopt internally modes of organizations compatible with rules set by liberal polities.[747]

(b) At the same time, this basic pattern of social organization has undergone a silent and long-hidden cataclysm, which only became easily noticeable with globalization: the massive introduction of limited liability corporations in the legal system in conjunction with the industrial revolution, starting in the nineteenth century,[748] has completely disrupted the balance of powers *and the constitutional structure of the Power System itself.* The progressive concentration of productive property rights within corporate structures started shifting the power structure in States' *internal* orders: the concentration of *property rights* on assets led to their reconstruction into *powers.* Economies of scale overwhelmed an economy of small proprietors, replacing them with large enterprises concentrating vast amounts of capital and employing many workers. Adam Smith's great hope that freeing up markets would dramatically expand the ranks of the self-employed had run its course. Many assume that the concentration of industrial power is the result of machine production. But the concentration of *control* does not come from the mechanization of industry; it comes from the concentration of *capital* – property rights – made possible thanks to the introduction of the limited liability corporation in the legal system.[749] As Nicholas Murray Butler, an American philosopher who once was president of Columbia University insisted:

> I weigh my words when I say that in my judgment the limited liability corporation is the greatest single discovery of modern times, whether you judge it by its social, by its ethical, by its industrial, or, in the long run, – after we understand it and know how to use it, – by its political effects. Even steam and electricity are far less important than the limited liability corporation, and they would be reduced to comparative impotence without it.[750]

Or, as Georges Ripert put it, without the public limited company, we would have had to do without the blast furnace, the steam engine and

---

[747] Supiot, *op cit*, note 627, starting at p. 137.

[748] Chayes, *op cit*, note 670, p. 35.

[749] *See* Lippmann, *op cit*, note 83, p. 13.

[750] *Ibid*, pp. 13–14. *See also* Miller, *op cit*, note 167, p. 21.

hydroelectric power.[751] And, in today's setting, we would have to do without all the subsequent technological inventions which required concentrations of capital for their development.

(c) With the industrial revolution and the vast concentrations of property rights made possible by recourse to the limited liability corporation, the pervasiveness of markets in labour brought manufacturing workers into an even deeper state of subjection than before.[752] From rights of autonomy designed to protect individuals' autonomy, concentrated property rights became *sources of heteronomy*, affecting the intellectual foundations of liberalism. There was both continuity and discontinuity in the process. Private ordering still has primacy. But it is now private ordering via private *firms* versus past private ordering via *individuals*.[753] They enabled the creation of private power structures (enterprises, notably) to which individuals became increasingly subjected. Concepts, institutions and doctrines that originated in an individual context, and whose applicability to organizations was at best questionable, were frequently used indiscriminately and unreflectively to deal with organizations as well.[754] States had to adapt. From 'nightwatchmen States', which only imposed the respect of property rights and the compliance with contractual obligations, they became 'welfare States' attempting to correct the negative consequences of unbalanced social relations created by the surge of corporate structures concentrating wealth, assets and contracts. One of the main reasons explaining this disruption lies in the fact that large enterprises developed within individualistic societies with no legal recognition of their existence as organizations, as a form of coordination of assets and of the individuals using them. These enterprises entered the legal world through *corporations*, which have legal personality and can be used to concentrate under one ownership structure various economic resources. The *enterprise's* lack of legal existence (as an organization) and the fact that its entry into the legal world has been made possible through the commercial corporation (or a group of corporations) resulted in a widespread confusion between the words and concepts of 'firm/enterprise' and 'corporation' and led to numerous misunderstandings in the social sciences. The worst of these developments is the so-called 'agency theory' which is the basis

---

[751] Ripert, *op cit*, note 43, p. 53.

[752] Anderson, *op cit*, note 270, pp. 35–36.

[753] *See* Gauchet, *op cit*, note 688, in particular, pp. 153–155, and Cohen, *op cit*, note 546, pp. 7–8.

[754] Dan-Cohen, *op cit*, note 23.

of the current legal models of 'corporate governance'. The disastrous consequences of this widespread erroneous theory are endless.[755] The inexistence of the firm as a positive legal concept is also the reason why legal scholars, like economists, did not develop any widely acknowledged theory of the enterprise.[756] The sole adequate theory analyses the enterprise as an autonomous legal order in competition/ cooperation with the State's own legal order.[757] It is with such a pluralistic legal theory that one can develop an accurate description and analysis of the structure of the Power System at the World Power System's level.[758] And it is also because of this issue that ordoliberals attempted to extend the objectives of liberalism. For them, it was not enough to protect the individual from the power of government, because governments are not the only threat to individual freedom.[759] However, the development of a legal theory of the enterprise has been hindered by legal positivists' approaches to law.[760] For positivists, law is inherently a production of the State and the idea that an enterprise could be a legal order in itself is anathema.[761] Still, there are minority pluralist approaches acknowledging the existence of legal orders on different levels than that of the State, whether on sub-national or supranational levels or as intertwined legal orders.[762] But they haven't led, so far, to an understanding of the World Power System as a

---

[755] Robé, *op cit*, note 600.

[756] Jacques Le Goff, 'Entreprise et institution; retour sur un débat crucial', in Jean-Pierre Le Crom (ed.), *Les acteurs de l'histoire du droit du travail*, Rennes: Presses Universitaires de Rennes (2004), pp. 83–104.

[757] Robé, *op cit*, note 192; Nikitas Aliprantis, 'L'entreprise en tant qu'ordre juridique', in N. Aliprantis et F. Kessler (eds.), *Le droit collectif du travail. Etudes en hommage à H. Sinay*, Francfort: Peter Lang (1994), p. 185.

[758] Jean-Philippe Robé, 'L'entreprise comme institution fondamentale de l'échange marchand', in Armand Hatchuel, Olivier Favereau and Franck Aggeri (eds.) *L'activité marchande sans le marché*, Colloque de Cerisy, Paris: Presse des Mines (2010), pp. 91–110.

[759] *E.g.* Gerber, *op cit*, note 89, pp. 36–37.

[760] *Ibid*, p. 34.

[761] Bruno Oppetit clearly stated: 'State positivism as an ideology cannot put up with other approaches. Legal positivism cannot tolerate any pluralistic approach'; Bruno Oppetit, 'La notion de source du droit et le droit du commerce international', 27 *Archives de philosophie du droit*, pp. 43–53 (1982), p. 47.

[762] The institutional theory is a pluralistic theory. *See* Eric Millard, 'Hauriou et la théorie de l'institution', 30/31 *Droit et Société*, pp. 381–412 (1995) and 'Sur les théories italiennes de l'Institution', in B. Basdevant et M. Bouvier (eds.), *Contrat ou institution: un enjeu de société*, Paris: Librairie Générale de Droit et de Jurisprudence (2004), pp. 31–46. Santi Romano developed a theory of legal pluralism and, in particular, the interesting concept of 'relevance'; *see op cit*, note 257.

pluralistic Power System. The State Power System – and this is a key point – is at the origin of a *knowledge system* (about law, here) which hinders the understanding of globalization.

(d) Faced with the rise of the power of enterprises and the resulting negative externalities, States, each in a position to react towards their *national* economies in the original liberal constitutional scheme, started producing *substantive law*, both normative and regulatory, protecting impacted interests through labour laws, social security laws, consumption laws, environmental laws and so on. In all the industrializing countries, State legislatures imposed increasingly stringent regulations, for example over railroads, insurance companies and the sellers of food and drugs, thereby limiting the set of issues about which the parties could freely contract.[763] Given industrial damages, the evolution of tort law led everywhere to a reduced role played by *fault* and the emphasis was put on the notion of *risk* associated with new production activities.[764] And for Justice Holmes, this changed the rationale behind certain theories to allocate liability. The fact that most putative new kinds of torts were now committed via railroads, via factories and the like meant that when deciding to make them actionable, one should take into account the advantages or disadvantages of forcing the general public to pay for the resultant costs through increased prices for the services and commodities generated by these businesses.[765] The logic behind the appropriateness or lack thereof of internalizing negative externalities (increasing prices via the judicial reallocation of the cost of damages) ex post was therefore clearly perceived by insightful jurists. And numerous administrative agencies were created to co-manage different aspects of the enterprises' life, proceeding to the reallocation of costs ex ante, via regulation.[766] Consciously or not, regulation was felt as more suitable since it was effectively dealing with organizational action and not with individuals' autonomy.[767] We then witnessed a true Constitutional Revolution of the State's role, one of its most

[763] *See* Fisher, Horwitz and Reed, *op cit*, note 41, p. 77.

[764] René Savatier, 'Le gouvernement des juges en matière de responsabilité civile', in *Recueil E. Lambert*, Glashütten im Taunus: Verlag Detlev Auvermann KG, vol. 1, pp. 453–466 (1ère edition, Librairie Générale de Droit et de Jurisprudence 1938). *See also* François Ewald, *L'État providence*, Paris: Grasset (1986).

[765] Fisher, Horwitz and Reed, *op cit*, note 41, p. 132.

[766] Jean-Philippe Robé, *L'entreprise et le droit*, Paris: Presses Universitaires de France (1999), starting at p. 74; reprinted in *Le temps du monde de l'entreprise – Globalisation et mutation du système juridique*, Paris: Dalloz (2015), starting at p. 100.

[767] Dan-Cohen, *op cit*, note 23, p. 136.

significant expressions being the evolution of US Supreme Court case law which, after having invalidated most of the laws adopted during the first New Deal, had to yield to the second one.[768] This evolution is what I called the *Second Constitutional Revolution*, the revolution of the transformation of the liberal State into the welfare and regulatory State. This evolution, however, took place on a *national* basis, and therefore on a *territorial* basis. As Ulrich Beck remarked:

> the dialectic of risk and the logic of insurance were first historically essential in establishing the nation-state's internal order. State insurance sharpened the border between the State's inside and its outside. It deepened its legitimacy. The State became the respected judge who mediated between the claims of its internal conflicting parties.[769]

But this means that increased competition among States to provide an accommodating legal environment to firms necessarily leads to a reduction of the State's legitimacy. Even the difficult adventure of the European integration is territorially based, and thus geographically limited. Norms being local,[770] the globalization of firms was bound to lead to State regulatory competition.

(e) As we have seen in Sections 3.4 and 3.5, internal and external sovereignty are two different concepts. Internal sovereignty can be allocated to numerous individuals or groupings. External sovereignty is the same for all States. Having a single conception of what a sovereign State is at the international level makes it possible to render compatible on the international scene institutions which are intrinsically very different. The fact is, however, that the way internal sovereignty operates has *also* a strong impact *externally*. The way China or Russia or the innumerable tax havens are internally organized has strong external effects. The existing international institutions inherited from the Bretton Woods system were designed after World War II for *liberal* States. After the implosion of the communist bloc, formerly socialist States were progressively integrated into the institutions of the liberal world economy. But the effective operation of liberalism requires

---

[768] Robert G. McCloskey, *The American Supreme Court*, Chicago: The University of Chicago Press (1960).

[769] Beck and Willms, *op cit*, note 49, p. 113.

[770] Although some States, and notoriously the US, have a tendency to apply some of their laws on an extra-territorial basis, like the Foreign Corrupt Practices Act ('FCPA').

the existence of a very complex institutional system. The market cannot exist by itself. It is necessary to have institutions which not only *stay* in their role, but also *play it*. It took centuries to develop liberal institutions in the areas of the world where they are indigenous. They cannot be imported as a package and superimposed on other social structures which have operated differently for centuries, where what matters is who you know, in which clan you are, which family you are from, what your ethnicity is, and so on. In North, Wallis and Weingast's parlance, no State can become an 'open access order' overnight.

Because of States' competition in the production of norms, the globalization of the economy has shifted the unstable balance of powers between official institutions (States and international organizations) and non-official ones (enterprises). The globalization of the Power System now challenges the Constitutional Revolution of the 'Welfare State' itself. Firms have taken advantage of the quasi abolition of economic borders to spread internationally and make use of the menu of locations offered by competing States to attract businesses.

So much so that we must now cope with global firms.

9

Coping with Firms

In the earlier chapters of this second part, I have addressed the concept of 'firm' and the need to differentiate it from the concept of 'corporation'. The firm is an organization performing an economic activity. The corporation is one of the legal devices used to legally structure large firms. All firms of a significant size are structured using a corporation or a group of corporations for the largest ones. Corporations are also used to legally structure the firm's 'Financial Structure' as I have defined this expression in Section 8.4.

I have then presented the features of business corporations which explain why they are so widely used to structure large businesses. The business corporation is a formidable tool to concentrate capital (real, like productive assets, or financial, like securities, shares or bonds) and although its use was originally restricted because of the dangers it represented for the liberal economic and political systems, economic development and the spreading of interstate and international economic exchange led to its widespread development and use. Multinational firms developed using these legal tools and, by extending on a global scale, they acquired the ability to make States compete to offer them attractive legal environments. This has led to the need to cope with firms, first on a national basis and, today, internationally.

We need to address the necessity to cope with firms as participants in the World Power System. The issue raised by the rise of private government has been spotted early on both in the US and in Europe. But the development of several promising schools of thought was stopped by the spread of the simplistic 'agency theory' which has led to biased firm governance worldwide. The bias extends to accounting rules which do not provide a full picture of the impact of a firm's operations and prevents firms from adapting their ways to the requirements of today's predicament. Addressing world issues such as climate change requires making decisions to change our ways of producing, travelling and consuming, inter alia.

These decisions are made by individuals as individuals or as agents of the institutions of the World Power System. At the roots of this System lie property rights which are rights of autonomy and are protected by the States and form part of the constitutional systems of government. The concentration of productive assets within the corporations which are used to legally structure large business firms has changed the effective operation of the 'global constitution'. Economic decisions within the World Power System are not made based on *prices* only. Within organizations they are made based on an *accounting* of the operations of the organization. To change these decisions, we need to amend the ways organizations account for their operations, considering the various forms of capital being used (financial and environmental for our purposes). Rob Gray puts it very clearly:

> We must ... first identify the cage in which we place ourselves through economic thought, and then escape that cage if we are to adequately address either changes in accounting in general, and protection and enhancement of the environment in particular.[771]

We will look at the issues raised by the fact that in an open economy, the competition among large business firms derivatively leads to a competition among States to offer firms accommodating legal environments. This limits the States' ability to internalize negative externalities and to redistribute income. Given the inherent defects of our divided State System, it is at the firm level that governmental rules must be developed so that firms integrate the consequences of their activities to a larger extent than they do today.

★★★

With the globalization of the largest firms, the official, public institutions of the World Power System are facing increased difficulties to internalize the interests insufficiently considered in the governance of firms. Climate change is a dire reality and we seem unable to address this most pressing issue. With regards to inequality, it has never been as high between the haves and haves not in the world.[772] This has led to a world of *Profits*

---

[771] Gray, *op cit*, note 680, p. 401.

[772] Since 2015, the richest 1 per cent has owned more wealth than the rest of the planet. Eight men now own the same amount of wealth as the poorest half of the world. And over the next 20 years, 500 people will hand over US$2.1 trillion to their heirs,

Without Prosperity.[773] It means that the ability to make decisions as a matter of principle towards the objects of property is concentrated and that the number of those who have lesser access to rights of autonomy increases. The unfairness and dangers of this state of affairs are immense. We are clearly lacking the institutions to internalize negative externalities in the world economy and to redistribute wealth, whereas there is consensus, as expressed by Bénabou and Tirole, on the need to have institutions in a position to fulfil these two political functions. The only debate is to what extent this must be done. With industrialization and large-scale production and distribution in enterprises structured around corporations, States started to reinvent themselves in the twentieth century and answered, in various ways, to the needs which were created and not addressed by the micro-powers in the Power System. Their role evolved. Beside protecting property rights as rights of autonomy as a matter of principle and enforcing contracts, they increasingly developed rules – of a judicial, regulatory or legislative nature, depending on the peculiarities of the local constitutional system of government involved – to internalize growing negative externalities and redistribute income to keep the open society operating. This mostly took place after major crises, such as the two world wars of the twentieth century and the Great Depression of the 1930s. Great crises open the door to great changes. But this new role played by the State was played on a local, national, i.e. territorial, basis. The fact is, however, that if States have roots which bind them to their territory and the population on it, enterprises have wings, as German sociologist Ulrich Beck aptly wrote.[774] Or, as written by David Kennedy:

> That corporate and financial actors move so easily while every public authority is constituted around a territorial jurisdiction as a matter of law *has effects.*[775]

Indeed. By definition, States are stuck with what they are: a combination of a territory, a population and an effective government over the other two components. States can, of course, adopt rules which have to be abided

---

see https://www.oxfamamerica.org/static/media/files/bp-economy-for-99-percent-160117-en.pdf. Or since 1980, the share of the world's wealth owned by the top 0.01 per cent has risen from 3 per cent to 8 per cent; *The Economist*, 15 December 2018.
[773] William Lazonick, 'Profits Without Prosperity', *Harvard Business Review*, pp. 47–55 (2015).
[774] *See generally* Ulrich Beck, *Pouvoir et contre-pouvoir à l'heure de la mondialisation*, Paris: Champs, Essais (2003).
[775] Kennedy, *op cit*, note 232, p. 834 (emphasis in original).

by on their territory;[776] and they still have their taxing authority. But with the international institutionalization of the freedom of movement of goods, services and capital, enterprises have the liberty to leave any State territory, or not to invest in it.

With globalization, the competition among firms has derivatively led to a competition among States to provide firms and those who control them via their Financial Structure with legal environments responding to their various needs. But in the process, the effectivity of the States' sovereignty has been eroded. And whilst States are in a competitive game, in the taxing area particularly, they still have to bear the weight of their territory and of their population; they still need to maintain the infrastructure, the education, justice, policing and other services provided by the other institutions which they are made up of. To maintain their effective operation, they need means. They need to collect taxes, which is made increasingly difficult over the mobile parts of the economic system which are heavily involved in a worldwide exercise of tax evasion. This is true at the firm level, and I have shown in our example in Chapter 8 some of the techniques which can be used to do this. But it is even more true at the level of the *Financial Structure* of firms in which the assets involved are all *incorporeal* (securities, trade names, brands, brand recognition, patents, copyrights, trademarks) and can be restructured very rapidly and indefinitely to adapt continuously to the evolving rules applying to them. In the present World Power System, only the locals can easily be taxed, and this increases the feeling of unfairness of the overall system. A vicious circle which, in the long run, would undermine the very foundations of our societies and of capitalism itself,[777] is in full operation. It could lead to a reversal of the process of conversion of violence into power I have described in Section 1.1. Without taxation, there is no proper education, no affordable health care, no proper infrastructure in roads, bridges and so on, which are required for the mere existence of a 'market economy', as we have seen in Chapter 4 and Section 4.5, in particular. Soon, legitimacy erodes too. And without legitimacy, there is no security and no property rights. And without all of the above, there can be no developed economy whatsoever.[778] Without correction, the present World Power System is on

---

[776] Although certain States attempt to apply, and sometimes succeed at applying, certain of their laws in an extra-territorial manner, such as the US rules against corruption under the Foreign Corrupt Practices Act of 1977. It is also the case for some antitrust rules.

[777] Early on, DeAnne Julius noted that 'there is a theoretical possibility that pressures in favor of policy convergence will drive the level of regulation so low that the foundations of the market itself are undermined'; Julius, *op cit*, note 690, p. 94.

[778] *See* Beck, *op cit*, note 774, p. 799.

a path to self-destruction. If we do not find the way to amend its mode of operation and reposition it within the identified Planetary Boundaries,[779] we risk societal collapse. It can arise via different paths: climate change and other environmental degradation which will lead to massive immigration movements; social unrest created by ever increasing social inequality – like the '*gilets jaunes*' movement in France in 2018 and 2019, just a little bit more serious; or the corporate undermining, via the exit strategies being used, of national welfare systems.[780] Basically it will come from an inability of the State System to fulfil the acknowledged State functions (providing physical and institutional infrastructures, internalizing negative externalities and correcting inequalities perceived as being excessive) via decentralized States.

9.1 Competing Firms and Competing States

Global firms and global investors have created for themselves, with the States' assistance, the liberty to invest where they want. After having obtained the freedom to freely incorporate, they became the beneficiaries of a series of international bilateral or multilateral treaties providing them the freedom to trade, to provide services, and to invest almost anywhere. We live in a world in which goods, services and investments move almost freely. The only factor of production which is prevented from moving freely are people, freedom of migration being extremely restricted. And in this regard, passports do not all have the same value.[781] Of course, once firms have made a physical investment in any given location, the assets invested locally fall under the jurisdiction of the State within which the investment has been made. But because firms have the choice to invest or not, they are in a position to strike bargains with States which grant them protection for their investment *against future changes in the law* of the State in which the investment is being made. Under a large global web of so-called Bilateral Investment Treaties (BITs) and Free Trade Agreements (FTAs) with investment chapters, States have granted corporations *international* legal rights. When an enterprise makes an investment in a country via a contract with the local State, the investment may benefit from protection under *international* law, and not merely local law, as is

---

[779] Steffen et al., *op cit*, note 59, p. 736.

[780] Beate Sjåfjel, 'Beyond Climate Risk: Integrating Sustainability into the Duties of the Corporate Board', 23 *Deakin Law Review*, pp. 1–22 (2018), p. 17.

[781] The ranking of passports by their total visa-free score is telling. *See* https://www. passportindex.org/byRank.php. The first African country – South Africa – ranks 96th.

the case for *local* investors. If the legal, corporate, vehicle used to make the investment is incorporated in a State having signed a protective BIT or FTA with the State hosting the investment, then the investment may benefit from the protections provided by the Treaty or the Agreement. It means that the contract between the corporation and the hosting State becomes an *international agreement under international public law*. The extraordinary outcome of this status is that the contractual provisions have *priority* over *later-in-time* conflicting local laws, including protective labour or environmental rules. These contracts trump domestic law as a matter of international law. Domestic law can in effect be frozen to the benefit of international investors.[782] Furthermore, via the corporation having made the investment, firms can enforce their rights through compulsory international arbitration: any dispute between the hosting State and the investing corporation is adjudicated by *private* arbitrators under international arbitration rules. And under the case law developed by these international arbitration tribunals, the value of the contracts 'internationalized' in this fashion is protected from the actions of the State deemed to be depreciating it. Investors are entitled to indemnification from the negative effects of new laws. This, of course, has a chilling effect on an improvement of local regulations to protect interests affected by negative externalities.

But there is *more*. A prospective investor may be a corporation created under the law of a State having no BIT or FTA agreement with the hosting State. To benefit from the protective web of international treaties, it is sufficient to create a *new subsidiary* under the law of a State having a favourable treaty, and the investor will be granted the sought-after protection. This has led to a considerable industry of treaty-shopping to identify under which treaty it is most favourable to invest given the nature of the investment, the sector of activity and so on.

But there is *even more*. It is often possible to do the treaty-shopping exercise *after* the investment. A company controlling another company is often provided treaty protection. If, for some reason, the investing entity does not benefit from the right degree of treaty protection, it is possible to change its direct or indirect shareholding *after the fact* to get the sought-after treaty protection. Given multinational enterprises' ability to create subsidiaries in their corporate structure with almost no limits, they have significant leeway to acquire treaty protection for their contracts with States even *after* the investment has been made.[783] Just like individuals can buy citizenships and passports and the protection coming with them

---

[782] *See* Arato, *op cit*, note 352, pp. 230–231.
[783] *Ibid*, p. 275.

(*see* Section 8.5), global firms can have access to the world menu of 'nationalities', irrespective of the absurdity of the notion for a corporate legal entity. Given this ability, they can take advantage of the enormous range of investment treaties.[784] And there is very little the hosting State can do to counter these moves.

As a consequence of all this:

> the multinational firm has become a powerful and increasingly autonomous international lawmakers – an author of its own rights and obligations under public international law. This transformation has come at stark cost to the State's capacity to regulate in the public interest, with only tenuous grounding in State consent.[785]

A major factor in this evolution lies in the fragmented nature of the investment regime in the World Power System. It consists of thousands of BITs and FTAs, interpreted by hundreds of arbitration tribunals, constituted on a one-off basis.[786] It makes it exceedingly difficult to amend the system because terminating or amending any single treaty would accomplish little: firms can simply restructure the ownership of the affected investments to use a corporation benefiting from another treaty.

One of the conclusions to be drawn from this state of affairs is that:

> the time has come for international lawyers to rethink the position of business firms within global legal space. ... international law has had trouble coming to grasps with the global business as a unified actor. The dogged focus on corporate form rather than the large-scale organization is a case in point ... It is worth returning to the grammar of public international law, to ask whether we must now conceive of the multinational firm as a unified semi-public actor for purposes of international law. ... Global firms can reshape the domestic law of their contracting partners in their own image – with tangible effects for the host State's populace. At the same time, their emergent power has no counterweight at the international level, in the form of international responsibility or other accountability mechanisms.[787]

---

[784] *Ibid*, pp. 276–280.
[785] *Ibid*, p. 230.
[786] *Ibid*, p. 289.
[787] *Ibid*, pp. 284–292.

Whereas the power of States historically grew through *territorial* conquest, peacefully via alliances or marriage or via armed invasion, the power of multinational firms grows with their increased *extraterritoriality*.[788] With many large economic actors whose presence cannot be taken as a given over the long term, States (which have to cope with their territories and populations, hard and slow to improve) are put in a position in which they need to be attractive for businesses. Otherwise, they do not have access to the tax resources required for their mere survival, let alone for the fulfilment of their internalizing or redistributive functions in a properly operating Power System. The operation of today's World Power System is the outcome of the combined operation of States, global markets and global firms.[789] Markets, States and enterprises have developed in symbiosis and each needs the others for its ultimate sustainment. But in today's stage of development of the World Power System, States need to be offering a legal environment which is not too expensive, i.e. a legal environment which does not 'excessively' internalize negative externalities (an activity which increases costs and therefore prices and therefore negatively affects firm competitiveness) or reallocate resources via taxation. This phenomenon leads to a race to the bottom, unless the States create coalitions, syndicates (under the name of 'international organizations' or 'international treaties'), to reduce competition among them. This leads to an insufficient offering by States and ultimately to a destructive surge of social violence and extremism in the political parties trying to get control of the Political Organs of the State.

At the same time, the doctrine of 'agency theory' is pushing firms to create short-term 'shareholder value' at the expense of other affected interests. A balance of the cost externalized in this manner and of the 'shareholder value' created would be the real indicator of the 'real value' created – if any – by firms. But the accounting system has been biased in favour of the sole accounting of 'shareholder value' creation or destruction, at the expense of any other form of accounting.

As we will see in more detail, the issue derives from a misunderstanding of the property rights involved and of the notion of property rights itself. It is urgent to understand that shareholders do not own corporations or firms, to understand firms as micro-political systems part and parcel of the Power System, and to develop proper rules of firm governance and accounting when they are active at the global level, without the internalizing and redistributing functions of a global State.

---

[788] Beck, *op cit*, note 774, p. 796.

[789] Charles-Albert Michalet, *Le capitalisme mondial*, Paris: Quadrige/Presses Universitaires de France (1976, 1998).

9.2 From Despotisms to Constitutional Government

For global firms, it is particularly important to develop our understanding that they are political systems which cannot be content to operate under a regime of despotisms as property and corporate law left to themselves entitle them to do. This ability derives from property rights. But as part of the Power System of society, the proper operation of these rights implies the existence of higher-level political institutions to eventually address the needs of those interests insufficiently taken into account by the autonomous play of private exchanges, as acknowledged by Roland Bénabou and Jean Tirole.[790]

In the early (1939) expression of this issue by Friedrich Hayek:

> the abrogation of national sovereignties and the creation of an international order of law is a necessary complement and the logical consummation of the liberal program.[791]

This is because:

> If goods, men, and money can move freely over the interstate frontiers, it becomes clearly impossible to affect the prices of the different products through action by the individual State. ... any burden placed on a particular industry by State legislation would put it at a serious disadvantage as opposed to similar industries in other parts of the Union. As has been shown by experience in existing federations, even such legislations as the restriction of child labor or working hours becomes difficult to carry out for the individual State.
>
> Not only would greater mobility between the States make it necessary to avoid all sorts of taxation which would drive capital or labor elsewhere, but there would also be considerable difficulties with many kinds of indirect taxation.

---

[790] Bénabou and Tirole, *op cit*, note 8, p. 1. *See also*, from another angle, Supiot, *op cit*, note 341, p. 130.

[791] Friedrich A. Hayek, 'The Economic Conditions of Interstate-Federalism', reprinted in *Individualism and Economic Order*, Chicago and London: University of Chicago Press (1948), p. 269.

> ... the federal government will have to take over the functions which the States can no longer perform and will have to do all the planning and regulating that the State cannot do.[792]

Even someone like Friedrich Hayek imagined the creation of a 'global State' as the answer to the issues of the expansion of a globalized economy over decentralized sovereign States. He knew markets cannot operate by themselves and that their outcome may require political correction. But we must deal with the likely possibility that there will *not* be a global constitutional convention where representatives of the world population sit down and create transnational institutions, a 'global State'.[793] And it is probably better that way. In the words of Gunther Teubner, a world State is a utopia, and a bad one at that.[794]

In an open world without a global State and with competing local States, some method must be found, however, so that global firms develop *internal* governmental rules making them internalize the interests affected. In his reflections upon the prospects for what would be a '*Second Enlightenment*',[795] Ulrich Beck wrote that the first task was to work out a realistic and effective notion of *cosmopolitan democracy*: the first job was to bring forth an image, an organizational model of a post-national, cosmopolitan and de-territorialized democracy.[796] He thought that we have to come up with

---

[792] *Ibid*, pp. 258–261.

[793] Beck and Willms, *op cit*, note 49, pp. 52–53. *See also* Kennedy, *op cit*, note 232, p. 858.

[794] Teubner, *op cit*, note 282, p. 8. For Joseph Weiler, the emergence of a World government would be '*a horrible thought in itself*'; Joseph H.H. Weiler, 'The Geology of International Law – Governance, Democracy and Legitimacy', 64 *ZaöRV*, pp. 547–562 (2004), p. 559.

[795] More than ever, we need to remember Kant's definition of the Enlightenment, which had to do *with the willingness to understand*: 'Enlightenment is man's emergence from his self-imposed immaturity. Immaturity is the inability to use one's understanding without guidance from another. This immaturity is self-imposed when its cause lies not in lack of understanding, but in lack of resolve and courage to use it without guidance from another. *Sapere Aude!* "Have courage to use your own understanding!"—that is the motto of enlightenment. ... It is so easy to be immature'; Immanuel Kant, *Perpetual Peace and Other Essays*, Indianapolis: Hackett Publishing Company (1983), p. 41. We have to emerge from the immaturity generated by the social sciences to make sense of the State System which is now fading and leaves room for the World Power System.

[796] Beck and Willms, *op cit*, note 49, p. 201.

political forms that will redefine and redistribute much of the sovereignty that has until now been concentrated at the national level in three directions: inwards towards society; downwards towards the local level; and outwards towards new decision-making networks and political arenas.[797]

But much of this 'redefinition and redistribution' of sovereignty has in fact already taken place via the definition of modern property rights and their concentration into corporate organizations used to run business firms.[798] Much of the institutional work has already been done by the autonomous operation of the Power System. What remains to be done – and it is still a gigantic task – is to bring these organizations under the rule of (a global constitutional) law and, if at all possible, under democratic rule. We need to find a way to combine the institutions of the first modernity (liberal sovereign and democratic territorial States, individual rights, property rights and contracts) and those of the second (the large firm, its Financial Structure and properly operating States in a position to internalize negative externalities and redistribute income). In Teubner's snappy expression:

> it is not the creation *ab ovo* of new constitutions in a constitution-free globality that is at stake, but rather the transformation of an already existing transnational legal system.[799]

Unlike the constitutional orders before it, the new global governance regime will not be imagined and built. The reason for this is that the key rule of this order was to be *found* rather than *made*.[800] It has been found. It is the notion of property right as a constitutional right of decision-making as a matter of principle which is at the root of the structuring of the organizations – the multinational enterprises and their Financial Structure – which have led to a restructuring of the operation of the World Power System.

Starting from the building block of property, it is possible to write a workable description of the world's legal order and to reinterpret our

---

[797] *Ibid*, p. 203.

[798] *See also* Giovanni Arrighi, *The Long Twentieth Century – Money, Power and the Origins of our Times*, London, New York: Verso (1994, 2006), pp. 80–81.

[799] Teubner, *op cit*, note 282, p. 8. *See also* Paolo Carrozza, 'Constitutionalism's Post-Modern Opening' in Martin Loughlin and Neil Walker (eds.), *The Paradox of Constitutionalism – Constituent Power and Constitutional Form*, Oxford: Oxford University Press (2007), pp. 169–187.

[800] *Contra, see* Kennedy, *op cit*, note 232, pp. 831–832.

partial institutions anew in constitutional terms. Globalization took place because of the inner legal structuring of open access order societies. It has rearranged the exercise of the prerogatives granted by liberal constitutional orders. Today's issue is to rearrange the use of these prerogatives under a constitutional regime ensuring their inclusiveness in that they should not lead to a destruction of the States providing the infrastructure, internalizing the negative externalities which must be internalized and the institutions which should exist to address inequalities. An understanding of property rights as political rights, as rights of decision-making as a matter of principle (micro-powers) in a political system comprising higher level political institutions (macro-powers) leads to an understanding of the need to constitutionalize firms understood as components of the World Power System. When the first Constitutions were adopted in the late eighteenth century, the State was the principal threat. In the United States, the Bill of Rights restrained the federal government; and the Fourteenth Amendment extended the restraint to the State governments. Today, the collective operations of large business firms take on aspects of governmental functions and decades ago already, Adolf Berle advocated that they should be governed with the same constitutional limitations as governments.[801]

With the global development of large firms, the micro-despotisms made possible thanks to their concentration of property rights over productive assets took considerable importance. What is at stake is the fact that multinational firms are not accountable towards all those directly affected by the use of their power. When the accountability issue arose with State governments, this led to the progressive introduction into the State System of democratic norm creation: institutions were implemented to the effect that those affected by the norms should have a say in their production. It started with the principle of 'no taxation without representation'.[802] This principle is fundamentally linked to an issue of transfer over property rights: if the principle is accepted that political institutions need resources, and thus need the transfer of resources from the 'private sector' of the Power System to their benefit, those who are going to bear the cost should collectively have a say to verify the existence of the need, its extent, and the associated cost – and thus the level of tax required.

During much of history, political philosophers have thought about the power of the State, how to limit it, how to submit its exercise to higher standards, protecting individual interests and the public interest; how to 'constitutionalize' public power. And, against all odds, these ideas have

---

[801] Berle, *op cit*, note 24, p. 19.

[802] *See* Section 4.3.

managed to reach pre-eminence, often via violent conflict. They led to the fact that State power is now often constitutionally limited, framed by rules. This was a major historic breakthrough. The ideals of eighteenth-century political theorists, often treated with great disdain at the time, are now deeply embedded in many of the routines of modern political life, from the language of the law to the institutions of liberal democracy. It is so much the case that it is not an exaggeration to claim that we are living a kind of normative theory.[803] But now has come the time to go beyond that and expand our understanding of the complexity of the Power System, of its density, of its structuring around micro- and macro-powers, and of the need to integrate businesses in our understanding of the deep structure of the Power System.[804] We must think about the ways in which it is possible to make them 'accountable', to subject them to 'constitutional' standards that maintain their decision-making autonomy, ensure consideration of the interests directly affected by the use of their prerogatives and make them face their responsibilities in case of malfunctions. Being 'responsible' does not only mean that one has to *correct* the damage created by one's actions; it also means that one has the obligation to try to *prevent* these consequences from occurring and that one will be held accountable for the fulfilment of this preventive obligation.[805]

An understanding of property rights as constitutional rights of decision-making as a matter of principle leads to a path through which an orderly globalization could be achieved 'bottom up' by realizing that firms are legal and political orders, that *global* firms are *global* legal and political orders and that they are part of the World Power System – and draw the consequences.

9.3 The Rise of 'Private' Government in the US, and Berle and Means' Real Message

In the US, the importance of the concentration of property rights in large organizations was clearly perceived by Adolf Berle and Gardiner Means in their famous 1932 study, *The Modern Corporation and Private Property*. Since then, much of their message has been distorted and many are those

---

[803] Anthony McGrew, 'Globalization beyond borders? Globalization and the reconstruction of democratic theory and politics', in McGrew, *op cit*, note 526, p. 241.

[804] *See generally* Pierre-Yves Néron, 'Business and the Polis: What does it mean to see Corporations as Political Actors?', 94 *Journal of Business Ethics*, pp. 333–352 (2010).

[805] Supiot, *op cit*, note 429, p. 146.

who make Berle and Means advocates of agency theory.[806] This is totally contrary to what Berle and Means tried to do in their book.

In the 1932 preface, Berle wrote that:

> Accepting the institution of the large corporation (as we must) and studying it as a human institution, we have to consider the effect on property, the effect on workers, and the effect upon individuals who consume or use the goods or services which the corporation produces or renders. This is the work of a lifetime; *the present volume is intended primarily to break ground on the relation which the corporation bears to property.*[807] [emphasis added]

Berle and Means are almost never cited among *property rights* analysts. It is surprising since they *themselves* wrote that the whole purpose of their 1932 work was to 'break ground on the relation which the corporation bears to property'. In 1932, they thought they could not achieve more, although they certainly thought that much more was needed. In their view, the analysis of the effect of the corporation on property, workers and consumers was 'the work of a lifetime' and they could not achieve it in a single book. So, they concentrated on *property*. Although it is almost completely forgotten, the conclusion of their work[808] is in line with the plan they set for themselves in the preface:

> … the enterprise assumes an independent life, as if it belonged to no one … the enterprise becomes transformed into an institution which resembles the State in character. The institution here envisaged calls for analysis, not in terms of business enterprise, but in terms of social organization. (…) Such a great concentration of power and such a diversity of

---

[806] *See generally* William W. Bratton and Michael L. Wachter, 'Shareholder Primacy's Corporatist Origins: Adolf Berle and The Modern Corporation', 34(1) *The Journal of Corporation Law*, pp. 99–152 (2008); Mark T. Moore and Antoine Rebérioux, 'Corporate Power in the Public Eye: Re-Assessing the Implications of Berle's Public Consensus Theory', 33 *Seattle University Law Review*, pp. 1109–1139 (2010).

[807] Berle's preface to the 1932 edition of Adolf A. Berle, Jr. and Gardiner Means, *The Modern Corporation and Private Property*, New Brunswick and London: Transaction Publishers (Ninth printing 2007, 1st edition 1932), p. liii.

[808] *See also* Michel Aglietta and Antoine Rebérioux, *Corporate Governance Adrift: A Critique of Shareholder Value*, Cheltenham: Edward Elgar (2005), pp. 261–262.

interest raise the long-fought issue of power and its regulation – of interest and its protection.[809]

Of course, Berle and Means did not and could not anticipate the fortune of the agency theory of the firm, which started long after their own work with a 1970 article by Milton Friedman.[810] They wrote their book prior to the spreading of the doctrine in the 'corporate governance' debate claiming that firm power should be used for the benefits of shareholders only, the defence of the other interests being the realm of 'political' institutions. When Berle and Means are presented as advocates of agency theory, their work is in fact turned *upside down* because the conclusion of their book is *in total contradiction* with the prevailing theory of the firm. With a deficient theory of the firm, shareholders' interests are now over weighted in firms' governance. But this is certainly not what Berle and Means advocated. The *very last words* of their book are very clear:

> … the modern corporation may be regarded not simply as one form of social organization but potentially (if not yet actually) as the dominant institution of the modern world. (…) The future may see the economic organisms now typified by the corporation, not only on an equal plane with the State, but possibly even superseding it as the dominant form of social organization. The law of corporations, accordingly, might well be considered as a potential *constitutional law* for the new economic State, while business practice is increasingly assuming the aspects of economic statesmanship.[811] [emphasis added]

It is hard to imagine that Berle and Means could ever have advocated that the 'potential constitutional law for the new economic State' had to be that managers must manage the firm in the shareholders' interests only and maximize short-term profits.[812]

---

[809] Berle and Means, *op cit*, note 807, pp. 309–310.

[810] Friedman, *op cit*, note 601.

[811] Berle and Means, *op cit*, note 807, p. 313.

[812] *See* William W. Bratton and Michael L. Wachter, 'Shareholder Primacy's Corporatist Origins: Adolf Berle and the Modern Corporation', 34(1) *The Journal of Corporation Law*, pp. 99–152 (2008); Jean-Philippe Robé, 'Les États, les entreprises et le droit – Repenser le système-monde', *Le Débat*, no 161, pp. 74–87 (2010). *See, generally*, Teubner, *op cit*, note 510. *See also* Larry Cata Baker, 'The Autonomous Global Corporation: on the Role of Organizational Law. Beyond Asset Partitioning and Legal Personality', 41 *Tulsa Law Review*, pp. 541–572 (2006).

A major issue in Berle and Means' work, however, is their constant confusion between the concept of 'corporation' and the concept of 'firm'. Berle and Means' path-breaking contribution on the understanding of the process of *'separation of ownership and control'*[813] was somewhat misleading in this regard.[814] Their thesis was that in the early twentieth century, a process had taken place whereby managers who did not own the firm/company (they did not make the distinction in their book[815]) now controlled it. In their analysis, however, they confuse two very different types of separations of ownership and control:

> It has long been possible for an individual to incorporate his business even though it still represents his own investment,

---

[813] Berle and Means, *op cit*, note 807.

[814] *See also* Ciepley, *op cit*, note 508, p. 147.

[815] In their book (*op cit*, note 807), Berle and Means constantly use the words 'firm' and 'corporation' as synonyms. For example, on page 7, they write that 'Though the American law makes no distinction between the private corporation and the quasi-public, the economics of the two are essentially different.' Since the distinction between private (or close) and public corporations is an issue of *corporate* (and securities) law, 'corporation' here really means 'corporation'. But when they write on page 313 that 'the modern corporation may be regarded not simply as one form of social organization but potentially (if not yet actually) as the dominant institution of the modern world', the word 'corporation' is used as a synonym of the word 'firm'. Later, Berle wrote an article with a promising title: 'The Theory of Enterprise Entity', 47 *Columbia Law Review*, pp. 343–358 (1947) (reprinted in Yuri Biondi, Arnaldo Canziani and Thierry Kirat (eds.), *The Firm as an Entity – Implications for economics, accounting and the law*, New York: Routledge (2007)). But he mostly addressed some *corporate law* issues created by the existence of groups of corporations and never treated the enterprise (or firm) as an organized economic activity. For example, Berle writes that 'whenever an enterprise is composed of more than one corporate entity, two distinct sets of relationships are entailed. The first consists of a body of relationships which the enterprise has with individuals… A second and wholly different set of relationships exist by reason of the distribution of liabilities or security holdings within the enterprise.' In Berle's mind, the enterprise seems to be some sort of composite *corporate* vehicle, which can comprise several corporate entities. It is not an organized economic activity comprising other contributors of resources beyond the shareholders. Berle advocates further that courts should be 'dealing frankly with the fact that an enterprise is itself an entity'; or that 'the enterprise, and not the incorporation papers, is the true entity'. But he was more concerned about reviving some sort of 'real entity' theory adapted to the phenomenon of groups of corporations rather than having a broader understanding of the firm as an organized economic activity. On the need to differentiate firms and corporations, *see* Lynn A. Stout, *Corporate Entities: Their Ownership, Control, and Purpose*, Cornell Law School Research Paper No 16–38 (2017).

his own activities and his own business transactions; he has in fact merely created a *legal alter ego* by setting up a corporation as the nominal vehicle. ... The corporate system appears only when this type of private or 'close' corporation has given way to an essentially different form ...: a corporation in which a large measure of separation of ownership and control has taken place through a multiplication of owners.[816]

In fact, strictly speaking, there are *two* separations of ownership and control in the development of a large firm: a first separation of ownership and control *takes place immediately at the incorporation stage*, as explained in Sections 6.9 and 6.10. The corporation is *not* an *alter ego* of the incorporator, as Berle and Means wrote. Treating a corporation as an *alter ego*, as a mere conduit of one's private affairs, can entail (for example) the dire consequences of committing embezzlement. Courts then disregard the corporate entity and hold the individual having abused the corporate form responsible for acts purportedly done in the name of the corporation but, in reality, done in the mere personal interest of the individual. Margaret Blair rightly points out that when a corporation is formed, initial investors not only commit a pool of capital to be used in the business, they also yield *control* over the business assets and activities to a board of directors that is legally independent of shareholders.[817] It derives from the fact that the 'pool of capital' is now *fully owned* by the corporation. From that moment on, the shareholders only own *shares* which do not give them any property right over the corporation or its assets. They have given up their right of decision-making as a matter of principle over these assets. They still have such a right; but over the *shares* they got because of their contributions. Without this strict separation between the ownership of the productive assets and the ownership of the shares, a market for shares would simply be impossible; just like there is no market in equity interests in partnerships.

The process Berle and Means described is a different process of separation of 'ownership and control', usually coming later in the history of any given firm, when directors, who *do not own a majority of the shares* in the corporation, come to *control* the day-to-day operations of

---

[816] Berle and Means, *op cit*, note 807, p. 5; emphasis added.

[817] Margaret M. Blair, 'Locking in Capital: What Corporate Law Achieved for Business Organizers in the Nineteenth Century', 51 *UCLA Law Review*, pp. 387–455 (2003), p. 393. And she rightfully insists: 'The separation of ownership and control is a feature, not a bug'; Margaret M. Blair, 'Why Lynn Stout Took Up the Sword Against Share Value Maximization', *Accounting, Economics and Law* (forthcoming, 2020), p. 4.

the corporation. That is a *second* separation of ownership and control: ownership of the *shares* and control of the *firm/corporation*. It is that moment when the directors do not have the right of decision-making as a matter of principle over a majority of the *shares of stock*. But separation of ownership of the productive *assets* used in the operation of the firm and control of the firm/corporation takes place earlier. Not distinguishing the two leads to a confusion about which change is at the origin of what. For example, the fact that company officers do not own the property they manage (it is owned by the corporation) does not derive from the fact that they do not own a majority of the shares issued by the corporation. It is due to the incorporation process, to the fact that it is the corporation as an autonomous legal person which owns the property operated by the managers. This change takes place instantaneously at the incorporation stage. And this first change was already in itself at the origin of a drastic evolution of the Power System: rights of autonomy designed for individuals were concentrated into heteronomous firms, acting as private governmental organizations, making decisions about the use of assets as a matter of principle over continuously increasing bundles of assets and contracts.

9.4 Legal Institutionalism in Europe

On the eastern side of the North Atlantic Ocean, like Berle and Means in the US, some writers also tried in the first decades of the twentieth century to develop an analysis of the firm going beyond its corporate and contractual structure.[818] In France, these analyses were in line with the so-called 'institution theory' developed by Maurice Hauriou and further developed by Raymond Saleilles and other authors.[819] By 1939, Jean Brethe de la Gressaye viewed the business firm as an institution, which is:

> the seat of a legal system of its own in that it elaborates and adapts it to its needs and its purpose. [In his words,] there is a Constitutional law of the institution determining the methods

---

[818] For an overall review, *see* Antoine Jeammaud, Thierry Kirat and Marie-Claire Villeval, 'Les règles juridiques, l'entreprise et son institutionnalisation: au croisement de l'*économie et du droit*', *Revue internationale de droit économique*, pp. 99–141 (1996).

[819] Saleilles, *op cit*, note 42.

of appointment and functions of the legislative, executive and judicial organs.[820]

Like Berle and Means, he realized that what was at stake was a *constitutional* issue. But no one realized that the constitutional system of government – this specific institutionalization of State power in the Power System – had to be thought about in connection with the surge of the large corporate firm starting from the concept of *property* as part of the decision-making process of society from micro-powers (individuals) up to macro-powers (States). Berle and Means hinted at it when they wrote that their book was 'intended primarily to break ground on the relation which the corporation bears to property'.[821] But they did not properly analyse the complexity of the evolution of the concept of property in a corporate economic system. And the European institutionalists did not even realize that this evolution was grounded in the notion of *property* at all and was a consequence of its concentration into large organizations via corporations.

In 1947, Paul Durand took another look at the notion of 'enterprise'. In his view, the absence of a legal concept of the business firm – the enterprise – came from the fact that the drafters of the Napoleonic Codes imagined that the legal relationships arising from economic life would be constructed based on generally available rules, notably contracts and property rights.[822] They did not anticipate the future emergence of the large-scale firm. But the advent of the firm made it difficult to analyse it within a legal framework that did not anticipate it. For Paul Durand, the firm is 'a society organized within political society in its image'. The paths which he thought were open to legal analysis were 'first to study the *constitution* of the society'.[823] Here again, the *intuition* that what is at stake is a *constitutional* issue is clear. According to Durand, with regards to 'the laws governing the operation of the firm', one can distinguish the 'order of the inner workings of the firm' on the one side and 'the external relations of the firm and the State' on the other.[824] Paul Durand concluded that the theory of the firm brings:

> a new vision of the world. While at the beginning of the nineteenth century, the organization of society was entrusted

---

[820] Jean Brethe de la Gressaye, 'Les transformations juridiques de l'entreprise patronale', *Droit social*, pp. 2–5 (1939), p. 3.

[821] Berle's preface to the 1932 edition of Berle and Means, *op cit*, note 807, p. liii.

[822] Paul Durand, 'Rapport sur la notion juridique d'entreprise', in 3 *Travaux de l'association Henri Capitant*, pp. 45–60 (1947), p. 45.

[823] *Ibid*, p. 49; emphasis in the original.

[824] *Ibid*, p. 56.

to a *single sovereign*, dominating the multitude of the subjects, modern society presents itself under the form of an organism. ... The economic and social organization comprises a whole series of gearings, formed by firms, each of them constituting a small complex world, both by its components and the laws of its internal functioning. A *revolution* has occurred.[825] [emphasis added]

As is apparent from these citations, a minority of authors understood that a silent *revolution* had occurred, and that *sovereignty* now belonged to many organizations. The pluralistic nature of the constitutional order was perceived early on. But what did not appear clearly to these authors is that the origin of this redistribution of sovereignty is to be found in the concentration of property rights into large organizations which end up creating significant counter-powers to State powers. This is because there was no understanding that what is concentrated – property – amounts to a concentration of rights of decision- and rule-making towards objects of property as a matter of principle. Someone like Durand, for example, searching for the origin of the power exercised by firms made a tragic mistake. He ruled out that property could play any role: 'property, being a right in rem over things, cannot explain a commanding power over people'.[826] Similarly, Michel Despax, citing Durand and Jaussand, wrote that one could not see how property, being a right over things, could explain the existence of a commanding power over people. He continued working with the illusion that the source of this power lies in the employment contract.[827] As we know from our analysis in the first part of this book, it is quite the opposite. Property gives authority to the owner over those who are making use of her property. It is what determines who commands within business firms. But making this common mistake about the nature of property, Durand and his followers prevented the understanding of the enterprise as a legal and political order and its position in the Power System. They adopted a kind of *Führerprinzip*, considering that the powers within a firm had no contractual origin but were 'inherent to the operation of the employer institution'.[828]

---

[825] *Ibid*, p. 60.

[826] *Ibid*, p. 48. On the combined evolution of the notion of property under civil and constitutional French law, *see* François Luchaire, 'Les fondements constitutionnels du droit civil', *Revue Trimestrielle de Droit Civil*, pp. 245–382 (1982).

[827] Michel Despax, *L'entreprise et le droit*, Paris: Librairie Générale de Droit et de Jurisprudence (1957), p. 226.

[828] Durand, *op cit*, note 822, p. 56.

9.5 Agency Theory and an Improper Mandate to Maximize Short-term Shareholder Value

Virtually all large business firms are legally structured using one or several corporations. Due to the first separation of ownership and control deriving from the creation of the corporation, those who are making use of the assets owned by corporations do not own them. They are corporate executives – not owners – and have access to the assets via the corporate law rules. They have *possession* (not *ownership*) of the productive assets and, as a logical consequence, they are, in connection with these assets, the despots at the lowest level of the political/legal Power System. The owner is the corporation. But acting as its *agents*, the corporate executives are the ones making the decisions as a matter of principle towards the property rights owned by the corporation. As the agent of an owner, like any owner, they must abide by the 'as-a-matter-of-exception-rules' set by the law. But on top of these restrictions applying across the board, they have one additional set of *restrictive* rules applicable to them because they are *agents*. On top of all the restrictive rules which would be applicable to any *individual* owner of the same assets, they are bound by the rules set by *corporate law* which determine what they can and can't do with the property owned by the corporation whose property they manage. They must manage in compliance with the rules of corporate law, which define in a very loose way the interests they must further and protect.

The current folklore is that corporate officers have a duty to *maximize* short-term shareholder value. But, in fact, nowhere do corporate officers and directors have a legally enforceable duty to *maximize* shareholder value.[829] And even in the US, as aptly written by Lynn Stout, 'U.S. corporate law does not, and never has, required public corporations to "maximize shareholder value" ... The idea is a fable'.[830]

---

[829] Lynn A. Stout et al., *The Modern Corporation Statement on Company Law* (2016), available at https://papers.ssrn.com/sol3/papers.cfm?abstract_id=2848833.

[830] Stout, *op cit*, note 604, pp. 23–25. Most authors entertaining the notion that courts insist that maximizing returns to shareholders is the sole aim of the corporation and that directors who fail to do so can be sued rely on a 1919 decision of the Michigan Supreme Court, *Dodge v. Ford Motor Company*. The court held in a *dictum* (i.e. a part of the decision which is a tangential observation and does not create precedent that future courts must follow) that 'there should be no confusion ... a business corporation is organized and carried on primarily for the profit of the stockholders. The powers of the directors are to be employed for that end'. What is extraordinary is that Michigan law has otherwise never been of much relevance in corporate law – which is State law. In addition, the case is almost a century old and did not involve a public corporation. The issue in the case related to the duties of a controlling shareholder

Most judicial opinions describe the directors' fiduciary duties as being owed 'to the corporation and its shareholders', which implies that the two are not the same.[831] This is mere logic since the corporation whose estate is being managed by the corporate executives is the owner of the productive assets and the counterparty to the contracts used to legally structure the firm. And it is a legal person *separate* from the shareholders for the many reasons I have described in Chapter 7. Of course, it is not an individual. But the legal system treats it as a legal person living its own, separate, autonomous legal life, having very similar rights and duties as those of an individual. The key question under corporate law is what interests those in charge of conducting the corporate affairs must have in mind when they make decisions on behalf of this legal person which, because it is a fictitious legal person, must live via the decisions and actions of real-life individuals.

Clearly, directors and officers – with a high degree of discretion – must have the stockholders' welfare as a goal. Their integration of other interests may be taken into consideration, but only as long as it can be presented as a means of promoting stockholder welfare.[832] The board of directors, however, has strong power to pursue its own vision of what is best for the stockholders. And that can include taking into account the interests of other stakeholders. As made very clear under Delaware law by the so-called 'Craigslist opinion', 'when directors decisions are reviewed under the business judgement rule, this Court will not question rational judgments about how promoting non-stockholder interests ... ultimately promote stockholder value'.[833] Great autonomy is therefore given under corporate law to take into account in the firm's management the various conflicting interests affected. The only cases in which the directors were blamed for pursuing other interests than those of the shareholders are the ones in which they *admitted* to having put other interests *ahead* of the

towards minority shareholders (the Dodge brothers wanted a dividend distribution to create a competing business and Henry Ford was refusing). And the case has never been validated by the Delaware courts, which are usually considered to be at the edge of corporate law. The only limited exception is the co-called 'Revlon duties': in a situation where the board plans to 'go private' – i.e. when a public corporation is about to stop being a public corporation – directors must embrace shareholder wealth as their only goal. *Ibid*, pp. 30–31.

[831] Stout, *op cit*, note 604, p. 28.

[832] *See generally* Leo E. Strine Jr., *The Dangers of Denial: The Need for a Clear-Eyed Understanding of the Power and Accountability Structure Established by the Delaware General Corporation Law*, University of Pennsylvania Law School, Institute for Law and Economics, Research Paper No. 15–08 (2015).

[833] *eBay Domestic Holdings, Inc. v. Newmark*, 16 A.3d 1, 34 (Del. Ch. 2010).

shareholders'.[834] But anybody can create a 'rational judgement' that caring about the natural environment, the clients and the workers, for example, promotes stockholder value at the end of the day. It is not corporate law which forces directors to endorse a narrow conception of short-term shareholder value. Ideology does. Corporate officers and directors have a strong *belief* in the pertinence of 'agency theory' because it is supported by most professional economists and the financial press generally. It has no basis in the reality of the legal system but operates as a strong incentive to maximize short-term 'shareholder value'. Consequently, the largest owners in our society – corporations – are ruled in the short-term interest of only one class of interested parties in firm management: the shareholders. And this is done in the name of a property right over the corporation which shareholders simply do not have, as seen in Chapter 7, and in the name of corporate law rules which simply do not exist.

To make things worse, missing the importance of the firm as part of the Power System and as an economic organization separate from the corporation(s) used to legally structure it has led to an improper *accounting* of its activities. Directed at the shareholders, lenders and other investors, and concentrated on financial capital as the only form of capital worth preserving in firm management, existing accounting rules are unable to effectively account for the full impact of a firm's activities. This is probably the single most important catastrophic consequence of 'agency theory'.

In his 1970 article,[835] Milton Friedman based his argument that 'The Social Responsibility of Business is to increase its Profits' on the false idea that shareholders own firms (or corporations – he did not make the difference) and that managers are their agents. We have seen why this is mistaken in Chapter 6.

But Milton Friedman developed a second line of arguments in the same article in favour of 'shareholder value maximization': a governance model giving the incentive to pursue 'shareholder value maximization' only is said to be socially beneficial because it maximizes the wealth created. Once this wealth is maximized, it is then up to political institutions to allocate its use. But neither firms nor their leaders – says Friedman – have anything to do with the allocation of the value created which is a political and not a business decision. We have developed sophisticated democratic political institutions to deal with allocation decisions and it is not up to business people to aim at anything else than maximizing value creation. Otherwise, they act as unelected politicians.

[834] Strine, *op cit*, note 832, p. 23.
[835] Friedman, *op cit*, note 601. For a critique, *see* Robé, *op cit*, note 158.

Milton Friedman's theory on the division of labour between 'private' and 'public' governance was based on the assumption that we live in a perfect normative environment integrating 'social' demands and, in particular, internalizing all the 'negative externalities' in the cost of producing goods and services (and thus, ultimately, in prices), via mandatory laws, regulations and taxes. Unfortunately, we have *never* lived in such an environment. With Friedman's assumption, governance issues are allocated in such a way that the role of the 'private' side of the Power System is simplified to the extreme (with the mandate to merely 'maximize wealth creation'), the complex issues of correcting the negative externalities and inequalities generated bearing only on the 'public' institutions. Of course, the institutions of public governance have *never* been able to fully address these most complex issues of our society. But the limited mandate given to 'private' institutions to simply 'maximize wealth' has made the life of public institutions even harder. What was hardly achievable in a world of relatively isolated national economies with an overarching State able to adjust its laws to an evolving economic system just can't be done in the present-day globalized economy. We are living today in a global economy where most large firms have a global footprint and operate in the anarchic world of a post-Westphalian State System without a global State. In the present context, the assumption that there is a 'public' normative system in place to provide the proper normative order so that firms can operate with the simplistic 'shareholder value' maximization mandate cannot be made. To 'maximize wealth', the management teams at the helm of large firms decide on the geographical allocation of the resources they control looking worldwide at the pros and cons of the various possible locations. Global firms choose among normative environments and make States compete to provide them with rules appropriate for the conduct of their activities. The contents of States' laws must be adapted for States' territories to remain as competitive places for the location of at least part of the production processes and/ or the accounting allocation of value creation in global value chains. In a globalized economy, it is the whole system of allocation of authority, of division of powers and of resources allocation which is affected by the firms' combined decisions. Public authorities, as well as the social and natural environments, bear to an unprecedented extent the consequences of choices made within private firms because globalization is negatively affecting States' internalizing capacities through laws and regulations. It is therefore impossible to assume in such an environment that all negative externalities are perfectly internalized by the political system of mandatory norm creation – as was done by Friedman. Shareholder value can be created without creating wealth, without creating real value.

But there is more: some 'negative externalities' are inevitable and involuntary side consequences of any economic activity. But because of the precepts of agency theory and its avatar of shareholder value maximization, other externalities are *intentionally produced* by firms: *externalizing costs* on the social or natural environments translates into profits. As written in 2015 by Leo Strine, the Chief Justice of the Delaware Supreme Court, given existing corporate governance rules:

> strong and effective externality regulation is important because the profit-pressure put on corporations by institutional investors is strong. ... stockholders will put pressure on corporate managers to seek as much profit as they can within the range of legally permissible conduct.[836]

Strine advocates adopting a sober and realistic view of corporate law as it presently exists and drawing the consequences:

> Under the current legal rules and power structures within corporate law, it is naïve to expect that corporations will not externalize costs when they can. It is naïve to think that they will treat workers the way we would want to be treated. It is naïve to think that corporations will not be tempted to sacrifice long-term value maximizing investments when powerful institutional investors prefer short-term corporate finance gimmicks. ... And it is naïve to think that institutional investors themselves will behave differently if action is not taken to address the incentives that cause their interests to diverge from those of the people whose funds they invest. ... we must recognize that directors are increasingly vulnerable to pressure from activist investors and shareholder groups with short-term objectives, and that this pressure may logically lead to strategies that sacrifice long-term performance for short-term shareholder wealth.[837]

But his realistic and sobering view of what is achievable via corporate law then cedes to an unrealistic hope:

> if interests such as the environment, workers, and consumers are to be protected, then what is required is a revival of effective

---

[836] Strine, *op cit*, note 832, pp. 33–34.
[837] *Ibid*, p. 38.

externality regulation that gives these interests more effective and timely protection. Critically, this externality regulation must be undertaken on a more global scale to match the regulatory structure to the scope of corporate conduct's impact in a globalizing economy.[838]

This suggestion is akin to the drawing of a plan to escape a desert island on the false assumption that there is a bridge. The reality is that the institutions 'to match the regulatory structure to the scope of corporate conduct's impact in a globalizing economy' are lacking. *The Dangers of Denial* are many and it is naïve to think that 'a revival of effective externality regulation ... on a more global scale' is accessible. It is simply not possible to expect global regulations (by whom?) to counterbalance the negative effects of the shareholder value ideology. By oversimplifying the issues of corporate governance in a globalizing world, the proponents of shareholder value maximization contribute to the existence of corporate governance systems which systematically *convert externalities* – costs imposed upon others and the environment, social and natural – *into profits*. And there is no one to adapt the laws to prevent this from happening.

There is one set of tools which remains to address the shareholder value issue, however, even without a new impetus correcting the *Shareholder Value Myth* in corporate governance: the rules of accounting. In many cases, an objective accounting of the value created by a *firm's* activity, considering all the costs and benefits involved, would show that some of the *profits* made do *not* correspond to *value* creation. But the notion that corporations (and therefore firms, in the mind of those who do not differentiate the two) should only seek to maximize *shareholder* value leads today to the exploitation of the difference between an accounting of the creation of *shareholder value* and an accounting of the *value created* (or destroyed) by the economic activity organized within a firm.[839] The reader may want to refer to my example in Section 8.3 where the profits made as a consequence of reorganizations *internal to the firm* vary widely and can be increased *without producing any additional widgets*. Irrespective of the understanding one has of the concept of 'value', no additional 'value' – no additional widget – is created in our example as a consequence of the various changes made in the organization which, however, increases

---

[838] *Ibid*, pp. 39–41.

[839] For a critique, *see* Yuri Biondi, 'The Pure Logic of Accounting: A Critique of the Fair Value Revolution', 1(1) *Accounting, Economics, and Law*, Article 7. Available at: https://www.degruyter.com/view/j/ael.2011.1.1/ael.2011.1.1.1018/ael.2011.1.1.1018.xml (2011).

'shareholder value'. In a world of State competition for the localization of firms' activities, of political failure at the international level and of imperfect norms, there may be a difference between the costs and benefits generated by a decision and their accounting translation. Firing well-paid employees in one location to hire lesser-paid ones in another country creates 'shareholder value'. Closing a regulated plant limiting pollution to open another one in a country in which the activity is unregulated creates 'shareholder value'. Reducing one's tax bill by localizing the accounting acknowledgement of value creation in a tax haven creates 'shareholder value'. But this can be done only because all the costs and benefits of any management decision are not taken into account in *financial* accounting. Some States benefit from this state of affairs – as is obvious for tax havens, which live on these gimmicks. But overall, in a world of State competition for the localization of firms' activities, of political failure at the international level and of imperfect regulations, there is usually a difference between the costs and benefits generated by business decisions and their accounting translation; i.e. there may be creation of 'shareholder value' by simply 'externalizing costs' (the cost of dismissed employees falling on employees and on the unemployment benefits systems; the cost of environmental pollution bearing on the local or global population, depending on the pollution at stake; or the cost of tax optimization falling on the taxpayers who do not have access to avoidance tricks). The spreading of the doctrine of shareholder value maximization has led to the widespread exploitation of this possibility.

Agency theory thus leads many firms to become organizations producing negative externalities *not as an ancillary consequence of their economic activity*, as is the case with any economic agent, *but as one of their main activities* – because it is an easy way to make profits. There are, of course, firms producing value and most firms probably produce both value and negative externalities. But shareholder value theory has prevented the development of accounting systems selecting those firms creating only 'real value'.

Looking at the sub-prime and subsequent financial and economic crisis, at environmental tragedies such as the extinction of many species of plants and animals, at climate change, at all sorts of instances of tax and legal dumping (due to the existence of tax and legal 'havens' provided by free-rider States), at the induced offshoring phenomenon (the use of corporate devices to locate the accounting acknowledgement of wealth creation in low-tax jurisdictions),[840] at increasing inequality and the debt

---

[840] *See generally* Palan, *op cit*, note 54.

crisis,[841] it is hard to agree that there are only '*some* imperfections in contracts and the laws' and that 'extremist views on shareholder value are [only] distasteful'.[842] The evidence is that negative externalities are large and pervasive; and existing models of corporate governance designed on the tenets of shareholder supremacy play their role in this state of affairs. By oversimplifying the issues of corporate governance in a globalizing world, the proponents of shareholder value maximization contribute to the existence of corporate governance systems which systematically convert externalities – costs imposed upon others and the environment, social and natural – into profits.

9.6 Rules of Accounting

Ronald Coase, who is one of the first economists having developed an institutional analysis of the firm, always insisted on the importance of accounting, considering that the theory of the accounting system is part of the theory of the firm.[843] For him, the reason for this was that while:

> outside the firm prices and therefore costs are explicit ... and are determined by the operation of the market, within the firm there are implicit costs ... but they are provided by the accounting system. This internal system takes the place of the pricing system of the market.[844]

Since *costs* are determined within firms by 'the accounting system' and not by *prices*, accounting rules play a key role in the measurement of the performance of the firm and in the organization of its operations. What is accounted for and how is a key determinant of the *firms'* activities because it determines how the *costs* of doing business are measured. A key audience of the accounts generated to measure the performance of a firm's activity should therefore be management itself.

When one makes the distinction between 'firm' and 'corporation', however, one immediately realizes that at present, the operations of the *firm* are guided by the accounting of the events and contracts taking place

---

[841] As of January 2019, the world level of debts amounts to $250,000 billion; *Le Temps*, 14 January 2019.

[842] Jean Tirole, *The Theory of Corporate Finance*, Princeton: Princeton University Press (2006), p. 61; emphasis added.

[843] *E.g.* Coase, *op cit*, note 198, p. 12.

[844] *Ibid*, p. 11.

at the level of the *corporation* (or corporations, for firms organized via a group of corporations), that is, at the level of its corporate structure. What is accounted for is *that part* of the firm's activity which gets translated into legal transactions or events to be accounted for at the *corporate* level, at the level of the specific *legal person(s)* used to legally structure the firm. The corporation has issued shares to raise the equity capital and the accounting of its operations concentrates on what affects this *financial* capital with, as we will see, quite a narrow understanding of what this means.

When the operations of an enterprise are structured using a group of corporations – a group of formally autonomous legal persons operating under a common controlling management structure – the accounting of the operations becomes more complex. Each legal person in the firm's legal structure has its own financials, its own balance sheet and profit-and-loss statements. These financial statements give a narrow view of the operations of each legal entity. Each legal entity's financials must in principle, at least formally, stand on their own feet. It must be so because each legal entity has its own creditors and debtors whose rights and obligations are towards the legal entity *only* (as a matter of principle) and not against the other legal persons in the group of corporations or the shareholders, as we have seen in Section 8.5. But to get a more realistic accounting view of the operation of the *group of corporations* as a whole, *consolidated accounts* have to be prepared, disregarding the existence of the subsidiaries as separate legal persons and treating the group as one single organization for accounting purposes. Anything internal has to be disregarded because it is not the outcome of third-party, *market* transactions. Internal transactions may therefore not have been made at *market* prices.

To deal with this issue, accountants have developed the idea of treating the group of *corporations* as an *entity* (although it is not a *legal* entity).[845] But this is for accounting purposes *only*, as the group of corporations *does not* exist at law as a separate legal entity having its own accounts. And this has also created some degree of confusion. Consolidating financial statements only leads to an adjustment of *corporate* accounting to deal with the fact that some transactions within the group of corporations occur among legal entities under common control. The economic conditions at which they take place may not be reliable and represent what would have happened on the market.

To consolidate financial statements, the first issue is to determine the perimeter of the accounting 'entity'. It is based on a notion of 'control'. The activities of all the legal entities under a common control are treated

---

[845] Biondi, Canziani and Kirat, *op cit*, note 815.

as the activities of one consolidated concern. The value of the equity stakes in the subsidiaries and sub-subsidiaries and so on are eliminated (to avoid double accounting of the same economic value) and the operations of all the entities deemed to be under a common control are treated as if they were the operations of one single accounting entity. This way, *only* transactions with the outside world, with a non-controlled seller or buyer of products or services, are accounted for.

But this is still 'corporate accounting' not 'firm accounting' since only the transactions or events occurring at the *corporate* level – at the level of the various *legal* entities used to structure the firm – within the legal system are accounted for. Only what affects *financial* capital, with a narrow understanding of what this comprises, is accounted for.

Accounting as a discipline has to deal with the practical problems of measurement in an ongoing society. Its objective is to provide the measurements needed to understand the outcome of a firm's operations and of other institutions not merely in equilibrium, as in prevailing economic models, but in the disequilibrium of a society's economic processes.[846] In this respect, traditional economic theory did not and still does not offer much help. The implicit assumption is that all the problems involving the complex issues in the accounting of ownership claims, for example, can be abstracted away via the broad principles of the price system.[847] The price system is certainly a formidable instrument to gather information and coordinate activities – as long as it works. But it does not always work. And the overall structure of microeconomic theory was so underdeveloped until recently that it was not ready to tackle the details of the micro-micro-economic reality faced by accountants.[848] Accountants had to solve empirical problems daily without having the luxury of waiting for economists to come up with an adequate analysis of the firm as an economic organization.

While accountants have not received much help from micro-economists to develop proper *firm* accounting given the poor state of the economic theory of the firm, accounting as a discipline has not been immune from the prevailing mantra of 'shareholder supremacy'. And this has led to a reduced scope of what is accounted for in financial accounting. Initially, accounting rules were developed to answer the needs of merchants, who were merely trading on the market. Their users were the merchants

---

[846] Martin Shubik, 'A Note on Accounting and Economic Theory: Past, Present and Future', 1(1) *Accounting, Economics and Law: A Convivium* (2011), Article 1, pp. 4–5. Available at: http://www.bepress.com/ael/vol1/iss1/1

[847] *Ibid*, p. 3.

[848] *Ibid*, p. 5.

themselves and their agents.[849] With the advent of the large business, corporate firm, a whole series of new issues and interested parties appeared: stockholders, creditors, suppliers, customers, neighbours, the natural environment and so on.[850] Stockholders want dividends, creditors want to be repaid, suppliers want to know about the credit of their contracting party, employees want to keep their jobs and prosper and so on. As a consequence of the existence of these various affected interests, generally accepted accounting principles (the so-called GAAPs) developed in many jurisdictions and were the result of social processes which required trade-offs among many parties with differing interests, goals and perceptions.[851] As a consequence, there are US GAAPs, Italian GAAPs, French GAAPs and so on. They are all different and measure performance differently.

With globalization and the increased 'financialization' of the economy via ever more sophisticated Financial Structures, it became apparent that local irreconcilable accounting rules were an obstacle to 'efficient' financial markets. The International Organization of Securities Commission (IOSCO) lobbied for the establishment of a single and universal international accounting standard, claiming that inconsistent, nationally imposed accounting standards create obstacles for investors when reading financial reports.[852] The International Accounting Standards Committee (IASC) issued a 'Conceptual Framework' in 1989 with the ambition to provide a basis for deciding which various accounting options should be removed or retained in the context of cross-border securities offering. For our purposes, the point of interest is that in the 1989 Conceptual Framework, the primary users of financial reporting were defined as 'present and potential investors, employees, lenders, suppliers and other trade creditors, customers, governments and their agencies and the public' (paragraph 9 of the 1989 Framework). There was an appreciation of the various stakeholders' interests in the content of the accounting information produced and offered. It does not mean that all these various interests were properly taken into account in the setting of the accounting rules. The point is that whatever importance was given to non-financial stakeholders, they disappeared as targeted '*users*' of the financials. In the 2010 Framework, the users of accounting information were reduced to include only 'investors, lenders and other creditors'. There is no consideration

---

[849] John Hicks, 'Capital Controversies: Ancient and Modern', 64(2) *The American Economic Review, Papers and Proceedings of the Eighty-sixth Annual Meeting of the American Economic Association*, pp. 307–316 (1974), at p. 310.

[850] Shubik, *op cit*, note 846, pp. 6–8.

[851] *Ibid*, p. 13.

[852] Zhang and Andrew, *op cit*, note 634, p. 19.

given to the needs of other stakeholders or to the provision of accounting information that is not financial in nature.[853] As mentioned in paragraph OB 10 of the 2010 IASB Conceptual Framework: 'Other parties, such as regulators and members of the public other than investors, lenders and other creditors, may also find general purpose financial information useful. However, these reports are not primarily directed to these other groups.' And in the March 2018 Revised Conceptual Framework, the objective of financial reporting remains to 'provide financial information that is useful to users in making decisions relating to providing resources for the entity'. As we will see in more detail later on, even if one takes into consideration only the needs of those who provide *financial* resources for the entity,[854] this is quite a narrow understanding of the information they require to make proper investment decisions. Under prevailing rules, they are actually getting very misleading information.

Since 2010, the IASB Conceptual Framework has been embracing a shareholder primacy perspective with a narrow notion of accountability.[855] What is accounted for has *changed* based on agency theory. As we have seen in Section 9.5, agency theory and the shareholder primacy doctrine have translated into a specific form of corporate governance. But this doctrine has also led to market-based accounting regulation led by the International Accounting Standards Board (IASB) whose standards have been implemented into European legislation to rule accounting for listed companies throughout Europe.[856] They assume that markets and the price system are the most suitable mode of economic exchange and of capital and asset valuation. As a consequence, in particular, the negative externalities generated by the firm activity remain *unaccounted for* since, by definition, they do not affect prices. And with regard to the determination of the assets affected by the firm's operations, a notion of 'control' is applied. In this perspective, many of the resources negatively affected by the firm's activity (air, water, workforce etc.) cannot be considered as forming part of the entity's assets because they are not 'controlled'. No one owns air, water or the employees. As a matter of illustration, in case

---

[853] Deegan, *op cit*, note 65, p. 452.

[854] It being understood that the revised framework only addresses the needs of financial resource providers in their decisions about buying, selling or holding equity or debt instruments, providing or settling loans and other forms of credit and voting, or otherwise influencing management's actions.

[855] Deegan, *op cit*, note 65, p. 452. *See also* Bernard Colasse, 'Comptabilité et vision de l'entreprise – Sur les normes comptables internationales', *Le Débat*, pp. 83–93 (2016).

[856] Yuri Biondi, *Better Accounting for Corporate Shareholding and Environmental Protection*, University of Oslo Faculty of Law Legal Studies Research Paper No 2014–28 (2014), p. 129.

of soil contamination, if the affected land is owned by the polluter, its value is depreciated in the financials. But if it is not owned, there will be a negative accounting impact *only* to the extent that there is a third party in a position to request indemnification. Externalities imposed upon the social and natural environment for which there is no third-party claimant are not accounted for. Only assets legally protected, and primarily *owned* assets, are being considered. Consequently, an accounting entity destroying all sea creatures and coastal vegetation in its local environment can be financially very successful: the abuse of the resources, being considered outside its 'control', is not accounted for.[857] We have already seen this phenomenon in Section 9.5 and earlier in this section: it is possible to create 'shareholder value' while not creating any 'real value' at all and actually while, in some cases, *destroying* real value.

Present-day international accounting rules are clearly in line with the doctrine of shareholder primacy and are part of the institutional setting which leads to a gigantic worldwide production of negative externalities. Many valuable resources are simply not owned or controlled. And their damage or destruction is thus not accounted for.

A viable theory of the firm must be accompanied with, and actually makes it possible to develop, an adequate theory of firm accounting.[858] With agency theory having biased the accounting of large firms in favour of the acknowledgement of short-term 'shareholder value', accounting is today very misleading and leads to the production of dramatic quantities of negative externalities – such as global warming, the issue I will concentrate on in the remainder of this book.

An enhanced accounting of the operations of *the firm*, comprising financial, environmental and social metrics would be much more effective to guide decisions about *the firm's* operations. To correct the damaging impact of improper accounting, the idea has been developed, for example, that 'triple bottom line accounting' should be used by management in making decisions.[859] The idea is that accounting should provide bottom line information about the use of financial capital, but also about the impact of the operations of the firm over the other forms of capital being used and affected by firm management, such as human and natural capital.

The theory of the firm offered in this book can lead to an improved accounting of its operations. Accounting is an important instrument to cope with firms. With an enhanced accounting system, we can rely on the

---

[857] Deegan, *op cit*, note 65, p. 453.

[858] Shubik, *op cit*, note 846, p. 5.

[859] John Elkington, *Cannibals With Forks: The Triple Bottom Line of 21st Century Business*, Oxford: Capstone (1997).

most formidable instrument invented to allocate resources among firms: the market. The financial market is not fulfilling its role today because its operators are not provided with adequate information. The market can assess which firms are better at producing shareholder value. We need to improve the information given to market participants for them to be in a position to identify and promote the firms which are better at producing real value as opposed to mere 'shareholder value'. We will see how by addressing the largest negative externality ever: climate change.

10

Towards a Sustainable
World Power System

So far in the second part of this book, I have distinguished the concepts of 'firm' and of 'corporation' and presented the extraordinary legal properties of corporations. I have explained why corporations are being used to legally structure the operations of virtually all large firms and their Financial Structure. Because of the properties of corporations, many firms have grown enormously and some of them are today significant participants in the World Power System not only as micro- but also as macro-powers. This is creating new challenges to cope with firms, as the historical methods used so far to deal with institutions of 'private' power based on the accumulation of property rights have merely been found at the State, national level, on a territorial basis, to internalize negative externalities and correct inequalities. In the absence of a global State and faced with State competition and governmental failure, we must find new ways to cope with global firms. One major issue is the prevailing 'agency theory' and the biased accounting rules which derive from this faulty doctrine.

As indicated in the General Introduction, I want to use World Power System analysis to tackle climate change. Those who still doubt the seriousness of this issue should read the calls made by scientists.[860] The issue is here and its treatment is urgent. Via the classical operation of the State System, States agreed in 2015 on the Paris Agreement which was viewed as a landmark achievement. It has always been insufficient, however, even assuming it would be implemented. But in addition, States do not respect their commitments. The latest round of discussions, held in Poland in 2018, only evidenced the insufficiency of the corrective measures taken. The reason for this is that this type of agreement can

---

[860] *See*, in particular, Figueres et al., *op cit*, note 1, pp. 593–597 (2017).

hardly work in the existing World Power System for the structural reasons detailed in this book. The issue is global, the commitments are local and their implementation would require the creation of local rules disadvantaging proactive States and their populations. The Paris Agreement does not work, it cannot work, it will not work.[861]

We must think differently, within the concepts and the set of constraints identified in this book.

★★★

The existing World Power System has led to – or at least has not prevented – the growth of major issues endangering the sustainability of human life on our planet.

Several planet boundaries are now being met, as we have seen in the General Introduction at pp. 20–24. Many of these issues derive from the defects of the State System – leading to insufficient measures to correct negative externalities and to reduce excessive inequalities – and addressing them via the State System is an impossible task.

In this chapter, I will mostly concentrate on the most serious one: climate change.

The globalization of the Power System is dissolving political, territorial and intellectual boundaries we thought eternal. But many of those commenting on it do not have much to offer. The theorists of postmodernism, neoliberalism and systems theory all agree that we are witnessing the end of politics as we knew it. But they disagree on almost everything else. They usually disregard the micro-structure of the World Power System which makes it hard for them to propose corrective actions to perceived issues. There was a remarkable absence of discussion of corporations in classical writers such as Locke, Rousseau, Kant, Hume or Bentham. But the same applies for more recent legal theorists or philosophers as well: there is nothing on corporations in Austin, Hart, Kelsen, Nozick, Ackerman, Dworkin or Rawls.[862] There is a widespread assumption of *individual* ownership and action despite obvious practical realities and an over-simple dichotomy between private right and public

---

[861] For a balanced view, *see* David Held and Charles Roger, 'Three Models of Global Climate Governance: From Kyoto to Paris and Beyond', 9(4) *Global Policy*, pp. 527–537 (2018).

[862] Walter Robert Goedecke, 'Corporations and the Philosophy of Law', 10 *Journal of Value Inquiry*, pp. 81–90 (1976), p. 81. *See also* Dan-Cohen, *op cit*, note 23.

action, liberal individualism and socialism.[863] Contemporary political philosophy is still wedded to an *individualistic* picture of society.[864]

The political structure of society is still perceived as the confrontation between the State, on the one hand, and the atomistically conceived individual on the other. This political individualism leads to the failure to address the political implications of the *organizational* structure of today's globalized society. In this perspective, the State appears as uniquely positioned in the Power System in terms of power, size and complexity. This translates into two deformed views: the first one consists in seeing the State as unique as a locus of coercive and potentially repressive force; and the other one is the equally false *opposite view* of seeing the State as the sole guardian of collective interests and endowed with a unique legitimacy to address collective issues not to be found anywhere else in the system.

The concentration of property rights into global organizations via the corporate system has fundamentally rearranged the effective operation of the political system. But political theory has not followed pace. And

> the failure of the international community to generate a sound framework for managing global warming is one of the most serious indications of the problems facing the multilateral order.[865]

Simultaneously, time is scarce to address the issues we are facing. With regards to climate change, which is our key priority, it is considered that if no serious action is taken within the next 15 years, the damage to the planet's climate will be irreversible. Sixty-eight world-class experts have actually published an article in the influential *Nature* indicating that if no serious action is taken in the next *three years* (this was in 2017 ...), it will be very hard to take the right measures afterwards in time to prevent destructive climate change.[866] It is almost certain that we will react too late to prevent dramatic climate change. But we still need to find out what will need to be done when the seriousness of the consequences will be felt and will force action.

This crisis is due to a production of CO_2 ancillary to human activities in excess of nature's capacity to absorb it. Nobody has a property right over nature's ability to absorb CO_2 and it is not a 'common' as is often

---

[863] Goedecke, *op cit*, note 862, pp. 82–83.

[864] Dan-Cohen, *op cit*, note 23, pp. 164–165.

[865] David Held, 'Reframing Global Governance: Apocalypse Soon or Reform!', in Held and McGrew, *op cit*, note 3, pp. 240–260, at p. 240.

[866] Christiana Figueres et al., *op cit*, note 1, pp. 593–597.

argued. It is not something 'owned in common'. It is simply not owned, just like a State or an enterprise or Saturn are not owned. There is no legal person having a property right over the resource in a position to transfer the right to own or use it. Nature is not an economic agent selling its production for a price going up and down depending on the demand level. When the resources it produces are being used, no price is being paid. Because it is not owned, nature's CO_2 absorbing capacity cannot be sold for a price. But it is still being used. And because no price is being paid when it is used, the *cost* of its use (a notion different from its *price*) is not included in the price system. It does not enter economic calculations, be it at the productive or the financial level. What could be included in the calculations is the cost of *restoring* the resource, such as planting a forest or building a carbon well using modern technology to absorb carbon in the atmosphere. But this is not done because no one (no owner) is able to present the bill, and the resources affected are considered to be *outside* the control of the polluting entity. We are in a typical case of negative externality, and climate change *is actually the largest negative externality ever created* by the market/price system. We are in a case where political intervention would be required in the Pigou–Bénabou–Tirole tradition. States have attempted to address the problem via the 2015 Paris Agreement. But they have done it through a typical State System international treaty: States agreed on *national* ceilings and then are supposed to implement them *locally*. But because they are in competition, States meet local resistance. Major States are in fact now exiting their commitments and we cannot base our future on such a feeble instrument. It does not work.

There is, however, another method to change the behaviour of millions of participants to the economic system to reduce our emissions of CO_2: via the accounting system, disclosure and investment adjustments because of the information made available to the market, and in particular financial markets.

10.1 The Challenge to Address the Global Issues

Addressing climate change in our World Power System requires finding the way to impact billions of decisions in the daily use of assets to make them more aligned with the preservation of our climate.

The challenge is daunting. We are on a collision course with our species' survival if we do not change. We know it. There are still some marginal discussions; but 100 per cent of the scientists working in this area agree on 90 per cent of the issues. There is agreement that we have a finite stock of CO_2 to emit if we want to limit global warning at any given level. To contain global temperature increases at 1.5°C, the emissions of CO_2 need to be reduced drastically (−45 per cent in 2030 compared with their level in 2010) to then reach 'carbon neutrality' by 2050, meaning that by then, we will have to stop emitting in the atmosphere more carbon than we take out. In the ideal situation, we will then only have *residual emissions* (i.e. those of the activities for which there is no substitute) but for which we will create 'negative emissions', i.e. carbon wells absorbing an equivalent amount of CO_2.[867] Then the increase in temperature will stabilize; and temperatures could be reduced if the 'negative emissions' (i.e. carbon absorption) become larger than the positive ones.

The issue is that the negative effects of the changes required to our modes of living to make them more congruent with our planet's CO_2 absorbing capacities would be felt rapidly while the positive ones would take time and will actually be imperceptible. The situation will get worse no matter what. Improvement will *not* be perceived because we will still live through dramatic events. They will just be less dramatic than those which would have occurred without the corrective measures. But it will not be felt. Most likely also, the internalization of the cost of CO_2 emissions, if it takes place early enough, will translate into an increase in prices and into a reduction of production and consumption. There will be an impression of a reduction in welfare. It will be the consequence of the fact that so far, significant costs imposed to our natural environment have not been accounted for and have not been included in the prices we paid for goods and services. We've had it too good for too long, and we have eroded our natural capital under the form of excessive consumption. We should have subtracted the cost of emitting CO_2 from GDPs (for States) and profits (for businesses) to have an accurate picture of the evolution.[868] But doing the right thing to put the measurement of our activities on the right path will mean that jobs will be lost before new ones will be created. Entire lines of business will disappear before new production will reach full speed. And the economic basis of certain States will be seriously eroded. There will be massive migration movements. Entire economic activities will have to stop in a disorderly manner. With so many unpleasant events, people will not get the feeling that their welfare is improving and that their efforts are leading to anything good. And simultaneously, action via the State System requires − for many jurisdictions − going through the democratic system and its short-term biases. Although the consequences of doing nothing are catastrophic, the

---

[867] *See* the 2018 *IPCC Report*, available at http://www.ipcc.ch/report/sr15/.

[868] Stiglitz, Sen and Fitoussi, *op cit*, note 66, pp. 159–160.

State System is inefficient at addressing a global issue of this magnitude; and democracy will be of no help, just as it has been of no help since the 1970s, when we first learned about these issues. There are too many tasks to tackle and short-term fixes get in the way of long-term solutions: rational politicians are led to cede to the pressures and demands of electoral majorities. They are just buying time.[869]

We seem to have reached the end of the dead end.

The whole purpose of developing the World Power System analysis was actually to assist in identifying *where* it is possible to act in this Power System and *how*. We need a system-level shift, taking most of our institutions as they are, but efficient at driving our economies towards long-term sustainability. The idea is to use the engines of globalization – multinational enterprises – as key forces for the changes required.

10.2 Re-engineering Multinational Enterprises

In addition to the States – which are and will remain key participants in the Power System, but which are inherently limited by what they are, i.e. *territorial* organizations in a *de-territorialized* economy – we have a wealth of systems of governance, both decentralized in numerous State jurisdictions and centralized in a unity of command at the world level. These governance systems are what we call 'multinational enterprises'. These numerous, specialized organizations, expert in their fields of activity, are all able to address within their organization, and sometimes up in their value chains, many of the critical global issues. This explains why it is so important to understand the effective micro-structure of the World Power System: it is a prerequisite to allocate duties and responsibilities *where* they can be met with today's configuration of the Power System. The traditional public/private allocation of prerogatives and responsibilities via property rights and State democracy does not work in a World Power System with a global economy structured via global business firms and States competing to attract them under their jurisdiction.

The idea is to make use of firms as the priority vehicles to adopt and implement the rules aligning firms' strategies with the requirements of the day. Enterprises and their Financial Structures are significant drivers

---

[869] Streeck, *op cit*, note 729, pp. 10 & 48. John Ruggie agrees that 'there is no going back to change the beginning. No silver bullet can reverse such a deep and wide systemic transformation. The only way to try and change the end is by identifying strategic points of intervention in what exists and to build on what seems to work'; Ruggie, *op cit*, note 619, p. 13.

in the convergence of the environmental, social and economic crises we are facing. The principal-agent, or agency, theory advocated by many mainstream economists has played a dramatic role in this evolution. But with an amended governance mandate, more in line with the real position of large multinational enterprises in the World Power System and untainted by the ideology of shareholder primacy, they can be turned into key contributors to the achievement of global sustainability goals.[870]

The concept is not at all to improve Corporate Social Responsibility (CSR) policies as they are understood today, as something which comes as a plus, a 'nice to have' after 'business as usual'.[871] Multinational enterprises are today very much part of the problem, having led to the need to think about new governmental rules. They can be made part of the solution by using their extraordinary capabilities. They can create global rules almost immediately enforceable worldwide and across their corporate structure. They often also have numerous means available to impact upstream on their full value chain. They are the organizations closest to the issues, in their concrete manifestations, both in their global dimension and in their local ones. These large firms are the first in line to be able to adjust their ways. And they control the intellectual and financial resources required. The strength of the method suggested is to use what firms are good at: gathering knowledge, making decisions and implementing them. The duties they have in connection with the products they create encompass the conditions of their production.[872] The change to be brought in the operation of business firms is an extension of their mandate, and a correlative adjustment of their accounting and reporting systems, of the incentives and compliance reviews. It is, of course, a very complex task. But compared with alternative grand plan solutions (which are not practical alternatives), it is relatively easy once the difference between 'real value' and 'shareholder value' is understood.[873]

---

[870] *See also* Sjåfjel, *op cit*, note 780, p. 2.

[871] This is all the more the case that recent research shows that there is a positive and statistically significant relationship between the conduct of CSR policies and profit shifting; *see* Iftekhar Hasan, Panagiotis Karavitis, Pantelis Kazakis and Woon Sau Leung, *Corporate Social Responsibility and Profit Shifting*, Working Paper, 19 January 2019, p. 33 (2019).

[872] Supiot, *op cit*, note 429, p. 156.

[873] *See* above in Section 8.3.

10.3 Starting with What We Have

As we have seen, beyond the 'State System' of world governance, there are unofficial participants in the World Power System. All the multinational enterprises are transnational economic and political systems, sometimes of very significant size. They fine-slice the operations in their value chains and place them, internally or externally, in the most cost-effective location, domestically and globally. Millions of decisions affecting the allocation of economic resources are made *within them* daily.

These organizations have governance systems deciding on strategies and on their implementation, with internal incentive mechanisms to ensure an alignment of the efforts of the members of the organization. They do not operate as a simulacrum of the price system, as many mainstream economists think. This is welcome given that the climate change issue to address is due to the *failure* of the market system to correct this negative externality. But for the official legal and political systems, these organizations have no existence. What does exist, as legal persons, are the *corporations* used to legally structure the business firms. And for the largest multinationals, their corporate structure is *a group of corporations* which has no single existence as such. Each corporation in the group is both subject to local laws and to the internal rules of the corporate organization to which it belongs. Acts within the organization, although they are the consequences of larger strategies, are attributed to various subsidiaries, with rare instances of 'piercing the corporate veil' where the effective decision-makers are brought to bear the negative consequences of their decisions.[874]

Beyond the corporate structure of each multinational enterprise, one can identify an even wider economic system. It is the full ecosystem of the global 'value chain' (also called 'global production network' or 'global supply chain'), with suppliers and sometimes distributors being both legally independent of, and economically very much integrated within, multinational enterprises (*see* Sections 6.6 and 6.7). The rising fragmentation of production has increased trade in intermediary goods. Many small and medium-sized enterprises (SMEs), often from developing countries, supply these goods and are integrated into global supply chains.[875] It is estimated that there are over 700 million workers employed directly and indirectly in global supply chains.[876]

---

[874] Noting that this is more common in antitrust matters. *See also* Ruggie, *op cit*, note 619, p. 13.

[875] *See* Ruggie, *op cit*, note 568, pp. 1–17.

[876] *See* the Business and Sustainable Development Commission, *January 2017 Report.*

Given the fact that about 80 per cent of world trade is in fact *intra-firm* trade (*see* Section 9.1), most international exchanges are subject to two relatively independent sets of rules: those created *by the State System* (at the local or international level); and those created *by the organizations* – the multinational enterprises – within which production and exchanges take place. Some have even predicted that 'the multinational firm is becoming the leading organization that "governs" the global economy, with the support of "local" States'.[877] The rules internal to global firms must be compliant with the local, territorial ones; they would be illegal otherwise. But they can be *more protective* of the interests affected than the local rules. For example, in March 2017, Danone adopted a Global Parental Policy which is applicable to its 100,000 employees worldwide and covers the first 1,000 days of every child born to one of Danone's employees. Anywhere.[878] This is a fantastic tool to project protective normativity worldwide.

Further, the authority of multinationals extends to certain contractors, franchisees and other types of non-equity counterparties. Through their Codes of Conduct or their procurement processes, they can require suppliers upstream in their value chain to adhere to social and environmental standards. It is considered that there are 500 million micro-, small- and medium-enterprises (MSMEs) around the world.[879] Many of them are not part of global supply chains. But they can still be influenced – taking into account the specificities deriving from their size and scope – by sub-procurement and requirement processes.

---

[877] Groupe de Lisbonne, *Limites à la concurrence – pour un nouveau contrat mondial*, Lisbonne: Fondation Gulbenkian, La Découverte (1995), p. 124.

[878] https://www.danone.com/content/dam/danone-corp/about-us-impact/policies-and-commitments/en/2017/2017_06_23_DanoneGlobalParentalPolicy.pdf. This is an interesting instance of legal pluralism, which is the key concept of a post-modern conception of the law, of a conception of different legal spaces superimposed, combined and mixed in our minds and actions. We live in a time of porous legality or legal porosity, in which multiple networks of legal orders constantly force us to make transitions and encroachments. Our legal life is characterized by the crossing of various legal orders, that is to say, the inter-legality. Inter-legality is the phenomenological counterpart of legal pluralism, which makes it the second key concept of a modern-day conception of law. Boaventura de Sousa Santos, 'Droit: une carte de la lecture déformée – Pour une conception post-moderne du droit', 10 *Droit et Société*, pp. 364–390 (1988), p. 382.

[879] Business Commission on Sustainable Development, *Ideas for Action for a Long-Term and Sustainable Financial System* (2017), p. 15. Available at: https://s3.amazonaws.com/aws-bsdc/BSDC_SustainableFinanceSystem.pdf.

The ability of multinationals to enforce their 'internal' norms across the globe offers an extraordinary opportunity to restructure world governance and make it compatible with the preservation of the planet's boundaries.

10.4 True Cost Accounting

To mobilize the potential offered by global firms, it is necessary to account differently for their operations. As we have seen in Section 3.2, in a situation where political action is difficult, a case can be made that action at the corporate level is a reasonable substitute.[880]

Multinational firms are operating in a space in which there is no encompassing political institution able to correct the negative consequences of their actions. This is particularly damaging because multinationals, given the mandate assigned to them by agency theory, make States compete to attract them. This leads to a race to the bottom in many regulatory areas. Although most of the literature on corporate social responsibility – in favour or against – addresses issues of gift making,[881] the key issue of today is the one of mitigating negative externalities, and not enough work is devoted to it. One reason for this lack of attention to the real issues we are facing is probably their sheer complexity in our World Power System with global firms and a divided State System. In such an environment, what is at stake is not determining whether firms must give to charities or not. What is at stake is the treatment of negative externalities which are inseparable from the production decisions made within firms.[882] And in these circumstances, the conclusion reached by Oliver Hart and Luigi Zingales is clearly that 'shareholder value maximization is not the appropriate goal for a company'.[883] With an adjusted mandate, multinational firms can compensate for the fact that they are active in States lacking institutional capabilities to internalize negative externalities or correct excessive inequality.

A major assumption at the root of the shareholder primacy model is that firms are deemed to be operating in regulatory environments internalizing all the negative externalities and correcting inequalities.[884] With this assumption, maximizing shareholder value maximizes 'real

---

[880] Hart and Zingales, *op cit*, note 319, and Bénabou and Tirole, *op cit*, note 8.

[881] Hart and Zingales, *op cit*, note 319, p. 6.

[882] *Ibid*, p. 27.

[883] *Ibid*, p. 28. *See also* Michael C. Jensen, 'Value Maximization, Stakeholder Theory and the Corporate Objective Function', 12 *Business Ethics Quarterly*, pp. 235–256 (2002), p. 239.

[884] Tirole, *op cit*, note 842, pp. 60–61.

value'. The profits correspond to the value created because there are no negative externalities to consider when measuring 'real value' creation.

With globalization, however, we are in a situation where firms operate in a regulatory environment in which all the negative externalities are *not* internalized by appropriate laws and taxes. In such an environment, profit maximization is *not* socially desirable.[885] And the public institutions to internalize negative externalities are lacking. There is a clear collective action issue with the State System, at the origin of many of the issues of our time.

A key issue, as we will see, is that the financials which guide the firms' operations and which are used as a basis of the incentive devices used within most firms (e.g. stock options or bonuses) do not reflect the full costs of the firm's operations and, therefore, its real value creation (or destruction). Like corporate governance, they have been tainted by agency theory. According to one former chair of the US SEC, financials increasingly tell an incomplete story.[886] This leads to ignoring substantial negative externalities, which are at the origin of, or contribute to, the existence of several global issues.

Similarly, politicians will not be able to react to the degradation of natural systems or be responsible for their choices in the management of the operations of the State if the natural resource assessment framework is not changed. The United Nations standard system of national accounts as it exists is totally unaware of the current changes in the environment.

Consequently, neither the accounting of private firms nor of public government have been able to alert us to the fact that brilliant economic performances can be hazardous to our future.[887] Neglecting the economic value of natural resources presents false data to policymakers – public and private – and reinforces the illusion of a dichotomy between the economy and the environment. Fictitious gains are shown instead of real losses: illusory gains in *income* are in fact losses in *wealth*.[888] With the limited scope of our accounting systems, depletion of (natural) capital appears as an income, just like in any well-structured Ponzi scheme. Via agency theory and the financialization of the economy, we are distributing future

---

[885] Antoine Rebérioux and Gwenaël Roudaut, 'Corporate Governance and Accountability', in *Handbook of the International Political Economy of the Corporation*, Cheltenham: Edward Elgar (2018), pp. 29–44, at p. 29.

[886] Elisse B. Walter (2017), *Sustainability Matters: Focusing on your Future Today*, (2017). Available at: https://corpgov.law.harvard.edu/2017/04/18/sustainability-matters-focusing-on-your-future-today/

[887] Stiglitz, Sen and Fitoussi, *op cit*, note 66, pp. 159–160.

[888] Robert Repetto, 'Accounting for environmental assets', 266(6) *Scientific American*, pp. 94–100 (1992).

under the form of accounting profits which correspond to a depletion of our natural capital.

10.5 Curing the Deficiencies of Accounting

That public accounts should be adjusted to appropriately account for the use of natural capital in public action should be a no-brainer.[889] Without this, it is simply impossible to evaluate the real efficiency of a State's operations.

But the same applies to business firms as well. For example, the top-100 emitting firms with listed shares are responsible for around a quarter of the global greenhouse gas emissions.[890] This is a huge proportion concentrated in a relatively small number of operators.

Within firms, decisions are being made based on the economic signals surrounding them, such as the price of labour and materials and the cost of taxes. But today's prices don't indicate to the decision-makers within firms the environmental or social externalities involved in the production of goods or services. The same, of course, also applies to consumers of the various productions of the firm, be it products or services or the financial instruments they offer on financial markets.

Today, accounting rules have been created to benefit the 'absentee shareholder', which is another consequence of the 'shareholder value' model. There is a dramatic lack of integration of the various interests affected by the accounting rules into the accounting rules themselves, as discussed in Section 9.6.

The numbers involved are immense. In 2012, a major analysis of unpriced environmental costs in the global economy looked at every primary production and processing sector – from agriculture, forestry, fisheries, mining, utilities and oil and gas exploration to cement, steel, pulp and paper, and petrochemicals. Across these sectors, it was evidenced that environmental externalities of US$7.3 trillion were unpriced in 2009 (the last year for which complete data was available), equivalent to 13 per cent of global GDP in that year, or nearly half of US GDP at the

---

[889] Although a first step should be the removal of the $450 billion in direct subsidies paid annually by States to fossil fuel companies, as well as the $5.2 trillion in annual indirect subsidies. *See, e.g.* Business Commission on Sustainable Development, *op cit*, note 879, p. 19.

[890] *The Emissions Gap Report 2017*, United Nations Environment Programme (UNEP), Executive summary.

time.[891] These costs are currently absent from corporate profit-and-loss accounts. They need to be internalized for decisions to be made with comprehensive accounting information. Curing damage *after the fact* will not do for two reasons. The first one is that it is an 'efficient' decision, based on existing rules, to pollute. Roy Shapira and Luigi Zingales, analysing in detail a real-life example in which a polluting company paid US$670 million *30 years after the fact*, found that in this example it was 'value-maximizing to pollute if the probability of getting caught was less than 19%. ... In other words, the decision to pollute was ex–ante optimal for the shareholders'. They concluded, apparently with some surprise, that:

> If the decision to pollute is not a product of incompetence or myopic fly-by-night companies, but rather a calculated, rational decision by a reputable company, perhaps socially harmful corporate behavior is more endemic and less solvable than we acknowledge.[892]

Indeed. The second reason is that with climate change, remediation will not be available anyway.

The ultimate objective is to have full-cost accounting. If all companies were accounting for the costs of the externalities they generate, then, consumers, investors and their financial intermediaries would be able to compare companies' *sustainability* performance by comparing their *financial* performance.[893]

Today, 93 per cent of the world's 250 largest companies report on sustainability; some even provide 'Integrated Reporting'. Of these, 75 per cent voluntarily abide by the Global Reporting Initiative (GRI), a multi-stakeholder framework for ESG reporting. But the information provided grants primacy to financial capital and the lack of a standardized system for reporting on environmental, social and governance (ESG) performance makes ESG analysis time-consuming and expensive. In its absence, different companies use different reporting standards.[894] The information provided is incomplete, lacks consistency and is not comparable between companies. This profusion of frameworks makes it very difficult to

---

[891] *See* Business and Sustainable Development Commission, *January Report* (2017), available at http://report.businesscommission.org/report, p. 64.

[892] Roy Shapira and Luigi Zingales, *Is Pollution Value-Maximizing? The DuPont Case*, NBER Working Paper No w23866 (2017). For other examples, *see* Stout, *op cit*, note 604, pp. 1–2.

[893] *See* Business and Sustainable Development Commission, *op cit*, note 891, p. 70.

[894] *Ibid*, p. 70.

compare sustainability reporting between companies in the same industry. When everyone uses different frameworks, there's no way to benchmark performance against competitors, or use high-performance scores to build trust among customers, staff and the public. And it is harder to make the case that investing in sustainability brings better returns. A 2017 study conducted by the large accounting firm PwC found that 82 per cent of the investors are dissatisfied with the comparability of sustainability reporting between companies in the same industry.[895]

As written by Michael Bloomberg, who chaired the Task Force on Climate-related Financial Disclosures (TCFD):[896]

> For the most part, the sustainability information that is disclosed by corporations today is not useful for investors and other decision-makers. ... The market cannot accurately value companies, and investors cannot efficiently allocate capital, without comparable, reliable and useful data on increasingly relevant climate related issues ...[897]

There are methodological issues to be addressed. But achieving 'true/full-cost accounting' is doable. For example, the sport lifestyle company PUMA published its Environmental Profit and Loss Account for the year ended 31 December 2010. According to PUMA's Chairman:

> the total results revealed that if we treated our planet as any other service provider, PUMA would have to pay €8 million to nature for the services rendered to our core operations ... An additional €137 million would be owed to nature from PUMA's supply chain of external partners ... we have to address the activities of our supply chain partners that generate 94% of our total environmental impact.

---

[895] Business and Sustainable Development Commission, *op cit*, note 891, p. 13.

[896] The Task Force on Climate-related Financial Disclosures was established by the Financial Stability Board (FSB) in late 2015. The Task Force developed voluntary recommendations on climate-related information that companies should disclose to help investors, lenders, and others make sound financial decisions. Numerous initiatives led by organizations such as the Principles for Responsible Investment (PRI), the World Business Council for Sustainable Development (WBCSD), the Institute of International Finance (IIF) and others are independently convening industry-specific working groups to drive implementation of the TCFD recommendations

[897] https://www.bloomberg.com/company/announcements/2015–bloomberg-impact-report-a-message-from-our-founder/

In financial terms, it means that the €202 million net profit made by PUMA in 2010 included free services received from nature of €145 million. The profit after adjustment of the environmental impact is, in fact, €57 million. It means that one way to increase its 'true value' creation is for PUMA to reduce its environmental impact. A 10 per cent reduction would increase its true profits by more than 25 per cent. This is true of any company generating negative environmental externalities. But with the numbers generated, PUMA now knows how much is at stake in each area of its operations.

The Environmental Profit and Loss Account is now being made at the level of the group of companies PUMA belongs to, i.e. Kering.[898] The numbers are not public and are made available to the group's top management only. But to lead other companies to embrace natural capital accounting, Kering has made its own methodology open source.

Richard Barker and Colin Mayer have developed an interesting method to determine how a 'sustainable corporation' should account for natural capital.[899] There is a need for two measures of profit: *financial profit*, as currently reported (the €202 million figure in the PUMA example); and *sustainable profit*, which is the hypothetical measure of how much financial profit would be if the activities of the firm were sustainable (the €57 million figure in the PUMA example – disregarding methodology issues). Barker and Mayer's starting point is that a corporation is sustainable if, at a minimum, it is *financially* viable. It must start being 'financially sustainable' because if it is not financially viable, there is no way it can be 'sustainable'; it will not have resources available to address its negative impact over the natural environment. Today, because of Friedman's doctrine that 'the business of business is to increase its profits', it is widely accepted that companies only need to be 'financially sustainable' and do not need to address the externalities they create. Addressing negative externalities is viewed as the role of governments. But as we have seen, there is a massive government failure at the level of the World Power System which pleads for a different kind of governance, based on a different kind of accounting. The case can easily be made that on its current trajectory with regards to climate change, economic activity cannot continue indefinitely. And the management of business firms is accountable to shareholders for the financial stability of their business model. Otherwise, their investors are purchasing financial securities they

---

[898] Among large firms having conducted similar experiments, one finds Norsk Hydro in Norway, Danish Steelworks and Watercare Services in New Zealand.

[899] Richard Barker and Colin Mayer, *How Should a 'Sustainable Corporation' Account for Natural Capital?*, Saïd Business School Research Papers, RP-15 (2017).

cannot properly value because environmental costs are not included in the numbers being used. Estimating the cost of the externalities imposed by the enterprise can be understood as a *currently measurable* proxy for risk exposure.[900]

It is hard to find out whether the stimulus for change will come from the corporate sector itself, from governments, from market pressure or from some kind of political action. But we know that we are on a collision course with the evolution of our climate and that corporate activity will ultimately need to become more sustainable or will disappear. It is *a present need* for investors to have the accounting information required to determine the environmental cost of doing business for firms to address it or else give way to more efficient competitors – those considering not only the preservation of financial capital, but of natural capital *as well* and *still* making profits. There is no realistic alternative in an open access order society.[901] And one can steer firm management in this direction through operational accounting.[902] A different way of accounting for the determination of profit-making is a way to bring about the *internal* changes that are needed in corporate action. The idea is to prevent claiming *revenue* when in fact what takes place is a destruction of *capital*. The strategic axis is to use the profit motive and the market. Not to do so would indeed be depriving ourselves of a powerful instrument to achieve our ends. The problem that companies face is not that they aim at making profits. It is that they do so within a framework of rules allowing value creation to be displayed when in fact capital is being destroyed. Somewhat ironically, the 'invisible hand' of the (financial) market is the most effective force at our disposal to make companies work for socially desirable purposes, as long as the full costs of their activities are accounted for.[903]

Proponents of corporate responsibility are wrong to put so much emphasis on the *content* of what companies decide rather than on *how* they decide – the decision-making process of the company itself. The type of 'responsibility' that must be developed in companies is not only the responsibility to respect the rules, but also the responsibility in its cognitive aspects – the sense that a person who is 'responsible' does not immediately translate her first impulse into action. She reviews her environment to take into account the consequences the action will have

---

[900] *Ibid*, p. 9.

[901] *Ibid*.

[902] Christopher Stone, *Where the Law Ends – The Social Control of Corporate Behavior*, New York: Harper and Row (1975), p. 38.

[903] *Ibid*, pp. 57–71.

on others; measures and weighs alternatives; and is ready to justify her decisions and actions.[904]

There are several approaches in the present literature on these responsibility, procedural and reporting issues.

The first approach is 'ESG reporting for shareholders' which reports on environmental performance insofar as it contributes to an understanding of items in the *financial statements*. But there is one single bottom line: *financial profit* for shareholders.

The second approach is 'stakeholder reporting'. Corporations report on their financial performance in the financial statements. And they report on their environmental performance in a *separate* document. The metrics may or may not be expressed in financial terms, and there is no commensurability for the financial statements, nor even among the various metrics used in the environmental report. This method is associated in practice with the Global Reporting Initiative.[905]

The third approach is 'stakeholder accounting'. As in the first approach, there is a single bottom line. But the financial accounts are revised to accommodate considerations of sustainability. For example, a liability for environment impact may be recognized even though no such liability would need to be recognized in conventional financial accounting, for example because there is no legal duty to eliminate the negative environmental impact. The financial statements are tweaked to be addressed to a different audience.

The fourth approach, the one I endorse, is 'sustainability accounting'. It maintains the existing system of corporate financial accounting but extends the accounting of the firm's operations to include the hypothetical transactions and events that would make the business sustainable with respect to its impact on natural capital.[906] This approach is sometimes called 'full-cost accounting'. Financial accounting and sustainability accounting are commensurable, both forming part of a *single system of accounting*, but with *two bottom lines* which are distinct but also *very much connected to each other*. The approach does not treat financial statements as inherently useless but seeks to address their limitations when it comes to measuring the sustainability of an organized economic activity – *a firm*. It takes into account the fact that other forms of capital than financial capital are being used and affected by the production process. Their current default value in financial accounting, however, is zero. Which means that the erosion of these forms of capital, when it occurs because of the

---

[904] *Ibid*, p. 217.

[905] https://www.globalreporting.org/Pages/default.aspx

[906] Barker and Mayer, *op cit*, note 899, pp. 11–12.

production process, is not accounted for. Since they are not on the balance sheet and there is no third party in a position to make an enforceable claim that the damage to these forms of capital should be compensated, some other method has to be found to protect them.

Financial accounting was simply not designed to incorporate considerations of the social and environmental impact of producing and accounting organizations.[907]

With regards to the natural environment,[908] negative impacts have always been there. But as long as we were within the planetary boundaries,[909] as long as nature could absorb these negative impacts, they could be addressed on an ad hoc basis via a series of measures in various legal systems. The situation today is different; survival is at stake for many species of plants and animals and humans and there is no encompassing polity to impose the appropriate rules. Sustainability accounting is the compass to use to drive human activity towards sustainability. It measures, reports and reconciles business activity from *both* a financial *and* a sustainability perspective.[910] While only the so-called 'genuine' obligations (those for which there is a legal or constructive obligation resulting from past events) are dealt with in the financial accounts, with full-cost accounting, the accounting of environmental use prevents the presentation of the accounting entity as a cash-generating machine for shareholders and investors when the environment is simultaneously damaged.[911] Natural capital must be preserved in addition to financial capital and be conceptualized in *physical terms*. A goal of *physical natural capital maintenance* must be applied to the accounting of the reporting entity. By applying a life-cycle approach to products and services, accounting for the reporting entity's environmental impact would transcend the fragmentation of the responsibility for environmental impact corporation by corporation or

---

[907] Deegan, *op cit*, note 65, p. 450.

[908] The preservation of social capital requires a different treatment. *See generally* Samuel Jubé, *Droit social et normalisation comptable*, Paris: Librairie générale de droit et de jurisprudence (2011). For example, human capital used by the firm can be valued as the present value of the income stream generated by the employees capitalized at a chosen capitalization rate. A workforce paid collectively $10 million at a capitalization rate of 5 per cent is worth $200 million. Given an attrition rate of 10 per cent in the industry considered (for example), the value of the human capital should be adjusted to $180. Any excessive attrition rate compared to the industry's average would translate into a loss of human capital; or training 'expenses' then become investments increasing the value of the human capital, etc.

[909] Steffen et al., *op cit*, note 59.

[910] Barker and Mayer, *op cit*, note 899, p. 12.

[911] Biondi, *op cit*, note 856, p. 132.

country by country. For CO_2 production, in particular, it is the full impact of the *firm* which is to be accounted for, irrespective of the location in any subsidiary or supplying entity or country upstream in the value chain.[912]

The key point of sustainability accounting is that it involves no attempt at giving natural capital any *price*. None is created by the price system and the attempts to create artificial markets for 'rights to pollute', for example, are notorious failures. The European Emission Trading Scheme has been so 'efficient' that the prices of the pollution rights have fluctuated widely with a general trend downwards, providing *no incentive* to reduce pollution.[913] The fact of the matter is that there cannot be any price for natural capital because no one owns it; and no one can. The fact that the price system cannot work to preserve this category of assets is not the outcome of some *market failure* to be corrected by creating artificial and non-performing 'markets'. It is a consequence of what property rights are; and there is none over certain categories of assets such as natural capital and, more specifically in our case, such as nature's CO_2 absorption capacity. The fact that some assets, organizations, or what-have-you cannot be priced is not the outcome of 'market failure' or 'imperfect definition of the property rights'. There are things which cannot be owned – the State, a firm, a landscape, the climate and so on – but this is not the outcome of any kind of 'failure'. The only 'failure' is to think that the market can be the sole arbitrator of all values. There are things the market cannot price but which still need to be preserved and valued. And any pricing would be artificial and would likely miss the target by either under- or over-shooting to protect the value considered.

From a sustainability perspective, it is the *physical maintenance* of the natural resources which is *an end in itself*. The notion of price is simply irrelevant. What matters is the *cost* of maintaining the natural resource. An accounting of what can be *priced* by the market must be supplemented by an accounting of unpriced *costs*. If a company is making 100 million dollars in profits but it would take a well costing 30 million dollars a year to absorb its CO_2 production over the accounting year, its real profits are 70 million dollars.

Sustainability accounting offers the immense advantage of placing the resources to be preserved outside the realm of economics.[914] Whereas with financial accounting there is absolute fungibility and unlimited substitutability among the assets and liabilities since only their *financial valuation* enters the financials, with sustainability accounting, fungibility

---

[912] *See also* Sjåfjel, *op cit*, note 780, p. 6.

[913] Deegan, *op cit*, note 65, p. 456.

[914] Barker and Mayer, *op cit*, note 899, p. 13.

and substitutability *is excluded*. It is the *physical integrity of the resource* which is to be preserved, irrespective of any valuation. What must be measured and integrated into calculations is the *cost* of physical restoration of the resource used. Financial accounting is aligned with mainstream economic thought in its *primary* reliance on market transactions and on the price system. But given the fact that certain forms of capital are not owned and cannot be owned, and their use cannot be priced because there can be no seller and buyer freely agreeing on a price, financial accounting needs to be *supplemented*. This has to be done to orient the guidance of economic activities towards sustainability by considering certain *costs* which cannot be *priced* by the price system.

Financial capital is at the heart of financial accounting.[915] It is a claim, not a resource.[916] It is *not* something considered to be owned by the accounting entity: it is treated as a *debt* towards shareholders which made it possible to acquire productive assets.[917] What the accountants call capital is really part of the resources contributed to the corporation and having made it possible to acquire the productive capital required to operate the firm. But eventually, the financial capital must be returned to the shareholders and, in the meantime, its use as a resource has to be paid for. It is not considered to be owned by the accounting entity. Corporate activity affects this value: increases are reported as *profits* and decreases are reported as *losses*. Profit measures the excess of the resources generated by a company during a period (income) over the resources it consumes during that same period (expenses). It is, of course, the reverse for losses. No profit can be evidenced to the extent financial capital is being *depleted*: this would not correspond to an *income*, but to a *reduction of wealth*, a *consumption of the financial capital* contributed by the shareholders.

What cannot happen to financial capital except in cases of fraud, i.e. a consumption of capital treated as an income (which is the essence of a Ponzi scheme, for example[918]), *does happen* with the other forms of capital used by the firm, such as environmental capital. The environmental capital (which is not owned either by the corporation) is being depleted in the production process and is not regenerated by the accounting entity. To

---

[915] *Ibid*, p. 18.

[916] *Ibid*, pp. 19–20.

[917] Henry P. Hill, *Accounting Principles for the Autonomous Corporate Entity*, New York: Quorum Books (1987), p. 8.

[918] In a Ponzi scheme, new contributions of capital by new investors are treated as income and are distributed to former contributors of capital. Capital contributions appear to be compensated; but there is no wealth creation by the entity distributing dividends. There is only depletion of the most recent contributions of capital. This, of course, can only last as long as there are new contributors of capital.

prevent such Ponzi schemes in social and environmental capital, the same norm of capital maintenance should apply to the *forms of capital other than financial capital being used* by accounting entities which they do not own – because they can't be owned. It is the case, for our purposes, for the use made of nature's CO_2 absorption capacity. As advised by the World Business Council For Sustainable Development (WBCSD) in its CEO Guide to the Sustainable Development Goals:[919]

> In order to measure, value and report their true value, true cost and true profits, companies need to go beyond financial capital accounting and incorporate natural and social capital as well.

As we have seen in Section 8.3, within the present system, resources for the shareholders can be generated without creating value: there can be increases in *shareholder value* without creation of any *real value*. This is because there are negative externalities which are not accounted for and the cost of correcting them would be higher than the shareholder value created.

This approach has the advantage of dismantling the misleading dichotomies between hard economics and soft ethics, pure finance and corporate generosity, responsibility towards shareholders and corporate social responsibility, hard law and soft law, and so on.[920] Investing in sustainable companies is not ethical, generous or socially responsible; it is just good old-fashioned long-term investing.

The sustainability of an accounting entity *is a key information to know and report*. This information is '*relevant*', which the IFRS March 2018 Conceptual Framework Project Summary defines as being 'capable of making a difference to the decisions made by users' of the information and it is '*faithful*' in that it 'faithfully represent[s] the substance of what it purports to represent'. Investors willing to invest in businesses which are sustainable in the long term do *not* have today the information they *need* to make the right decisions.[921] They do not get this '*relevant*' and '*faithful*' information. And there are investors urging companies to adopt a long-term perspective who would value this information. Sustainability

---

[919] https://www.wbcsd.org/Overview/Resources/General/CEO-Guide-to-the-SDGs, p. 19. The WBCSD comprises almost 200 world companies working together to accelerate the transition to a sustainable world. *See also* the *SDG Compass*, which provides guidance for companies on how they can align their strategies as well as measure and manage their contribution to the realization of the SDGs; https://sdgcompass.org/.

[920] Sjåfjel, *op cit*, note 780, p. 13.

[921] *Ibid.*

accounting, which is much more *'faithful'* than mere financial accounting is quite *'relevant'*, at least for a large class of *'users'*, and would allow them discriminating among firms with a future and the rest.

Maybe more importantly, sustainable firms have a clear interest in creating and diffusing this information. They should take the lead in creating a dynamic in which their unsustainable competitors would need to adapt or else disappear. They can demonstrate that they could survive even in a world which would take the natural environment seriously. And if and when restrictive regulations will come because of the seriousness of the consequences of our collective lack of foresight, the investors in these firms will fare better than those remaining invested in unsustainable firms. The competitive advantage of firms making it known via hard numbers that they are sustainable would be clear in all the markets in which they operate: the markets for equity, for debt and for the products and services they sell to their clients. Not to mention the labour market to hire the best, responsible, employees. This is particularly important to attract and retain the young generation.

Board directors have a general duty of loyalty and care. To fulfil their mission, they should discover whether the company they are overseeing is managing a firm which is sustainable or not. A case can be made that this is part of their duties. Here and now. Some even claim that good faith initiatives based on scientific evidence and reasonable economic assumptions should be taken to safeguard a company's continuing prosperity and its sustainability.[922] But in any case, it is clearly in the interest of at least part of the stockholders to know if the company in which they are invested is being managed in a sustainable manner or not. The *reverse*, i.e. resisting against the provision of sustainability accounting, is harder to defend. The present and future value of all claims against a company is affected by its sustainability – or lack thereof.

With regard to shareholders, investors, clients, customers, as well as regulators, with access to the information regarding a firm's sustainability or progress towards sustainability, they can adjust their decisions and push for a restoration of the damaged resources or withdraw their investment or business. This is particularly acute for equity investors – shareholders – because it goes against the grain of today's mantra that companies should maximize short-term shareholder gains. Apart from any moral consideration (and there is no question that many shareholders do have moral considerations) an equity investor needs to know if the company he invested in is sustainable. Without this information, everything else

---

[922] *See generally* Sarah Barker, *Directors' Personal Liability for Corporate Inaction on Climate Change*, Governance Directions, pp. 21–25 (2015), especially p. 25.

being equal, two companies can be valued equally when in one, sooner or later, the value of the equity will be negatively affected while the other one, because it is sustainable, will thrive. With the right information made available, 'the subpolitics of investment could be forged into an instrument of power'.[923] A substitute to an unachievable 'revival of effective externality regulation ... on a more global scale'[924] would be in operation.

For downstream net destructions of natural capital, individuals can be made responsible for their own decisions. And States can prohibit or restrict the use of destructive assets, such as excessively polluting cars, and so on. The classical allocation of duties among property rights owners and political institutions works – at least it can.

With an enhanced accounting system, we can rely on the most formidable instrument invented to allocate resources among *firms*: the market. The financial markets are *not* fulfilling their role today because their operators are *not* provided with the right information. The market can assess which firms are better at producing *shareholder* value. But as we know, this concept is different from the concept of *real* value: firms can create *shareholder value* while not creating any real value or even while destroying *real value*. We need firms to improve the information given to market participants for them to be in a position to identify and promote the firms which are better at producing real value as opposed to mere 'shareholder value'.

10.6 Concluding Remarks

Property rights are legal rights. They are fundamental rights for the individuals enjoying their prerogatives and building blocks for the institutional operation of the polities defining and enforcing them. Developing an above-ground notion of 'economic property' rights would create even more obstacles to the understanding of the operation of property in our society than we already have with social sciences structured around the fading State System. This is because property is a constitutional right of decision-making as a matter of principle. It leaves open the possibility that the decisions made autonomously by owners generate negative externalities and inequalities unaccepted by the polity. The acknowledged role of political institutions is to provide infrastructure; but also to correct negative externalities and inequalities, when the polity feels the need to have them corrected. Via the institution of property,

[923] Beck and Willms, *op cit*, note 49, p. 219.
[924] As proposed by Leo E. Strine Jr: *op cit*, note 832, pp. 39–41.

market institutions are inseparable from political institutions in a position to correct the outcome of the autonomous operation of property rights and other liberties. Western society has built over time a system of allocation of prerogatives in society which coherence is demonstrated by its parallel development in the history of numerous States and of their populations and its inscription in their constitutions. Having political democratic institutions was a requirement to make the price system work in an open industrializing society.

With globalization, this allocation of prerogatives is fundamentally challenged.

The key to engage this is to understand the importance of business corporations. They have concentrated property rights, the rights of decision- and rule-making as a matter of principle over productive assets. These have been used to create multinational firms which can play States against one another in a race to the bottom. The States' internalizing function and the correction of inequalities are seriously affected, to the point that humanity's survival is now at risk if we do not find an alternative way to internalize negative externalities and deal with inequality.

Economic theory has not been able to catch up so far with this evolution because of a generalized lack of understanding of property rights. The autonomous operation of the market cannot suffice at the global level: there is no world State to make the market work.

We need to integrate *costs* which have *no market price* into the accounting of the performance of large, international business organizations. This should be done to measure the impact of States' operations as well. This can be done via the accounting system, which can then generate additional information to be given to improve the operation of what are now defective markets in a defective State System.

Sooner or later, unsustainable businesses will crash out of business. Equity investors in these firms will lose the value of their investments.[925] This can take place in a relatively orderly fashion or via chaos. The most likely scenario is, of course, chaos, given our preference for the present over the future. But equity investors have a right to know *now* whether

[925] Impact models are hard to build but they generally underestimate the magnitude of the issue. See *generally* Stern, *op cit*, note 64. The mean expected losses in discounted, 2015 value terms, are $4.2 trillion by 2100, which is roughly equivalent to the value of all the oil and gas companies in the world, or the entire Japanese GDP. But if warming goes higher and if one applies a lower discount rate – which is appropriate given the societal dimension of the issue – the losses can go as high as $43 trillion with a 6° increase, which is more than 60 per cent of the 2015 market capitalization of all the world stock markets: https://eiuperspectives.economist.com/sites/default/files/The%20cost%20of%20inaction_0.pdf

the enterprises in which they are invested are sustainable or whether they are on a path towards unsustainability. They have a right to get this information *now* about the business models of the firms they have invested in. And asset managers have a fiduciary duty to reduce the climate risks embedded in their investment portfolios.[926] By forcing companies to generate this information, they and the directors who will respond to their legitimate request, will make it a market obligation to become sustainable or else, for lack of equity investment, they will have to leave room for firms which can do so. This will certainly lead to disruptions. But we still have the choice between a chaotic and violent adaptation process or relatively orderly disruptions eliminating firms incompatible with our survival.

---

[926] https://eiuperspectives.economist.com/sites/default/files/The%20cost%20of%20 inaction_0.pdf

Epilogue

I started writing this book on 1 January 2016. At the time I was working on another book titled *The Genealogy of Globalization*. I thought I was almost done. But I realized that I couldn't write it in an intelligible way without first working out in detail the concepts of property rights and of the World Power System. This is the reason for the present book. It presents how the World Power System has evolved thanks to the operation of modern property as a right of decision-making and rule-making as a matter of principle towards objects of property. The concentration of these prerogatives over productive assets in large enterprises due to the corporate revolution has led to the growth of negative externalities and very large inequalities. Consequently, States have adapted their laws. But now States are under competitive pressure in their legal offering due to globalization. We need to find new ways to correct what some call 'market failures', taking into account that we are also facing a massive 'governmental failure' at the same time. In this book, a suggestion has been made to put us in a position to address the largest negative externality of all time: climate change. The idea is to provide more comprehensive accounting information to the market. The real profit or loss of every type of accounting entity must be measured taking into account their full impact on all the various forms of capital they use.

What is missing from this book is an explanation of what was so special about European history that led to the worldwide spread of legal concepts originally created in Europe which have played an instrumental role in the structuring of global political and economic institutions.

This exercise in reverse engineering the World Power System is the object of *The Genealogy of Globalization*.

Bibliography

ACKERMAN, Bruce A., *Private Property and the Constitution*, New Haven: Yale University Press (1977).

ADAMS, Henry Carter, *Relation of the State to Industrial Action and Economics and Jurisprudence. Two Essays*, New York: Columbia University Press (1954).

AGLIETTA, Michel and Antoine REBÉRIOUX, *Corporate Governance Adrift: A Critique of Shareholder Value*, Cheltenham: Edward Elgar (2005).

ALCHIAN, Armen A., 'Specificity, Specialization and Coalitions', 140 *Journal of Institutional and Theoretical Economics*, pp. 34–49 (1984).

ALCHIAN, Armen A. and Harold DEMSETZ, 'Production, Information Costs and Economic Organization', 62(5) *American Economic Review*, pp. 777–795 (1972).

ALEXANDER, Gregory S., 'Property as a Fundamental Constitutional Right? The German Example', 88(3) *Cornell Law Review*, pp. 733–778 (2003).

ALEXANDER, Gregory S., *The Global Debate Over Constitutional Property – Lessons from American Takings Jurisprudence*, Chicago and London: The University of Chicago Press (2006).

ALIPRANTIS, Nikitas, 'L'entreprise en tant qu'ordre juridique', in N. Aliprantis et F. Kessler (eds.), *Le droit collectif du travail. Etudes en hommage à H. Sinay*, Francfort: Peter Lang, p. 185 (1994).

ALLEN, Douglas W., 'Comment on Hodgson on Property Rights', 11(4) *Journal of Institutional Economics*, pp. 711–717 (2015).

AMERICAN BAR ASSOCIATION, *The Report of the Task Force of the ABA Section of Business Law Corporate Governance Committee on Delineation of Governance Roles and Responsibilities*, 1 August (2009).

AMIAUD, André, 'L'évolution du droit des sociétés par actions', in *Le droit privé au milieu du XXe siècle – Etudes offertes à G. Ripert*, tome 2, pp. 287–295, Paris: Librairie générale de droit et de jurisprudence (1950).

ANDERSON, Elizabeth, *Private Government – How Employers Rule Our Lives (and Why We Don't Talk about It)*, Princeton: Princeton University Press (2017).

ARATO, Julian, 'Corporations as Lawmakers', 56(2) *Harvard International Law Journal*, pp. 229–295 (2015).

ARDANT, Gabriel, *Histoire de l'impôt, Livre I*, 'De l'antiquité au XVIIe siècle', Paris: Fayard (1971).

ARDANT, Gabriel, 'Financial Policy and Economic Infrastructure of Modern States and Nations', in Charles Tilly (ed.) *The Formation of National States in Europe*, Princeton: Princeton University Press (1975), pp. 164–242.

ARRIGHI, Giovanni, *The Long Twentieth Century – Money, Power and the Origins of our Times*, London, New York: Verso (1994, 2006).

ARROW, Kenneth J., *The Limits of Organization*, New York: WW Norton & Co. (1974).

ASSEMBLÉE NATIONALE, *Constitution française, présentée au Roi par l'Assemblée Nationale le 3 septembre 1791*, Dijon: Imprimerie P. Causse (1791).

AUDIER, Serge, *Le colloque Lippmann – Aux origines du néo-libéralisme*, Editions Le Bord de l'Eau (2008).

BAKER, Larry Cata, 'The Autonomous Global Corporation: on the Role of Organizational Law. Beyond Asset Partitioning and Legal Personality', 41(3) *Tulsa Law Review*, pp. 541–572 (2006).

BARKER, Richard and Colin MAYER, *How Should a 'Sustainable Corporation' Account for Natural Capital?*, Saïd Business School Research Papers RP-15 (2017).

BARKER, Sarah, 'Directors' Personal Liability for Corporate Inaction on Climate Change', February *Governance Directions*, pp. 21–25 (2015).

BARNARD, Chester I., *The Functions of the Executive*, Cambridge & London: Harvard University Press (1938, 1968).

BARNAVE, *Introduction à la révolution française; texte présenté par Fernand Rudé*, Paris: Armand Colin, Cahiers des Annales No 15 (1960).

BARTELSON, Jens, *A Genealogy of Sovereignty*, Cambridge: Cambridge University Press (1995).

BARZEL, Yoram, *Economic Analysis of Property Rights*, Cambridge: Cambridge University Press (1989).

BARZEL, Yoram, *A Theory of the State: Economic Rights, Legal Rights, and the Scope of the State*, Cambridge: Cambridge University Press (2002).

BEAUD, Michel, *Le système national mondial hiérarchisé*, Paris: AGALMA, La Découverte (1987).

BEAUD, Olivier, 'La notion d'État', 35 *Archives de Philosophie du Droit*, pp. 119–141 (1990).

BEAUD, Olivier, 'L'histoire du concept de constitution en France – De la constitution politique à la constitution comme statut juridique de l'État', 3 *Jus Politicum* (2009).

BECK, Ulrich, *Pouvoir et contre-pouvoir à l'heure de la mondialisation*, Paris: Champs, Essais (2003).

BECK, Ulrich, 'Reframing Power in the Globalized World', 29(5) *Organization Studies*, pp. 793–804 (2008).

BECK, Ulrich and Johannes WILLMS, *Conversations with Ulrich Beck*, Cambridge: Polity Press (2004).

BELLEY, Jean-Guy, 'L'État et la régulation juridique des sociétés globales – Pour une problématique du pluralisme juridique', XVIII (1) *Sociologie et sociétés*, pp. 11–32 (1986).

BELLEY, Jean-Guy, 'L'entreprise, l'approvisionnement et le droit. Vers une théorie pluraliste du contrat', 32(2) *Les Cahiers de Droit*, pp. 253–299 (1991).

BELLEY, Jean-Guy, *Le contrat entre droit, économie et société*, Québec: Les éditions Yvon Blais Inc. (1998).

BÉNABOU, Roland and Jean TIROLE, 'Individual and Corporate Social Responsibility', 77(305) *Economica*, pp. 1–19 (2010).

BERLE, Adolf A., Jr., 'The Theory of Enterprise Entity', 47(3) *Columbia Law Review*, pp. 343–358 (1947).

BERLE, Adolf A., Jr., *Power Without Property – A New Development in American Political Economy*, New York: Harcourt, Brace and Company (1959).

BERLE, Adolf A., Jr., 'Property, Production and Revolution', 65(1) *Columbia Law Review*, pp. 1–20 (1965).

BERLE, Adolf A., Jr. and Gardiner MEANS, *The Modern Corporation and Private Property*, New Brunswick and London: Transaction Publishers (Ninth printing 2007, 1st edition 1932).

BILLIER, Jean-Cassien, *Le pouvoir*, Paris: Armand Colin (2000).

BILLIER, Jean-Cassien and Aglaé MARYIOLI, *Histoire de la philosophie du droit*, Paris: Armand Colin (2001).

BIONDI, Yuri, 'The Enterprise Entity and the Constitution of the American Economic Republic', 1(3) *Accounting, Economics, and Law*, Article 2 (2011), available at: http://www.bepress.com/ael/vol1/iss1/7.

BIONDI, Yuri, 'The Problem of Social Income: Another View of the Cathedral', 34 *Seattle University Law Review*, pp. 1025–1047 (2011).

BIONDI, Yuri, *Better Accounting for Corporate Shareholding and Environmental Protection*, University of Oslo Faculty of Law Legal Studies, Research Paper No 2014-28 (2014).

BIONDI, Yuri, 'The Firm as an Enterprise Entity and the Tax Avoidance Conundrum: Perspectives from Accounting Theory and Policy', *Accounting, Economics, and Law* (2017).

BIONDI, Yuri, Arnaldo CANZIANI and Thierry KIRAT (eds.), *The Firm as an Entity – Implications for economics, accounting and the law*, New York: Routledge (2007).

BIOY, Xavier (sous la direction de), *La personnalité juridique*, Toulouse: Presses de l'Université Toulouse 1 Capitole (2013).

BLAIR, Margaret M., *Ownership and Control – Rethinking Corporate Governance for the Twenty-First Century*, Washington DC: The Brookings Institution (1995).

BLAIR, Margaret M., 'Locking in Capital: What Corporate Law Achieved for Business Organizers in the Nineteenth Century', 51(2) *UCLA Law Review*, pp. 387–455 (2003).

BLAIR, Margaret M., 'The Neglected Benefits of the Corporate Form: Entity Status and the Separation of Asset Ownership from Control', in Anna Grandori (ed.) *Corporate Governance and Firm Organization: Micro foundations and Structural Forms* (2004), pp. 45–66.

BLAIR, Margaret M., 'Why Lynn Stout Took Up the Sword Against Share Value Maximization', *Accounting, Economics and Law* (forthcoming, 2020).

BLAUFARB, Rafe, *The Great Demarcation –The French Revolution and the Invention of Modern Property*, Oxford: Oxford University Press (2016).

BLOCH, Marc, *Feudal Society*, Los Angeles: Manyon (1970).

BOBBIO, Norberto, *Il futuro della democrazia*, Torino: Einaudi (1984, 1991).

BOBBIO, Norberto, *The Age of Rights*, Cambridge: Polity Press (1996).

BOTTOMLEY, Stephen, *The Constitutional Corporation – Rethinking Corporate Governance*, Aldershot: Ashgate (2007).

BOURDIEU, Pierre, 'Les juristes, gardiens de l'hypocrisie collective', in Chazel, F. and J. Commaille (sous la direction de), *Normes juridiques et régulation sociale*, pp. 95–99, Paris: Librairie générale de droit et de jurisprudence (1991).

BOWLES, Samuel and Herbert GINTIS, 'The Power of Capital: on the Inadequacy of the Conception of the Capitalist Economy as 'Private'', 14(3–4) *The Philosophical Forum*, pp. 225–245 (1983).

BOWLES, Samuel and Herbert GINTIS, *Democracy and Capitalism: Property, Community and the Contradictions of Modern Social Thought*, New York: Routledge (1986).

BRATTON, William W. and Michael L. WACHTER, 'Shareholder Primacy's Corporatist Origins: Adolf Berle and the Modern Corporation', 34(1) *The Journal of Corporate Law*, pp. 99–152 (2008).

BRAUDEL, Fernand, *Civilisation matérielle, économie et capitalisme, XVe–XVIIIe siècles*, tome 1 'Les structures du quotidien: le possible et l'impossible', Paris: Armand Colin (1979).

BRAUDEL, Fernand, *Civilisation matérielle, économie et capitalisme, XVe–XVIIIe siècles*, tome 2 'Les jeux de l'échange', Paris: Armand Colin (1979).

BRAUDEL, Fernand, *Civilisation matérielle, économie et capitalisme, XVe–XVIIIe siècles*, tome 3 'Le temps du monde', Paris: Armand Colin (1979).

BRAUDEL, Fernand, *La dynamique du capitalisme*, Paris: Arthaud (1985).

BRETHE DE LA GRESSAYE, Jean, 'Les transformations juridiques de l'entreprise patronale', *Droit social*, pp. 2–5 (1939).

BREWSTER, Kingman Jr., 'The Corporation and Economic Federalism', in Edward S. Mason (ed), *The Corporation in Modern Society*, Cambridge: Harvard University Press (1959), pp. 72–84.

BUCHANAN, John, Dominic Heesang CHAI and Simon DEAKIN, 'Empirical analysis of legal institutions and institutional change: multiple-methods approaches and their application to corporate governance research', *Journal of Institutional Economics*, pp. 1–20 (2013).

BURDEAU, Georges, *L'État*, Paris: Editions du Seuil (1970).

BURNS, James Henderson (ed.), *Histoire de la pensée politique médiévale – 350–1450*, Paris: Presses Universitaires de France (1988, French edition 1993).

BUSINESS COMMISSION ON SUSTAINABLE DEVELOPMENT, *Ideas for Action for a Long-Term and Sustainable Financial System* (2017), available at: https://s3.amazonaws.com/aws-bsdc/BSDC_SustainableFinanceSystem.pdf.

BUSINESS AND SUSTAINABLE DEVELOPMENT COMMISSION, *January Report* (2017), available at http://report.businesscommission.org/report.

CARBONNIER, Jean, *Flexible droit*, Paris: Librairie générale de droit et de jurisprudence (4ème édition 1979, 9ème édition 1998).

CARROZZA, Paolo, 'Constitutionalism's Post-modern Opening' in Martin Loughlin and Neil Walker (eds.), *The Paradox of Constitutionalism – Constituent Power and Constitutional Form*, Oxford: Oxford University Press (2007), pp. 169–187.

CARY, William L., 'Federalism and Corporate Law: Reflections upon Delaware', 83 *Yale Law Journal*, pp. 663–705 (1974).

CASSESE, Sabino, 'The Rise and Decline of the Notion of State', 7(2) *International Political Science Review*, pp. 120–130 (1986).

CERNY, Philip C., 'Globalization and the Changing Logic of Collective Action', 49(4) *International Organization*, pp. 595–625 (1995).

CHAMPAUD, Claude, *Le pouvoir de concentration de la société par action*, Paris: Sirey (1962).

CHANDLER, Alfred D., *The Visible Hand – The Managerial Revolution in American Business*, Cambridge: Belknap Press (1979).

CHANDLER, Alfred D., 'Organizational Capabilities and the Economic History of the Industrial Enterprise', 6(3) *Journal of Economic Perspectives*, pp. 79–100 (1992).

CHANDLER, Alfred D., *Scale and Scope – The Dynamics of Industrial Capitalism*, Cambridge: Belknap (1994).

CHANTEAU, Jean-Pierre, 'Le droit et la régulation des pouvoirs dans l'économie-monde', 22 *Revue de la Régulation – capitalisme, institutions, pouvoirs*, Automne (2017).

CHAVAGNEUX, Christian, 'Can States Regain Fiscal Sovereignty Over Globalized Business?', in Jean-Philippe Robé, Antoine Lyon-Caen and Stéphane Vernac (eds.), *Multinationals and the Constitutionalization of the World Power System*, with a Foreword from John Gerard Ruggie, London & New York: Routledge (2017).

CHAYES, Abram, 'The Modern Corporation and the Rule of Law', in Edward S. Mason (ed.), *The Corporation in Modern Society*, Cambridge: Harvard University Press (1959), pp. 25–45.

CHAZAL, Jean-Pascal, 'La propriété: dogme ou instrument politique? Ou comment la doctrine s'interdit de penser le réel', 4 *Revue trimestrielle de droit civil* (2014).

CHEUNG, Steven N.S., 'The Contractual Nature of the Firm', 26(1) *Journal of Law and Economics*, pp. 1–21 (1983).

CHEVALLIER, Jacques, 'L'État de droit', *Revue de Droit Public*, pp. 313–380 (1988).

CIEPLEY, David, 'Beyond Public and Private: Toward a Political Theory of the Corporation', 107(1) *American Political Science Review*, pp. 139–158 (2013).

CIPOLLA, Carlo M., *Before the Industrial Revolution – European Society and Economy, 1000–1700*, London: Routledge (1976).

COASE, Ronald H., 'The Nature of the Firm', 4(16) *Economica N.S.*, pp. 386–405 (1937).

COASE, Ronald H., 'The Problem of Social Costs', 3 *Journal of Law and Economics*, pp. 1–44 (1960).

COASE, Ronald H., 'Accounting and the Theory of the Firm', 12 *Journal of Accounting and Economics*, pp. 3–13 (1990).

COASE, Ronald H., 'The Institutional Structure of Production', 82(4) *The American Economic Review*, pp. 713–719 (1992).

COASE, Ronald H., 'The Nature of the Firm – Influence', in Oliver E. Williamson and Sidney G. Winter (eds.), *The Nature of the Firm – Origins, Evolution, and Development*, Oxford: Oxford University Press (1993), pp. 61–74.

COASE, Ronald H., 'Accounting and the theory of the firm', in Yuri Biondi, Arnaldo Canziani and Thierry Kirat (eds.), *The Firm as an Entity – Implications for economics, accounting and the law*, New York: Routledge (2007), pp. 82–91.

COASE, Ronald H., 'Saving Economics from the Economists', (December) *Harvard Business Review*, p. 36 (2012).

COHEN, Julie E., *Between Truth and Power – The Legal Construction of Informational Capitalism*, Oxford: Oxford University Press (2019).

COHEN, Morris R., 'Property and Sovereignty', 13 *Cornell Law Quarterly*, pp. 8–30 (1927).

COLASSE, Bernard, *La crise de la normalisation comptable internationale*, 17 Association française de comptabilité, pp. 156–164 (2011).

COLASSE, Bernard, *Introduction à la Comptabilité*, Paris: Economica (2013).

COLASSE, Bernard, *Dictionnaire de comptabilité – Compter / conter l'entreprise*, Paris: La Découverte (2015).

COLASSE, Bernard, 'Comptabilité et vision de l'entreprise – Sur les normes comptables internationales', *Le Débat*, pp. 83–93 (2016).

COLE, Daniel H., 'Economic property rights as "nonsense upon stilts": a comment on Hodgson', 11(4) *Journal of Institutional Economics*, pp. 725–730 (2015).

COLE, Daniel H. and Peter Z. GROSSMAN, 'The Meaning of Property Rights: Law versus Economics?', 78 *Land Economics*, pp. 317–330 (2002).

COMMONS, John R., *Legal Foundations of Capitalism*, Madison: The University of Wisconsin Press (1968, 1st edition 1924).

CONRAD, A., 'Constitutional Rights of the Corporate Person', 91 *Yale Law Journal*, pp. 1641–1658 (1981–1982).

COX, Robert W., 'Democracy in Hard Times: Economic Globalization and the Limits to Liberal Democracy', in Anthony McGrew (ed.), *The Transformation of Democracy? Globalization and Territorial Democracy*, Cambridge: Polity Press (1997), pp. 49–72.

CROXTON, Derek, 'The Peace of Westphalia of 1648 and the Origins of Sovereignty', 21(3) *The International History Review*, pp. 569–591 (1999).

CROZIER, Michel and Erhard FRIEDBERG, *L'acteur et le système. Les contraintes de l'action collective*, Paris: Seuil (1977).

DAHL, Robert A., *A Preface to Economic Democracy*, Berkeley and Los Angeles: University of California Press (1985).

DALLAS, Mark P., Stefano PONTE and Timothy J. STURGEON, 'Power in Global Value Chains', 26(4) *Review of International Political Economy*, pp. 666–694 (2019).

DAN-COHEN, Meir, *Rights, Persons and Organizations: A Legal Theory for Bureaucratic Society*, Berkeley: University of California Press (1986).

DANIELSEN, Dan, 'Local Rules and a Global Economy: An Economic Policy Perspective', 1 *Transnational Legal Theory*, pp. 49–115 (2010).

DEAKIN, Simon, 'Tony Lawson's Theory of the Corporation: Towards a Social Ontology of Law', 41 *Cambridge Journal of Economics*, pp. 1505–1523 (2017).

DEAKIN, Simon and Alain SUPIOT, *Capacitas – Contract and the Institutional Preconditions of a Market Economy*, Oxford: Hart Publishing (2009).

DEAKIN, Simon, David GINDIS, Geoffrey M. HODGSON, Kainan HUANG and Katharina PISTOR, 'Legal Institutionalism: Capitalism and the Constitutive Role of Law', 45 *Journal of Comparative Economics*, pp. 188–200 (2017).

DEEGAN, Craig, 'The accountant will have a central role in saving the planet … really? A reflection on "green accounting and green eyeshades twenty years later"', 24 *Critical Perspectives on Accounting*, pp. 448–458 (2013).

DEEGAN, Craig, 'Twenty-five years of social and environmental accounting research within *Critical Perspectives on Accounting*: Hits, misses and ways forward', 43 *Critical Perspectives on Accounting*, pp. 65–87 (2017).

DEMSETZ, Harold, 'Toward a Theory of Property Rights', 57(2) *American Economic Review*, pp. 347–359 (1967).

DEMSETZ, Harold, 'The Theory of the Firm Revisited', 4(1) *Journal of Law, Economics and Organization*, pp. 141–161 (1988).

DEMSETZ, Harold, *The Economics of the Business Firm – Seven Critical Commentaries*, Cambridge: Cambridge University Press (1995).

DEMSETZ, Harold, 'Book review of *Firms, Contracts and Financial Structure*, by Oliver Hart', 106(2) *Journal of Political Economy*, pp. 446–452 (1998).

DESPAX, Michel, *L'Entreprise et le Droit*, Paris: Librairie générale de droit et de jurisprudence (1957).

DEUTSCH, Karl W., 'State Functions and the Future of the State', 7(2) *International Political Science Review*, pp. 209–222 (1986).

DIMAGGIO, Paul J. and Walter W. POWELL, 'The Iron Cage Revisited: Institutional Isomorphism and Collective Rationality in Organizational Fields', 48 *American Sociological Review*, pp. 147–160 (1983).

DOCKES, Pierre, *L'espace dans la pensée économique du XVIe au XVIIIe siècle*, Paris: Flammarion (1969).

DODD, Merrick E., 'American Business Association Law a Hundred Years Ago and Today', in A. Reppy (ed.), *Law, A Century of Progress, 1835–1935*, New York: New York University Press (1937), vol. 3, pp. 254–293.

DOWNING, Brian M., 'Medieval Origins of Constitutional Government in the West', 18 *Theory and Society*, pp. 213–247 (1989).

DUGUIT, Léon, *Les transformations du droit public*, Paris: Hachette Livre (1913).

DUPUY, Jean-Pierre, 'Epistémologie de l'économie et analyse de système', in Jacques Lesourne (ed.), *La notion de système dans les sciences contemporaines*, tome 2, Aix-en-Provence: Librairie de l'Université (1981).

DURAND, Cédric, *Le capital fictif*, Paris: Les Prairies Ordinaires (2014).

DURAND, Paul, 'Rapport sur la notion juridique d'entreprise', in *Travaux de l'association Henri Capitant*, vol. 3, pp. 45–60 (1947).

DURAND, Paul, 'L'évolution de la condition juridique des personnes morales de droit privé', in 1 *Le droit privé français au milieu du xxe siècle – Etudes offertes à G. Ripert*, pp. 138–159, Paris: Librairie générale de droit et de jurisprudence (1950).

DWORKIN, Ronald, *Law's Empire*, London: Fontana Press (1986).

EASTERBROOK, Frank H. and Daniel R. FISCHEL, 'Limited Liability and the Corporation', 52 *University of Chicago Law Review*, pp. 89–117 (1985).

EASTERBROOK, Frank H. and Daniel R. FISCHEL, *The Economic Structure of Corporate Law*, Cambridge: Harvard University Press (1991).

ELIAS, Norbert, *La civilisation des mœurs*, Paris: Calmann-Lévy (1939, 1969, 1979, 1991).

ELIAS, Norbert, *La dynamique de l'Occident*, Paris: Calmann-Lévy (1939, 1969, 1975).

ELY, James W. Jr., *The Guardian of Every Other Right – A Constitutional History of Property Rights* (2nd edition), Oxford: Oxford University Press (1998).

ELY, John Hart, *Democracy and Distrust:. A Theory of Judicial Review*, Cambridge: Harvard University Press (1980).

ELY, Richard Theodore, *Property and Contract in Their Relations to the Distribution of Wealth*, Vols. 1 and 2, New York: The Macmillan Company (1914).

EWALD, François, *L'État providence*, Paris: Grasset (1986).

EWALD, François (ed.), *Naissance du Code civil*, Paris: Flammarion (1989).

FAMA, Eugene F., 'Agency Problems and the Theory of the Firm', 88(2) *Journal of Political Economy*, pp. 288–307 (1980).

FALK MOORE, Sally, *Law as Process. An Anthropological Approach*, London: Routledge & Kegan Paul (1978).

FAMA, Eugene F. and Michael C. JENSEN, 'Separation of Ownership and Control', 26(2) *Journal of Law & Economics*, pp. 301–325 (1983).

FATOUROS, Arghyrios, 'Problèmes et méthodes d'une réglementation des entreprises multinationales', *Journal du Droit International*, pp. 495–521 (1974).

FAVEREAU, Olivier, *Entreprises: La grande déformation*, Collège des Bernardins, collection Parole et Silence (2014).

FAVEREAU, Olivier, 'The Economics of Convention: From the Practice of Economics to the Economics of Practice', 44 *Historical Social Research*, pp. 25–51 (2019).

FAVEREAU, Olivier and Jean-Philippe ROBÉ, 'RSE et propriété de la firme', in José Allouche (ed.), *Encyclopédie des ressources humaines*, Paris: Vuibert (2012).

FERRERAS, Isabelle, *Critique politique du travail – Travailler à l'heure de la société des services*, Paris: Les Presses de Sciences Po (2007).

FERRERAS, Isabelle, *Gouverner le capitalisme?*, Paris: Presses Universitaires de France (2012).

FERRERAS, Isabelle, *Firms as Political Entities – Saving Democracy Through Economic Bicameralism*, Cambridge: Cambridge University Press (2017).

FIGGIS, John Neville, 'Respublica Christiana', 5 *Transactions of the Royal Historical Society*, Third Series, pp. 63–88 (1911).

FIGUERES, Christiana, Hans Joachim SCHELLNHUBER, Gail WHITEMAN, Johan ROCKSTRÖM, Anthony HOBLEY and Stefan RAHMSTORF, 'Three Years to Safeguard our Climate', 546 *Nature*, 29 June, pp. 593–597 (2017).

FISCHEL, Daniel R., 'Race to the Bottom Revisited: Reflections on Recent Developments in Delaware's Corporation Law', 76 *Northwestern University Law Review*, pp. 913–945 (1981).

FOHLEN, Claude, 'Société anonyme et développement capitaliste sous la monarchie censitaire', *Histoire des entreprises*, pp. 65–77 (1960).

FOHLEN, Claude, 'Société anonyme et développement capitaliste sous le Second Empire', *Histoire des entreprises*, pp. 65–79 (1961).

FONTANELLI, Filippo, 'Romano and l'ordinamento giuridico: The Relevance of a Forgotten Masterpiece for Contemporary International, Transnational and Global Legal Relations', 2(1) *Transnational Legal Theory*, pp. 67–117 (2011).

FOSS, Kirsten and Nicolai FOSS, 'Coasian and Modern Property Rights Economics', 11(2) *Journal of Institutional Economics*, pp. 391–411 (2014).

FOSSEN, Anthony van, 'Passport Sales: How Island Microstates Use Strategic Management to Organize the New Economic Citizenship Industry', 13(1) *Island Studies Journal*, pp. 285–300 (2018).

FOUCAULT, Michel, *Surveiller et punir*, Paris: Gallimard (1974).

FOUCAULT, Michel, *Dits et écrits – 1954–1988*, tome II (1970–1975), Paris: Éditions Gallimard, Bibliothèque des sciences humaines (1994).

FOUCAULT, Michel, *Dits et écrits – 1954–1988*, tome III (1976–1979), Paris: Éditions Gallimard, Bibliothèque des sciences humaines (1994).

FOUCAULT, Michel, *Dits et écrits – 1954–1988*, tome IV (1980–1988), Paris: Éditions Gallimard, Bibliothèque des sciences humaines (1994).

FOUCAULT, Michel, *Il faut défendre la société, Cours au Collège de France, 1976*, Paris: Gallimard-Seuil, collection 'Hautes Etudes' (1997).

FOUCAULT, Michel, *Sécurité, Territoire, Population, Cours au Collège de France, 1977–1978*, Paris: Gallimard-Seuil, collection 'Hautes Etudes' (2004).

FOUCAULT, Michel, *Naissance de la Biopolitique, Cours au Collège de France, 1978–1979*, Paris: Gallimard-Seuil, collection 'Hautes Etudes' (2004).

FRANCOIS, Lucien, *Le cap des tempêtes – Essai de microscopie du droit*, Deuxième édition, Bruylant, LGDJ (2012).

FREEDEMAN, Charles E., 'Joint-Stock Business Organizations in France, 1807–1867', 39(2) *Business History Review*, pp. 184–204 (1965).

FREEDEMAN, Charles E., *Joint-Stock Enterprises in France 1807–1867: From Privileged Company to Modern Corporation*, Chapel Hill: University of North Carolina Press (1979).

FREEMAN, R. Edward, *Strategic management: A stakeholder approach*, Cambridge: Cambridge University Press (1984).

FREEMAN, R. Edward, Jeffrey S. HARRISON, Andrew C. WICKS; Bidhan L. PARMAR and Simone DE COLLE, *Stakeholder Theory – The State of the Art*, Cambridge: Cambridge University Press (2010).

FREUND, Ernst, *The Legal Nature of Corporations*, Chicago: The University of Chicago Press (1897).

FRIED, Barbara H., *The Progressive Assault on Laissez Faire – Robert Hale and the First Law and Economics Movement*, Cambridge: Harvard University Press (1998).

FRIEDMAN, Lawrence M., *A History of American Law*, New York: Simon & Schuster (1973).

FRIEDMAN, Lawrence M., *Total Justice*, New York: Russell Sage Foundation (1985).

FRIEDMAN, Milton, 'The Social Responsibility of Business is to Increase its Profits', *The New York Times*, 13 September, pp. 32–33, 122 & 126 (1970).

FUKUYAMA, Francis, 'The End of History?', 16 *The National Interest*, pp. 3–18 (1989).

FUKUYAMA, Francis, *The Origins of Political Order – From Prehuman Times to the French Revolution*, New York: Farrar, Strass and Giroux (2011).

FULLER, Lon L., *The Morality of Law*, New Haven: Yale University Press (2nd edition 1969).

FURUBOTN, Eirik G. and Svetozar PEJOVICH, 'Property Rights and Economic Theory', 10(4) *Journal of Economic Literature*, pp. 1137–1162 (1986).

GAILLARD, Emmanuel, *Le pouvoir en droit privé*, Paris: Masson (1985).

GALBRAITH, John Kenneth, *The Economics of Innocent Fraud – Truth for our Time*, Boston & New York: Houghton Mifflin Company (2004).

GALIANI, Sebastian and Itai SENED (eds.), *Institutions, Property Rights and Economic Growth – The Legacy of Douglass North*, Cambridge: Cambridge University Press (2014).

GAUCHET, Marcel, *L'avènement de la démocratie – I – La révolution moderne*, Paris: Gallimard (2007).

GAUCHET, Marcel, *L'avènement de la démocratie – II – La crise du libéralisme*, Paris: Gallimard (2007).

GAUCHET, Marcel, *L'avènement de la démocratie – IV – Le nouveau monde*, Paris: Gallimard (2017).

GERBER, David J., 'Constitutionalizing the Economy: German Neo-liberalism, Competition Law and the "New" Europe', 42 *American Journal of Comparative Law*, pp. 25–84 (1994).

GHESTIN, Jacques, 'La notion de contrat', *Dalloz, Chronique*, pp. 147–156 (1990).

GIANNINI, Massimo Severo, 'Gli elementi degli ordinamenti giuridici', 8 *Rivista trimestriale di diritto pubblico*, pp. 219–240 (1958).

GIDDENS, Anthony, *The Consequences of Modernity*, Cambridge: Polity Press (1991).

GILPIN, Robert, *The Political Economy of International Relations*, Princeton: Princeton University Press (1987).

GILPIN, Robert, *Global Political Economy – Understanding the International Economic Order*, Princeton: Princeton University Press (2001).

GIRARD, Bernard, *Responsabilité sociale des entreprises: retour sur un article de Milton Friedman*, Les cahiers de la CRSDD, no 04–2013 (2014).

GLEESON-WHITE, Jane, *Six Capitals – The Revolution Capitalism Has to Have, Or Can Accountants Save the Planet?*, Sidney: Allen & Unwin (2014).

GOEDECKE, Walter Robert, 'Corporations and the Philosophy of Law', 10 *Journal of Value Inquiry*, pp. 81–90 (1976).

GOMEZ, Pierre-Yves, *Le Gouvernement de l'entreprise*, Paris: InterEditions (1996).

GOMEZ, Pierre-Yves and Harry KORINE, *Entrepreneurs and Democracy – A Political Theory of Corporate Governance*, Cambridge: Cambridge University Press (2008).

GOTHOT, Pierre, 'François Rigaux ou la chute des masques', in *Nouveaux itinéraires en droit. Hommages à François Rigaux*, Bruxelles: Bruylant (1996), pp. 4–25.

GOTTLIEB, Gidon, 'Relationism: Legal Theory for a Relational Society', 50 *University of Chicago Law Review*, pp. 567–612 (1983).

GRAEBER, David, *Debt – The First 5,000 Years*, Brooklyn & London: Melville House (2011, 2012, 2014).

GRAY, Rob, 'Accounting and Environmentalism: An Exploration of the Challenge of Gently Accounting for Accountability, Transparency and Sustainability', 17(5) *Accounting, Organization and Society*, pp. 399–425 (1992).

GRENIER, Jean-Yves and André ORLÉAN, 'Michel Foucault, l'économie politique et le libéralisme', 5 *Annales, Histoire, Sciences Sociales*, pp. 1155–1182 (2007).

GROSSI, Paolo, *L'Europe du droit*, Paris: Faire l'Europe, Seuil (2011).

GROSSMAN, Sanford and Oliver D. HART, 'The Costs and Benefits of Ownership: A Theory of Vertical and Lateral Integration', 94(2) *Journal of Political Economy*, pp. 691–719 (1986).

GROUPE DE LISBONNE, *Limites à la concurrence – pour un nouveau contrat mondial*, Lisbonne: Fondation Gulbenkian, La découverte (1995).

GUNDER FRANK, André, *ReORIENT; Global Economy in the Asian Age*, Berkeley, Los Angeles & London: University of California Press (1998).

GURVITCH, Georges, *Le temps présent et l'idée du droit social*, Paris: Vrin (1931).

GURVITCH, Georges, *Eléments de sociologie juridique*, Paris: Aubier (1940).

GURVITCH, Georges, *La déclaration des droits sociaux*, Paris: Vrin (1946).

GUSTAFSSON, Harald, 'The Conglomerate State: A Perspective on State Formation in Early Modern Europe', 23(3–4) *Scandinavian Journal of History*, pp. 189–213 (1988).

HABERMAS, Jürgen, *La paix perpétuelle*, Paris: Cerf, collection 'Humanités' (1996).

HADARI, Yitzhak, 'The Structure of the Private Multinational Enterprise', 71 *Michigan Law Review*, pp. 729–806 (1969).

HAGGARD, Stephan, Andrew MACINTYRE and Lydia TIEDE, 'The Rule of Law and Economic Development', 11 *Annual Review of Political Science*, pp. 205–34 (2008).

HALDANE, Andrew G., *Who Owns A Company?*, Speech given by Andrew G. Haldane, Chief Economist, Bank of England, University of Edinburgh Corporate Finance Conference, 22 May (2015).

HALE, Robert L., 'Coercion and Distribution in a Supposedly Non-Coercive State', 38(3) *Political Science Review*, pp. 470–494 (1923).

HALE, Robert L., 'Force and the State: A Comparison of "Political" and "Economic" Compulsion', 35 *Columbia Law Review*, pp. 149–201 (1935).

HALE, Thomas, David HELD and Kevin YOUNG, *Gridlock: Why Global Cooperation is Failing When We Need It Most*, Oxford: Polity Press (2013).

HALE, Thomas and David HELD et al., *Beyond Gridlock*, Oxford: Polity Press (2017).

HALPÉRIN, Jean-Louis, *Histoire du droit privé français depuis 1804*, Paris: Presses Universitaires de France (1996, 2001).

HALPÉRIN, Jean-Louis, *Histoire des droits en Europe de 1750 à nos jours*, Paris: Flammarion (2004).

HAMILTON, Walton H., 'Property – According to Locke', 41 *Yale Law Journal*, pp. 864–880 (1932).

HANSMANN, Henry and Reiner KRAAKMAN, 'The End of History for Corporate Law', 89(2) *Georgetown Law Journal*, pp. 439–468 (2001).

HARBRECHT, Paul P., 'The Modern Corporation Revisited', 64 *Columbia Law Review*, pp. 1410–1428 (1964).

HART, Herbert L.A., *The Concept of Law*, Oxford: Oxford University Press (1961).

HART, Oliver D., 'An Economist's View of Fiduciary Duty', 43(3) *University of Toronto Law Journal*, pp. 299–313, Special Issue on Corporate Stakeholder Debate: The Classical Theory and Its Critics (1993).

HART, Oliver D., 'Corporate Governance: Some Theory and Implications', 105 *Economic Journal*, pp. 678–689 (1995).

HART, Oliver D., 'Incomplete Contracts and the Theory of the Firm', in Oliver E. Williamson and Sidney G. Winter (eds.) *The Nature of the Firm – Origins, Evolution, and Development*, New York and Oxford: Oxford University Press (1993), pp. 138–158.

HART, Oliver D., *Firms, Contracts and Financial Structure*, Oxford: Oxford University Press (1995).

HART, Oliver D. and John MOORE, 'Property rights and the theory of the firm', 98 *Journal of Political Economy*, pp. 1119–1158 (1990).

HART, Oliver D. and Luigi ZINGALES, *Companies Should Maximize Shareholder Welfare Not Market Value*, ECGI Working Paper Series in Finance No 521/2017 (2017).

HASAN, Iftekhar, Panagiotis KARAVITIS, Pantelis KAZAKIS and Woon Sau Leung, *Corporate Social Responsibility and Profit Shifting*, Working Paper, 19 January (2019).

HAURIOU, Maurice, *Principes de droit public*, Paris: Dalloz (1910, 2010).

HAURIOU, Maurice, 'La théorie de l'institution et de la fondation (essai de vitalisme social)', 4 *Cahiers de la nouvelle journée*, Paris: Bloud & Gay (1925), pp. 89–128.

HAURIOU, Maurice, *Aux sources du droit – Le pouvoir, l'ordre et la liberté*, Caen: Bibliothèque de Philosophie Politique et Juridique, Textes et documents, Université de Caen (1933, 1986).

HAURIOU, Maurice, *Précis élémentaire de droit administratif*, Paris: Sirey (1938).

HAYEK, Friedrich A., *Individualism and Economic Order*, Chicago and London: University of Chicago Press (1948).

HEINSOHN, Gunnar and Otto STEIGER, *Ownership Economics – On the foundations of interest, money, markets, business cycles and economic development*, London & New York: Routledge (2014).

HELD, David, *Democracy and the Global Order – From the Modern State to Cosmopolitan Governance*, Stanford: Stanford University Press (1995).

HELD, David, 'Elements of a Theory of Global Governance', 42(9) *Philosophy and Social Criticism*, pp. 837–846 (2016).

HELD, David, 'Reframing Global Governance: Apocalypse Soon or Reform!', in David Held and Anthony McGrew (eds.), *Globalization Theory – Approaches and Controversies*, Cambridge: Polity Press (2007), pp. 240–260.

HELD, David and Anthony McGREW (eds.), *Globalization Theory – Approaches and Controversies*, Cambridge: Polity Press (2007).

HELD, David and Charles ROGER, 'Three Models of Global Climate Governance: From Kyoto to Paris and Beyond', 9(4) *Global Policy*, pp. 527–537 (2018).

HENDERSON, W.O., *The Genesis of the Common Market*, London: Frank Cass & Co. Ltd. (1962).

HICKS, John, 'Capital Controversies: Ancient and Modern', 64(2) *The American Economic Review, Papers and Proceedings of the Eighty-sixth Annual Meeting of the American Economic Association*, pp. 307–316 (1974).

HILL, Henry P., *Accounting Principles for the Autonomous Corporate Entity*, New York: Quorum Books (1987).

HINNA-DANESI, Fabrizio, 'Mafia – Politique – Entreprise', *Les Petites Affiches*, 20 mars, no 35, p. 19 (1996).

HOBHOUSE, Leonard Trelawny, 'The Historical Evolution of Property in Fact and in Idea', in The Bishop of Oxford (ed.), *Property, its Duties and Rights*, London: Oxford University Press (1913), pp. 1–31.

HODGSON, Geoffrey M., *On the Institutional Foundations of Law: The Insufficiency of Custom and Private Ordering*, 43(1) Journal of Economic Issues, pp. 143–166 (2009).

HODGSON, Geoffrey M., 'Editorial Introduction to "Ownership" by A.M. Honoré' (1961), 9(2) *Journal of Institutional Economics*, pp. 223–255 (2013).

HODGSON, Geoffrey M., *Conceptualizing Capitalism – Institutions, Evolution, Future*, Chicago and London: The University of Chicago Press (2015).

HODGSON, Geoffrey M., 'Much of the "economics of property rights" devalues property and legal rights', 11(4) *Journal of Institutional Economics*, pp. 683–709 (2015).

HODGSON, Geoffrey M., 'What Humpty Dumpty might have said about property rights – and the need to put them back together again: a response to critics', 11(4) *Journal of Institutional Economics*, pp. 731–747 (2015).

HODGSON, Geoffrey M., 'Taxonomic Definitions in Social Sciences, with Firms, Markets and Institutions as Case Studies', *Journal of Institutional Economics*, pp. 1–18 (2018).

HOFFMANN, Sabine, 'Property, possession and natural resource management: towards a conceptual clarification', 9(1) *Journal of Institutional Economics*, pp. 39–60 (2013).

HOHFELD, Wesley Newcomb, 'Some Fundamental Legal Conceptions as Applied in Judicial Reasoning', 23(1) *Yale Law Journal*, pp. 16–59 (1913).

HORWITZ, Morton, 'The Transformation in the Conception of Property in American Law 1780–1860', 40 *University of Chicago Law Review*, pp. 248–290 (1973).

HUNT, B.C., *The Development of the Business Corporation in England, 1800–1867*, New York: Russell & Russell (1969, 1st edition 1936).

IACOBUCCI, Edward M. and George G. TRIANTIS, 'Economic and Legal Boundaries of Firms', 93 *Virginia Law Review*, pp. 515–570 (2007).

ICRICT (Independent Commission for the Reform of International Corporate Taxation), *Declaration of the Independent Commission for the Reform of International Corporate Taxation*, June (2015).

INGBER, Léon, 'Le pluralisme juridique dans l'œuvre des philosophes du droit', in J. Gilissen (ed.), *Le pluralisme juridique*, Bruxelles: Editions de l'Université de Bruxelles (1972), pp. 57–84.

IRELAND, Paddy, 'Property, Private Government and the Myth of Deregulation', in Sarah Worthington (ed.), *Commercial Law and Commercial Practice*, Oxford: Hart Publishing (2003), pp. 85–123.

IWAI, Katsuhito, 'Persons, Things and Corporations: The Corporate Personality Controversy and Comparative Corporate Governance', 47(4) *American Journal of Comparative Law*, pp. 583–632 (1999).

JACKSON, Robert, *Sovereignty*, Cambridge: Polity Press (2007).

JEAMMAUD, Alain and Antoine LYON-CAEN, 'Droit et direction du personnel', *Droit Social*, pp. 56–69 (1982).

JEAMMAUD, Antoine, Thierry KIRAT and Marie-Claire VILLEVAL, 'Les règles juridiques, l'entreprise et son institutionnalisation: au croisement de l'économie et du droit', *Revue internationale de droit économique*, pp. 99–141 (1996).

JENSEN, Michael C., 'Value Maximization, Stakeholder Theory and the Corporate Objective Function', 12 *Business Ethics Quarterly*, pp. 235–256 (2002).

JENSEN, Michael C. and William H. MECKLING, 'Theory of the Firm: Managerial Behavior, Agency Costs and Ownership Structure', 3(4) *Journal of Financial Economics*, pp. 305–360 (1976).

JOHNSON, Paul, *Making the Market – Victorian Origins of Corporate Capitalism*, Cambridge: Cambridge University Press (2010).

JUBÉ, Samuel, *Droit social et normalisation comptable*, Paris: Librairie Générale de Droit et de Jurisprudence (2011).

JULIUS, DeAnne, *Global Companies and Public Policy – The Growing Challenge of Foreign Direct Investment*, London: Pinter Publishers, Royal Institute of International Affairs (1991).

KANT, Immanuel, *La philosophie de l'histoire*, Paris: Denoël (1947).

KANT, Immanuel, *Perpetual Peace and Other Essays*, Indianapolis: Hackett Publishing Company (1983).

KANTOROWICZ, Ernst H., *The King's Two Bodies – Study in Medieval Political Theology*, Princeton: Princeton University Press (1957).

KATZ, Larissa, 'The Regulative Function of Property Rights', 8(3) *Econ Journal Watch*, pp. 236–246 (2011).

KATZ, Larissa, 'Governing through Owners: How and Why Formal Private Property Rights Enhance State Power', 160 *University of Pennsylvania Law Review*, pp. 2029–2059 (2012).

KATZ, Larissa, 'Property's Sovereignty', 18 *Theoretical Inquiries in Law*, pp. 299–328 (2017).

KAY, John, 'Is it meaningful to talk about the ownership of companies?', *Financial Times*, 11 October (2015).

KELSEN, Hans, 'L'essence de l'État' (traduction H. Thévenaz), 17 *Cahiers de philosophie politique et juridique*, Caen: Presses Universitaires de Caen (1990, 1ère édition 1926), p. 17.

KELSEN, Hans, *Théorie pure du droit* (traduction H. Thévenaz), Editions de la Baconnière, collection 'Être et penser, cahiers de philosophie', no 37 (1953, 1988).

KELSEN, Hans, *Théorie pure du droit* (traduction Charles Eisenmann), deuxième édition, Paris: Bruylant/Librairie Générale de Droit et de Jurisprudence (1962, 1999).

KELSEN, Hans, *General Theory of Norms* (traduction Michael Hartney), Oxford: Clarendon Press (1991).

KELSEN, Hans, *General Theory of Law and State*, Clark, New Jersey: The LawBook Exchange (1945, 2007).

KENNEDY, David, 'The Mystery of Global Governance', 34 *Ohio Northern University Law Review*, pp. 827–860 (2008).

KEOHANE, Robert O., *After Hegemony – Cooperation and Discord in the World Political Economy*, Princeton: Princeton University Press (1984).

KINLEY, David, 'Human Rights, Globalization and the Rule of Law: Friends, Foes or Family?', 7(2) *UCLA Journal of International Law and Foreign Affairs*, pp. 239–264 (2002).

KLEIN, Daniel B. and John ROBINSON, 'Property: A Bundle of Rights? Prologue to the Property Symposium', 8(3) *Econ Journal Watch*, pp. 193–204 (2011).

KOKKINI-IATRIDOU, D. and P.J.I.M. DE WAART, 'Foreign Investments in Developing Countries – Legal Personality of Multinationals in International Law', 14 *Netherlands Yearbook of International Law*, pp. 87–131 (1983).

KOLBEN, Kevin, 'Integrative Linkage: Combining Public and Private Regulatory Approaches in the Design of Trade and Labor Regimes', 48(1) *Harvard International Law Journal*, pp. 203–256 (2007).

KOTZUR, Markus, 'Universality – A Principle of European and Global Constitutionalism', 6 *Historia Constitucional* (2005).

KRIEGEL, Blandine, 'La défaite de la justice', in *La Justice, L'obligation impossible*, Paris: Collection Autrement, Série Morales (1994).

LA PORTA, Rafael, Florencio LOPEZ-de-SILANES and Andrei SHLEIFER, 'The Economic Consequences of Legal Origins', 46(2) *Journal of Economic Literature*, pp. 285–332 (2008).

LANDEMORE, Hélène and Isabelle FERRERAS, 'In Defense of Workplace Democracy: Towards a Justification of the Firm-State Analogy', *Political Theory*, pp. 1–29 (2015).

LANE, Frederic C., 'Economic Consequences of Organized Violence', 18(4) *Journal of Economic History*, pp. 401–417 (1958).

LARDEUX, Gwendoline, 'Qu'est-ce que la propriété ? Réponse de la jurisprudence récente éclairée par l'histoire', *Revue trimestrielle de droit civil*, pp. 741–757 (2013).

LARRERE, Catherine, *L'invention de l'économie au XVIIIe siècle – Du droit naturel à la physiocratie*, Paris: Presses Universitaires de France (1992).

LAURENT, Alain, *Histoire de l'individualisme*, Paris: Presses Universitaires de France (1993).

LAZONICK, William, 'Profits Without Prosperity', *Harvard Business Review*, pp. 47–55 (2015).

LAZONICK, William, Matt HOPKINS, Ken JACOBSON, Mustafa ERDEM SAKINC and Öner TULUM, *US Pharma's Financialized Business Model*, Institute for New Economic Thinking, Working Paper No 60 (2017).

LEFEBVRE-TEILLARD, Anne, 'L'intervention de l'État dans la constitution des S.A.', 59 *Revue Historique de Droit Français et Etranger*, pp. 383–418 (1981).

LEFEBVRE-TEILLARD, Anne, 'Liberté d'entreprendre, structures juridiques et rôle de l'État', in Alain Plessis (ed.), *Naissance des libertés économiques – Le décret d'Allarde et la loi Le Chapelier*, Paris: Histoire Industrielle (1993), pp. 283–288.

LEFEBVRE-TEILLARD, Anne, 'La Révolution, une période décisive pour les sociétés par actions', *Revue des Sociétés*, pp. 345–358 (1989).

LÉVY-BRUHL, Henri, *Histoire juridique des sociétés de commerce en France aux XVIIe et XVIIIe siècles*, Paris: Domat Montchrestien (1938).

LINDBLOM, Charles E., *The Market System – What It Is, How It Works, and What to Make of It*, New Haven & London: Yale University Press (2001).

LIPPMANN, Walter, *An Inquiry into the Principles of The Good Society*, Boston: Little, Brown and Company (1938).

LOCKE, John, *Two Treatises of Government*, Cambridge: Cambridge University Press (1960, 1963, 1988).

LUCHAIRE, François, 'Les fondements constitutionnels du droit civil', *Revue Trimestrielle de Droit Civil*, pp. 245–382 (1982).

LUHMANN, Niklas, 'The Self-Reproduction of Law and its Limits' in Gunther Teubner (ed.), *Dilemmas of Law in the Welfare State*, Berlin: De Gruyter (1986), p. 113.

LUHMANN, Niklas, 'La constitution comme acquis évolutionnaire', 22 *Droits*, pp. 103–125 (1995).

LUHMANN, Niklas, *Observations on Modernity*, Stanford: Stanford University Press (1998).

LYON-CAEN, Antoine, 'Le pouvoir entre droit du travail et droit des sociétés', *Revue de Droit du Travail*, Septembre, pp. 12–17 (2010).

LYON-CAEN, Antoine and Gérard LYON-CAEN, 'La doctrine de l'entreprise' in *Dix ans de droit de l'entreprise*, Paris: Librairie Technique (1978), pp. 601–621.

MACNEIL, Ian R., 'Economic Analysis of Contractual Relations', in P. Burrows and C.G. Veljanowski, (eds.), *The Economic Approach to Law*, London: Butterworths (1981), pp. 61–92.

MACNEIL, Ian R., 'Relational Contracts: What We Do and Do Not Know', *Wisconsin Law Review*, pp. 483–526 (1985).

MACPHERSON, C.B., *The Political Theory of Possessive Individualism – Hobbes to Locke*, Oxford: Oxford University Press (1962, 2011).

MAINE, Henry Sumner, *L'ancien droit – considéré dans ses rapports avec l'histoire de la société primitive et avec les idées modernes*, translation of *Ancient Law* (1861), NuVision Publication LLC (2008).

MAITLAND, Frederic W., 'Moral Personality and Legal Personality', 6(2) *Journal of the Society of Comparative Legislation*, pp. 192–200 (1905).

MALAFOSSE, Jehan de, *Le droit à la nature*, Paris: Editions Montchrestien (1973).

MARTIN, Isabelle, 'Prendre la puissance économique au sérieux: jalons pour une appréhension relationnelle des contrats au sein des réseaux de production', 57(1) *Les Cahiers de Droit*, pp. 55–97 (2016).

MARTIN, Xavier, *Mythologie du Code Napoléon – Aux soubassements de la France Moderne*, Bouère: Editions Dominique Martin Morin (2003).

MAYALL, James, *Nationalism and International Society*, Cambridge: Cambridge University Press (1990).

McCLOSKEY, Robert G., *The American Supreme Court*, Chicago: The University of Chicago Press (1960).

McGREW, Anthony, 'Globalization Beyond Borders? Globalization and the Reconstruction of Democratic Theory and Politics', in Anthony McGrew (ed.), *The Transformation of Democracy? Globalization and Territorial Democracy*, Cambridge: Polity Press (1997), pp. 231–266.

McGREW, Anthony, 'Organized Violence in the Making (and Remaking) of Globalization', in David Held and Anthony McGrew (eds.), *Globalization Theory – Approaches and Controversies*, Cambridge: Polity Press (2007), pp. 15–40.

MENARD, Claude and Mary M. SHIRLEY, 'The future of new institutional economics: from early intuitions to a new paradigm?', 10(4) *Journal of Institutional Economics*, pp. 541–565 (2014).

MENARD, Claude and Mary M. SHIRLEY, 'The Contribution of Douglass North to New Institutional Economics', in Rafe Blaufarb (ed.), *The Great Demarcation – The French Revolution and the Invention of Modern Property*, Oxford: Oxford University Press (2016), pp. 11–29.

MERRILL, Thomas W., 'Property and the Right to Exclude', 77 *Nebraska Law Review*, pp. 730–755 (1998).

MERRILL, Thomas W., 'The Property Strategy', 160 *University of Pennsylvania Law Review*, pp. 2061–2095 (2011–2012).

MERRILL, Thomas W., 'Property and Sovereignty, Information and Audience', 18 *Theoretical Inquiries in Law*, pp. 417–445 (2017).

MERRILL, Thomas W. and Henry E. SMITH, 'What Happened to Property in Law and Economics?', 111 *Yale Law Journal*, pp. 357–398 (2001).

MERRILL, Thomas W. and Henry E. SMITH, 'The Property/Contract Interface', 101(4) *Columbia Law Review*, pp. 773–852 (2001).

MESTRE, Jean-Louis, 'Le Conseil constitutionnel, la liberté d'entreprendre et la propriété', *Dalloz, Chroniques*, pp. 1–8 (1984).

MICHALET, Charles-Albert, *Le capitalisme mondial*, Paris: Quadrige/Presses Universitaires de France (1976, 1998).

MILLARD, Éric, 'Hauriou et la théorie de l'institution', 30/31 *Droit et Société*, pp. 381–412 (1995).

MILLARD, Éric, 'Sur les théories italiennes de l'Institution', in B. Basdevant and M. Bouvier (eds.), *Contrat ou institution: un enjeu de société*, Paris: Librairie Générale de Droit et de Jurisprudence (2004), pp. 31–46.

MILLER, Arthur S., 'Toward the "Techno-Corporate" State? An Essay in American Constitutionalism', 14(1) *Villanova Law Review*, pp. 1–73 (1968).

MILLER, Arthur S., *The Modern Corporate State: Private Governments and the American Constitution*, Westport: Greenwood Press (1976).

MIRABEAU, Victor Riqueti, Marquis de, *Théorie de l'impôt*, sans lieu d'édition [Paris], ni nom d'éditeur [Chaubert et Hérissant] (1760).

MIROWSKI, Philip and Dieter PLEHWE (eds.), *The Road from Mont Pelerin – The Making of the Neoliberal Thought Collective*, Cambridge: Harvard University Press (2009).

MONTESQUIEU (Charles de Secondat, baron de La Brède et de), *De l'Esprit des loix, ou Du Rapport que les loix doivent avoir avec la Constitution de chaque gouvernement*, Genève: Barillot & Fils (1748).

MONTESQUIEU (Charles de Secondat, baron de La Brède et de), *Œuvres de Monsieur de Montesquieu. Nouvelle édition, revue, corrigée, considérablement augmentée par l'auteur* [publié par F. Richer], Londres: Nourse (1767).

MOORE, Mark T. and Antoine REBÉRIOUX, 'Corporate Power in the Public Eye: Re-Assessing the Implications of Berle's Public Consensus Theory', 33 *Seattle University Law Review* 1109–1139 (2010).

NECKER, Jacques, *Compte-rendu au Roi*, Paris: Imprimerie Royale (1781).

NEGRI, Antonio, *Le pouvoir constituant – Essai sur les alternatives de la modernité*, Paris: Presses Universitaires de France (1992).

NELSON, R.R. and S.G. WINTER, *An Evolutionary Theory of Economic Change*, Cambridge: The Belknap Press of Harvard University Press (1982).

NÉRON, Pierre-Yves, 'Business and the Polis: What does it mean to see Corporations as Political Actors?', 94 *Journal of Business Ethics*, pp. 333–352 (2010).

NGUYEN QUOC DINH, Patrick DAILLER and Alain PELLET, *Droit international public*, Paris: Librairie Générale de Droit et de Jurisprudence (4th edition 1992).

NONET, Philippe and Philip SELZNICK, *Law and Society in Transition – Toward Responsive Law*, New York: Octagon Books (1978).

NOREL, Philippe, *L'histoire économique globale*, Paris: Seuil (2009).

NORTH, Douglass C., *Structure and Change in Economic History*, New York: W.W. Norton (1981).

NORTH, Douglass C., *Understanding the Process of Economic Change*, Princeton: Princeton University Press (2005).

NORTH, Douglass C. and Robert Paul THOMAS, 'An Economic Theory of the Growth of the Western World', XXIII *Economic History Review* (2nd series), pp. 1–17 (1970).

NORTH, Douglass C. and Robert Paul THOMAS, *The Rise of the Western World – A New Economic History*, New York: W.W. Norton (1973).

NORTH, Douglass C., John Joseph WALLIS and Barry R. WEINGAST, *Violence and Social Orders – A Conceptual Framework for Interpreting Recorded Human History*, Cambridge: Cambridge University Press (2009).

NOZICK, Robert, *Anarchy, State and Utopia*, Oxford: Blackwell (1974, 1993).

OECD, *2017 Background Brief – Inclusive Framework on BEPS*, available at: https://www.oecd.org/ctp/background-brief-inclusive-framework-for-beps-implementation.pdf.

OLIVIER-MARTIN, François, 'La France d'ancien régime, État corporatif', 5 *Annales de droit et de sciences politiques*, pp. 690–702 (1937).

OLIVIER-MARTIN, François, 'Le déclin et la suppression des corps en France au XVIIIe siècle', in 2 *Etudes présentées à la Commission Internationale pour l'Histoire des Assemblées d'États*, Louvain: Bureau du recueil, Université de Louvain (1937), pp. 149–163.

OLIVIER-MARTIN, François, *Histoire du droit français des origines à la Révolution*, C.N.R.S. (1992, réédition de 1948).

OLSON, Mancur, 'Dictatorship, Democracy and Development', 87(3) *American Political Science Review*, pp. 567–576 (1993).

OSTROM, Elinor, *Governing the Commons – The Evolution of Institutions for Collective Action*, Cambridge: Cambridge University Press (1990, 2008).

PADOA-SCHIOPPA, Antonio, 'Conclusions: modèles, instruments, principes', in Antonio Padoa-Schioppa (ed.), *Justice et législation*, Paris: Presses Universitaires de France (2000), pp. 394–434.

PAILLUSSEAU, Jean, 'L'efficacité des entreprises et la légitimité du pouvoir', 74 *Les Petites Affiches*, 19 juin, p. 17 (1996).

PALAN, Ronen, 'Tax Havens and the Commercialization of State Sovereignty', 56(1) *International Organization*, pp. 151–176 (2002).

PALAN, Ronen, *The Offshore World – Sovereign Markets, Virtual Places and Nomad Millionaires*, Ithaca: Cornell University Press (2003, 2006).

PALAN, Ronen, Richard MURPHY and Christian CHAVAGNEUX, *Tax Havens – How Globalization Really Works*, Ithaca: Cornell University Press (2010).

PALAN, Ronen, 'International Political Economy of Past and Futures and the Rise of ARMAs', Draft prepared for 'A Retrospective on the Work of Susan Strange: Structure, Power, Knowledge, and Norms', Princeton University, 10–11 January (2014).

PENNER, J.E., 'The "Bundle of Rights" Picture of Property', 43(3) *UCLA Law Review*, pp. 711–820 (1995–96).

PERROW, Charles, 'A Society of Organizations', 20(6) *Theory and Society*, pp. 725–762 (1991).

PETTIT, Philip, 'Two Fallacies about Corporations', in Subramanian Rangan (ed.), *Performance and Progress: Essays on Capitalism, Business, and Society*, Oxford: Oxford University Press (2015), pp. 379–394.

PEZZINO, Paolo, 'La mafia, l'État et la société dans la Sicile contemporaine (XIXe et XXe siècles)', 13(49) *Politix*, pp. 13–33 (2000).

PHILLIPS, Richard, Hannah PETERSEN and Ronen PALAN, *Estimating the Share of Corporate Income and Profits Controlled by OFC-Based Subsidiaries* (forthcoming).

PICQ, Jean, *Une histoire de l'État en Europe – Pouvoir, justice et droit du moyen âge à nos jours*, Paris: Les presses de Sciences Po (2009).

PIETRI, Antoine, '"Property" or "possession": just a matter of semantics ... or Paradigm?', MPRA Paper No 67096, posted 8 October, 22:38 UTC (2015).

PIGOU, Arthur Cecil, *The Economics of Welfare*, London: Palgrave Macmillan (4th edition 1932, reprint 2013).

PIRENNE, Henri, *Medieval Cities: Their Origins and the Revival of Trade*, Princeton: Princeton University Press (1925).

PISTOR, Katharina, *The Code of Capital – How the Law Creates Wealth and Inequality*, Princeton and Oxford: Princeton University Press (2019).

PITTE, Jean-Robert, *Histoire du Paysage Français*, tome 2, 'Le profane: du XVIe siècle à nos jours', Paris: Tallandier (1989).

PLANTEY, Alain, *De la politique entre les États – Principes de diplomatie*, Paris: Pédone (2e édn, 1991).

PLESSIS, A. (ed.), *Naissance des libertés économiques – Le décret d'Allarde et la loi Le Chapelier*, Paris: Histoire Industrielle (1993).

POLANYI, Karl, *La grande transformation*, Paris: Gallimard, Bibliothèque des sciences humaines (1944, 1983).

PONTE, Stefano and Timothy STURGEON, 'Explaining Governance in Global Value Chains: A Modular Theory-Building Effort', 21(1) *Review of International Political Economy*, pp. 195–223 (2014).

POPPER, Karl, *La société ouverte et ses ennemis*, tome 1, 'L'ascendant de Platon'; tome 2, 'Hegel et Marx', Paris: Seuil (1979).

RADIN, Margaret J., 'Property and Personhood', 34 *Stanford Law Review*, pp. 957–1015 (1982).

RAJAN, Raghuram and Luigi ZINGALES, 'Power in a Theory of the Firm', *Quarterly Journal of Economics*, pp. 387–432 (1998).

RAWLS, John, *A Theory of Justice*, Oxford: Oxford University Press (1972).

REBÉRIOUX, Antoine and Gwenaël ROUDAUT, 'Corporate governance and accountability', in *Handbook of the International Political Economy of the Corporation*, Cheltenham: Edward Elgar (2018), pp. 29–44.

REICH, Charles A., 'The New Property', 73 *Yale Law Journal*, pp. 733–787 (1964).

RENARD, Georges, *La philosophie de l'institution*, Paris: Sirey (1939).

RENAUT, Alain, '*État de droit et sujet de droit*', 24 *Cahiers de philosophie politique et juridique*, Caen: Presses Universitaires de Caen (1993), p. 51.

RENNER, Karl, *The Institutions of Private Law and their Social Functions*, New Brunswick & London: Transaction Publishers (1949, 2010).

REPETTO, Robert, 'Accounting for Environmental Assets', 266(6) *Scientific American*, pp. 94–100 (1992).

RICHARD, Jacques, *Comptabilité et développement durable*, Paris: Economica (2012).

RICHARD, Jacques, 'The Dangerous Dynamics of Modern Capitalism (from Static to IFRS' Futuristic Accounting)', 30 *Critical Perspectives on Accounting*, pp. 9–34 (2015).

RICHARDSON, G.B., 'The Organization of Industry', 82 *Economic Journal*, pp. 883–96 (1972).

RICHARDSON, Gary, 'Guilds, laws, and markets for manufactured merchandise in late-medieval England', 41 *Explorations in Economic History*, pp. 1–25 (2004).

RIGAUX, François, *Droit International privé*, tome 1, 'Théorie générale', Bruxelles: F. Larcier (1977).

RIPERT, Georges, *Les aspects juridiques du capitalisme moderne*, Paris: Librairie générale de droit et de jurisprudence (1951).

RIPSTEIN, Arthur, 'Property and Sovereignty: How to Tell the Difference', 19 *Theoretical Inquiries in Law*, pp. 243–268 (2017).

RIQUEUR, Paul, *Le juste*, Paris: Editions Esprit (1995).

RIZZOLI, Fabrice, 'Pouvoirs et mafias italiennes: Contrôle du territoire contre État de droit', 132 *Pouvoirs*, pp. 41–55 (2010).

ROBÉ, Jean-Philippe, 'L'entreprise en droit', 29 *Droit et société*, pp. 117–136 (1995).

ROBÉ, Jean-Philippe, 'L'ordre juridique de l'entreprise', 25 *Droits*, pp. 163–177 (1997).

ROBÉ, Jean-Philippe, *L'entreprise et le droit*, Paris: Presses Universitaires de France (1999).

ROBÉ, Jean-Philippe, 'Conflicting Sovereignties in the World Wide Web of Contracts – Property Rights and the Globalization of the Power System', in Graf-Peter Calliess, Andreas Fischer-Lescano, Dan Wielsch and Peer Zumbansen (eds.), *Soziologische Jurisprudenz, Festschrift für Gunther Teubner*, Berlin: De Gruyter Recht (2009), pp. 691–703.

ROBÉ, Jean-Philippe, 'Enterprises and the Constitution of the World Economy', in Fiona Macmillan (ed.), 2 *International Corporate Law*, Hart Publishing (2003), pp. 45–64.

ROBÉ, Jean-Philippe, 'Les États, les entreprises et le droit – Repenser le système-monde', 161 *Le Débat*, pp. 74–87 (2010).

ROBÉ, Jean-Philippe, 'L'entreprise comme institution fondamentale de l'échange marchand', in Armand Hatchuel, Olivier Favereau and Franck Aggeri (eds.), *L'activité marchande sans le marché*, Colloque de Cerisy, Paris: Presse des Mines (2010), pp. 91–110.

ROBÉ, Jean-Philippe, 'The Legal Structure of the Firm', 1(1) *Accounting, Economics, and Law*, Article 5, available at: http://www.bepress.com/ael/vol1/iss1/5 (2011).

ROBÉ, Jean-Philippe, 'Being Done with Milton Friedman', 2(2) *Accounting, Economics, and Law*, Article 3 (2012).

ROBÉ, Jean-Philippe, 'Science v. Ideology: A Comment on Lynn Stout's New Thinking on "Shareholder Primacy"', 2(2) *Accounting, Economics, and Law*, Article 7 (2012).

ROBÉ, Jean-Philippe, *Le temps du monde de l'entreprise – Globalisation et mutation du système juridique*, Paris: Dalloz (2015).

ROBÉ, Jean-Philippe, 'L'actionnaire est-il un créancier résiduel?' in Philippe BATIFOULIER, Franck BESSIS, Ariane GHIRARDELLO, Guillemette de LARQUIER and Delphine REMILLON (eds.), *Dictionnaire des conventions – Autour des travaux d'Olivier Favereau*, Villeneuve d'Ascq: Presses Universitaires Septentrion (2016), pp. 24–29.

ROBÉ, Jean-Philippe, Antoine LYON-CAEN and Stéphane VERNAC (eds.), *Multinationals and the Constitutionalization of the World Power System*, with a Foreword from John Gerard RUGGIE, London & New York: Routledge (2016).

ROE, Mark J., 'Delaware's Competition', 117 *Harvard Law Review*, pp. 588–646 (2003).

ROMANO, Santi, *The Legal Order*, London: Routledge (1946, 2017).

ROSANVALLON, Pierre, *Le capitalisme utopique – Critique de l'idéologie économique*, Paris: Seuil (1979).

ROSE, Carol M., 'Property as the Keystone Right?', 71 *Notre Dame Law Review*, pp. 329–369 (1996).

ROSS, Alf, 'On the concepts "State" and "State Organs" in Constitutional Law', 5 *Scandinavian Studies in Law*, pp. 111–129 (1961).

ROUGIER, Louis, *Les mystiques économiques; comment l'on passe des démocraties libérales aux États totalitaires*, Paris: Librairie de Médicis (1938).

ROUSSEAU, Jean-Jacques, *Du Contract Social; ou Principes du Droit Politique*, Amsterdam: Marc Michel Rey (1762).

RUGGIE, John Gerard, 'International regimes, transactions, and change: embedded liberalism in the postwar economic order', 36(2) *International Organization*, pp. 379–415 (1982).

RUGGIE, John Gerard, 'Taking Embedded Liberalism Global', in David Held and Mathias Koenig-Archibugi (eds.), *Taming Globalization: Frontiers of Governance*, Cambridge: Polity Press (2003), pp. 93–129.

RUGGIE, John Gerard, 'The Multinational as Global Institution: Power, Authority and Relative Autonomy', *Regulation and Governance*, pp. 1–17 (2017).

RUGGIE, John Gerard, 'The Social Construction of the UN Guiding Principles on Business and Human Rights', in Surya Deva (ed.), *Handbook on Business and Human Rights*, London: Edward Elgar (2018).

RUGGIE, John Gerard, *The Paradox of Corporate Globalization*, M-RCBG Faculty Working Paper Series 2020-01 (2020).

SALEILLES, Raymond, *De la personnalité juridique*, Paris: Librairie nouvelle de droit et de jurisprudence A. Rousseau (1910) (Editions La Mémoire du Droit, 2003).

SASSEN, Saskia, *Territory, Authority, Rights – From Medieval to Global Assemblage*, Princeton: Princeton University Press (2006).

SASSEN, Saskia, *La globalisation. Une sociologie*, Paris: Gallimard (2007, 2009).

SCHMITT, Carl, *Le nomos de la terre*, Paris: Presses Universitaires de France (1988, 2001).

SCHMITT, Carl, *Théorie de la Constitution*, Paris: Presses Universitaires de France (1989).

SCHUTZ, Anton, 'Saint Augustin, l'État et la "bande de brigands"', 16 *Droits*, pp. 71–82 (1992).

SCIULI, David, *Corporate Power in Civil Society – An Application of Societal Constitutionalism*, New York: New York University Press (2001).

SEARLE, John R., 'What is an Institution?', 1(1) *Journal of Institutional Economics*, pp. 1–22 (2005).

SEAVOY, Ronald E., *The Origins of the American Business Corporation (1784–1855) – Broadening the Concept of Public Service during Industrialization*, Westport: Greenwood Press (1982).

SEIDL-HOHENVELDERN, Ignaz, *Corporations in and under International Law*, Cambridge: Cambridge University Press (1987).

SELZNICK, Philip, 'Legal Institutions and Social Control', 17 *Vanderbilt Law Review*, pp. 79–90 (1963).

SELZNICK, Philip, *Law, Society and Industrial Justice*, New York: Russell Sage (1969, 1980, 1983).

SEN, Amartya, *Ethique et économie*, Paris: Presses Universitaires de France (1987, 1993).

SERRES, Michel, *Le contrat naturel*, Paris: Editions F. Bourin (1990).

SEVE, René, 'La théorie du droit selon John Austin – Le positivisme tel qu'il devrait être?', 13 *Cahiers de philosophie politique et juridique*, Caen: Presses Universitaires de Caen (1988), p. 69.

SEWELL, William H., *Gens de métiers et révolutions – Le langage du travail de l'Ancien Régime à 1848*, Paris: Aubier Montaigne (1983).

SHAPIRA, Roy and Luigi ZINGALES, *Is Pollution Value-Maximizing? The DuPont Case*, NBER Working Paper No. w23866 (2017).

SHINN, James and Peter GOUREVITCH, *How Shareholder Reforms Can Pay Foreign Policy Dividends*, Council on Foreign Relations (2002).

SHUBIK, Martin, 'A Note on Accounting and Economic Theory: Past, Present and Future', 1(1) *Accounting, Economics and Law – A Convivium*, Article 1 (2011), available at: http://www.bepress.com/ael/vol1/iss1/1.

SIMON, Herbert A., *Administrative Behavior: A Study of Decision-Making in Administrative Organizations*, New York: Free Press, Fourth Edition (1997).

SINGER, Joseph William, 'Democratic Estates: Property Law in a Free and Democratic Society', 94 *Cornell Law Review*, pp. 1009–1062 (2008–2009).

SJÅFJELL, Beate, 'Redefining the Corporation for a Sustainable New Economy', 45(1) *Journal of Law and Society*, pp. 29–45 (2018).

SJÅFJELL, Beate, 'Beyond Climate Risk: Integrating Sustainability into the Duties of the Corporate Board', 23 *Deakin Law Review*, pp. 1–22 (2018).

SLOBODIAN, Quinn, *The Globalists – The End of Empire and the Birth of Neoliberalism*, Cambridge: Harvard University Press (2018).

SMITH, Adam, *The Wealth of Nations*, New York: The Modern Library (1994).

SMITH, Henry E., 'Property is not just a Bundle of Rights', 8(3) *Econ Journal Watch*, pp. 279–291 (2011).

SOTO, Hernando de, *The Mystery of Capital – Why Capitalism Triumphs in the West and Fails Everywhere Else*, New York: Basic Books (2000).

SOUSA SANTOS, Boaventura de, 'Droit: une carte de la lecture déformée – Pour une conception post-moderne du droit', 10 *Droit et société*, pp. 364–390 (1988).

SOUSA SANTOS, Boaventura de, *Toward a New Common Sense: Law, Science and Politics in the Paradigmatic Transition*, New York: Routledge (1995).

SOUSA SANTOS, Boaventura de, *Toward a New Legal Common Sense: Law, Globalization, And Emancipation*, London: Butterworths (2nd edition 2002).

SPENGLER, Joseph J., 'The Problem of Order in Economic Affairs', in J.J. Spengler and W.R. Allen (eds.), *Essays in Economic Thought: Aristotle to Marshall*, Chicago: Rand McNally and Co. (1960), pp. 6–34.

SPRUYT, Hendrik, *The Sovereign State and its Competitors*, Princeton: Princeton University Press (1994).

STEFANIK, Kirsten, 'Rise of the Corporation and Corporate Social Responsibility: The Case for Customary International Law', 54 *The Canadian Yearbook of International Law* (2016).

STEFFEN, Will et al., 'Planetary Boundaries: Guiding Human Development on a Changing Planet', 347 (6223) *Science*, p. 736 (2015).

STERN, Nicholas, 'The Structure of Economic Modeling of the Potential Impacts of Climate Change: Grafting Gross Underestimation of Risk onto Already Narrow Science Models', 51(3) *Journal of Economic Literature*, pp. 838–859 (2013).

STEWART, Megan A., 'Civil War as State-Making: Strategic Governance in Civil War', 72 *International Organization*, pp. 205–226 (2018).

STIGLITZ, Joseph, Amartya SEN and Jean-Paul FITOUSSI, *Richesse des nations et bien-être des individus*, Paris: Odile Jacob (2009).

STONE, Christopher, *Where the Law Ends – The Social Control of Corporate Behavior*, New York: Harper & Row (1975).

STOPFORD, John, M., Susan STRANGE and John S. HENLEY, *Rival States, Rival Firms – Competition for World Market Shares*, Cambridge: Cambridge University Press (1991).

STORY, Jonathan, 'Le système mondial de Susan Strange', 2 *Politique étrangère*, pp. 433–447 (2001).

STOUT, Lynn A., *The Shareholder Value Myth – How Putting Shareholders First Harms Investors, Corporations and the Public*, San Francisco: BK Business Books (2012).

STOUT, Lynn A., *Corporate Entities: Their Ownership, Control, and Purpose*, Cornell Law School Research Paper No 16–38 (2017).

STOUT, Lynn A. et al., *The Modern Corporation Statement on Company Law* (2016), available at https://papers.ssrn.com/sol3/papers.cfm?abstract_id=2848833.

STRANGE, Susan, *The Retreat of the State – The Diffusion of Power in the World Economy*, Cambridge: Cambridge University Press (1996).

STRANGE, Susan, *States and Markets*, London: Pinter Publishers (1988, 2nd edition 1994).

STREECK, Wolfgang, *Buying Time – The Delayed Crisis of Democratic Capitalism*, London: Verso (2014).

STRINE, Leo E. Jr., *The Dangers of Denial: The Need for a Clear-Eyed Understanding of the Power and Accountability Structure Established by the Delaware General Corporation Law*, University of Pennsylvania Law School, Institute for Law and Economics, Research Paper No 15–08 (2015).

SUPIOT, Alain, *Critique du droit du travail*, Paris: Presses Universitaires de France, Collection 'Les voies du droit' (1994).

SUPIOT, Alain, 'The Dogmatic Foundations of the Market', 28(4) *Industrial Law Journal*, pp. 321–345 (2000).

SUPIOT, Alain, 'Le droit du travail bradé sur le "marché des normes"', *Droit Social*, pp. 1087–1096 (2005).

SUPIOT, Alain, *Homo Juridicus – Essai sur la fonction anthropologique du droit*, Paris: Editions du Seuil (2005).

SUPIOT, Alain, *L'esprit de Philadelphie – La justice sociale face au marché total*, Paris: Editions du Seuil (2010).

SUPIOT, Alain, 'The public–private relation in the context of today's refeudalization', 11(1) *I-Con* 129–145 (2013).

SUPIOT, Alain, *La gouvernance par les nombres – Cours au Collège de France (2012–2014)*, Paris: Fayard (2015).

SUPIOT, Alain, 'État, entreprise et démocratie', in Pierre Musso (ed.), *L'entreprise contre l'État*, Paris: Editions Manucius (2017), pp. 13–31.

TAX JUSTICE NETWORK, The, *The Cost of Tax Abuse – A briefing paper on the cost of tax evasion worldwide* (2011), available at: www.tackletaxhavens.com/Cost_of_Tax_Abuse_TJN%20Research_23rd_Nov_2011.pdf.

TESTU, François Xavier, 'La distinction du droit public et du droit privé est-elle idéologique?', *Dalloz, Chronique*, p. 345 (1998).

TEUBNER, Gunther, 'The Many-Headed Hydra: Networks as Higher-Order Collective Actors', in Joseph McCathery, Sol Picciotto and Colin Scott (eds.), *Corporate Control and Accountability – Changing Structures and the Dynamics of Regulation*, Oxford: Oxford University Press (1993), pp. 41–60.

TEUBNER, Gunther, 'The King's Many Bodies: The Self-Deconstruction of Law's Hierarchy', 31(4) *Law and Society Review*, pp. 763–788 (1997).

TEUBNER, Gunther (ed.), *Global Law Without a State*, Aldershot: Dartmouth (1997).

TEUBNER, Gunther, 'Global Private Regimes: Neo-Spontaneous Law and Dual Constitution of Autonomous Sectors in World Society', in Karl-Heinz Ladeur (ed.), *Globalization and Public Governance*, Aldershot: Ashgate (2004), pp. 71–87.

TEUBNER, Gunther, 'Societal Constitutionalism: Alternatives to State-Centered Constitutional Theory', in Christian Joerges, Inger-Johanne Sand and Gunther Teubner (eds.), *Transnational Governance and Constitutionalism*, Oxford: Hart Publishing (2004), pp. 3–28.

TEUBNER, Gunther, *Constitutional Fragments – Societal Constitutionalism and Globalization*, Oxford: Oxford University Press (2012).

TEUBNER, Gunther, 'Societal Constitutionalism – Nine Variations on a Theme by David Sciulli', in Paul Blokker and Chris Thornhill (eds.), *Sociological Constitutionalism*, Cambridge: Cambridge University Press (2017), pp. 313–340.

THOMAS, Yan, 'La valeur des choses: Le droit Romain hors la religion', 6 *Annales, Histoire, Sciences Sociales*, pp. 1431–1462 (2002).

TILLY, Charles, 'Reflections on the History of European State-Making', in Charles Tilly (ed.), *The Formation of National States in Western Europe*, Princeton: Princeton University Press (1975).

TILLY, Charles, *Contrainte et capital dans la formation de l'Europe – 990–1990*, Paris: Aubier (1990, 1992).

TIROLE, Jean, *The Theory of Corporate Finance*, Princeton: Princeton University Press (2006).

TØRSLØ, Thomas, Ludwig WIER and Gabriel ZUCMAN, *The Missing Profits of Nations*, 5 June 2018, available at: https://gabriel-zucman.eu/files/TWZ2018.pdf.

TROPER, Michel, *Pour une théorie juridique de l'État*, Paris: Presses Universitaires de France, collection Léviathan (1994).

UMBECK, John, 'Might Makes Right: A Theory of the Formation and Initial Distribution of Property Rights', 19(1) *Economic Inquiry*, pp. 38–59 (1981).

UNIVERSITY OF OSLO, DEPARTMENT OF PRIVATE LAW, *The Sustainable Companies Project Report* (2013), available at: https://www.jus.uio.no/ifp/english/research/projects/sustainable-companies/.

VAREILLES-SOMMIÈRES, Marquis de, 'La définition et la notion juridique de propriété', *Revue trimestrielle de droit civil*, pp. 443–495 (1905).

VELDMAN, Jeroen, 'Politics of the Corporation', 24 *British Journal of Management*, pp. 18–30 (2013).

VINER, Jacob, 'Adam Smith and Laissez Faire', in *Adam Smith, 1776–1926*, Chicago: University of Chicago Press (1928), pp. 116–155.

WALLERSTEIN, Immanuel, *World-Systems Analysis – An Introduction*, Durham & London: Duke University Press (2004).

WALTER Elisse B. (2017), *Sustainability Matters: Focusing on your Future Today* (2017), available at https://corpgov.law.harvard.edu/2017/04/18/sustainability-matters-focusing-on-your-future-today/.

WEILER, Joseph H.H., 'The Geology of International Law – Governance, Democracy and Legitimacy', 64 *ZaöRV*, pp. 547–562 (2004).

WHITTAKER, Simon, 'Public and Private Law-Making: Subordinate Legislation, Contracts and the Status of "Student Rules"', 21(1) *Oxford Journal of Legal Studies*, pp. 103–128 (2001).

WILLIAMS, Joan, 'The Rhetoric of Property', 83 *Iowa Law Review*, pp. 277–361 (1997).

WILLIAMSON, Oliver E., 'The Modern Corporation: Origins, Evolutions, Attributes', 19(4) *Journal of Economic Literature*, pp. 1537–1568 (1981).

WILLIAMSON, Oliver E., *The Economic Institutions of Capitalism*, New York: Free Press (1985).

WOLF, Edward Nathan, 'Recent Trends in Households' Wealth, 1983–2009: The Irresistible Rise of the Household Debt', 2(1) *Review of Economics and Institutions*, Article 4 (2010).

XIFARAS, Mikhail, 'The Global Turn in Legal Theory', 29(1) *Canadian Journal of Law and Jurisprudence*, pp. 215–243 (2016).

ZENATI, Frédéric, 'Pour une rénovation de la théorie de la propriété', (2) avril–juin *Revue Trimestrielle de Droit Civil*, pp. 305–323 (1993).

ZENATI, Frédéric, 'L'immatériel et les choses', 43 *Archives de philosophie du droit*, pp. 79–95 (1999).

ZHANG, Ying and Jane ANDREW, 'Financialization and the Conceptual Framework', 25 *Critical Perspectives on Accounting*, pp. 17–26 (2014).

ZINGALES, Luigi, 'In Search of New Foundations', LV(4) *Journal of Finance*, pp. 1623–1653 (2000).

Index

A

absolute monarchy 160
absolute property rights 74
absolutism 89
acceptability 174–5
accountants, empirical problems and
    322
accounting
    assets and 324–5
    bottom line information 325
    consolidated accounts 321
    corporations as entities and 321
    curing the deficiencies of 338–49
    firms and 315
    full cost accounting 339, 340, 343
    improper 325
    negative externalities and 325
    objective of 322
    practical problems of measurement
        322
    shareholder supremacy and 322
    theory of 320
    true cost accounting 336–8
    universal standard for 323
    value of 325–6
accounting organizations 26
accounting profits 275
accounting rules 249, 293, 315, 318,
    320–6
    benefiting absentee shareholders 338
    corporations and 321
    irreconcilable 323
    performance measurement and 320
    present-day international 325
    shareholder primacy and 325
accounting system 249
Adams, Henry Carter 13n28, 243–4
Adkins v. Children's Hospital (1923) 180
administrative agencies 290
after-tax profits 252, 253
agency, possession and 67–9

agency theory 35, 67, 208, 227, 259,
    288–9, 293, 300
    accounting and 324
    Berle and Gardiner 306, 307
    negative externalities and 319
    shareholder value and 313–20
    support for 315
agents 90
    of corporations 245
agreed bonds 203
agricultural economy 6
Alchian, Armen 72
Alexander, Gregory 104n284
Allen, Douglas 41n79
American Declaration of Independence
    (1776) 59
American Economic Association meeting
    (1896) 243–4
Anderson, Elizabeth 173, 213
Apple 214
arbitrage 257, 277
arbitrariness 154, 160, 161
arm's length price 272, 277, 278
Aron, Raymond 189
Arrow, Kenneth J. 4n8
    on the coercive power of firms 12
Article 2 (French Declaration, 1789) 6,
    9n18, 58–9
Article 5 (French Declaration, 1789) 108
Article 16 (French Declaration, 1789)
    101
Article 544 (French Civil Code) 74, 85
Article 14.2 (Fundamental Statute) 104
assets 234–5, 248
    accounting and 324–5
    bundled 209
    see also productive assets
auditing 235
authority
    obeying 12
    power and 7n15

autonomous exchange 66
autonomy 8, 203
  efficiency and 11–14
  heteronomy and 13
  of individuals 12, 13, 15, 285
  limiting of 109
  multinational enterprises and 281
  organizations and 25
  Organs of the State 100–2
  owners and 82, 103, 108, 165–6
  private 94
  private prerogatives and 94, 95
  private property and 96
  reduction of 13
  right of *see* rights of autonomy

B

Bakeries Act 180
bandit rationality 138–9
Barker, Richard 341
Barry, Norman 57
barter exchange 143
Barzel, Yoram 46, 63n146, 64
Bates, Robert 65n152
Bavarian government 159
Beck, Ulrich 291, 295, 302–3
Bénabou, Roland 4–5, 301
beneficial owners 263
Bentham, Jeremy 46, 202–3
BEPS (base erosion and profit shifting) 276
Berle, Adolf 12n24, 68, 99, 209, 304, 305–10, 311
Bermuda black hole 265
Bilateral Investment Treaties (BITs) 297, 298, 299
Bill of Rights 6
  in England 59, 149
  in France 17
  in the US 17n47, 304
Blackstone, William 85
Blair, Margaret 309
Bloch, Marc 146
Bloomberg, Michael 340
Bolshevik revolution 103
Boston Harbour 149
bottom line information 325
Bouvines, Battle of 149
Brandeis, Justice Louis 18, 69, 189
Braudel, Fernand 129, 131, 246
Bretton Woods system 119, 291
Brewster, Kingman 108
Britain
  freedom of incorporation 19

  legislative changes in 18–19
  see also England
British Virgin Islands (BVI) 280, 281
bundle of rights theory 78–82
business corporations *see* corporations
business firms *see* firms
Butler, Nicholas Murray 287

C

Cap Gemini 266n682
capital 26–7, 212, 246
  concentration of 243, 243n661, 287
  corporations and 231, 309
  destruction of 342
  environmental 346
  financial 247, 321, 322, 342, 344, 346
  human 344n908
  locking in 235–6
  mystery of 48
  natural 342, 343, 344, 345, 349
  productive 275
  real 247, 275
  shares of the form of 246
  social 344n908
capital gains 273
capitalism 48, 122–3
  appearance of 224
  dual type of property rights and 225
  early 131
  European development of 161
  evolving legal system and 90
  liberalism and 189–90, 191
  rise of 246
  see also modern capitalism
carbon dioxide (CO_2) 26–7, 329–30
  cost of restoration 330
  cost of use 330
carbon neutrality 331
Carbonnier, Jean 9n19
Cary, William 18
case law 230–1n640, 298
Cayman Islands 280, 281
Central African Republic 156
chain of contracts 211, 215
Chandler, Alfred 200, 244n663
Cheung, Steven 211, 212, 214, 215
China, property and 7
Christendom 121, 122
cities 129, 130
citizen, concept of 222
city-leagues 130, 158
city-States 130, 158

Civil Code (French) 15n37, 74, 91, 202, 203
  Article 544 74, 85
civil law 84–5
civil servants 159–60
civil society 7
climate change 1, 22, 22–3, 124, 294, 327
  destructive 329
  global issues of 330–2
  insufficient corrective measures taken 327–8
  irreversible damage, potential of 329
  issues facing 330–1
  Paris Agreement (2015) and 21
  reducing global temperature 331
  see also carbon dioxide (CO_2)
clusters of contracts 206–7, 210, 211, 212, 215
CO_2 *see* carbon dioxide (CO_2)
coalitions 111, 137, 138–42
Coase, Ronald 42, 71–2, 79, 198–9, 212–13, 212–13n615
  on accounting 320
  on firms 200
  on planned enterprises 271
  'The Problem of Social Cost' 81–2
Cobden-Chevalier treaty (1860) 19
Code law 84
The Code of Capital (Pistor) 43
Code of Commerce (1807) 17
coding 43
coercion 96–7
Cohen, Morris 118
Colbert, Jean-Baptiste 16, 127–8
Cold War 123
Cole, Daniel 41, 42–3
collective power 170
colonization 122, 286
commerce 129
common law 84–5, 127
Commons, John R. 40n72
communism 1, 7, 122–3
  property and 75
Compagnie des Indes Occidentales 16
Compagnie des Indes Orientales 16
Compagnie Générale for Insurance and Big Adventures 16
compulsory international arbitration 298
compulsory transfers 154–5
concentrated property rights 288
Conceptual Framework (IASC, 1989) 323
Conceptual Framework (IASC, 2010) 324

Conceptual Framework Project Summary (IFRS, 2018) 347
consolidated accounts 321
consolidated financial statements 321–2
Constitution 6
  autonomy from the Organs of the State 100–2
  fundamental rights and 88–9, 100
  government majorities and 88
  individual freedoms under 101
  liberal 171
  of liberal States 132
  power in times of peace and war 104–5
  prerogatives 90, 132
  private prerogatives 90–1, 92, 94–100
  protection against governmental abuses 88
  public government 88
  restrictive view of 89
  rules defining fundamental rights 88
  small-scale despotisms and 102–4
constitutional government 311
  despotisms and 301–5
constitutional law 121
  internal sovereignty and 132
constitutional legal system 167
constitutional orders 303
Constitutional Revolution (1937) 181
  see also First Constitutional Revolution; Second Constitutional Revolutions
constructivism 63n146
Continental Congress 149
contract enforcement 56, 57
contract law 203–4
contract negotiation 72–3
contracting entities 222
contracts 99, 143–4, 201
  clusters of 206–7, 210, 211, 212
  creation of voluntary relationships 202
  duration of 206
  firms and 207, 209
  firms versus corporations 268–9
  from status to 202–4
  incompleteness of 236, 237
  between multinational enterprises 270
  networks of 204
  nexus of 231, 238
  stable exchange and 205–7
  types of 206
  unregulated subordination 204
Copernican revolution 245
corporate accounting 322

corporate executives 313
  restrictive rules against 313
corporate governance 67, 282–4, 307, 324
  oversimplification of 318
  shareholder value myth 318
corporate law 18, 308n815, 314
  constraints on contracts and prices 270
  corporate agents and 67
  corporate executives and 313
  development of 14–20, 24
  discretion of directors under 314
  misunderstandings about 227
  sober and realistic view of 317
corporate nationality 125
corporate officers 67
corporate organizational society 272
corporate organizations 125
corporate ownership 67
corporate personality 221, 230, 235
corporate personhood 230
  key feature of 234
  locking in capital 235–6
corporate persons 187, 230
corporate powers 170
corporate prerogatives 238–40
  characteristics of 239
  heteronomous 239
  mandatory 239
  non-transferable 239
  public interest and 239
  qualified 239
corporate property 185, 186
corporate responsibility 342–3
Corporate Social Responsibility (CSR) 336
  policies 333
corporate system 12, 25
corporate tax 273
corporate tax revenue
  base erosion and profit shifting ('BEPS')
    276
  loss of 275
corporation law, liberalization of 245
corporations 187–8, 220–1
  accounting and 321
  Adam Smith and 188
  agents and 245
  as an alter ego 309
  concentration of power 170
  corporate danger 188–9
  creation of 187
  definition of 192, 195
  directors and managers of 67–8
  early formation of 243

as entities 321
eternal life of 235
fallacies about 238
fear of 185
features of 227–40
as fictions 220
firms and 192, 195, 195–200, 207, 268–82
foundations of 242
Fourteenth Amendment and 62n142
from liberalism to capitalism 191
initial investors in 309
international legal rights and 297–8
legal personality of 219, 229–31
legal persons and 199, 220, 314
legal structuring of firms 241–2
as a legal vehicle 199
legally treated as individuals 13
limited liability 7, 20, 25, 244, 245, 287
managing businesses 224–5
as owners of assets 232–3
ownership of 233–4
perception of 185–6
political role of 223
pool of capital in 309
pre-French revolution 16–17
pre-US Constitution 15
private powers and 188
privatization of 16
productive assets and 224
protection of assets 235
quasi-public 170
railroads and 244
raising capital 231
relocation of 269
residual control rights and 236–8
share ownership and 270
shareholders and 67–8
short-term interest of shareholders and
  315
stability of 236
State affairs and 243–6
subsidiaries of 269
universal use of 242
see also firms; incorporation;
    multinational enterprises;
    organizations
cosmopolitan democracy 302
costs 271, 319
  accounting system and 320
  environmental 249
  labour 251, 257
  positive transaction costs 81–2, 83
  see also transaction costs

Cox, Robert 177
Craigslist opinion 314
credit 48
creditors 234–5
criminals 138
crises 295
cross-border trade 271

D
damages 101–2
Danone 335, 335n878
de facto rights 204
De Soto, Hernando 9, 45n87
    The Mystery of Capital 9, 48
debt 284n730
Declaration of Independence (1776) 149
Declaration of the Rights of the Inhabitants
        of the Commonwealth of
        Massachusetts 93n247
decolonization 122, 286
Delaware 280
Delaware law 314
democracy 103
    despotism and 163–82
    elected majorities and 88
    marginally living in 171–2
    process of 89
    property rights and 98
    unrestrained 89
Democratic Republic of Congo 156
Demsetz, Harold 56n121, 72, 232, 233
deregulation 15
derivative rights 48, 225
Despax, Michel 312
despotisms
    constitutional government and 301–5
    construction of 171
    democracy and 163–82
    small-scale 102–4, 171
directors
    Craigslist opinion 314
    duties of 314
    stockholder welfare and 314–15
disorganized violence 138
dividends 231
division of labour 129, 133, 188
    markets and government 5
division of power 132
Dodge v. Ford Motor Company (1919)
        313–14n830
domestic law 298
Double Irish 265
due process 178–9

Duguit, Léon 118–19
Durand, Paul 311–12, 312
Dutch Sandwich 265

E
Earth System Processes 20–1
economic development 48
economic due process 179
economic exchange 129
economic expansion 128–9
economic knowledge 45–6
economic liberalism 17
economic property 65
economic property rights 47–9, 64, 349
economic theorists
    on firms 197
    general language of 198
    specialized language of 198
    use of words 'firm' and 'corporation'
        198
economic theory 34–5, 350
    traditional 322
economic thought, nineteenth century 191
economics
    law and 117–18
    politics and 91, 109, 118
    the State and 118
economy, environment and 337
Edict of Paulette 128
efficiency 4
    autonomy and 11–14
Ely, Richard 39n70, 120
embezzlement 309
Emissions Gap Report (2017) 22
employees 72
    co-determination rights and 104
    employment contracts and 70, 72–3
    repressive rules and practices against
        76–7
employment agreements, termination of
        175
employment contracts 70, 72–3, 213
    as a contract of subordination 99
    legal difference between owners and
        non-owners 71
employment relations 203–4
end of history theory 1
enforceable rights 55
England
    absolute property rights in 74
    Bill of Rights 59, 149
    centralized royal courts of 127
    Common Law in 127, 203

England (continued)
    contract law in 203–4
    from status to contract 203–4
    King's Court 127
    Norman Conquest 127
    rule of law in 127
English Common Law 85
English Private Limited Company 19
Enlightenment 302n795
enterprise, theory of 289
entrepreneurs
    creating firms 207–8
    liability of 210–11
    unincorporated businesses 208–10
environment
    economy and 338
    unpriced environmental externalities
        and 338–9
environmental capital 346
environmental costs 249
environmental crisis 188
equality 50
equity investors 35, 348–9, 350–1
ESG (environmental, social and governance)
    reporting 339, 343
EU, loss of corporate tax revenue 275
Eucken, Walter 45, 190
Eurocentrism 161–2
European Emission Trading Scheme 345
European State System 122
exchange value 64
external sovereignty 119, 291
externality 14n35
externality regulation 318
extortion 138

F
Fama, Eugene F. 209n608, 238
Family Offices 263, 266n682
fault 290
feudal aids 159
feudal society 146
feudal system 130
feudal theory 130
feudalism 129
    taxation under 157
Fifth Amendment (US Constitution) 6, 60,
    61, 178
    due process clause 178
    procedural safeguards 61
finances 133
financial accounting 319, 343–4, 345, 346
financial assets 224

financial capital 247, 321, 322, 342, 344,
    346
financial capitalism 241, 246
financial equity 27
financial markets 247, 248
financial profit 341
financial reporting 323, 324
financial statements 321, 343
Financial Structure 276, 279, 281, 284, 296,
    303, 332–3
    evolution of 260
    of firms 247–8, 259–68
    intangible assets of 277
    legitimate reasons for 261
    sophistication of 323
    State law and 267
financial sustainability 341
financial system 225
financialization of the economy 225, 247
financials 337
firm accounting 322
firms 207–8
    allocation of resources of 13–14
    as alternatives to market exchanges 199
    as a chain of contracts 215
    coercive power of 12
    competing 296, 297–300
    contract negotiations and 72–3
    contracts and 207, 209
    coping with 293–326
    as counter markets 270–1
    created by individual entrepreneurs
        207–8
    deficiency theory of 307
    definition of 192, 195, 196n570
    differences from corporations 192, 195,
        195–200, 207
    differentiated from Financial Structure
        247–8
    directing resources 212–13
    economic activity of 199, 210
    as economic organizations 199
    economic theory of 197
    as an entity 210
    existing theories of 35
    freedom to trade 297
    giving orders to employees 213
    importance of 216–17
    improper accounting of 315
    incorporeal assets of 296
    inputs and outputs 249, 250
    interaction with the State 248–59
    intra-firm trade 271

law of property and 72
legal analysis of 311
legal person and 196n570, 199, 207, 210
legal relationships within 67–8
legal structure of 197, 208, 215
limits of 214–16
management of 267
markets and 217
negative externalities and 319
as a nexus of contracts 209
organization of 267
as participants in the World Power
  System 293
prerogatives of 173
as a private government 173
as a proprietorship 199
raising capital through share issues 231
rights to individuals, benefiting from
  173
role in World Power System 200
sustainability of 27
theory of 311–12, 325
tools for costs reduction 257
value creation and 249
versus corporations 268–82
in the World Wide Web of Contracts
  211–14
see also corporations; Financial Structure;
  global firms; multinational
  enterprises; organizations
First Constitutional Revolutions 245
First Constitutions 304
Fitoussi, Jean-Paul 23
foraging order 110
force 56–7
  of the State 58
foreign firms 275
Fossen, Anthony van 279–80
Foucault, Michel 8, 96–8
Fourteenth Amendment (US Constitution)
  62, 178, 304
  due process clause 178
  equal protection clause 62n142
France
  ancien régime 17, 74, 148, 150, 202
  Bill of Rights 17
  business corporations in 16–17
  Civil Code 15n37, 74, 85, 91, 202, 203
  declaration as sovereign State 128
  different languages of 145n425
  different legal rules in 145n426
  difficulties raising taxes 153–4
  Explanatory Memorandum 19

free trade treaties 19
freedom and rights of individuals 17
freedom of incorporation 19–20
from status to contract 203
General Estates 153–4
grandes écoles 150
King's sovereignty 126
legal monism in 17
limited liability companies 19
limited liability corporations 17
line between public and private 150
office holders 159
origins of the State 127–8
'pré carré' doctrine 158
privileges in 154
protectionist climate in 19n55
rural law of 74
tax exemptions for mobility 149
taxation 149–50
trade in 130
weights and measures 145n427, 147–8
franchise restrictions 222
franchisees 192
Frankfurter, Felix 24
free incorporation 20
Free Trade Agreements (FTAs) 297, 298,
  299
freedom of contract 3, 71, 99, 175, 203
freedom of enterprise 3–4
freedom of incorporation 188, 241, 267–8
French Constitution (1791) 59, 201, 202,
  203
  Fundamental Provisions Guaranteed by the
    Constitution 202
French Declaration of the Rights of Man
  and Citizen (1789) 9n18, 91, 201–2
  Article 2 6, 58–9
  Article 5 108
  Article 16 101
  rules limiting autonomy of 109
French Revolution (1789) 17, 74, 128
  metric system and 148
  reasons for 154
Freund, Ernst 68, 232
Friedman, Milton 208, 307
  public and private governance 316
  shareholder value maximization 315
Führerprinzip 312
Fukuyama, Francis 1, 93n247, 109n289
full cost accounting 339, 340, 343
Fuller, Lon 50
fundamental rights 88–9, 89, 100
  right to property 100

Furubotn, Eirik 66–7, 121
fuse 264

G

General Agreement on Tariffs and Trade
    (GATT) 120
general capacity, rule of 201
general language 198
General Partners 264
generally accepted accounting principles
    (GAAPs) 323
German Basic Law 95n255
Germany
    Article 14.2 (Fundamental Statute) 104
gift making 336
gilets jaunes movement 297
Global Compact 282
global economy 316
global enterprises 18
global firms
    internal government rules for 302
    as political systems 301
Global Parental Policy (Danone) 335
global regulations 318
Global Reporting Initiative (GRI) 339, 343
global rules 333
global State 302
global supply chains 334, 335
global value chain 334
global warming 329
globalization 2, 122, 169, 337
    open access order societies and 304
    planned enterprises and 271
    property rights and 20
    shareholder value and 274
    World Wide Web of Contracts and 205
globalization of enterprises 269–70
globalization of the economy 269–70
governance 316
government
    democratic process of 89
    intervention in markets 4
    interventionism 164
    prerogatives 90
    private sphere of 3
    property and 5–8
    public sphere of 3
Gray, Rob 259, 294
Great Depression 164
great empires 142
greenhouse gas emissions (GHGs) 22, 338
Grenier, Jean-Yves 98n263
Grossi, Paolo 103

Grossman, Peter 42–3
Group of Lisbon (1995) 205
Gunder Frank, André 161–2

H

Haldane, Andrew G. 227n636
Hale, Robert 70, 70–1n168, 77–8
Harlan, Justice 179
Hart, Oliver 29, 53–4, 236, 237, 336
    theory of ownership 83–4
Hauriou, Maurice 310
Hayek, Friedrich 189, 301–2
Held, David 123, 124
Henri IV 128
Henry, James 281n720
heteronomy 94, 96, 99, 203
hierarchy 126
High Middle Ages 128
HNWI (High Net Worth Individuals)
    266n682, 281
Hobbes, Thomas 140
Hobhouse, Leonard T. 12n27, 13n29
Hohfeld, Wesley 79
Holmes, Justice Oliver Wendell 69, 180,
    290
Holy Roman Germanic Empire 126
Honoré, Anthony 15, 47, 81
horizontal market transactions 212
household responsibility criteria 222
households 207, 207n599
Hughes, Chief Justice 181
human capital 344n908
human rights 140–1
humanity, challenges facing 1
hunter-gatherer societies 110

I

ideology 315
illegally owned goods 65, 65n151
illegitimate possession 63, 64, 65
IMF (International Monetary Fund) 276
immaturity 302n795
impact models 350n925
impersonal relationships 48, 50
income, redistribution of 4
incompleteness of contracts 83
incorporation
    consequences of 218–19
    converting of property rights and 232
    freedom of 188, 241, 267–8
    multiplication of property rights and
        224–5
    process of 217–18

individual entrepreneurs *see* entrepreneurs
individual rights 57
individuals
    autonomy of 12, 13, 15, 285
    freedom and rights post-French
        Revolution 17
    freedoms of 101
    not governed by Organs of the State
        134–5
    notion of 221
    private property and 15
    self-government of 108
    as slaves 221–2
    as small-scale sovereigns 285
Industrial Revolution 24, 288
industrialization 108, 187, 245, regulation
inequality 294–5
Institute of International Finance (IFF)
    340n896
institution theory 310
institutional pluralism 127
institutional theory 289n762
institutions, failings of 1
Integrated Reporting 339
intellectual property assets 274
intermediary goods 334
internal sovereignty 126–32, 291
    constitutional law and 132
internal trade 143
International Accounting Standards Board
    (IASB) 324
International Accounting Standards
    Committee (IASC) 323
international agreements 298
international arbitration tribunals 298
international economic exchanges 25, 270
International Labour Organization (ILO)
    103
international law 115, 119, 125, 299
    international sovereignty and 132
    multinational firms and 125
International News 69
International Organization of Securities
    Commission (IOSCO) 323
international public law 121, 298
international sovereignty 121–6
    basis of 124–5
    international law and 132
    origins of 122
international taxation 124
international trade
    within multinational enterprises 270,
        271

organized by multinational enterprises
    271
interstate commerce powers 62
interventionism 164
intra-enterprise exchanges 269–70
intra-enterprise global trade 283
intra-firm exchange 25
intra-firm trade 271, 335
intra-group interest payments 273
intra-organizational rule 171
inversion 265
investment 160–1
investment funds 26
investment treaties 299
investors 298
invisible hand 139, 342
IP, corporate tax avoidance on 277
Ireland
    foreign direct investment in 275–6n702
    taxation in 275, 275–6n702
Ireland, Paddy 227

J
Jefferson, Thomas 59
    property distribution 98
Jensen, Michael 238
Jersey 280
joint-stock companies 17
joint-stock corporations 188
Jubé, Samuel 344n908
judge-made law 84
judges 100n274
Julius, DeAnne 296
juristic person 223
justice 155–6
    monetary taxation as 158
justice system 114

K
K2 265
Kant, Immanuel 302n795
Kelsen, Hans 101n276, 170
    on a proper understanding of property
        168–9
Kennedy, David 295
Kering 341
in-kind transfers 129
Kleptotours 265n681
knowledge system 290

L
la Gressaye, Jean Brethe de 310–11
labour 54

labour costs 251, 257
Lafayette, Marquis de 59
laissez-faire constitutionalism 178–9
land 54
large-scale law 167
large-scale political system 167
Laundromat 265
law 4, 50
    contingency situation 88
    economics and 117–18
    limitations of 78
    as limited derogations 100–1
    neglect of, in North's analysis 112
    open access orders and 112, 117
    Organs of the State and 133–6
    pluralistic nature of 100n274, 166
    World Power System and 119n324
    see also legal system; rules
law enforcers 135
law of contracts 179
law of persons 201
law of status 201
law offenders 135
legal absolutism 103
legal entities 321
legal fictions 219, 220, 229, 237
legal imputation 90, 92
legal institutionalisation 310–12
legal institutions 41
legal knowledge 45–6
legal monism 17
legal objects (property) 73
legal orders 96, 96n257, 140, 167, 170, 221
    autonomous, small-scale 172
legal origins enthusiasts 84
legal personality 49–51, 93, 210
    of corporations 219, 229–31
    groups/institutions not having 223–4
    importance of 220
    and the State 229
legal persons 49, 50, 140
    citizens and 222
    corporations as 220, 314
    as equals 221
    firms and 196n570, 199, 207, 210
    importance of 223–4
    persons and 222
    prerogatives of 92
legal pluralism 164, 335n878
    from official to unofficial 168–71
    property and 166–8
legal property 65
legal property rights 47, 64

Legal Realism movement 79
legal relationships, in corporations and firms
    67–8
legal revolution 24–5
legal separateness 229
legal subjects (individuals) 73
legal system 42–4
    conceptions of the State 121
    historical process of 56–7
    market economy and 143
    property and 44–5
    understanding of 44
legality *see* rule of law
legally owned goods 64, 65
legitimacy 115–16
legitimate possession 63, 63n145, 64
legitimate violence 113–14, 116
    see also organized violence
Lenin, Vladimir Ilyich 103
liability partitioning 234–5, 236
liberal constitutionalism 103, 181
liberal democracy, economic liberalism and
    17
liberal individual rights 238
liberalism 119, 291–2
    capitalism and 189–90, 191
liberalization movement 245–6
liberty
    Article 2 (French Declaration) 9n18, 60
    Fifth Amendment (US Constitution)
      60, 178
    Fourteenth Amendment (US
      Constitution) 178
liberty of contract 179, 180, 187
    invalidation of 181
Liggett v. Lee (1933) 189
limited access order 110–11
limited liability corporations 17, 20, 25,
    244, 245, 287
Lippmann Colloquium (1938) 189, 191
Lippmann, Walter 43, 58, 75
liquidity 236, 248
local laws 268
local States 118
Lochner, Joseph 180
Lochner v. New York (1905) 180
Locke, John 5, 9, 10, 140
    political philosophy of 54, 55, 60
    on property 54, 55
    property and possession 63
    Second Treatise of Government 54, 55
locking in capital 235–6
long-term contracts 72

losses 346
Louis XVI 147, 154
Luhmann, Niklas 73
Luxembourg 280
    taxation in 275

M

Macpherson, C.B. 54n116
macro-powers 7–8, 82
    evolution of 129
Mafia 139
Magna Carta (1215) 149, 178
Maine, Henry Sumner 176–7, 201, 202
mainstream economic analyses 144
Maitland, Frederic 169–70n505
Malta, taxation in 275
management services, payment of 273, 274
Marjolin, Robert 189
market
    as a collective choice 11
    government intervention in 4
    role of 4
market competition 270
market contracts 72
market economies 25, 142–3
    development of 143
    exchanges mediated via money 158–9
    purposive contracts and 205
    in a sophisticated society 58
    States and 87n227, 144–5, 156
    transaction costs in 72, 156
market exchange economy 144
market exchange(s) 146–7, 158
    deep institutionalization of 147
market prices 272, 278
market society 142, 145, 147, 150
    delusion of 272
markets
    firms and 217
    global spread of 119–20
    marginal to the Power System 216–17
    norms and institutions of 119
    political protection of 302
    World Wide Web of Contracts and 216
Marxism 42, 98
Massachusetts Bay Colony 149
as-a-matter-of-exception-rules 313
maximizing shareholder value 227
Mayer, Colin 341
Means, Gardiner 305–10, 311
means of production 6
medieval law 73–4
micro-despotisms 304

micro-powers 8, 82
microeconomic theory 322
Microsoft 211, 212, 214
Miller, Arthur S. 70n167
minimum wage 180, 181
Mirabeau, Victor Riqueti, Marquis de 141,
    141n407, 150–1, 152–3, 285–6
    on arbitrariness 160
    on taxation 159
'The Missing Profits of Nations' (Tørslø et
    al.) 275, 278
modern capitalism 246–8
The Modern Corporation and Private Property
    (Berle and Gardiner) 305–6, 307,
    308, 308n815
*The Modern Corporation Statement on Company
    Law* (Stout et al.) 227
Modern State 148–51
modern taxes 148–51
monetary economy 129, 137–8
monetary exchange economy 142
monetary exchanges 147, 157
money 143
    circulation of 158
Mont Pelerin Society 189
MSMEs (micro-, small- and medium-
    enterprises) 335
multinational enterprises 18, 125, 195,
    196n570
    accountability of 304
    advantageous use of legal systems 269
    authority of 335
    Codes of Conduct 335
    corporate structure of 334
    development of 288
    economic system of 334
    economic transactions between
        subsidiaries 272
    extraterritoriality of 300
    global development of 304
    global rules 333
    governance systems 334
    growing power of 300
    independence of 306–7
    inexistence as a legal institution 268–9
    internal norms of 335, 336
    internal trade 270
    as international lawmakers 299
    legal structuring of 224
    low-tax jurisdictions and 273
    means available 333
    organizational autonomy of 281
    political institutions and 336–8

multinational enterprises (continued)
  power of 18
  price manipulation within 270, 272
  re-engineering of 332–3
  resources of 281
  rules for 335
  tinkering with costs and prices 271
  visible profits in accounts 275
  see also corporations; firms
The Mystery of Capital (De Soto) 9, 48

N
Napoleonic Codes 311
National Assembly 154, 201
national, concept of 223
Nationally Determined Contributions (NDCs) 21–2
natural capital 342, 343, 344, 345, 349
natural capital accounting 341
natural persons 222
natural rights 6, 57
  invention of 57
  notion of 57
natural state 110–11, 112, 146
nature 330
Nature 22, 329
'The Nature of the Firm' (Coase) 71–2, 212
Necker, Jacques 147, 157–8
negative emissions 331
negative externalities 4, 14, 20–4, 176, 316, 317
  accounting and 325
  climate change and 330
  internalization of 290, 337
  large and pervasive 320
  production decisions and 336
neo-classical economic theory 143
neo-liberals 191
neoliberalism 2, 189
new institutional economics 72
New Property 120
New York Court of Appeals 178
nexus of contracts 231, 238
nightwatchman States 14, 30, 89, 164, 176, 288
'no taxation without representation' principle 304
Norman Conquest 127
normative theory 305
norms 172
North, Douglass 49–50, 51, 109, 110–13, 143, 172

O
obeying authority 12
objective rights 140
objects of property 25
  appropriation by the State 165
  corporations' creation of 244
  illegitimate 64, 65
  owners and 34, 39
  rights and 42, 48
  rights of decision-making over 10, 34, 53
  shares as 231–4
objects of rights 65, 222
Occidental culture 221
OECD (Organization for Economic Co-operation and Development) 276
official legal pluralism 169
offshoring phenomenon 319
Olson, Mancur 57, 138–9
open access orders 49–50, 78, 111, 220
  impersonality and 50, 107, 111
  law and 112, 117
open access society 49, 186
open order society 113, 146, 153
operational accounting 342
Oppetit, Bruno 289n761
optimization schemes 265
orders 53
  versus prices 72–5
ordo-liberalists 189, 289
organizations
  autonomy rights of 25
  internal institutional structure of 172
  see also corporations; firms
organized crime 281
organized violence 109–10
  role of 113–18
  State monopoly of 110, 113–14, 115, 117, 151–2, 156, 157
  see also legitimate violence
Organs of the State 87, 89, 90–4
  administrative 133–6
  administrative functions of 134
  autonomy and 100–2
  concept of 92
  laws applicable to individuals 134–5
  political 133–6
  political appointees 134
  political decision-making organs of 134
  prerogatives 186
  property, autonomy from 100–2
  public prerogatives 90, 92–3
  rule-making organs of 134
  State to State variations 91

Orléan, André 98n263
owners 11
    autonomy of 82
    contracts and 99
    exempt from legal duties 95
    as lawmakers 75–8
    managerial autonomy of 103
    of objects of property 34, 39, 53
    as part of the Power System 102
    prevented from integration as Organs of
        the State 101
    of productive assets 212
    reduced autonomy of 165–6
    right of decision-making as a matter of
        principle 20, 34, 39n70, 53, 67, 77,
        78–82, 86
    rules limiting autonomy of 108
    self-government of 96
    sovereignty of 53
ownership
    Article 554 (Civil Code) 74
    definition of 85
    Hart's theory of 83–4
    incidents of 81
    liability for damages 101–2
    private prerogatives and 96–100
    residual rights of control of 83, 84
    right as a matter of principle 78–82, 84
    shared 74–5
ownership and control, separation of 308–9,
    309–10

P

paper profits 275
Paris Agreement (2015) 21–2, 124, 327,
    330
    failure of 328
peasants 157
Peckham, Justice 180
Pejovich, Svetozar 40n73, 66–7, 121
Penner, J.E. 79–80, 81
person, concept of 221, 222
personal liberty 80
personal rights 79, 80
personhood 229
persons, contracts and 222
physical natural capital maintenance 344,
    345
Pigou, Arthur Cecil 4
Pirenne, Henri 129
Pistor, Katarina 43
planetary boundaries 21, 297, 344
Planetary Life Support Systems 20–1

Polanyi, Karl 143
Polanyi, Michael 189
police forces 116
police power 179
political decolonization 286
political economy 87n227
political entrepreneurs 114, 115, 127
political individualism 329
political institutions 282
    allocation decisions of 315
    evolution of 148, 150
    higher-level 301
    joining international institutions 122–3
political philosophers 304–5
political power 7
political regulation 172
political system 102
    right to property and 100
political theory, eighteenth century 305
politics, economics and 91, 109, 118
pollution 345
Ponzi schemes 346, 346n918, 347
Popper, Karl 111, 129
positive transaction costs 81–2, 83
possession 9, 28
    agency and 67–9
    definition 47–8
    in French law 63n145
    granting rights of 64
    physical force and 56–7
    property and 41n78, 48, 53, 63
    secondary importance of 62–4
possessive individualism 54n116
postmodernism 98
Pound, Roscoe 179
power 3
    authority and 7n15
    definition 14n34
    inequality in 77
    struggle for 75
    in times of peace and war 104–5
    transformation of violence into 115–16,
        144
Power System 10–11, 23, 45
    appearance as open 174
    competition in 174
    complexity of 89, 90, 305
    democratic institutions of 103
    despotism of property in production 103
    economic and political spheres in 174
    evolution of 24–7, 61, 187
    globalization of 328
    history of 285–6

Power System (continued)
    liberal 17, 134
    markets and 216–17
    micro-institutional reality 272
    mode of operation of 173–4
    notion of 7
    operating in an impersonal manner 220
    operation of 82
    organized components of 272
    origins of 141
    owners as part of 102
    power of owners in 77
    private sphere of 90–1
    property as a building block of 85–6
    property in 14–20, 53, 58
    public government 181
    public sphere of 90–1
    recent dynamic of 285–92
    relays in 171–3
    resource allocation 109
    rules of 103
    unbalanced evolution of 191
    see also World Power System
prerogatives 90–1, 132, 186
    of firms 173
    of legal persons
    in state of nature theories 141
    subjective 238
    see also corporate prerogatives; private
        prerogatives; public prerogatives
prescribed bonds 203
price system 322, 345, 346
prices 25, 53, 181
    within multinational enterprises 271–2
    versus orders 72–5
primary markets 248
Principles for Responsible Investment (PRI)
    340n896
private autonomy 94
private exchanges 301
private government(s) 173
    in the US 305–10
private heteronomy 96–100
private law, property and 45
private legal orders 170
private-made law 187
private monetary exchange 145
private ordering 288
private organizations 270
private power structures 288
private prerogatives 90–1, 94–100, 186
    characteristics of 239
    differences from public prerogatives 92

individuals and 95–6
    ownership and 96–100
    rights of autonomy and 94, 95
    as a subjective right 95
    transferability of 95
private property 49, 87
    public property and 120–1, 133
    right of autonomy of 96
    unrestrained use of 108
private sphere 3, 7, 90–1
private systems 171
privileges 154
'The Problem of Social Cost' (Coase) 81–2
production 103
productive assets 10
    corporate executives and 313
    corporations and 224
    owners of 212
    private property and 11–12
    property over 224
    rights of decision-making over 34, 212
productive capital 275
productive goods 246
productive property 13
profit and loss 251, 274
profit maximization 337
profits 346
    in low-tax jurisdictions 273, 276
    shareholder value and 274
    shifting of 276, 277–8
    taxation of 275
    value creation and 318
Profits without Prosperity (Lazonick) 294–5
Progressivism 177
property
    abuses of 108
    as a building block of the Power System
        85–6
    as a circumscribed list of actions 81–2
    coercive power of 75
    common-sense perceptions of 39–40
    concentration of 24–7, 191, 238–40
    as a constitutional prerogative 56–62
    constraints of 166
    content of 166
    deprivations of 178
    extra-legal notions of 41
    giving power over people 96–8
    government and 5–8
    as a legal concept 10
    legal personality and 49–51
    legal pluralism and 166–8
    liability for decision-making 102

managerial authority over 70
as a method of allocation of government
    authority 165–6
modern day 46–7
notion of 9
owners of *see* owners
possession and 41n78, 47n78, 48, 53, 63
in the Power System 14–20
private law and 45
in production and consumption 99
protection by and against the State 58
redistribution of 176
reduced autonomy of owners 165–6
regulation of 15
relationship to the State 53
securitization of 48
as a social concept 56
social organization and 7
social side of 66
sovereignty and 107–36
as a spontaneous institution 40
and the State 65–7
things and rights 8–11, 39–40
understanding of 168–9
unequal distribution of 98
as a value-enhancing institution 64–5
see also objects of property
property owners *see* owners
property rights 10, 24
autonomous operation of 66
concentration of 78, 288
constitutional protection of 165
de facto rights and 204
democracy and 98
economic notion of 40
exchange of 211
impersonal 132
incorporation and 224–5
and the law 41–2
legal notion of 41
as legal rights 34
legal system and 42–4, 44–5
modern notion of 109
of multinational firms 195
post-French Revolution 74
of private persons 49
of public persons 49
reasonableness of 180
sovereignty and 118–21
theory of 83–4n219
understanding of 44–5
violence and 110
protective laws 164

Protestantism 121
public assets 133
public authorities 316
public borrowing 243
public force 153
public governance 316
public institutions 316
public limited companies 287–8
public-made law 187
public necessity 59
public normative order 316
public normative system 316
public prerogatives 90–1, 94, 95
    characteristics of 92–3, 95, 239
    differences from private prerogatives 92
public property 49
    private property and 120–1, 133
public sphere 3, 90–1
public systems 171
Puerto Rico, taxation in 275
PUMA 340, 341
pure market transactions 205, 211
pure sale and purchase transactions 192,
    205, 206, 212, 215

R
'race to efficiency' 18, 246
'race to the bottom' 18, 246
railroads 244
RBC Wealth Management 266n682
real capital 247, 275
real economy 225
real entity theory 308n815
real productive assets 263
real rights 79, 80
real value 319, 349
real value destruction 259
Realists 81
regime *capacitaire* 222
regime *censitaire* 222
regulation 15, 17, 290
Reich, Charles 120
relocation of businesses 269
Renner, Karl 80
Republicanism 98
residual control rights 83, 84, 236–8
residual emissions 331
resources, efficient use and allocation of 11,
    13–14
Revised Conceptual Framework (2018) 324
Revlon duties 314
Richardson, Katherine 22–3
Rigaux, François 168

right of decision-making as a matter of principle 20, 34, 39n70, 53, 67, 77, 78–82, 86, 166
  constitutional decentralization of 285
  directors and 310
  owners and 165, 236
  shareholders and 309
  unrestrained use of private property 108
  violence and 110
right of personal liberty 80
right of principle *see* owners
right to exclude 69–72
right to fire 69, 70
right to hire 69
right to organize 69, 70
rights 6
  enforceable 10
  existence of prior to the State 140
  as a matter of principle 78–82
  over shares 225
  over things 225
  property and 8–11
rights in personam 79, 80
rights in rem 79, 80, 85
rights of autonomy 10, 94, 95, 166, 186
  employees 99
  freedom of contract and 99
  private property and 95, 96
rights of individuals 173
Ripert, Georges 287
risk 290
risk partitioning 265
Robinson Crusoe (Defoe) 56–7
Rockström, Johan 22–3
Romano, Santi 96n257
Röpke, Wilhelm 189, 190, 191
Ross, Alf 89
Rougier, Louis 135, 189–90
Round Trip 265
Rousseau, Jean-Jacques 94n249, 140
royalties 270, 274
Rueff, Jacques 189
Ruggie, John Gerard 195–6
rule of law 116, 127, 303
rules 75–6
  applied in an impersonal fashion 94
rules of accounting *see* accounting rules
Rüstow, Alexander 189

S
Saleilles, Raymond 19–20, 310
Salin, Pascal 144n422

Santa Clara v. Southern Pacific (1886) 230–1n640
scandals 94
Schmitt, Carl 91
Schütz, Alfred 189
Sciuli, David 170
sea trade 155
Second Constitutional Revolutions 164, 174, 176–82, 291
  in 1937 181
Second Enlightenment (Beck) 302
Second Treatise of Government (Locke) 54, 55
secondary markets 248
security 231
self-employed 287
self-interest 4
Selznick, Philip 205
Sen, Amartya 23
Shapira, Roy 339
share capital 247, 260
shared ownership 74–5
shareholder primacy model 324, 336
shareholder supremacy 322
shareholder value 25, 26, 247, 258, 259, 274, 300, 349
  agency theory and 313–20
  creation of 26
  externalizing costs and 319
  firm managers and 267
  hiring and firing of employees 319
  maximizing 276, 313
  means of creating 319
  through profits shifting 276
shareholder value maximization 315, 316, 317, 318, 319, 336–7
shareholders 67–8, 219, 224, 225
  corporations' assets and 235, 236
  dividends and 231
  limited liability of 235
  liquidity and 236, 248
  ownership of firms and 227, 227n636, 232
  powers of 234
  removal from business operations 247
  rights of 233
  short-term interests of 315, 317
  voting rights 232
shareholders welfare 235
shares 68, 225
  as autonomous objects of property 231–4
  as a form of capital 246
  issuing of 231

Simon, Herbert 73, 216
Singapore Sling 265
Single Malt 265
slavery 221
small-scale despotisms 102–4
SMEs (small and medium-sized enterprises) 334
Smith, Adam 4, 188, 287
    duties of sovereignty 190
    mistake of 190–1
social behaviour 111
social capital 344n908
social contract theories 140
social orders of human history 110–11
social organization 7
'The Social Responsibility of Business is to Increase its Profits' (Friedman) 208
social rights 120, 164
social sciences, intellectual production of 2
socialism 6
socialists, property and 202–3
society
    organization of 4
    organizational structure of 329
    political structure of 329
soft law 282, 282n723
sole and despotic dominion 81, 85
Sons of Liberty 149
sovereignty
    duties of 190
    of firms 312
    internal sovereignty 126–32
    international sovereignty 121–6
    property and 107–36
    property rights and 118–21
    redefinition of 303
    redistribution of 303, 312
    States' trading of 279
Soviet Union 123
specialized language 198
specific objects of property 60
Spruyt, Hendrik 128
stable exchange, contracts and 205–7
stakeholder accounting 343
stakeholder reporting 343
Stamp Act (1765) 149
Starbucks 213–14
State act 92
State affairs 243–6
State constitutional law 172
State contract law 217
state family laws 167–8
State insurance 291

State law 78, 169
    Financial Structure and 267
state of emergency 159
State of law 39, 93, 114
    functions of 186
    states operating in accordance with 120
    taxation and 151
    violence in 116, 144
state of nature theories 5–6, 53, 140, 141
    effective prerogatives in 141
    John Locke and 54–5, 63
State positivism 289n761
State power 7
State System 3–5
    divided 25, 33
    globalization of 122
    inefficiency of addressing global issues 332
    operation of 131
    Treaties of Westphalia and 131
State, the 90–4
    administering laws in an impersonal manner 93, 116, 142, 144, 186
    agents of 90
    Constitutional Revolution of 290–1
    as a consumer of resources 144
    as a corporate person 186
    credit and 153
    double monopoly of 152
    economic role of 65
    economics and 118
    enforcement system of 64, 65
    England, development of 127
    evolution of 89
    extension of protection services 176
    as a facade institution 122
    France, development of 127–8
    freedom of individuals and 101
    governing of 133
    interaction with firms 248–59
    legal imputation 90
    legal personality and 229
    legitimacy in international law 115
    legitimate use of violence 71
    market economy and 144–5
    modern 148–51
    monopoly of legitimate violence 110, 113–14, 115, 117, 151–2, 156, 157
    nightwatchman role of 14, 30, 89, 164, 176
    origins of 137
    perception of 329
    physical force of 58

State, the (continued)
  political philosophers and 304–5
  power to seize private property 60
  procedures to prevent abuse of powers
    114
  property and 65–7
  protection of property 64
  resources and taxes 133
  separation of functions 101
  services of 116, 133, 142–8, 144, 155
  social unrest and 114
  as a systematic unity of authorities 93
  taxation and 151–4
  see also welfare State
stateless societies 156
States 288
  absolute sovereignty of 286
  access to money 142
  attractive to businesses 300
  autonomy of individuals 285
  competing 297–300
  competing local legal environments in
    269
  competition among 18, 82, 191
  competition between legal systems 272
  decentralization of authority 285–6
  development of 14, 142
  development of rules 295
  developmental stage of 139
  enabling laws 172
  erosion of sovereignty 296
  gridlock 124
  increase of 122
  institutional arrangements 123
  internal affairs of 285
  internal law of 281
  internal trade and 143
  international community of 123
  international law and 282
  intra-enterprise exchanges within 269–70
  justice and 155–6
  legal environments of 300
  limitation of powers 286
  local 118
  market economies and 156
  as market players 269
  and markets 87n227
  multipolarity of 124
  problems, dealing with 124
  protection of property 8
  protective demands of the population 283
  recognition, importance of 125
  reinvention of 295

  relationships with other States 123
  resources of 8, 155, 282
  sea trade and 155
  services of 155
  soft law and 282
  as sovereign public powers 283
  sovereignty of 82, 132, 282, 284, 285
  and a State of law 120
  substantive law 290
  tax evasion of corporations and 296
  tax resources of 8, 278–9
  tax revenue, loss of 279, 296
  tax systems of 272–3
  taxation and 155
  territorial character of 131
  territorial control of 283
  trading of sovereignty 279
  wealth creation of 145–6
statutes 108
Stewart, Megan 115n310
Stiglitz, Joseph 23
stock exchanges 248
stockholders 314–15, 317, 323
Stout, Lynn 196, 227, 233n646, 313
Strange, Susan 85–6n227
Strine, Leo 317
sub-prime market 319
subjective prerogatives 238
subjective rights 140
subjects of rights 222, 223
substantive law 290
suppliers 199, 204, 206, 207, 213, 214, 215
supply contracts 249
Supreme Court 24, 77, 88, 178–9, 180, 181
sustainability 27
  accounting and 341
  companies' reporting on 339
  competitive advantage of 348
  inconsistent reporting between
    companies 339–40
  investment in 347, 347–8
  stakeholder accounting and 343
sustainability accounting 343, 344, 345,
    345–6, 347–8
Sustainable Development Goals (SDGs) 347
sustainable profit 341
Sutherland, Justice 181
system of natural liberty 190

T
taille 130
Task Force on Climate-related Financial
    Disclosures (TCFD) 340, 340n896

tax havens 275, 278, 280–1, 319
tax laws 153, 272–3
tax revenue 278
tax system, efficient 147
taxation 133, 137
  applied in an impersonal manner 153
  arbitrariness of 154, 160
  as a constitutive exchange 153
  in the early Middle Ages 159
  evasion of 296
  events and 159
  in France 149–50, 153–4
  from compulsion to modern taxation 154–61
  in an impersonal manner 153
  in Ireland 275, 275–6n702
  loss of corporate tax revenue 275
  in Luxembourg 275
  in Malta 275
  mandatory payment of 155
  military needs of the State and 152
  modern 148–51
  of peasants 157
  practical issues in 151–4
  in Puerto Rico 275
  regular dates and 159
  regularity of 159, 160
  revenue, loss of 275–80, 284
  small island countries and 279–80
  State monopoly of 152
  State violation of principles of 154
  States and 155
  under feudalism 157
  in the US 275, 277
  without representation 148, 149
territorial states 130
Teubner, Gunther 302, 303
'The Theory of Enterprise Entity' (Berle) 308n815
Theory of taxation (Mirabeau) 150–1, 152–3
The Virginia Declaration of Rights 59
things, property and 8–11, 39–40
Thirty Years' War 122
TINA (There Is No Alternative) 198
Tirole, Jean 4–5, 301
Tørslø, Thomas 274
tort law 290
Total group 213
towns 130
Toyota 211, 212, 214
trade 128–9
  growth of 130

intra-firm trade 335
  reduction of internal barriers to 147
trade deficits 280
trade surpluses 280
transaction costs 42, 72, 83, 156
  positive 81–2, 83
treaty protection 298
treaty-shopping 298
triple bottom line accounting 325
true cost accounting 336–8
Trump, President Donald 22
truth effects 126
Two Treatises of Government (Locke) 5

U
ultra-liberal economists 156
ultra-liberalism 156
UNCTAD report (2018) 271, 277
Understanding the Process of Economic Change (North) 112
unitary taxation and formulary apportionment approach 277, 278
United Nations Environment Programme (UNEP) 22
United Nations Framework Convention on Climate Change (UNFCCC) 21
United Nations (UN) 123
United States of America (USA)
  American Supreme Court 182
  Bill of Rights 17n47, 304
  centralization of political power 182
  corporate tax avoidance on IP 277
  correcting unbalances 175–6
  Declaration of Independence (1776) 149
  economic regulation by State governments 61–2
  industrialization of 177
  laissez-faire constitutionalism of 178–9
  loss of corporate tax revenue in 275
  national federal State 182
  private government in 305–10
  Progressivism 177
  property ownership in 60–1
  protection of Afro-Americans 62
  'race to efficiency' 246
  'race to the bottom' 246
  railways 244
  regulatory race 18
  see also States; US Constitution
unlimited liability 245
unofficial legal pluralism 170
urban centres 130

US Constitution 15
    Fifth Amendment 15, 60, 61, 178
    Fourteenth Amendment 62, 178, 304
    Framers of 61

V
value 216, 249, 258–9, 318
    see also shareholder value
Vauban, Sébastien Le Prestre de 158
Viner, Jacob 190
violence 109
    control of 111
    disorganized violence 138
    property rights and 110
    by the State 71
    transformation into power 115–16,
        144
    see also force; legitimate violence;
        organized violence
Violence and Social Orders (North et al.) 49,
    151
violent organizations 110
*The Visible Hand – The Managerial Revolution
    in American Business* (Chandler)
    244n663
voluntary exchange economy 117
voluntary transfers 155
von Mises, Ludwig 189

W
wage relationship 204
Waite, Chief Justice 230–1n640
Wallerstein, Immanuel 119n324
Wallis, John Joseph 49–50, 51, 109, 110–13,
    172
war 104–5
War of Independence 149
Washington consensus 2
wealth
    concentration of 266, 266n682,
        266n683, 266n684, 284,
        294–5n772
    redistribution of 4, 295
The Wealth of Nations (Smith) 190
Weber, Max 114
weights and measures 145n427, 147–8
Weingast, Barry 49–50, 51, 109, 110–13,
    172
welfare States 164, 176, 288
West Coast Hotel Co. v. Parrish (1937) 181
Westphalian treaties 122, 131
Wier, Ludvig 274
Williamson, Oliver E. 83, 244n663

World Business Council for Sustainable
    Development (WBCSD) 340n896,
    347, 347n919
World Health Report (2013) 266n682
World Power System 1, 5
    climate change *see* climate change
    corporate law in 18
    corporations and 242
    despotism of property in production 103
    economic and political systems in 65
    economic decisions within 294
    fragmented investment regime in 299
    global issues 330–2
    globalization of enterprises and 282–3
    governmental challenges to 182
    issues facing 185
    lacking political unity 187–8
    law and 119n324
    legal structure of 171
    micro-structure of 328, 332
    multinational firms and 195
    operation of 300
    outdated understanding of 10–11
    path to self-destruction 296–7
    as a pluralistic Power System 289–90
    relationship between property rights and
        sovereignty 119
    restructuring of 303
    role of firms in 200
    shortcomings of 231
    sustainable 327–51
    taxation of locals 296
    threat to sustainability 328
    understanding the operation of 224
    unofficial participants in 334
    world system analysis and 119n324
    see also Power System
World Wide Web of Contracts 124, 161,
    201–5, 206
    boundaries between firms 192
    distortion of 279
    firms in 211–14
    globalization and 205
    as a legal structure 205
    markets and 216
    networks of 204
    participants to 204
    variety of 205

Z
Zingales, Luigi 209n608, 336, 339
zone of acceptance 73
Zucman, Gabriel 274

www.ingramcontent.com/pod-product-compliance
Lightning Source LLC
Chambersburg PA
CBHW070900030426

42336CB00014BA/2263